James Martin Peebles

Around the World

Or, Travels in Polynesia, China, India, Arabia, Egypt, Syria, and other...

James Martin Peebles

Around the World
Or, Travels in Polynesia, China, India, Arabia, Egypt, Syria, and other...

ISBN/EAN: 9783744757775

Printed in Europe, USA, Canada, Australia, Japan

Cover: Foto ©Andreas Hilbeck / pixelio.de

More available books at **www.hansebooks.com**

AROUND THE WORLD:

OR,

TRAVELS IN POLYNESIA, CHINA, INDIA, ARABIA, EGYPT, SYRIA,

AND OTHER

"HEATHEN" COUNTRIES.

BY

J. M. PEEBLES,

AUTHOR OF "SEERS OF THE AGES," "JESUS,—MYTH, MAN, OR GOD," "SPIRITUALISM DEFINED AND DEFENDED," &c., &c.

"I can not rest from Travel: I will drink
Life to its lees." — TENNYSON.

BOSTON:
COLBY AND RICH, PUBLISHERS,
9 MONTGOMERY PLACE.
1875.

Entered according to Act of Congress, in the year 1874, by
J. M. PEEBLES,
In the Office of the Librarian of Congress, at Washington.

Stereotyped and Printed by
RAND, AVERY, & CO., BOSTON.

PREFACE.

"WHAT I saw" in China, India, Arabia, Egypt, Syria, and other heathen countries, is expressive of this volume's distinctive characteristics. It abounds in precisely such facts about the South-Sea Islanders, Chinese, Hindoos, Arabs, Syrians, and other Asiatics, with the peculiarities of their social and religious life, as all Americans ought to know.

Among other reasons, the author visited Polynesia, Asia, and Africa, to personally inform himself touching the difference between life in America, and life in the Orient; and also to more fully understand the real condition of the heathen. He has endeavored to describe what came under his observations with fairness, and a true moral independence. It is quite time that the "heathen" members of a common humanity, and heirs to a conscious immortality, should be described by travelers as they are, giving them the benefit of that "charity which thinketh no evil."

A portion of the contents of this book appeared in "The Banner of Light," under the heading "*Letters of Travel.*" These have been revised, and a large amount of such original matter added as relates to the laws, customs, phenomenal manifestations, and ancient religions, born and cradled under the sunny skies of Asia.

The natural tendency of travel is to give breadth to thought, freedom to philosophy, and a fresh impetus to the humanitarian sentiments of the soul.

"*Ex Oriente lux!*" In "prehistoric pile," in Greek mystery, and Druid circle, in Shemitic prophecy, and Egyptian symbol, as in the science and culture of the present, we read the progress, and the future possibilities, of all tribes and nationalities.

" Over space the clear banner of mind is unfurled,
And the habits of God are the laws of the world."

AROUND THE WORLD.

CHAPTER I.

HAMMONTON TO CALIFORNIA.

TRAVEL is an educator. Seeing, in connection with reason and consciousness, is knowing. And knowledge is the stepping-stone to wisdom.

Since seeing, then, is knowing, why not see the world? why not traverse lands and seas? why not further lift the veil from Isis? and why not lay the marvelous treasures of antiquity at the feet of the golden present?

If essential spirit, as Oriental sage and seer have taught, is causation; if the spiritual is the real; and if this objective life is but the shadow-world of effects, — then, that parliaments of angels should conceive plans above to be executed on earth, is both possible and natural. All conscious intelligences must necessarily sympathize. None of us are wholly our own. Uncontrollable circumstances affect, and unseen powers influence us. As mirrors reflect, so mystics, aided by ministering angels, often outline the future. A scroll is now unrolling, a vision fulfilling. The journey enzones the world, *viâ* California, Sandwich Islands, New Zealand, Australia, China, India, Arabia, Egypt, Palestine, Central Europe, and England, to

"The land of the free, and the home of the brave."

ACROSS THE CONTINENT.

What a marvelous country, stretching from these commercial cities, that, like star-dust, dot the Atlantic coast, to the wave-washed shores of the Pacific! Considering extent of territory, variety of climate, grandeur of scenery, mineral resources, and free institutions, it is worth something to be an American citizen. The distance from our residence in Hammonton, N.J., to San Francisco, is some thirty-five hundred miles. A week's travel spans prairie and mountain. Telegraphic wires and iron-belted highways have quite annihilated time and space. Tunneling the English channel, sailing in air-ships through cloud-lands, and exploring the islands that stud the open polar sea, are achievements just ahead of us. Surely life is a rush forward, a struggle 'mid contending forces; and, scientifically considered, progress is the key-word of the country.

ALONG THE WESTERN ROUTE.

As Nile bottom-lands to Syria in the period of the patriarchs, so are broad prairie-fields to the East. It is these that fill our national granaries. Passing them, it seemed that peach-orchards fairly reeled under their fruitage, while vineyards unveiled to us their purple clusters. Swiftly whirling by cornfields, they rustled and swayed like waving forests. Pleasant things for the palate, beauty for the eye, lands for the toiler, minerals for the miner, wealth for the industrious, friends for the worthy, books for the student, and religious enthusiasm for souls great and liberal — *these* are among the charms of the sunset States.

The "Far West," and the Great American Desert, are alike the myths of our geography days. Most of these wasted lands may be made productive by irrigation. The surging tide of immigration, instead of stopping, as formerly, in Illinois, Indiana, Minnesota, Iowa, and Nebraska, pushes across the once trackless desert, scales the Rocky Mountains, and secures a foothold in Nevada, Utah, and California.

The intelligence of this age excels its integrity and morality. The higher call is for the solid, rather than the sensational; for constructors, rather than ruthless, reckless iconoclasts.

Omaha, on the western bank of the Missouri, numbers nearly twenty thousand. Here George Francis Train made a large portion of his fortune. The old state-house, a magnificent building, situated upon the highest point in the city, is to be devoted to educational purposes.

Pullman's palace sleeping-cars are luxurious. Eating-houses are numerous; charges one dollar currency. The Platte is a lazy, shallow stream, skirted with light timber. Along this river lies the old emigrant trail, marked by an occasional grave. Pawnee Indians were standing around every station. Reticent, they seemed sad. They·are fading away. The embers of their council-fires are cold. Oh, my countrymen, feed them generously, treat them justly, kindly, in these their dying days!

NORTH PLATTE CITY, AND CHEYENNE.

Accompanying Col. S. F. Tappan, Gens. Sheridan, Sherman, Terry, Harney, and other members of the Congressional Indian Commission, westward a few years since, here at North Platte was held our first peace-council. It was a thrillingly interesting occasion. The Indians flocked in by hundreds. The Brule Sioux chief, Spotted Tail, made a peace speech. Gen. Sherman cross-examined him. Gen. Harney admitted that he had never known an Indian chief the first to break a treaty. If belief in a future conscious identity, and intelligible communications from the spirit-world, constitute an individual a Spiritualist, then this Sioux chief is a Spiritualist. So, doubtless, are the chiefs and medicine-men of the other tribes.

Aug. 15 we reached Cheyenne, the capital of Wyoming. It is the most populous town between Omaha and Ogden. The Black Hills in the distance were crowned with snow. The railway cuts each side of Cheyenne show volcanic matter, mixed with marine fossils. A rolling ocean once swept over these plains and mountains. Here are found beautiful moss agates. They are for sale, with rare mineral specimens, at nearly every station. If London is the paradise of books, and Persia of roses, the West is the Elysian land of geologists and mineralogists.

Wyoming is woman's political Eden regained. Suffrage is here guaranteed her as a constitutional right. And yet only about half of the women in Cheyenne use this ballot privilege. Why is it? Are there not far more *women* than men opposed to universal suffrage? Laramie was the first place in the world where a female jury was impaneled.

Sherman is the highest railway point on the Pacific route, named in honor of Gen. Sherman. It is eight thousand two hundred and forty-two feet above the level of the sea. The air here is light, pure, and bracing. It is just the place for an astronomical observatory. The mountain-peaks are weird and magnificent; while the general plateau is covered with short grass, sage-brush, and stunted pines. Desolate as the region seemed, blackbirds were chattering upon telegraph-wires, swallows were cutting curious angles, and eagles sailed and circled above the mountain hights. Life and activity flame everywhere. The universe is God's house; this earth, one of the smaller apartments. Entering, we found it already furnished. What a carpet!—the emerald grass. What a ceiling!—the frescoed sky. What tapestried pillars!—the granite rocks. What a front-door!—the flaming sunrise. What a rear-door!—the sunset, through which the day goes down into shadow-lands. What a chandelier!—the sun and stars. What fields for explorations!—the interstellar spaces of infinity. Surely, as the Mohammedan says, "Allah is great and good."

ECHO CAÑON, AND OGDEN.

Oh for an ocean of imagery in which to dip the pen! Echo Cañon is entered at the little station of Castle Rock. The elevation is nearly seven thousand feet. Huge sandstone bluffs line the right-hand side of the cañon. These have been worn and torn by storms, till, in the distance, they present the appearance of old feudal castles. The engine leaps, plunges, down the defile. The perspective produces dizziness. Along the route westward from these castles and snowy ravines, are the "Devil's Gate," "Devil's Pulpit," "Devil's Slide," and the "Witches' Cave,"—names strictly orthodox.

Ogden is the famous junction of the railways. Tourists leave here for a peep at Salt Lake City. This half-way house, one thousand and thirty-two miles west of Omaha, claims a population of four thousand, a majority of whom are Mormons. Such as have left polygamy and its practices, for the purity of Spiritualism, are called "apostates." They are quite numerous. Why so many hot springs in these regions? and from whence the perpetual internal heat? A circus in full blast, our lecture was slimly attended. Ring-master's whips and grinning clowns are more inviting to the masses than literature, spiritual lectures, or such materializations as may be seen at Moravia and other Meccas noted for their demonstrations of immortality.

A venerable gentleman in Ogden, once a Latter-Day Saint, now a devoted Spiritualist, gave us a thrilling account of the inside workings of Mormonism, even to the ceremonial "endowments,"—washing, anointing with oil, and the clothing in white. Other of these rites, Israelitish and Phallic, are secret.

UTAH, AND SALT LAKE.

With a mongrel population of some twenty thousand, Salt Lake is claimed and considered the "Zion of our God." The location, in some respects, is admirable.

Each city lot, originally containing an acre and a quarter, blossoms now something like the poet's Eden. Irrigation from a pure mountain stream is the secret of this luxuriant growth. Externally, Salt Lake may be considered the city of crystal streams, and handsome fruit-orchards. Industry is the rule, rather than the exception, among these Mormons. Let us approve where we can. Successful co-operative stores have been formed in nearly all the districts. They are modeled largely after those in England.

The railway from Ogden passes along the shores of Salt Lake, the "Dead Sea" of America. The farms, irrigated and well tilled the whole distance, were burdened with ripened grain, and the orchards loaded with inviting fruit. Such cultivation quite surprised us. Only one mile from the Tabernacle, there is a full-flowing, warm sulphur spring; while the twin peaks of the Wahsatch Mountains, a few miles distant, are white with perpetual snows. They are eleven thousand feet high.

This inland Salt Lake, nearly a hundred miles in length, and forty in width, has seven islands, three of which are well adapted to grazing. The Mormon Church owns them. The waters of this lake are so excessively salt, that nine pailfuls will make one of salt. In 1850 it required only from three to five. Swarming with insect life, this rippling body has risen from twelve to fifteen feet within a few years. This has freshened the waters. Utah Lake should not be confounded with Salt Lake. The former is a beautiful sheet of fresh water, whose outlet is the River Jordan. The Territory abounds in scriptural names. There are over thirty incorporated cities in Utah; and the mineral wealth is inexhaustible.

JOSEPH SMITH, THE PALMYRA SEER.

The original Mormon temple is still standing in Kirtland, Ohio. Roaming through the deserted aisles of the quaint structure with one of the first "Latter-Day Saints," he gave me a full description of the eccentricities and spiritual marvels connected with the modern Mahomet, Joseph Smith. His seership was trustingly relied upon, and his clairvoyant gifts paraded as proofs of his Messiahship.

When in this "superior condition," his visions were as original as weird and witching. Furthermore, he conversed daily with spirits and angels.

In a letter written in 1842, by Joseph Smith, to "The Chicago Democrat," edited by John Wentworth, this founder of the "Latter-Day Saints" lifts the curtain, and gives us a peep at his visional experiences:—

"While fervently engaged in supplication, my mind was taken away from the objects with which I was surrounded, and I was inwrapped in a heavenly vision, and saw two glorious personages, who exactly resembled each other in features and likeness, surrounded with a brilliant light, which eclipsed the sun at noonday. They told me that all religious denominations were believing in incorrect doctrines, and that none of them was acknowledged of God as his church and kingdom; and I was expressly commanded to 'go not after them.' . . .

"On the evening of the 21st of September, A. D. 1823, while I was praying, a light like that of day burst into the house, and filled the whole room. The appearance produced a shock that affected the whole body. In a moment a personage stood before me, surrounded with a glory yet greater than that with which I was already surrounded. This messenger proclaimed himself to be an angel of God, sent to bring the joyful tidings that the covenant which God made with ancient Israel was at hand to be fulfilled. . . .

"On the 6th of April, 1830, the 'Church of Jesus Christ of Latter-Day Saints' was first organized in the town of Fayette, Seneca County, State of New York. Some few were called and ordained by the Spirit of revelation and prophecy, and began to preach as the Spirit gave them utterance; and, though weak, yet were they strengthened by the power of God; and many were brought to repentance, were immersed in the water, and were filled with the Holy Ghost by the laying-on of hands. They saw visions, and prophesied. Devils were cast out, and the sick healed by the laying-on of hands. . . .

"We believe in the same organization that existed in the primitive Church, viz., apostles, prophets, pastors, teachers, evangelists, . . . in the gift of tongues, prophecy, revelation, visions, healing, interpretation of tongues, &c."

All denominational religions originated in spiritual manifestations. Guatama Buddha, Jesus, Mahomet, Swedenborg, and Joseph Smith, all had visions, and saw angels. In the beginning of Mormonism, polygamy was undreamed of. Excrescences attach themselves to the thrifty trunk, rather than the tender sapling.

THE MORMON TABERNACLE.

A nondescript, — spheroidal-shaped and arched. It holds some ten thousand people. The organ is said to be equal to any in the United States. The music, the Sunday we attended, was heavy, but not soul-inspiring. While Elder Andrews was preaching, the deacons distributed the " Lord's Supper,"— bread and water. This latter is cheaper and better than any intoxicating symbol. The officiating clergyman dwelt largely upon the persecutions of the saints. They had been "pushed westward like the Indian;" their prophet Joseph, and his brother Hiram, were " murdered in 1844 in Carthage Gaol;" their president had been "arrested as a criminal;" and more afflictions at the hands of the Gentiles awaited them. It was a transitional period with their church. The sermon was pathetic, practical, and not devoid of all merit. There were about five thousand present. Polygamy, of its own unnaturalness, is declining. The system, considered by itself, has not a redeeming trait. There is less sealing of wives each year. And yet the churchal doctrine taught is, that the more wives, the greater glory to the man; the more children, the greater glory to the woman. This appears plausible when the Mormon doctrines are elaborately elucidated.

THE MORMON PRESIDENT.

Brigham Young is a native of Whitingham, Windham Co., Vt. Risking the laugh — this was *also* our birthplace. Armed with letters from United-States Senators, the Shaker Elder F. W. Evans, and others, we found easy access to the private sanctum of the Latter-Day Prophet. Ere an hour had elapsed, the interviewing was mutual. Our acquaintance with polygamy practices, and other phases of social life, in Turkey, deeply interested this prince of polygamists. He sharply questioned us; and, Yankee-like, we quizzed him. Mormons insist that plurality of wives is the only cure for prostitution and the social evil.

Calm and dignified, Mr. Young's appearance is considerably in his favor. He is rather short, and decidedly stout built. The forehead is full, the perceptives exceeding the reflectives. The complexion is light, hair thin, and gait moderate. He must have seen over seventy winters. While affable and easy in manner, he is at the same time subtle and penetrating. There is a vein of vanity, too, plainly visible in his constitution. He likes attention, — must be a leader, or nothing. Though on excellent terms with himself, he is too incomplete for a moral hero, and too selfish for a saint. He has hugged his passion of a "Latter-Day" Zion, modeled after the polygamy patriarchs of old, till it now scorches him like a brand. When he dies, there will be divisions in the flock. The bishops and other leaders are cunning and shrewd. There are several aspirants for the president's office. The humbler officials and itinerating elders are the religious workers. The bishops are generally rich; while President Young, a theocratic despot, through tithing and financial speculations, has become a millionaire.

MORMON DOCTRINES.

Since the Pacific Railway made the Atlantic States and Utah neighbors, Mormon theology and practices have become well understood. In the general conception, their doctrines are Mosaic; in construction, conglomerate; and, in execution, despotic. It is really the resurrected religion of Moses, Solomon, and David, veneered and slightly modernized.

Denying the existence of one eternal God, — essential spirit, — they believe in a plurality of gods, all of whom have wives, who were once mortals dwelling on material planets. The highest god of whom the Mormons profess any knowledge is "Elohim." His laws are the edicts of will, and his government sternly patriarchal. This deity, say they, is no omnipresent spirit, but a personal being, with body, bones, and flesh, but no blood. He dwells in the planet *Kolob*, near the center of our system. This planet, quite unknown to astronomy, revolves upon its axis once in a thousand years, which to the "Lord is as one day."

They believe spirit to be refined matter, and spirits to be constituted of material atoms. There are four orders of intelligences, — gods, angels, spirits, men. Both the Christian Bible, and Book of Mormon, are equally authoritative: neither is infallible. Revelations and spirit-ministrations have been the common property of all ages. All faithful Mormon saints become gods after death, creating, peopling, and governing worlds.

SPIRITS AS WORLD-BUILDERS.

Ignoring the Spiritualist's conception that God — the absolute Good — governs the universe by immutable law, and forms worlds, and systems of worlds, upon the principle of evolution, Mormons adopt the antiquated theory that spirits make worlds, — such starry worlds as sparkle in the measureless spaces of infinity. The erratic Scaliger, of the fourteenth century, put forth the same notion. North advanced the idea in his "Republic." It is the "dodge" of babyish atheists.

The divine scale downward, in their creed, runs thus: Elohim, Jehovah, Adam, Jesus, Joseph Smith, Brigham

Young, the Latter-Day Saints, and then the Gentile world generally. It is the chief employment of gods, angels, and spirits to manufacture and people worlds. Adam was the son, the representative son, of the god who made this earth. Accordingly, he is its ruling spirit. All the " righteous in Zion " will create, people, and govern worlds for their own glory. Morally speaking, they commence the nuclei of their future kingdoms now, present wives and children becoming hereafter. their subjects. Spirit-begetting, world-building, and star-engineering in the future world, — *these* are heavenly employments in the eyes of Mormons. For spirits, remember, having created worlds, and established laws for their government, run them mechanically through space, something as engineers run their trains, or schoolboys roll their hoops.

If a Pleiad fade, or planet disappear, may it not be owing to the careless sky-engineering of a neophyte, — some thoughtless spirit, who failed to whistle in season, " Down with the brakes " ?

STRANGE THEORIES.

Exercise of the procreative functions in the realms of immortality, as Mormons teach, naturally necessitates organic bodies, — not the " spiritual body " mentioned by Paul, but the resurrection of the veritable physical body, as originally taught in the decline of Egypt's greatness. Not only will the literal " body come up," say these religionists, but the very garments also in which it was buried. As Adam was first made, then Eve, so the man is first raised, then the wife, — " *the* wife " whom the saint most loved. After this they are " called up " — resurrected — in the order of the sealing. With the " saints," marriage is a sacrament, and for eternity. If not sacramentally sealed, the marriage ends at death. Each family is a clan, and the father the chief. President Young has fourteen or fifteen wives, and some forty or more children. Family worship is conducted in his household night and morning. In all relations, whether private or public, he is a theocratic dictator. He once said this publicly: "By the wave of my hand, I can move this people as I will. . . . I have a right to dictate to the Church in all things, either temporal or spiritual,— even to the ribbons the women wear."

Progression, they believe, extends to the next life. All may be saved, either here or hereafter, except the "sons of perdition,"— apostate Mormons. These are not to be eternally damned in hell-fire, but destroyed, disintegrated, returning back to their primal elements. This is what was meant by the "second death." They preach the continuance of "spiritual gifts," and affirm that President Young has been so overshadowed or entranced by their prophet-founder, when speaking, that his "gestures seemed, and voice sounded, precisely like Joseph Smith's." When first occurring, this created intense excitement. They are loth to accept any spiritual manifestations now, however elevated, unless coming through the adherents of the Church. In this they resemble the Roman Catholics.

Though upwards of seventy, Brigham Young, dreaming of an empire, is endeavoring to establish the order of Enoch,— a Utopian project of despotic communism. This scheme, which puts individual rights, property, and the liberty of conscience, into the hands of priest and president, is meeting, and deservedly so, with a most potent opposition. Prophets are criticised nowadays, and anathemas have lost their sting.

HOW TO DEAL WITH POLYGAMY.

That which is not just is not law. Governments, the statuary enactments of fallible men, are necessarily imperfect. And yet considering society, and the low moral condition of large classes, restraints and laws, with their legitimate penalties, are indispensable.

Mormonism is Asia-imported; and its devotees are doubtless

sincere. Plurality of wives they consider a religious duty, based upon the Bible, and a revelation on celestial marriage, given at Nauvoo in 1843. They also quote Christian authorities in its support, such as John Milton, Rev. Martin Madan, and the more recent Rev. Dr. D. O. Allen, missionary of the American Board for twenty-five years in India. These "foreign missionaries," including Episcopalians, Presbyterians, Baptists, &c., in general conference at Calcutta, unanimously came to the following conclusion:—

"If a convert, before becoming a Christian, has married more wives than one, in accordance with the practice of the Jewish and primitive Christian churches, he shall be permitted to keep them all; but such a person is not eligible to any office in the Church."

Polygamy being part of a religious system rooted in the Old Testament, based upon the examples of patriarchs and prophets, upon the approval of eminent Christian writers, and honestly accepted by an industrious body of religionists as a divine institution, and the highest order of social life, how can it legitimately come under Congressional legislation? Admitting it true that public opinion in republics constitutes the basis of legislative proceedings, still minorities have rights. These rights are sacred. To stolidly disregard them endangers liberty. Legislation, to enforce what a majority may denominate morality, is simply usurpation. Neither Congrsss, nor any other body of men, has a right to dictate a creed, or standard of morality, for individuals. It is impossible to legislate wisdom or virtue into any people. The true methods lie deeper. Right generation, ante-natal conditions, and educational manipulations, — these are the underlying forces of progress and redemption.

ANTICHRIST AND POLYGAMY.

Pending the Reformation in Germany, during the early part of the sixteenth century, those great reformers, Luther, Melancthon, Zwingle, and Bucer, held a solemn consultation at Wittenburg on the question, "Whether it is contrary to the divine law for a man to have two wives at once?" and decided unanimously that it *was not;* and, upon the authority of this decision, Philip, Landgrave of Hesse, actually married a second wife, his first being still alive. This fact is recorded in D'Aubigné's History of the Reformation, and by other authors of that period.*

Rev. Gilbert Burnet, Bishop of Salisbury, eminent as a theologian, wrote a tract upon the question, " Is a plurality of wives in any case lawful under the gospel?" Here is an extract:—

"Neither is it [a plurality of wives] anywhere marked among the blemishes of the patriarchs. David's wives, and store of them he had, are termed, by the prophet, God's gift to him; yea, a plurality of wives was made in some cases a duty by Moses' law; when any died without issue, his brother, or nearest kinsman, was to marry his wife, for raising up seed to him; and all were obliged to obey this, under the hazard of infamy if they refused it; neither is there any exception made for such as were married. From whence I may faithfully conclude. that what God made necessary in some cases to any degree can in no case be sinful itself; since God is holy in all his ways."

While some Christians, and *all* Utah Mormons, accept polygamy as biblical and divine in origin, only about one family in ten of the latter practices it. The responsibilities are too vital and potent. Household inharmonies are unpleasant. And then, children must be cared for, expenses met. Few, it is commonly believed, have wives sealed to them from vile sensual motives : still the look is unspiritual.

The equality of the sexes stoutly wars against polygamy. As an institution, it is semi-barbaric. Intelligence, and the soul's moral consciousness, condemn it. In Utah it is wilting under the frost-seal of a death that can know no resurrection. The more intellectual of the young, among these Latter-Day Saints, are not Mormons. They do not

* Hon. W. H. Hooper's Plea for Religious Liberty, p. 14.

follow their fathers, but incline to the ways of the Gentiles. Let polygamy perish, then, as it inevitably must, under the weight of an inherent social injustice. Reason, conviction, conscience, and moral purity, — *these* as motives, as spiritual forces, are wiser methods to employ in its overthrow, than persecution, or impassioned Congressional interference.

LIBERALISM IN SALT LAKE.

Seldom have we met a nobler self-sacrificing band of independent thinkers. The more enthusiastic of them are converts from Mormonism, — men esteemed in the church as elders, and one of them a veritable apostle. Showing their faith by their works, these enterprising souls have erected, and neatly furnished, a magnificent hall, *The Liberal Institute*, for educational purposes. This devotion to the principles of harmonial philosophy ought to inspire, if not shame, many Eastern organizations into the necessity of constructing commodious edifices for lyceums and lectures.

"The Utah Magazine," conducted by F. L. T. Harrison and W. S. Godbe, was a pioneer in the direction of religious freedom. Sorely did its calm yet keen utterances trouble Brigham Young, and those who considered him quite infallible. One of the startling declarations of the president in these times was this: "*It is my right to dictate to the church in all things, either temporal or spiritual, — even to the ribbons the women wear.*" If opposed in his dictatorship, he substitutes bitterness for logic, and abusive expletives for words of reason. The velvety paw could suddenly and easily change to the lacerating claw.

While Mr. Harrison was yet in the church of the Latter-Day Saints, he wrote thus, touching the marvels attending the itinerating elders and speakers in the Mormon fraternity: —

"When Joseph Smith inaugurated our church, nearly forty years ago, it burst upon the world as a revelation of spiritual power. The main peculiarity of our system was, that we asserted the necessity of close and constant intercommunication between this and the heavenly worlds. . . .

"'Abroad among the nations,' we had plentiful corroboration that this theory was no idle dream, but based on facts. Wholesale spiritual manifestations did there attend us. Our sick were then healed by the hundred. During the great cholera year in England, among about thirty thousand Latter-Day Saints, scarcely one succumbed to the disease. We were rich in spiritual manifestations; we felt angelic presence, even if unseen; we lived in an atmosphere that made us feel every day very near to God and the heavenly world."

The guest of Senator Fitch and lady, the recipient of personal kindnesses from others, we have only pleasant memories of Utah, its people, and scenery.

CALIFORNIA.

Landing upon the Pacific coast, fifteen years since, an invalid, I can only now exclaim, What changes! What a marvelous growth! The State has a population of some six hundred thousand; the city of San Francisco, one hundred and fifty thousand.

The Orient with its treasures, and the Occident with its untold energies, meet in this city, that has sprung up as if by the sorcerer's art. Vigor, vigilance, and public-spiritedness constitute the red globules that flow in the body politic. Pioneer Californians are truly hospitable. El-Dorado men are proverbially generous. Those possessing fortunes are certainly more liberal with them than the same number in the bleaker Atlantic cities. Money should be yoked to education, and idealism harnessed to practical uses. Citizenship here is a conglomerate. It reminds me of Constantinople.

PRESSING IMPROVEMENTS ARE NEEDED.

Arise, then, O sunset city of gold, and deck thyself! Telegraph Hill is an unsightly landmark. The sea-tourist passing the "Golden Gate" expects something different. And then, the dreary heights of Russian Hill might easily be covered with verdure. Black Point also might be made to bloom like the rose. What opportunities for landscape artists! Transformations and suburban decorations pay even property-holders. If there's a praiseworthy *mania*, it is the laying out of beautiful gardens, noble avenues, and mammoth parks. Inspired we feel to preach a sermon to the citizens of California, upon the importance of putting shade-trees around their houses, and books into them. Home presupposes a library, a cabinet, a conservatory, an orchard, and a grove with weird, winding paths for walking and meditation.

"Who loves a library, still his Eden keeps;
Perennial pleasures plants, and wholesome harvests reaps."

How easily the interior towns of this thrifty State might be made to rival the villages in the Atlantic States, by putting out ornamental shrubbery! In a hot, dusty summer's day, what is more inviting than the cooling shadows of graceful evergreens, or the serried lines of maples and elms that interlace and arch public highways? And then, why not plant fruit-trees all along the wayside? Why not have the gardens of the Hesperides in our midst to-day? Why not have a heaven on earth, with the divine will fully done? When half-dreaming of heaven, with its homes of love, dreaming of the spirit-gardens that hang and float in ether spaces above us, our brain throbs and brims in ecstasy.

THE SAN FRANCISCANS.

Old heads guide the feet that tread this new city. Enterprise is the password, victory the psalm. Enthusiasm anywhere is existence, and earnestness its own great reward. Financially Californian cups run over. This is the trouble, — the material overriding the spiritual.

The two themes of excitement just now are continental railways and Arizona diamond-fields. Reality or sham diamond stocks sell readily; and emigrants, vying with miners, are hurrying along the trails of the troublesome Apaches.

The Chinese question remains a puzzle. Hard coin is likely to continue the circulating currency. Exchange is found a profitable business.

The present has been a year of unprecedented prosperity all along the Pacific shores. Californians tell us they can spare twelve million quintals of wheat from their coast this season, and have enough for home-consumption. Lacking vessels and railway conveyances, quantities must remain unsold. English and other foreign nations control the great shipments. They can afford to underbid our ship-owners. Congress would do well to turn its attention from railway corporations and subsidies to American shipping interests, and their necessary relations to the great trading-marts of the world.

THE FRUIT AND THE VINE.

Tons of melons, peaches, pears, apricots, figs, grapes, &c., during this September month, and much earlier, literally blockade Oakland Wharf and the front streets. Passing, one naturally asks, How can they be disposed of? The markets are cloyed, and it will not pay to transfer them to the Western States. The Pacific Railway at present is a perfect monopoly. When those other lines projected are constructed, fares and freights must necessarily be reduced. Soulless corporations threaten the life of the country. Oh for Congressmen that cannot be bought!—for judges who are rigidly just!

This State seems determined to excel in other things than gold-mines and mammoth trees. Think of a single squash weighing two hundred pounds! Last year the Santa Barbara grape-vine produced nearly seven tons of grapes. R. B. Blowers, a substantial land-owner of Woodland, Yolo County, took us into his Chili clover-field, which he pastures four months, and then mows five times during the year. This Chili variety of clover is excellent for grazing purposes, and exceedingly nourishing as hay. It has a small white blossom, strikes its roots down ten and twelve feet into the deep, rich soil, and often produces twenty-four tons to the acre. Ranches do best when thoroughly irrigated. The agricultural and horticultural outlook of the whole State is full of promise. Rice-growing on Sherman Island has proved a complete success.

Oranges of fine flavor are to be had in all parts of the State, ripening from November to April. Three varieties of lemons grow in the Southern Coast District. Two counties, Yolo and San Joaquin, have produced four million bushels of wheat in a season. Large fields often average from ninety to one hundred bushels to the acre.

The low "tule" lands, if reclaimed, would produce immense crops of rice; an important matter considering California's sixty thousand population of Chinese. Peach orchards fringe the rivers; while beautiful vineyards either dot·the valleys, or shingle the rugged sides of the Sierra Nevadas. What California most needs to-day is a fresh immigration of sober, industrious, energetic men.

RELIGIOUS TENDENCIES.

Countries, like individuals, have their aural emanations. There is less restraint west than east of the Rocky Mountains. Thought free, the intellect clear, liberalism fruits out spontaneously in California. Residing anywhere in the stirring, pulsing West, broadens the vision, expands the emotional nature, and inspires a most generous toleration.

Our lectures upon the harmonial philosophy and social life in Turkey were delivered in Mercantile Library to audiences intelligent and critical. Mr. Kendrick was the presiding officer. The progressive lyceum was full of promise. Dr. Dunn drilled officers and pupils in calisthenic exercises. Rev. Herman Snow, one of God's faithful shepherds, has ever at hand a choice assortment of liberal and Spiritualist books. This is the head-center of liberalism in the city, and the only liberal bookstore worthy the name upon the Pacific Coast.

Hon. S. J. Finney, though much absorbed in matters pertaining to legislation, continues the same brave defender of equal rights, and broad humanitarian principles, that he was in the Atlantic States. Though criticising loose, illogical literature; though ignoring the immoralities of "sexual freedom;" though protesting against the imposture, and money-catching charlatanism, so frequently fastening itself upon Spiritualism, — he has never denied the divine principles underlying the Spiritual philosophy. In a letter to us, dated Sept. 1, he writes, among other things, this: —

"I hear that I am reported, in the East, as having thrown Spiritual science overboard. Well, the *liars* are not all dead yet!"

There exists among reformers a most deplorable want of good-will and mutual esteem, attributable, evidently, to envy and jealousy. This weakness was so common among artists in Swift's time, that he wrote, —

> "What *artist* would not grieve to see
> His brother *paint* as well as he?"

Every man of genius has a way of his own. Let him have it. A rational individuality is commendable.

It is said that Cowley despised the genial, natural Chaucer; that Fielding ridiculed Richardson; that Wilkes sneered at the prolific book-maker Gibbon; and that the contemporaries of Newton twitted him of being a dreamer among the stars, and an almanac-maker among men. It was thoughtful in Paul to write, "In honor preferring one another." The Pacific shores are rich in great, full-blossomed souls.

To-morrow, the 11th of September, 1872, we embark upon the steamer "Idaho." Our old friend Dr. E. C. Dunn is to accompany us on our voyage.

The passage to Australia, with a fair sea, requires about thirty-five days, possibly forty. Starting, light-hearted, we throw backward kind thoughts and good-will to all. The following tender lines written by Edward Pollock, the young and gifted Californian poet, seem appropriate : —

"There's something in the 'parting hour'
  Will chill the warmest heart ;
Yet kindred, comrades, lovers, friends,
  Are fated all to part.
But this I've seen, and many a pang
  Has pressed it on my mind, —
The one who goes is happier
  Than those he leaves behind.

Have you a friend, a comrade dear,
  An old and valued friend?
Be sure your term of sweet concourse
  At length will have an end.
And when you part, — as part you will, —
  Oh! take it not unkind
If he who goes is happier
  Than you he leaves behind.

God wills it so, and so it is :
  The pilgrims on their way,
Though weak and worn, more cheerful are
  Than all the rest who stay.
And when, at last, poor man, subdued,
  Lies down, to death resigned,
May he not still be happier far
  Than those he leaves behind?"

CHAPTER II.

THE SANDWICH ISLANDS. — SOUTH-SEA ISLANDS, AND SÉANCES AT SEA.

OUR steamer wriggles like a revolving auger. Our crew, a nautical commonwealth, is getting social. There are two princes aboard, — Prince Augustus, Duke of Saxe, who married the Brazilian emperor's daughter; and Prince Philippe, having a high grade in the Austro-Hungarian army. They are modest, thoroughly-cultured gentlemen. To know is to admire them.

Spirit speaks through forms. Souls largely fashion the houses they inhabit. An individual's life-aims can no more be concealed than fire. Faces and voices, fingers and feet, all reveal character. Repairing to the stateroom assigned us on "The Idaho," Aaron Knight,* entrancing Dr. E. C. Dunn; said in substance, —

"On this voyage, stretching in the distance, we can not only speak to you face to face, but can fix such an electric atmosphere around you as will add to your comfort and spiritual unfoldment. The two spirit circles, ever a unit in purpose, are all present. Our combined power you well understand, and yet the laws of nature are our masters. Should your bodies go down to rest on coral reefs, we shall be present to welcome and minister to your resurrected spirits."

* Aaron Knight, the spirit guardian of Dr. Dunn, entranced him some seventeen years since in Battle Creek, Mich.; giving at the time his name, the family name, his earthly residence in Yorkshire, Eng., and about the length of time he had been in the spirit-world, — nearly two hundred years. Subse-

How calm the sea! What a quiet life, reading by day, and gazing by night at the glittering stars, — those shining altar-lamps set in the heavens by the finger of the Eternal! A change, — rough and rolling, the ocean! Would you escape sea-sickness, walk the deck in defiance of dashing waves. Exercise a plucky will-power: no compromise. Grace aside, it is *grit* that leads to glory on the ocean.

INNER DREAMS.

Half dreaming, let us philosophize. I fancy myself a sort of moral equation. Consciousness is the algebraic " equal ; " eternity, the unknown quantity. Laws are deific methods. Mathematical laws are universal. Every atom, every particle of iron circulating in my body, follows the law of its strongest attraction, — follows it mathematically. Results are true to their producing causes. Moral equations, because relating to moral actions, and the moral possibilities of the soul, admit of self-solution only. I am the problem. I solve myself.

The genius of this intellectual age requires the abolition of war, of flag and cannon, of whip and personal Devil, — ay, more, the gradual yet complete reconstruction of government, jurisprudence, theology. Oh for the coming man, the

quently he told me of the old walled city of York, once capital of the kingdom; of the York Minster, and its weird pictures; of the River Ouse, St. Mary's Abbey, and of his brother the Rev. James Knight, ordained in London, — *all* of which were as utterly unknown to me as to Mr. Dunn.

When appointed to a consular post in Asiatic Turkey, by Pres. Grant, I resolved, upon reaching England, to identify this spirit, if possible. Accordingly accompanied by Robert Green, Esq., of Brotherton, I went to York, and then to the " Will Office; " where, after long searching, aided by the clerk, we found the *brother's name*, Rev. James Knight, A.M., who, as Aaron Knight had frequently informed us, preached in London, York, and other prominent cities. This is the record, transcribed in the clerk's own hand: —

"24th of October, 1714, James Knight, A.M., was ordained deacon in the Savoy Chapel, London, and priest in the same chapel on the following Sunday."

From the Institution Book in the Archiepiscopal Registry, York.

YORKSHIRE, ENGLAND.

The identity of river, abbey, minster, pictures, family name, Rev. James Knight, was perfect, and the *test* one of the most interesting and important in the records of phenomenal Spiritualism.

constructor! Oh for self-denial, and more moral heroism! Why cringe and cower? Why lean like a half-dipped candle, and cautiously inquire for the winning way? Alone, — alone with truth, is a majority!

WHEN DOES THE SOUL BEGIN TO EXIST?

"I looked, and, behold, a door was opened in heaven," exclaimed the Revelator John. The harmonial philosophy recognizes this open door, — these golden gates ajar.

Sitting at four o'clock in our stateroom with Dr. Dunn, he was immediately entranced, the conversation turning upon pre-existence. Mr. Knight, the controlling spirit, said, that, "While making no pretensions to infallibility, still I must say that I consider the theory of 're-incarnation,' that is, the re-incarnating of resurrected and immortalized souls back into gross earthly bodies again, as neither necessary in the divine economy, nor true. in fact; but the theory of the soul's conscious pre-existence is true."

What is the soul, Mr. Knight?

"A potentialized portion of God, the divine principle, the spirit *esse*, the keystone that crowns with a fadeless immortality.

"This germinal soul, beginning to accrete spiritual substance and physical matter, takes the human form from the sacred moment of embryonic conception."

But, if the human form has a beginning, must it not have an end? as only circles are endless.

"It is not very safe, in reasoning, to apply circles, angles, or mathematics in any form, to mind. Ending does not imply an abrupt finality, neither annihilation. Both the spiritual and physical bodies are continually ending in time. Never at two different moments are they precisely the same. Change pertains to all matter, to all substance. The term 'creation' should give place to 'evolution,' 'unfoldment.' The divine method is by the law of evolution.

If the undisputed axiom be true, that 'Ex nihilo nihil fit,' 'from nothing nothing comes,' then 'man uncreate,' — man once absolutely and literally out of, never *in*, conscious being as individual man! This renders the existence of man a positive impossibility. Further: if certain combinations, conditions, and principles go to form or make up the sum total of man, more potent laws and conditions, with other and superior disintegrating forces, may unmake him. While spirit manifestations demonstrate a future existence, pre-existence lays the foundation of, and proves the endlessness of, that existence in the beautiful home-lands of heaven."

THE INDIVIDUALITY OF SPIRITS.

An Irish spirit, Michael O'Brien, entrancing the doctor, sharply reproved me for not calling *him*, when he came, "brother," as I did others.

Pleading guilty, I said, "What has been your occupation to-day?"

"Well, bracing you up a little, fixing the atmosphere around the medium, and studying metaphysics, — surely, a jaw-twister, *that*. With the assistance of Mr. Knight and the circle, I am going to make a scholar, Jamie, I am *that*."

"What have you seen in the better land to-day?"

"Faith, I'm always seeing here in spirit-life. I see now a whole shoal of spirits around us, some of whom want to control *you*. They all have their own notions and plans, whether Catholics or Protestants, Chinamen or Indians; and, I may as well say, Irishmen, though I'm a Kilkenny Irishman myself. The spirit-world is very much like the world you are in: you'll find it so, you *will*."

Parisi, an Italian spirit, positive and commanding in style, comes when he has something to communicate, and never from calling. Controlling, and speaking of the origin of life, he incidentally referred to the moon's inhabitants.

"But our astronomers," said I, "pronounce the moon uninhabited, having no atmosphere."

"It matters little to me what your astronomers, in their

earthly blindness, may or may not say. There is an atmosphere pertaining to your earth, to the moon, to the planets, to every orb, every object, and entity in nature. The most refined atmosphere relating to any star in the range of your telescopic system is one of the Pleiades, third of the series. There are other planets in interstellar realms far in advance of this, however. Earthly astronomers know nothing of them; nor very little, as yet, of their neighbor the moon, with its atmospheric strata, and swarming inhabitants. The science of astronomy among mortals is yet in its swaddling-clothes. They should talk with becoming modesty. . . .

"Most certainly. There are old Oriental cities, precious stones, treasures and statuary, buried in deltas, and imbedded under mountains of sands. These, by the aid of clairvoyance, and the citizens of the heavens who lived in remote antiquity, might and *will* be unearthed when mortals become unselfish enough to wisely appropriate such immense treasures."

Aaron Knight, influencing, said, "Spirits have infinitely better facilities for moral progress than mortals; but as to how they use them is a matter of choice. I am no fatalist. Neither men nor spirits are mere things, but moral actors. . . . Certainly, there are planets whose surfaces are so refined, fruits so sublimated, and atmospheres so ethereal, that the inhabitants peopling them, though having an outer envelope comparable to the physical body, do not die as the term 'death' is understood by you. They gradually throw off the external vesture in particled emanations, but do not for a moment cease to be conscious. . . . Spirits are, of course, fallible. Many of them do not understand either the laws or the effects of psychological control as they should. Mediums are both benefited and injured by magnetic influences. This depends upon the wisdom and motives of the intelligences. . . . The guardian, other things being equal, can the most effectually impress a medium. All mediums should have in attendance organized circles of spirits. This is a shield and a safeguard. No effective medium is ever left entirely alone. Some member of the sympathizing circle continues with him, to minister as necessity demands. . . .

"No: none retrograde as a whole. There is no law of absolute retrogression. While mortal or spirit may retrograde morally, they may at the same time be advancing intellectually; a man, while declining physically, may be progressing spiritually. Action must ultimate in progress in some direction. Upward, as one of your poets wrote, 'all things tend.'"

THE SANDWICH ISLANDS.

This ocean-embosomed cluster of isles, nine in number, has some sixty-five thousand inhabitants. When discovered by Capt. Cook, the group was supposed to contain full four hundred thousand. Remnants of mounds, temples, and ruins indicate it. During the second voyage of this navigator, a difficulty arising, a high chief was killed by one of the captain's party. The slain chief's brother swore revenge. In the midst of the fray, Capt. Cook himself shot a man. The natives, who had previously supposed him a god, found him decidedly human. Though finally killing him through retaliation, they dissected his body for anatomical purposes. History and legend agree that these natives were never cannibals.

The entrance to the harbor is through a passage in the coral reefs that girdle the island of Oahu. Seen from the harbor, Honolulu is exceedingly beautiful. The city, embowered in fresh green foliage, numbers six thousand; the district, twelve thousand, only about two thousand of whom are white. The Hawaiian Hotel, and the public buildings generally, would do honor to any larger city. The gardens are decidedly tropical. They are irrigated from mountain streams. Fruit clogs the market. Sugar-plantations and pulu-fields plead for more workmen. The "labor-question" here, as elsewhere, awaits solution. All men are about as lazy as they can afford to be.

It is very common to see native women trooping along the streets horseback. Some were richly though quaintly attired in long riding-habits. They all, like the Turkish and Arab women of the East, ride astride their poor-bred horses; and some deck themselves in ribbons and othelo flowers. Their dresses are entirely loose and flowing, *all* the weight coming upon the shoulders.

On the outskirts of the city, 'mid tropical shrubbery and graceful palms, I saw taro growing, the original Hawaiian food of the natives. It thrives on soil that can be flooded. Exceedingly nutritious, it not only tastes, but, when steamed in their stone ovens, looks, very much like huge, rough Irish potatoes.

From this taro, they make their *poi* by pounding it into a semi-fluid consistency, and then storing it in gourds and calabashes. It is eaten by dipping one — if very thin, two — fingers into the pot of *poi*, and thrusting them quickly into the mouth.

THE MORALS OF OAHU.

These Hawaiians are considered by some ethnologists as vestiges of the Semitic stock. Others think to the contrary. It is certain that the primitive poetry of these natives bears a striking resemblance in style to the Hebraic. They practiced, when discovered, circumcision, and had what corresponded to the Israelitish " house of refuge." They had three orders of priests, — Kaula, prophets; Kilo, magicians or ghost-seers; and Kahunas, the teachers. They have a tradition among themselves, that they came from Tahita. Europeans brought among them liquors and syphilis, and taught them war upon the principles of Christian civilization. As a people, these aborigines are rapidly dying off from the island. Civilization, such as it is, hastens their inevitable doom. In twenty years there will probably be no Kanackas, pure-blooded natives, left upon the Hawaiian Islands. Their moral degeneracy has kept pace with their physical. Though nominally Christianized, their "easy virtue" is patent in the flocks of half-castes that throng the city and mountain districts. If missionaries have not filled the brains of these poor heathen with intelligence, and exalted moral principles, they have managed to fill their own purses.

Morals are at a low ebb. Many white men — Germans, French, Portuguese, and some Americans — live with native women unmarried. This is considered no social disgrace, since commenced many years ago by distinguished officials. Color is no bar to office or position.

The government of these islands is a constitutional monarchy. Queen Emma, who traveled through Europe and our country a few years since, became queen by marriage.

Kalakaua is the present king. He has a fine literary taste, and seeks this class of men as privy councilors.

Though belief or unbelief in no way affects the truth, still the belief of a man, if held in earnest, and woven into the spiritual frame of mind, must necessarily exert a controlling influence upon the springs of action, and leave its impress upon the life. The natives originally believed in good and bad spirits, in a future life, and the return of their departed from the land of shades. Their idols were the images of deified mortals. Dr. Damon, a resident of Honolulu, or some of the Polynesian groups, for thirty years, assured us that these aborigines all believed in a future existence when first visited by missionaries. The belief bubbles up spontaneously in the souls of all tribes and races.

HAWAIIAN SPIRITISM.

Candid research will ultimately force the concession that the lowest and most degraded tribes have deep-rooted ideas of gods, spirits, and a future existence. Otherwise, they are not men, but monkeys, apes, baboons, chimpanzees, gorillas! Man devoid the cranial organs of hope, veneration, conscientiousness, ideality, and spirituality, is not a wholeness, — is *not* man. With these organs, he necessarily conceives of another and superior state of existence. His notions may be rude; still they are germinally bedded in truth. Under all skies, man naturally believes in the superhuman, in the return of departed ancestors, and the care of guardian spirits. This is pre-eminently true of this Hawaiian branch of the Polynesians. Faith of this kind is so rooted in their souls' soil, that thirty years' missionary drillings have in no way eradicated it.

Bennett, after describing, in his historic sketches, their mythology, and the "*tabu* imposed by the chiefs," says there was always a "class among them who practiced sorcery and conjuration, and offered prayers to the spirits." Richardson assures us, that, in all past times, "they dealt in divination, calling upon the spirits of their dead to assist them in war, and bless them in peace. Their gods were the spirits of departed heroes."

A strong effort was early made to convert Kamehameha I. to the Christian religion. The purpose signally failed. He listened, however, with great gravity to the churchal argument for the "necessity of faith in Christ;" and then, says Jarvis, he coolly replied, —

"By faith in your God, you say any thing can be accomplished, and the Christian will be preserved from all harm. If so, cast yourself down from yonder precipice; and, if *you* are preserved, I will believe."

It was a clincher!

SINGULAR SOCIAL CUSTOMS.

Naturally trusting and affectionate, Hawaiian men, when meeting in their more primitive times, embraced and kissed, as do women in civic life. Missionaries, forgetting Paul's injunction, "Salute the brethren with a holy kiss," have taught them a different way of salutation. Their priesthood was hereditary. Each chief, before the consolidation in a kingdom, had his family priest, who accompanied him to battle. In Christian countries this class of men is called chaplains, praying for victory through war, in the name of the Prince of peace!

In the better period of these islanders, a falsehood was considered a fearful offense, and fœticide was unknown. The male child then born, and now also, takes the preference. This is the case in the Christian kingdoms of Europe. Lunatics were supposed by these Sandwich Island people to be obsessed by angry spirits.

In their old traditionary ages, the man had but one wife. Marriage ceremonies, as such, were unknown. Wooing for a season, the parties commenced living together, and, if reciprocally pleasant, the union was understood to be permanent; if unhappy, however, they mutually agreed to separate. If children were born into their rude homes, it was then considered disgraceful to annul the marital relation. They are exceedingly fond of their children, and in every department of life are naturally kind and generous.

INTELLECTUAL DECLINE.

Though doubtless true,

"That through the ages one unceasing purpose runs,"

still there are lost Edens of civilization and culture. If literature and art, like the nationalities they crowned, have had their ebb and flow, so civilized countries and island tribes have had their golden ages now dead and buried. Extant monuments, mammoth ruins, and exhumed scrolls, substantiate the position.

Who has not been charmed while reading, in Baldwin's "Pre-Historic America," of that ancient Peruvian road extending over marshes, ravines, rocky precipices, and the great chain of the Sierras, — strongly walled on each side, and quite as long as the two Pacific railroads? These macadamized roads were constructed, according to Gomara, long before the reigns of the Incas. Humboldt, examining them, writes, —

"Our eyes rested continually on superb remains of a paved road of the Incas. The roadway, paved with well-cut dark porphyritic stone, was twenty feet wide, and rested on deep foundations. This road was marvelous. None of the Roman roads I have seen in Italy, in the South of France, or in Spain, appeared to me more imposing than this work of the ancient Peruvians."

So there are remnants of a magnificently paved road around the Isle of Maui, one of the Hawaiian group. It was constructed long ages ago by a king of the island, named Kahihapilani, who was expecting his sister from the island of Hawaii. This masonry, as well as templed ruins, point to a once high, but now entombed civilization.

And, what is equally interesting, the native poets of the Hawaiian Islands were an order by themselves, something like the Druidic bards of Briton. These were called Kàhumeles (poet-bards) in ancient times, and were not unlike the Homeric balladists, and Grecian rhapsodists. Their chant-like poems were handed down from father to son; and they proudly sung that in the halcyon ages their ancestors came from Asia. Their poems, drawn from natural scenery, were weird and musical, but neither measured nor rhythmical. This is true of those old compositions of the Vedic ages.

Declining and degenerate, the Hawaiians have no genuine poets now. Some, however, excel in music and mathematics. Natives constitute the missionaries' choirs. Many of the old Hawaiian chants in praise of their chiefs and their gods have been committed to writing by Judge Fanander, for the purpose of publication. Fortunately, while attending a natives' "hula-hula" dance in the queen's gardens, I listened to some of these meles, or ballad-songs.

RECENT PHENOMENA.

The apostolic "discerning of spirits" is a gift as common in "heathen" as Christian lands. The Sandwich Islanders, though frequently seeing and conversing with departed spirit friends, speak of their manifestations with great reserve; because the missionaries have assured them that all such phenomena were the "devices of the Devil."

The gentlemanly editor of "The Pacific Advertiser," and an old resident of Honolulu, Mr. Sheldon, narrated to us several interesting incidents relating to Spiritism in his own family, and others among the natives of the islands.

CHAPTER III.

THE POLYNESIAN RACES.

"THE steamer 'Nevada' sails to-day, Sept. 26, four o'clock, for New Zealand," reads "The Morning Honolulu Bulletin."

What a day of bustle, — coaling, loading, transferring, packing! The beeves have been driven in from the mountains by the natives. Panting, frightened, and fevery with heat and rage, they are roped on the wharf by the sailors, beaten, thrown to the ground, and tied with strong hempen cords. Then while bellowing, struggling, and frothing at the mouth with very madness, they are dragged by marine tackling up into the vessel to be killed and eaten by passengers on the voyage. And the crew — sadly do we say it — greedily ate the fevered bodies of those poor, bruised, dead animals! In the year 2000, meat-eating will be considered a monstrous practice, only paralleled by the cannibalism of the South Seas.

THE DAILY OUTLOOK.

Sunny are these days, sailing 'mong the Pacific Islands, decked in the rich and gorgeous drapery of the tropics.

> "Oh! soft are the breezes that wave the tall cocoa,
>   And sweet are the odors that breathe on the gale;
> Fair sparkles the wave as it breaks on the coral,
>   Or wafts to the white beach the mariner's sail."

The Bishop of Oxford describes the inhabitants of Polynesia as "children of nature, children of the air, children of light, children of the sun, children of beauty, taking their greatest pleasure in the dance." Though these paradisaical isles sparkle like gems in the Pacific, the origin of the races peopling them is a study. Ethnology and comparative philology can at most but point to the quarries whence nationalities and tribes were hewn. From the rich table-lands of India, and the undulating valleys of Iran, came those primeval emigrants that gave to the West culture and intellectual activity. But the extreme East, the Micronesians and the Polynesians of the Pacific, whence these intertropical races? During our week's stay on the Hawaiian group of islands, and others since, the natives, their customs, laws, languages, and religious ideas, have been a constant theme of thought and study.

It is generally conceded that the languages spoken by the millions of Polynesians have the same common structure, with such differences as may be resolved into dialects resulting from long non-intercourse.

When a native New Zealander and Hawaiian meet, though more than four thousand miles apart, they are so closely connected lingually, that they very soon engage in a free interchange of ideas. This, in some degree, is true of the Marquesan, Tahitan, Samoan, and others of the Polynesian stocks. The system of "taboos" in some form runs through all the Southern Polynesian families.

THE MICRONESIANS.

Glance at the location of your island neighbors in Oceanica. Have we not all one father? Are we not brothers all? The numerous Caroline, Ascension, Gilbert Islands, and others adjacent, evidently belong to the Micronesian division, and were peopled either by the Indo-Chinese, or Northern Malayan races. The ruins on Ponapi, one of the Caroline group, built entirely of basaltic prisms, indicate a marvelous civilization in the past. The present natives have no conception why nor by whom such massive walls, parapets, and vaults were constructed. The present race upon the Gilbert Islands has stout physical developments, high cheek-bones, fine straight hair, black and glossy. The aquiline nose is the rule, and the cerebrum is largely developed. They are less savage than some of their trafficking visitors.

Swarms of children, innocent of any clothing, flock to the harbor upon each landing. So prolific are they yet, on the greater number of these islands, and so uncontaminated with the diseases of foreign civilizations, that their population is deliberately limited by practicing abortion to prevent too great a number of hungry mouths. They should study the Malthusian method of depopulation, or welcome to their sea-girt shores Shaker missionaries to initiate celibate communities.

THE MARSHALL ISLES.

These are a large group of the Micronesian family, ranging from 4½° to 12° north latitude. They were first discovered by the Spaniards in 1529, and called by them the "good gardens." The inhabitants were straight, light-colored, and strangely tattooed. Their dress was decidedly Adamic, — fig-leaves and mats about their loins! At present the men wear full beards, are energetic, and very hospitable. The women are dressed in fine matting, have long black hair, and decorate themselves profusely in shell-jewelry. Ocean travelers consider them beautiful, though minus corset and waterfall, pannier and paint.

They traverse the seas with large retinues, are eminently clannish, and count nobility of descent on the mother's side. While worshiping deities, they hold the spirits of their ancestors in great reverence. They are skilled, say European residents in their midst, in every kind of "incantation and necromancy." They consult their mediums when in a state of ecstasy, and heal by beating and striking the diseased part. Consecrated groves, and sacred spots, are common among them. Their desolate cemeteries are in waving groves of cocoanut trees; and weird-shaped paddles lift their blades for tombstones. They are evidently of Japanese extraction.

THE SAMOANS, OR NAVIGATORS.

These very important islands, a sort of half-way steamship house in the Pacific, for recruiting, repairing, and re-provisioning, lie between latitudes $13\frac{1}{2}°$ and $14\frac{1}{2}°$ south, and about 170° west longitude. Our captain made a short call at this group, — nine in number, — too short for our individual purpose. They are volcanic in origin, safe to approach, and partially belted with coral reefs. Pago-Pago is a deep, land-locked harbor on the south side of Tutuila. Upolu is the most thickly populated, containing twenty thousand inhabitants. Our gentlemanly commander, J. H. Blethen, had permitted us to study his maps and charts of this densely-wooded group of isles — gems of the ocean — before reaching them. The afternoon approach was too grand and gorgeous for the pen to paint. The sea was a polished mirror; the sky, glass; the sun, well adown the western spaces, gold; and the scattering clouds, crimson and purple, were chariots of fire.

The steam checked, and the vessel at rest, the natives flocked to us like birds to a banquet. Physically, they are a splendidly-made race, with full, high foreheads, wavy beards, and white, exquisitely-set teeth. They are light in color, and quick in motion. They have dark-brown hair, eyes black and expressive. The occasional reddish hair seen had been bleached. Honest and trusting, they are evidently of Indo-Malayan origin.

The women are well-formed, healthy, handsome, and, what is more, are famed for their chastity. Both men and women go as naked as new-born babes, except weirdly-woven leaves and sea-grass aprons around their loins. Our passengers bought of them war-clubs, fans, fruits, head-gearings, birds, baskets, spears, and shells. Missionaries are among them. Already they exhibit hopeful signs of civilization in wishing to barter for tobacco, whiskey, fancy-colored clothing, and lime preparations for bleaching their hair. Some of these natives bleach or color the hair red; Americans, black: tastes differ.

The scenery upon these islands is transcendently beautiful. Cascades are numerous, the valleys fertile, and vegetation varied and luxuriant. Tropical fruits, cocoanuts, pineapples, bananas, citrons, bread-fruit, oranges, limes, sugarcane, coffee, taro and dye-wood trees abound in rich profusion. The largest portion of Upolo has a fine garden soil, where large springs of pure water bubble up, and flow in thousands of little streams toward the sea. The whole group is exceedingly valuable. Action has already been taken by the United States toward annexation.

Among the code of laws drawn by these native chiefs, to be recognized in commercial relations between the United States and the Samoan Islands, are the following: —

"5th. All trading in distilled or spirituous liquors, or any kind of intoxicating drink, is absolutely prohibited. Any person so offending shall be fined one hundred dollars on conviction before a mixed court. All such liquors found on shore, and kept for sale or barter, shall be seized and destroyed. If any native is found intoxicated, the individual who has supplied him with drink shall pay a fine of ten dollars. If any foreigner be found drunk or riotous, he shall pay a fine of ten dollars.

"6th. Any person found guilty of offering inducement to a native female to prostitute herself to a foreigner, to pay a fine of ten dollars; and any native female found guilty of prostituting herself to a foreigner, to pay a fine of twenty dollars."

And these Samoan chiefs are called " savages," " degraded heathen," to whom tobacco-using, wine-drinking Christian missionaries must be sent to save them from hell!

I can but deplore that conceited ignorance which characterizes two classes of Americans, — radical rationalists who crankly assert that there " are islanders in the Pacific, and ferocious tribes in Africa, that have not the faintest idea of God or another state of existence;" and pompous clergymen who everlastingly prate about the "polluted and fiendish *heathen*" of Oceanica.

THE FEEJEES.

Islands, like individuals, have their reputations. Those dotting an ocean which covers one-third of the entire surface of the globe should be more thoroughly surveyed and explored. The Feejees, constituting quite an archipelago, contain one hundred and fifty-four islands, seventy of which are inhabited. They are governed by chiefs. The natives, though dark-hued, are noble in mien, shrewd, and enterprising. Missionaries have given them a hard name. Bear in mind the Feejeean side of the story has neither been heard nor published. They stoutly deny having been aggressors, yet admit themselves good at retaliation. A. G. Findlay, F. R. G. S., says, —

"These islanders have been misrepresented. Late visitors speak very highly of their honesty, cleanliness, refinement, and virtue."

The men have heavy, bushy heads of hair, and wear full beards. When discovered by the navigator Tasman, they knew nothing of the venereal diseases that accompany Christian civilization. The taint of syphilis is not yet common among them. They had, when first visited, no idols. They believed in transmigration and immortality. They worshiped in caves and groves. They also had their mediums, who, when in ecstatic states, foamed at the mouth; but every utterance breathed in this rude trance-condition was carefully noted as the voice of a god.

They build their houses in cocoanut groves. Often they are umbrella-shaped, and rudely thatched. It requires little or no labor to sustain life. Enterprise is little more than a dream all through these equatorial regions. The English are aiming to get full control of the Feejee group for cotton-growing, and a military basis.

HOW WERE THESE ISLANDS PEOPLED?

What the camel is to the Arab, the horse to the Asian Mongul, the canoe is to these islanders. In the construction of their *proas*,—sea-crafts made of bread-fruit wood,—they display great talent. The better class of them will carry a hundred men in the open sea. The sails and rigging are managed with great dexterity. They provision these *proas* with cocoanuts, taro, preserved bread-fruit, &c.; which, with their skill in fishing, enables them to sustain voyages for several months. This partially explains the method by which the different and widely separate Pacific isles may have been peopled. The Malay race—nomads of the sea—whether for adventure, commerce, or plunder, had but to put their wives and utensils into their canoes, and, drifting with the prevailing trade-winds, were sure to reach some island, intermingling with the inhabitants; or, if uninhabited, establishing a new race.

Not only have these Polynesian natives swift-sailing canoes, but they have rudely-constructed maps of their own invention, made of large tropical leaves, and sticks, tied in straight and curved lines, indicating ocean winds and currents. And, further, Japanese and Chinese junks have been blown to sea, performing long voyages, and finally stranding, with their occupants, upon distant islands. Bancroft tell us that these have even reached the continent of America.

In December, 1832, one of these junks was wrecked on Oahu, near Honolulu, after having been tempest-tossed eleven months. Only four, out of a crew of nine, survived. The population of Lord North's Island must have originated in some way similar to this, as it is over a thousand miles distant from any other land.

Furthermore, the mariner's compass is not new. Navigation is old as tradition. China was known to Egypt more than three thousand years before the Christian era, and a commercial intercourse maintained between the countries.

Africa was circumnavigated by ancient Egyptian mariners; and among the relics of that old civilization may be traced indications of an acquaintance with the American coast. In that period the geography of the world was well understood. Ancient spirits inform me that many of these Pacific islands are the unburied prominences of a submerged Polynesian continent having an immense antiquity. The speech of this great oceanic nation, derived from the primitive Sanscrit of say fifteen thousand years since, tinged with the Indo-Malay, lies at the base of the present Polynesian languages. Remnants of the ancient Sanscrit have been discovered in the highlands of Central Africa.

Our captain, unrolling his Pacific charts one day, directed my attention to the locations of over sixty islands, definitely marked by the old navigators, that have entirely disappeared, sunk in fathomless depths. In consonance with these cataclysmic changes, Mr. Brace, in his "Races of the World," assures us that both Dana and Hale notice evidences of a gradual subsidence of islands even within the historic period; the ruins of temples on Bānabē, for instance, being found partly submerged by the sea. Biblical dogmatists have sought to trace relations, and draw parallels, between the Israelitish "lost tribes" and the Polynesians. This theory vanishes like mist, however, when it is considered that the Hebrews themselves were derivatives, — the refuse and clannish outlaws sloughed off from the mature civilization of Egypt. Burrowing with, these Hebrews borrowed their religious notions from, the lower castes of the Egyptians. They were afterwards modified into Mosaic theology. And Egypt, be it remembered, received her religious doctrines largely from India.

CIVILIZED TREATMENT OF THE ISLANDERS.

The testimony of missionaries and explorers is alike uniform, that Pacific traders have, with few exceptions, exhibited the worst traits of meanness, injustice, and rank dishonesty.

Dr. Damon of Honolulu said a certain shipmaster, dealing with the Marshall Islanders, agreed to pay for cocoanut-oil a fixed amount of tobacco; but, in place, delivered "boxes filled with pieces of old tarred ropes cut up to correspond in length with tobacco-plugs." This was civilization! Another merchant trader, dealing with them, sold them for "stipulated brandies, kegs filled with salt water."

Two captains of whalers from Massachusetts under friendly pretenses coaxed several chiefs aboard; then, moving out into the harbor, demanded a heavy ransom for their delivery. Others, aflame with passion, have with basest motives induced the native women to come upon their vessels. And, when these poor natives have retaliated, the cry has been "savages," "cannibals," "fiendish heathen!"

When the New-Zealand aborigines were at war, a few years since, with the English for the illegal seizure of their lands, the unsuspecting Maoris were unprepared for an attack, because it was the Christian sabbath. They had been taught that Christian soldiers would neither attack nor fight on the Lord's Day. And yet, on this sacred day, they rushed out well-prepared, attacking and butchering hundreds of the trusting heathen. The wrongs, deceptions, and diseases of civilization have been so burnt into the bodies and souls of these aborigines, that they distrust everybody with a white skin. Are they blamable?

The distinguished Rosser sadly says, —

"It is painful to be obliged to report that disease is now being rapidly introduced even among the Ralik Islanders by whale-ships passing the islands, and which now permit natives with females on board their vessels. How sad that the safe residences of missionaries among them should be the causes of attracting physical and moral death to their shores! With but few exceptions, the contact with the representatives of civilization serves to render their diseases more deadly, and their vices more vicious."

So far as missionaries have taught these islanders to read and write, taught them the industries of civilization, they have done a good work. On the other hand, their shrewd, selfish conduct, and theological dogmas, have proven a curse to the native mind. To get a correct opinion of the millions peopling the Pacific islands, their manners, habits, purposes, laws, and religious convictions, one must see and converse with *them*, with old voyagers, explorers, and non-sectarian residents.

CHAPTER IV.

OCEANICA TO AUCKLAND.

To-day, Oct. 2, we crossed the equator. The weather is oppressive, the sun scorching. Only the sea, and its refreshing breezes, save us from suffocation. We are yet in the line of the south-east trade-winds.

The sunsets are gorgeous. It is a fitful season for meditation. Some poet thus sings of man's origin: —

"Heaven's exile, straying from the orb of light."

Who at times does not feel himself an exile, a prisoner? The world is a hotel. The soul is imprisoned in the body; and a fashionable conservatism would make us all moral prisoners by compelling conformity to the shams of society. Why not sleep each alone, as did Pythagoras? Why not wear linen only, as did Apollonius? Why not wear the hair and beard long, as did sage and *savant* in the palmy period of the lost arts? If shaving at all, why not be consistent, shaving away the eyebrows, and even the hair, as do the Chinese?

Louis XII. ascended the French throne at the age of nine, beardless. His courtiers, famous for their cringing servility, rushed to the barbers, and came away clean-faced. That stern old state counselor, Sully, refused to shave, as he had previously done under the reign of King Henry IV. These vain, face-scraped courtiers often made merry at the attorney's odd appearance. Sully, bearing their jests for a time, said to the king, "Sire, when your father of glorious memory consulted me upon important affairs, the first move he made was to turn away all apes and buffoons from his court!" This silenced the French dandies.

Our floating institution darts like an arrow from crest to crest. The passengers are jolly in defiance of the discomforts. Why not make the best of every thing? Why peddle pains and aches to excite and elicit sympathy? Any thing but a peevish, fault-finding disposition. John the Revelator heard "music," not complaining, in heaven. The wise patiently submit to life's destiny, having learned to "labor and to wait." All this mental unrest, this hot seething, this stern struggling, this toiling up the steeps, this magnetic fire that comes pouring down from the higher realms, is only

"The spirit of the years to come,
Yearning to mix itself with life."

Watching the tremulous waves, this morning, while baptized by a dripping shower, I yearned to stand upon their white crests, and have all the world's dust washed away from my garments, making my heart so warm, so sunny, so like a bank of fresh, fragrant flowers, that the careworn and weary earth would delight to thereon rest, in faith and trust.

My fellow-passengers have engaged to-day in all kinds of amusements,— sleight-of-hand, trickery, story-telling, and ventriloquizing in imitation of pigs and puppies; any thing to be heroes. My *mania* for books makes me an odd one. The pleasure is exquisite. Blessings on book-makers! Oh that men would think more, write more, converse more, and talk less!

Blab and witty words are cheap. Books all afire with the personalities of their authors nourish the soul. Pythagoras enjoined not only purity and patience, but seven years' silence, upon certain of his students, as preparatory steps to wisdom. This way, this way, O Samian!

Public speaking on the ocean is more novel than pleasant. Invited by a committee, through the purser James V. Lavery, to address the officers and passengers upon the divine principles of the spiritual philosophy in their relation to immortality, we so did, Dr. Dunn following in a most interesting manner. In accordance with an arrangement between the doctor, his attending spirit-guides, and ourself, previous to sailing, we held semi-weekly séances for spirit-communications. In answer to several inquiries, Mr. Knight said, —

"We can not well draw the line of demarkation between physical matter and spirit-substance, they so interblend and over-lap. There are atoms, and molecular particles of physical matter, in their highly sublimated state, more ethereal perhaps than some portions of spirit-substance. This unsteady upward-reaching is seen in every direction. There possibly may be gorillas with reason flaming up to a higher point than in some of the lowest tribes of men. But mark, *they*, the gorillas, have reached their acme ; while these lower tribes have but just started in the line of human possibilities.

"All insects, all venomous reptiles, and brutes, are tottering and imperfect structures ; and it is illogical to predicate immortality of imperfection. The arch can not stand without the keystone. . . .

"By your request, I have inquired of John who was meant by the 'elect lady,' in his second epistle ; and the gist of the response was, the phrase *elect lady*, a symbolical expression, referred to the Christian religion in its purity. This lady elect was the lady of his faith, the most spiritual religion of that age. Spirituality pertains to the feminine, intellectuality to the masculine."

A strange controlling intelligence now comes, making the medium exceedingly spasmodic. Listen! It is a weird, unknown tongue. What does it mean ? . . . He has gone, and Mr. Knight comes to explain : —

"This spirit was a chief of the Oahu Island, who lived in a mortal body over a century since. He desired to inform you that himself and his people believed in spirit-intercourse when on earth, though it was connected with much superstition. Since his transition, he has progressed rapidly ; and still he cherishes a deep interest in the remnants of his race. He is very desirous to have you remain on the islands you have left, and preach true doctrines, in contradistinction from the false and gloomy theology that is being taught by missionaries."

Another change. Swailbach, a German spirit, comes. The accent is unmistakable.

"I have just taken possession to say that I had visited these natives as a spirit many times in the past. They are Aryanic rather than Semitic in origin. In a very remote period, this root-race moved southeasterly from the high plateaus of India, through Malayan lands, towards the Pacific islands."

Do you understand the language of these natives?

"Not as they speak it in their mortal bodies; and yet I can converse freely with them when disrobed of mortality. Ours is largely soul language. The movement of a muscle, throbbing of a nerve, or slightest facial expression even, of a spirit, is language, and self-interpreting. Study of many earthly languages, unless for the purpose of teaching, is time unwisely spent. Languages, earthly in origin, like nationalities, gradually fade away as spirits ascend and unfold interiorly, the tendency being from the special to the universal."

Aaron Knight, again controlling, said,—

"Those failing to make the right marks along the pathway of human life have to retrace their steps after entering spirit-life. There is a band of explorers with us. They are properly naturalists. Some of them are very ancient spirits. . . . We are now passing over the ruins of a grand old city, which had vast surburban forests. The petrified remnants indicate a likeness to the mammoth trees of California. They were an enlightened race. The people lived in stone houses, and were engaged in mechanical and pastoral pursuits. They were the progenitors of your American mound-builders. Were your clairvoyant eyes opened, you would this moment see under *débris*, sands, and sea-plants, the scattered remnants of a long-forgotten civilization. As volcanic isles and lofty mountains have been thrust up from the ocean's depths, so islands and continents have sunk 'mid commotions unknown to earthly history. The sinking of the new Atlantis continent some nine thousand years before the Platonian period, as mentioned by Plato, Solon, and the Egyptian priests, is no myth."

USES AND ABUSES OF SPIRITUAL SÉANCES.

"*You*, and multitudes of others," exclaimed the spirit Knight, "should never sit in circles. Many of the best mediums on earth have never even attended a séance. And yet for scientific observations, or for obtaining physical manifestations, circles help to more readily concentrate the magnetic forces. But to see clairvoyants, to see the impressional, or the truly inspired, sitting in promiscuous circles, holding hands, and imbibing diverse aural exhalations, is to us mentally painful.

"Morbid and nervously sensitive natures require, or think they require, a constant change. They have a *mania* for the stimulus of séances, not understanding that promiscuous magnetic blendings are as injurious to the soul as sexual promiscuity is to the body. These, *all* these practices opposed to the natural laws of life, yield but thorns for the flesh, and obsessions for the spirit. . . . Every mortal has a guardian, and often this guardian spirit does not wish the individual to become a medium. Spiritualists seem to greatly lack wisdom relating to the nature and mission of mediumship. Only the few are fitted for it."

HATS AND BALD HEADS.

Overboard went a hat. It broke the lull of the hour. Did the winds reason? What do men wear hats for, — those tall, silken, stove-pipe, cylinder-shaped hats?

Indians in the West, and Polynesians in the Pacific, have no bald heads. These natives, taught by Nature, let God's sunshine and cooling breezes fan their bare heads. Is there not much to be learned of "savages"?

In Christ's Hospital, the "Blue-Coat School," London, founded by Edward VI., the boys, even the seniors, all go bareheaded. This was a condition of the endowment. And, though they thread city streets in the hottest weather, there has never a case of sunstroke been known among them.

THE ITALIAN TEACHER.

To-day Parisi Lendanta controlled the medium again. He is an Italian spirit, profound and peerless. Among other things he said, —

"We are now passing over mountain ranges towering up from the bottom of the ocean. These lofty rocky eminences serve somewhat to hold the waters in check, and render them 'Pacific.' This ocean has no such raised plateau across the bed-surface as has the Atlantic. Owing to its uneven depths, and rough volcanic ridges, it would be difficult to cable."

His elucidation of the atmospheric and electric stratifications above us was singularly philosophical. It is impossible to fully report him. He flourished near the close of the Middle Ages, — that period which elapsed between the decline of ancient learning, and the revival. The Dark Ages are said to have ceased about the year 1400. They terminated, however, at various times in the different countries of Europe. The destruction of feudalism, the invention of printing, and the discovery of America by Columbus, mark the general period of resurrection from the darkness of the mediæval ages.

I find this spirit, Parisi, perfectly familiar with the histories of Petrarch, Tasso, Dante, Ariosto, and other Italian *littérateurs*. Dante's ideal of the old Latin poets was Virgil, much of whose fame was owing to the Fourth Eclogue, interpreted by churchal fathers as a prophecy of Jesus Christ. Virgil quoted Livy and Lucan to prove that gods and angels had wrought spiritual marvels through mortals during all the ages of antiquity. The sibylline oracles should be extensively read by scholars.

ONE OF THE SOUTH-SEA ISLANDS.

Oct. 20. — Safely in Auckland, New Zealand, distant from New York nearly nine thousand miles. The city, built upon high land, looks fresh and vigorous. The gardens come down close to the sea. Exclusive of suburbs, it numbers about twelve thousand. Natives in the province of Auckland, divided into five tribes, number twenty-five thousand. June and July are the coldest months of the year; and January and February, corresponding to July and August in England and America, are the warmest. Neither serpents, nor noxious reptiles of any species, have been found upon the New-Zealand islands. Toads and frogs are also unknown. Has some Saint Patrick here lifted his magic wand? The original inhabitants call themselves Maori. They are a dark race, but athletic, brave, ingenious, and intelligent. Efforts to Christianize them have not been very successful. In the New-Zealand group they number forty or fifty thousand. Racially they belong to that branch of the Polynesians that are of Indo-Malayan origin. They have handsome black hair, straight or aquiline noses, and well-balanced brains. They tattoo themselves.

It is just the opening of spring-time now in New Zealand. The delicate blossoms are falling from plum and peach trees, and the gardens are beautiful. The English oak is putting out its emerald leaves, and flowers fill the air with their fragrance. I spent a pleasant afternoon with the Rev. Samuel Edgar, a liberal-minded Congregational clergyman. He offered me the use of his pulpit, and influence also, to sustain a course of lectures upon Spiritualism. Six or seven days more of sailing will bring us to Melbourne, Australia, *viâ* Sydney, queen city of the Pacific.

CHAPTER V.

AUSTRALIA.

SYDNEY, noted for its beautiful harbor and magnificent scenery, is far less American, say travelers, than Melbourne. It was in April, 1770, that Capt. Cook, on a voyage of discovery in the southern seas, entered a haven near Port Jackson, to which he gave the name of Botany Bay, in honor of Dr. Solander, an eminent Swedish botanist accompanying him. The settlement started encouragingly, and for a time was made a depot for English criminals. But, the harbor proving unsafe, the site for a city was thought ineligible. Subsequent cruising in the vicinity discovered, through an inlet called Port Jackson, a commodious and most magnificent harbor. Soon a canvas tent was erected, and sites for buildings marked out. The fleet speedily removed from Botany Bay, ten miles distant, to this port, now named Sydney.

The parks, recreation grounds, and botanic gardens are among the first places of resort to which strangers direct their steps. These gardens are clothed with plants and flowers from every known part of the world. They comprise about forty acres, sloping down to and fringing the harbor. Tropical foliage and fruitage gladden the eye. Oranges do well. The trip to Parramatta, some fifteen miles from Sydney, is delightful. It can be reached by road, rail, or water. Oranges, lemons, apple, pear, loquat, apricot, peach, and other excellent fruits, together with extensive vineyards stocked with superior kinds of grapes, may be seen growing in the greatest luxuriance all through these regions.

The temper and tone of this city, numbering one hundred and fifty thousand, are conservative, self-opinionated, and gold-clutching, — uninviting conditions, certainly, for angel-ministry. There are, however, candid investigators, and some avowed believers. Among the latter is the Hon. J. Bowie Wilson, ex-member of the legislature. This gentleman has traveled extensively in America. The Rev. Dr. Stanley, formerly a Unitarian clergyman, Mr. Gale, employed in the post-office, and several others, are deeply interested in those subjects pertaining to the spiritual philosophy.

THE LANDING.

Locked up in floating prisons for fifty days, over ten thousand miles of sea, it was exquisitely refreshing to pass the "heads," sailing up the harbor, more properly an inland sea, and reaching Melbourne, the largest and wealthiest of the Australian cities.

Awaiting the arrival of our steamer, "The Hero," was a committee of gentlemen, who, after extending hands of fellowship, and greetings of good-will, conducted us to the hospitable residence of Mr. McIlwraith, one of the city councilors. A dinner was in waiting. This part of the pleasing programme concluded, a stroll on solid *terra firma* was richly enjoyed.

MELBOURNE.

This city, the capital of Victoria, and the finest in the southern hemisphere, has a population approaching two hundred thousand. It stretches along, dotting and fringing both banks of the Yarra to within some seven miles of its mouth. Though quite English in architectural appearance, Melbourne, considering its age, is a magnificent city. Its climate and geographical situation, as well as its extensive suburban parks, lawns, and gardens, can elicit only praise from travelers.

The principal streets are wide, well-paved, and brilliantly lighted in evening-time with gas. Along the curb-stones, in some of the streets, run rippling streams of pure water. There is no doubt of its being a decidedly healthy city. Epidemics are almost unknown. It is said that the first case of hydrophobia has yet to occur. Could dogs, pleading, ask for a healthier, better paradise? Nothing surprises me so much in this country as the museums, fine public libraries, and free reading-rooms. The city library contains over two hundred and fifty thousand volumes. Others connected with the university, or other public institutions, are nearly as large, and accessible daily, free of charge. This is a blessing to the poor. The parliament "Education Bill," making education secular and compulsory, was bitterly opposed by bishops, priests, and aristocrats. This was to have been expected. The priesthood in all lands aims to keep the people in ignorance, or to so monopolize their education as to turn it into sectarian channels. Education is the key-word of the age. Schools should be *free*, and education compulsory, under all skies. In the ratio that mental and moral instruction is enforced, crime diminishes. To this end Barlow says, "It may be safely pronounced that a State has *no right to punish a man* to whom it has given *no previous instruction.*" Sir Thomas More writes to this effect in his "Utopia:" "If you suffer your people to be *ill-educated,* and their manners to be corrupted from their infancy, and then *punish* them for those crimes to which their first education *disposes* them, what else is to be concluded from this, but that you *make* thieves, and then *punish* them?"

PARKS AND GARDENS.

If flowers are the alphabets of angels, gardens are the delights of gods and good men. The Melbourne Botanic Gardens, beautifully situated on the south bank of the flowing Yarra, some half a mile from the city, cover an area of a hundred and fourteen acres, and abound in almost an innumerable number of trees, shrubs, plants, and ornamental flowers, snowy, crimson, and golden. The palms and ferns are exceedingly fine; and the deep emerald of the tropical foliage is, on this December day, absolutely magnificent.

The city and suburbs comprise in the aggregate not less than two thousand five hundred acres. These reserves are not mere enclosures, but most of them are laid out, planted, and ornamented in the most approved style.

The eucalyptus is the national tree. There are some thirty species, the wood being excellent for ship-building and railroad-ties. The foliage is beautiful, and the leaves are said to have a therapeutic value. These eucalypts back in the gullies and mountains rival, if not excel, the renowned forest-giants of California. Mr. Klein, measuring a eucalyptus on the Black Spur, found it four hundred and eighty feet high. The minster spire of Strasbourg has been pronounced the highest of any cathedral on the globe, sending its pinnacle to the height of four hundred and sixty-six feet; the great pyramid of Cheops is four hundred and eighty feet in height; and yet these eucalyptus trees would completely overshadow spire and pyramid.

AMUSEMENTS AND MORALS.

Cricket, football, racing, shooting, bay-fishing, and boating on the Yarra, have their daily devotees. Holidays are frequent. At these seasons, arcades, stores, offices, are closed, business put aside, and the old become young again.

Pictures necessarily have backgrounds. There is everywhere, in social life, the sunny and the shady side. In this city, sin abounds. Jails push out their forbidding fronts. Criminals are flogged. This is a blotch upon penal legislation. Gold is chief among the gods worshiped. Mines and wines, wool and wheat, are the staple productions of the country. Few are so poor that they cannot indulge in colonial wines and tobacco. Hotels and saloons are tended, with few exceptions, by young women termed "bar-maids."

Handsome ones are sought to fascinate young men. It is the old story of Eve and the apple. Women not only "bet" at the races, but some are bitten with the *mania* of gambling. The most eloquent of the Melbourne clergymen lectures on "Christmas carols," wears diamonds, sings comic songs, and "tips the glass fashionably." Prosperous sinners are petted, poor ones pitched into purgatory. The serpents of the press shake their rattles at all reformers. But to published facts. The following telling paragraph was clipped from "The Melbourne Age." The author expresses himself: —

"Gratified that a correspondent has called attention to the state of immorality existing among the *upper class of society*, among which I think we may count a greater number of hoary-headed *old libertines*, for our population, than any other community in the world. And what else can be expected, when we find that among the legal, the medical, ay, and the *reverend professions*, among our legislators, our magistrates, and our highest civil servants, are to be found the men who foster these nurseries of vice into which innocent girls are decoyed, and damned body and soul together? What else can we expect, when we know that among these libertines are married men who have marriageable daughters of their own, to their infinite shame and disgrace be it said? What else can we expect, when we know that numbers of the higher officers of the police frequent these dens, not to keep them in check, but to indulge in the vilest profligacy and vice? It is well known that there are what are called 'respectable' brothels, that the common constables, and the inferior officers of police, are not allowed to interfere with; that, when any 'distinguished' visitors of an airy turn of mind come to Melbourne, they are introduced to one or other of these places and the occupants by a gentleman in Melbourne holding a very high position in the government service, and who acts in all such cases as the procuror (!) for the procuresses."

Over four thousand "outcast women," known to the police as such, parade the streets after nightfall; while as many more amateurs remain in their dens, awaiting the calls of the carnally-minded. These classes walk in the most prominent thoroughfares, and lounge upon rustic seats in parks and gardens in evening-time. The colonial cities of Australia, like mining countries generally, are famous for unchastity. The cause of this cancerous condition of society is largely owing to the prevalence, and practical influences, of Orthodox theology. If these sinning parties believed in the certainty of retribution, and the abiding presence of ministering spirits, they would immediately turn from the error of their ways. In Spiritualism, as a Christ-baptism, is the world's hope.

CLIMATE.

Pale and low in the south-west of clear New-England skies, swings the sun these wintry days of January. Here, in Victoria, it is nearly vertical, and the heat quite oppressive; while the maddened dust-clouds that whirl and waltz along the streets of Melbourne are fearful to encounter. When it rains in these regions it pours.

Considering the latitude and marine position, Victoria can but enjoy a climate quite genial to Europeans and Americans. Approximating the tropical, it constantly reminds me of New Orleans, and the Gulf States generally. The weather is excessively warm only during the prevalence of the hot northerly winds. They are something like the California winds in the valleys of the interior, only more scorchingly withering. The hottest of all the months is January, the coldest July. A thin ice, and occasionally frosts, are seen during the winter months, June, July, and August. These frosts vary in different portions of the country, depending upon the elevation above the level of the sea. The haying season is over in January, immediately after which the farmers commence harvesting their wheat.

A BROAD OUTLOOK.

Though an immense island, Australia may reasonably be considered a continent. Its length, from east to west, is over two thousand five hundred miles, and its breadth nearly two thousand; the northern part, approaching the equator, being about four thousand miles to the south-east of India, and four thousand to the south of China. It is estimated to contain three million square miles; fifty times the size of England, and one hundred that of Scotland. It is divided into Victoria,—Melbourne, the capital,—New South Wales, Queen's Land, South Australia, and Western Australia. Each of these colonies is governed by councils,—legislative bodies something like the houses of parliament,—under the superintendence of a governor appointed by the Queen of England. Victoria has an area of 86,831 square miles. It is very nearly as large as all of Great Britain, exclusive of her islands in the seas. A chain of hills traverses the whole colony, called the Dividing Range. The snowy Alps form the boundary between Victoria and New South Wales. They range from five thousand to six thousand feet above the level of the sea. The rivers of Victoria are neither serviceable for steamers, nor magnificent in appearance. Many of them dry up during the summer months. To this the Yarra, on the banks of which the metropolis is situated, is an exception. The country back in the distance contains numerous salt and fresh water lakes and lagoons. They are generally shallow, except when happening to be the craters of extinct volcanoes.

Reflecting upon personal favors, and treasuring pleasant memories of Mr. Bright, Walker, Terry, Tyerman, Sanders, Gill, Stowe, and others, we were deeply indebted to Councilman McIlwraith, for introductions to city officials; to Dr. Motherwell, for drives to Dr. Howitt's, and other suburban localities; and to Mr. Carson, the horticulturist, for taking us through pleasant country villas towards the mountains. The fields and farming-lands along the way, hedged around with sweet-brier, were under excellent cultivation. Why do not landless Englishmen flock hither, and till these waiting waste lands?

Mr. Carson has in his fruit-orchard thirty varieties of oranges, several varieties of lemons, Japanese loquats, and nearly all the varieties of European fruits. Walking through the market with Dr. Dunn, on a January morning, I saw ripe raspberries, currants, gooseberries, blackberries, plums, apples, apricots, almonds, and pears. . . .

When these Australian colonies cut themselves entirely loose from English domination, constituting an independent federation, they will develop their hidden resources, and reveal more fully the richness of their intellectual capacities.

RUSH TO THE GOLD-FIELDS.

If rock-embosomed crystals are subterranean flowers, metals may be considered mineral trees in process of development. Tradition has it that a Pyrenees shepherd, in 1849, was the first to discover gold in Australia. The attention of settlers at this period was directed principally to the raising of sheep and cattle. Finding small bits of the "precious metal," previous to this time, had not been considered of sufficient importance to turn the scattered settlers from their agricultural pursuits. If the pluckiness of the American Stanley, in discovering Dr. Livingstone, put to shame the conceit and stupidity of certain Englishmen, the enterprise of California miners was quite as conspicuous in revealing the auriferous stores of Australia's hidden wealth. Those famous gold discoveries upon the Pacific slopes aroused the attention of practical men to renewed prospecting operations for gold in Victoria, New South Wales, and other portions of Australia.

Profitable fields were soon discovered and developed. Gold was found in great profusion at Clunes early in 1850.

O reeling, clutching world! how long will gold remain your god? Licenses were issued for digging on Sept. 11, 1851. Immense yields were daily reported. The excitement was soon at white heat. Ordinary occupations were forsaken, and the whole social condition of the country suddenly changed. Attorneys forsook the courts, merchants their counting-rooms, clerks their desks, clergymen their pulpits; all hastening pell-mell to the diggings. Provisions went up, and prices for labor were enormous. The rush from England seemed a very panic; and priests quite forgot the passage, " Lay not up for yourselves treasures on earth." Many Americans filled their purses, and returned to their native land, preferring the eagle to the colonial lion. The scene has completely changed. Surface-digging is no longer profitable; but the tertiaries and the quartz veins seem absolutely inexhaustible.

VICTORIA. — EQUALITY OF THE SEXES.

In citizenship Australia is eminently cosmopolitan. In the streams of immigration to this quarter of the globe, the English born have been foremost, the Irish second, and the Scotch third. This close social proximity, these family alliances, cementing living representatives, will not only break down old barriers, but ultimately develop an Australian type of people deeply interesting to ethnologists.

"Male and female," are they not about equal? Statistics leave no doubt of this fact; which, by the way, presents an unanswerable argument against polygamy. Nature's census says, "equal;" and Nature's teachings say, "monogamic marriage, and chastity in the married life."

Equality in the number of the sexes is one of the first conditions necessary to the development of any people into a full, healthy national growth. There is a sad disproportion, however, in some portions of Australia. An admirer of Malthus gave me these figures. In the year 1838, there were but fourteen females to every one hundred males; but at the census in 1861 there were sixty-four females to every one hundred males. The disproportion is still less at the present time. Such inequality of ratio must necessarily affect the morals of a country. A recent census assures us that there are a million and a half more of women than men in England. What does this mean? Does not the fact foreshadow revolution?

ANGEL-MINISTRY IN MELBOURNE.

No longer "local," the Spiritual philosophy, with attending phenomena, has believers and advocates in all enlightened countries. Spiritualism rests upon the evidence of the senses, the testimony of seers and sages, patriarchs and prophets, Jesus and the apostles, the early Church fathers, the French prophets, Torquato Tasso, Madame Guyon, Swedenborg, Ann Lee, George Fox, the Wesleys, and millions of our fellow-countrymen. The banner of Spiritualism, in some form, floats to-day beneath all skies; and he who fights it fights the proofs of a future existence, fights spirits and angels, Jesus and Almighty God.

Though there had been here and there a Spiritualist in the colonies for several years, importing occasionally pamphlets and books from London and Boston, Spiritualism took no organic form till less than three years since. The city society was organized under the name of "The Victorian Association of Progressive Spiritualists." This association has sustained speaking regularly by Messrs. Nayler, Bright, Ross, Walker, and others. The Rev. Mr. Tyerman, a recent convert from the English Church, addressed the society each Sunday for the term of six months.

Mr. W. H. Terry commenced investigating in 1861. He is a healing-medium, bookseller, and earnest worker. He is also editor and proprietor of "The Harbinger of Light." This journal succeeded "The Glow-worm," published by Mr. Nayler.

The committee inviting us to these distant shores, I find to be solid, substantial, and honorable gentlemen. Some of them occupy prominent positions in the city. Mr. Stanford, an American, is the brother of Ex-Gov. Stanford of California, who, at present, is the president of the Central Pacific Railway.

The reception was truly complimentary. Over two hundred ladies and gentlemen assembled in Masonic Hall to extend hands of fellowship to American strangers. Every face was wreathed in smiles. The hall, tastefully decorated with flowers and evergreens, presented a gay and attractive aspect. The exercises were varied, and deeply interesting. The president, Mr. J. Ross, delivered the congratulatory address. The speeches, music, refreshments, and conversations made up an enjoyable evening.

A promising Children's Progressive Lyceum had been organized a few weeks before our arrival. Mr. Terry was elected conductor, and Mr. G. A. Stowe secretary. The flags and badges were beautiful. Dr. Dunn aided them in perfecting the work. It could not have fallen into better hands.

PERSECUTION BY THE PRESS.

Heaven save sensitive reformers in all lands from the mockery of an unprincipled press, from priestly throats that vomit falsehood, and churchal tongues that delight to lap blood! Though addressing audiences in all the American States, except Florida and Texas, upon the unpopular yet progressive movements of the age, I was never so unjustly criticised, basely misrepresented, and shamefully vilified, as by a portion of the daily Victorian press. Not content with this, I was burlesqued in "The Weekly Punch," and pantomimed in the theaters. The personal abuse commenced with the delivery of the first lecture in Temperance Hall. This was expected. Accordingly, Mr. Charles Bright, a literary gentleman contributing to "The Daily Argus," was sufficiently far-seeing to secure a superb short-hand reporter. And while a slimy, policy-seeking press was pouring out venom, the lecture of the "vulgar blasphemer" appeared in print, entitled "Spiritualism Defined and Defended," ably prefaced by Charles Bright, and published by W. H. Terry.

The following written by a man interested in "The Melbourne Daily Telegraph," — organ of the clergy, — and appearing afterwards in "The Dunedin Morning Star," reveals the *animus* of a large portion of the religious and secular press, touching Spiritualism and its expositors: —

"If the 'Seer of the Ages' get your length in earth-life, you had better treat him well; for I can assure you, you will seldom find his equal. If his spirit should get the length of 'Arabula' before his body reaches N. Z., — I don't know the latitude of this place, viz., '*Arabula*,' but I refer you for information to 'The Arabian Nights,'— you should get *his hide stuffed*, and preserve him to posterity; the 'ages,' I fear, shall nevermore look on his like again. I can not better begin to describe him than by giving a few of the delicate epithets bestowed on this Mr. Peebles in all the newspapers, town and country: an 'impudent American, an 'impious pretender,' a 'long-haired apostate,' a 'specious humbug,' a 'rabid lunatic,' an 'uncouth revivalist,' a 'vulgar blasphemer,' a 'long-haired apostate!' These figures of speech might be indefinitely multiplied, and yet half the truth would not be told. This 'great and good man' (Peebles) in speaking works himself up to a frenzy, while with bloodshot eyes, and rolling tongue, and foaming mouth, he tells the opinion that some 'heathen Chinee' had formed of Christianity away somewhere in the Far West. He then maudles over a Yankee story about some poor youth mourning for his granny, whom he had never seen, and who came from 'Arabula' to pat him on the head. . . . On every occasion of his public appearance, the same hysterical females, the same half-crazed, wild-looking men, are to be seen ready to swallow any thing and every thing; the more absurd the better. They cry, 'The new and beautiful faith!' 'There is no God, but Peebles is a prophet.'"

In the strength of a high-toned Spiritualism, giving assurance of attending angels, and a blissful immortality, a man may richly afford to bear all insult, all falsehood, and all railing at his country, or at his Spiritual convictions, from the unclean lips of priests, and the paid minions of the press.

Australian journalism lacks the energy of the American, the culture of the French, and the dignity of the English press. The distinguished William Howitt never wrote a pithier paragraph than this: —

"Many persons who have attended *Spiritual séances* of various kinds, and satisfied themselves of their *reality*, express their surprise that the press, as a body, remain doggedly *unconvinced*. Why should they be surprised? It is simply an affair of Hodge's *razors*. Journals, whether of news or literature, like those celebrated razors, *are made to sell*. So long as the press thinks it will *pay better* to abuse Spiritism than to profess it, it will continue to do so; but should the writers for the press hear to-day, or any day, that the public is gone over to Spiritism, they will all, to a man, be zealous Spiritists the next morning. Then, and not a day earlier, nor a day later, will the press be *convinced*. Their logic all lies in the three celebrated words, pounds, shillings, pence."

The clairvoyance and healing-gifts of Dr. Dunn were underrated and maliciously ridiculed in the dailies, calling out in the end several spicy rejoinders. The city was in quite an uproar. Passing the streets, I frequently heard, " There ! *there* he goes, that old long-haired Spiritualist!"

Spiritualists and liberalists, sufficient for the occasion, resolved upon a new line of tactics, that of appealing from the press to the public. Accordingly, immediately following our first course of six lectures in *Temperance Hall*, the committee unitedly resolved to take possession of a larger and more fashionable place for the second series. Luckily they secured the Prince of Wales Theater. The first Sunday, there were over twenty-five hundred present. The following Sunday evening, the proprietor opened the upper gallery, and there were full three thousand in attendance. The platform was filled with gentlemen of standing and position in society; and the congregational singing was excellent. " The Melbourne Press" met with a sudden conversion. In a single night its snarls turned to songs, and all was fair as a summer's morning.

" The Daily Express" mentioned the meeting very handsomely. " The Daily Herald" said, " An immense crowd of people assembled again last night to hear the American Spiritualist expound the new religion. He was evidently in earnest, and at times eloquent." " The Daily Telegraph" thus prefaced a fine report: " A crowd filled the Prince of Wales Theater last evening, from pit to ceiling. The assemblage was intelligent and orderly, listening to the lecture entitled, '*Spiritualism becoming Universal.*' " " The Daily

Melbourne Age," previous to its abstract of the discourse, said, "The theater was so crowded, that, even though the upper gallery was opened, many people were compelled to stand."

"The Journal," referring to the immense assemblage, said, "The points relating to spirits returning to earth were well put, riveting the closest attention." . . . This modification, this change of base, on the part of the press conductors, entitle them to little credit. The new and more tolerant position was forced upon them. "Can the Ethiopian change his skin?" The press has three creed-words, "Will it pay?"

There are honorable exceptions, however. It is only justice to say that "The Melbourne Daily Argus" and "The Ballarat Star" treated us fairly from the commencement.

AUSTRALIAN ARROGANCE.

Men considered in England below mediocrity, failures financially and intellectually, pendulums vibrating between shadows and nothing, when reaching Melbourne, the Paris of Australia, scrambled for high positions. What they had not, they assumed to have. Wasps are largest when first hatched. It was only in 1851 that the gold-fever rose to its highest pitch in Victoria. The country is still comparatively new, the city youthful. And then, isolated too from the leading countries of the world, England and America, it would naturally trundle into the ruts of colonial conceit and self-sufficiency. That there is a venomous prejudice in Melbourne, on the part of many, against Americans, admits of no denial. This, commercial men of New York, and the wool-buyers of New-England, may distinctly understand. Possibly the "Alabama awards" and the "San Juan Settlement" may have had something to do with the feeling. Where envy and jealousy exist, they should not be pushed out too prominent. The gossamer web so very thin half reveals the hidden poison. The penal element of the past tinctures and tones Australian society. Such a moral virus must necessarily linger. Horse-racing is well patronized by ladies. At the hurdle-races large amounts change hands. The public mind of the city, if not in a fevery, is at least in a state of chronic unrest. Humility, toleration, and a genuine cosmopolitan nobility, would be excellent antidotes to counteract the deadly influences of arrogance and assumption. The passage of the "Education Bill" was a timely act.

The evangelical theologians of Australia, proud and persecuting, are zealous in missionary efforts to save the heathen. On the other hand, Confucian mandarins in Australia, and Buddhist mandarins of China, as well as many Brahmans of India, seriously contemplate organizing missionary movements to elevate and morally enlighten certain heathen and Pagan nations, called "Christians." *

Before my eyes lies an evangelical work with the following title: "A Declaration for Maintaining the True Faith, held by all Christians, concerning the Trinity of Persons in one only God, by John Calvin, against the Detestable Errors of Michael Servetus, a Spaniard; in which it is also proved

---

* "The Maryborough Advertiser," Queensland, Australia, of April last, has the following: "At a numerous meeting of Chinese residents in Melbourne, it was resolved, in view of the deplorable Paganism which prevails, to establish a mission in Victoria, to bring its benighted inhabitants to a knowledge of Confucius, and of the pure morality which he taught. . . . Grateful for the protection enjoyed under the laws of Victoria, and desirous also of reciprocating the zealous efforts of British missionaries in China, the Chinese residents of Melbourne purpose to send English-speaking and highly educated Mandarins into the metropolis and country towns of Victoria, to wean the inhabitants, if possible, from the degrading worship of that god who bears the name of Mammon. Our sacred books tell us, 'Contentment furnishes constant joy; much covetousness, continual grief. To the contented, even poverty is joy. To the discontented, even wealth is a vexation.' Now, we perceive that, among the idolaters and Pagans calling themselves Christians, there is much covetousness, and no contentment. Therefore we desire, as fellow-beings created by the same divine Power, to bring our Victorian brethren to a knowledge of the truth as it is in Confucius, and convert them from the error of their ways." Then follow directions to subscribers, the honorable secretary, &c. — See "Human Nature," Aug. 1, London.

that it is *lawful to punish Heretics, as this Wretch was justly executed in the City of Geneva.* Printed at Geneva, 1554." In a letter dated February, 1546, Calvin says, "If Servetus come to Geneva, I will exercise my authority in such a manner as not to allow him to depart alive." In another, of Sept. 30, 1561, he writes, "Do not fail to rid the country of such zealous scoundrels, who stir up the people to revolt against us. Such monsters should be exterminated, as I have exterminated Michael Servetus, the Spaniard." This is the real genius of evangelical Christianity in Melbourne.

THE SPIRIT OF THE CHURCH.

Read the history of Queen Elizabeth. Study the horrible secrets of that English Inquisition known as the High Commission Court and the Star Chamber. Through it heretics and scholarly free-thinkers were brought to the block. In after years John Bunyan was imprisoned, George Fox hunted and vilified, and Ann Lee banished. Persecutions, fetters, dungeons, fires, swords, and inhuman butcheries, have ever been the attendants of Christianity. And, what is more, these red-handed Christians have justified their murderous proceedings by quoting the commands of Scripture, "If thy brother, thy son, or the wife of thy bosom . . . say, Let us go and serve other gods, . . . thou shalt surely kill him; . . . thou shalt stone him with stones that he die" (Deut. xiii. 6, 10).

"If any man or woman be a wizard or witch, that is, consult 'familiar spirits,' they shall surely be put to death" (Exod. xxii. 18; Lev. xx. 27).

"If any child or children, above sixteen years old, and of sufficient understanding, shall curse or smite their natural father or mother, he or they shall be put to death" (Exod. xxi. 15, 17; Lev. xx.). Also, "A stubborn and rebellious son, above sixteen years of age, which will not obey the voice of his father, or the voice of his mother, . . . such son shall be put to death" (Deut. xxi. 18, 21).

That reigning Protestant Christian, Henry VIII., issued, in harmony with Bible commands, this edict: —

"If any person, by word, writing, &c., do preach, teach, or hold opinions, that in the blessed sacrament of the altar, under form of bread and wine, after the consecration thereof, there is not present, *really*, the *natural body and blood of our Saviour Jesus Christ*, or that *in the flesh, under form of bread, is not the very blood of Christ*, or that *with the blood, under the form of wine, is not the very flesh of Christ*, as well apart as if they were both together, then he shall be adjudged a heretic, and *suffer death by burning*." *

When persecuting "Bloody Mary" — a devoted Christian by profession — was reproved for those merciless butcheries perpetrated for Christ's sake, she replied, "As the souls of heretics are hereafter to be eternally burning in hell, there can be nothing more proper than for me to imitate the divine vengeance by burning them on earth."

Wherever a purse-proud Christianity has gained the most power, it has most obstructed the march of civilization, as in Spain and Italy. Guizot, the great historian of civilization in France, tells us that "when any war arose between power and liberty, the Christian Church always planted itself on the side of power, against liberty." This churchal Christianity in our midst is the importation of the dark ages, the horrid nightmare of the world. It is immoral in its tendency; for it sends good moral men to hell, and the lifelong wicked to heaven, if soundly orthodox. According to the sectarist's belief, a man may commit all manner of crimes, — lie, swear, cheat, steal, and murder, — then comply with the "conditions of salvation," and swing from the gallows to glory!

Consult the records of capital punishment. Nearly every victim attended, during the last weeks of imprisonment, by the clergy, makes full confession, repents, believes, and with a spasm leaps from hemp to heaven. For proof, we are

---

* Pickering's Statutes, vol. iv., p. 471.

referred to the repentant "thief upon the cross," and all closing up with the hymn, —

> "While the lamp holds out to burn,
> The vilest sinner may return."

Some of the most distinguished scientists and learned jurists in England are deists, — disbelieving in immortality, revelation, and the miraculous conception. This, on church-al grounds, seals their damnation. There are many good men in churches, however, — good and excellent in spite of the demoralizing tendencies of their creeds.

The immortal fathers of American independence were theists. Abraham Lincoln was an "infidel." He made no profession of Christianity. He had no "saving faith in the atoning blood of the Lord Jesus." He was neither converted, "born again," nor baptized. He joined no Christian church, and yet was hurled, with a "fell shot," from a theater into eternity! And, if the orthodox creed be true, Lincoln, the martyred president, is in hell, — wailing this moment with the *damned in hell!* If so, let it be my doom. I would prefer hell — whatever it may be — with Lincoln, Franklin, Jefferson, Adams, Madison, Washington, Shakspeare, Byron, Burns, Shelley, Edgar A. Poe, Dickens, Humboldt, and the whole galaxy of political, intellectual, and moral lights of the world, to that little jasper-walled heaven of the sectarian Christian, where a few lonesome, long-visaged saints, saved through another's merits, wave palms, and serenade the Jewish Jehovah for ever! Orthodox Christianity, with its fanaticism, superstition, and cramping creeds, is rapidly sinking, in enlightened countries, into hopeless decrepitude and remediless decay. It has failed to save the world. Professing Jesus, it has practiced Moses. Its sun is setting, its corpse awaiting burial.

Quietly drinking the cup, patiently receiving the poisoned arrows of secular and sectarian spite, I forwarded to the Victoria press no retaliatory replies: neither did I correct the purposed misrepresentations of the reporters. Return " good for evil," and " blessing for cursing," — *these* were among the divine teachings of the Master. Thorns precede moral victories. When they " persecute you in one city, flee ye into another," was the command of the gentle Nazarene. Accordingly, I resolved to bear witness to the truth in other and distant localities.

PROVINCIAL CITIES.

Ballarat. — Accompanied by Mr. Watson and other friends, I found myself, upon a sunny morning, stowed away in a stage-coach, ticketed for Ballarat, a city lying about one hundred miles from Melbourne in a northerly direction. It is five thousand feet above the level of the sea, has fifty thousand inhabitants, is famous for mining interests, enterprising in railway matters, and prints five dailies, one of which, " The Ballarat Star," is a leading journal in the colony. It reported our lectures, delivered in Alfred Hall, fairly and handsomely. Mr. John Finlay, residing at Gracefield, some three miles from the city, is a zealous Spiritualist, reformer, and Shaker, praying continually for a more rapid spread of the Millennial Church. He has thought seriously of emigrating to Mount Lebanon, America, to join the fraternity of Shakers. He is the master in a fine suburban academy.

The stranger at Ballarat sees nothing but prosperity among the gold-diggers. The wages of the miners average about forty-five shillings — English money — per week. They work eight hours a day, thus reaching that acme of the workman's bliss, —

> " Eight hours for work, and eight for play ;
> Eight for sleep, and eight shillings a day."

Castlemaine. — Formerly a rich alluvial mining-town. Three thousand Chinamen at one time either walked its streets, or camped around the outskirts. Nearly all nationalities being represented, they studied toleration, and sang, —

> "With spades and picks we work like bricks,
> And dig in gold formations."

The city was named after an Irish peer. It numbers at present some seven thousand, is lighted with gas, has an excellent library, publishes two spicy dailies, and is surrounded by a rough agricultural and vine-growing country. Here I found a fine congregation of Spiritualists, ministered to each Sunday by Mr. G. C. Leech, a prominent attorney, and gentleman of culture.

Lecturing in Mechanics Institute, Mr. Leech occupied the chair. The building was densely crowded. Though there have been marvelous physical manifestations in this city, bigotry is still rampant. The pious Archdeacon of Castlemaine, "whose face doth shine," . . . is a violent opposer of Spiritualism.

Sandhurst, — a wide-awake city, originally called Bendigo, claims twenty-five thousand inhabitants. It is the headquarters of vast quartz ranges pronounced absolutely inexhaustible. The buildings are fine; and every thing, save the public garden, indicates enterprise and thrift. Our lectures were delivered in the Rifles' Orderly Hall ; Mr. Denovan, an ex-member of the Colonial Parliament, presiding. This gentleman is as universally esteemed as brave in the utterance of his convictions.

Geelong — with a population of twenty thousand, situated upon Corio Bay — struggled sharply to gain the pre-eminence over Ballarat. The struggle proved a failure. The city was named after a native chief, and is noted for its harbor, botanical gardens, suburban orchards, and beautiful vineyards. The Spiritualists, exceedingly coy, need an infusion of moral firmness and spinal stiffening. Our lecture was delivered in Mechanics Institute, and fairly reported.

Stawell — quite a distance from Melbourne — contains a

large number of free-thinkers and Spiritualists; the latter unnecessarily divided upon the subject of re-incarnation. They have an organized society, and a fine edifice for Sunday meetings, — the Lyceum Hall. Mr. B. S. Nayler was their settled speaker.

GATHERED FRAGMENTS.

The general enterprise of Australia; the genial climate; the magnitude of the cities; the gardens, beautiful parks, and choice libraries, of Melbourne, — far exceeded my preconceived opinions. But neither the culture, the broad toleration, nor the advanced condition of Spiritualism, met my expectations. Considered conservative in America, even to standing upon the border-lands of Christian Spiritualism, I did not even dream of being called by the Melbourne press, "Yankee adventurer," "long-haired apostate," "vulgar blasphemer!" In the end, however, a grand moral victory was achieved: to God and good angels be all the praise! Dr. Dunn gave a lecture upon Spiritualism in Temperance Hall, followed by a séance for physical manifestations. It was exceedingly satisfactory. His healing and clairvoyant powers were richly appreciated by those who tested his gifts, and attended his séances.

Not forgetting the "testimonial," the illuminated scroll, publicly presented me through Mr. Bright; the fine album from Mr. Terry; nor the interesting soirée gotten up for us at the parting, — I take pleasure in testifying that it was never my good fortune to meet more honorable and generous men, or nobler women, than those gracing the ranks of Spiritualism in Victoria. All my relations with them were harmonious and pleasant. Their personal kindnesses I can not forget. And, though never privileged with meeting them all again this side the peaceful river of death, I shall meet them, *know* them, and *love* them in heaven, where mornings of progress know no setting suns.

THE AUSTRALIAN NATIVES.

The aboriginal inhabitants of Australia are called "black men." They are not black, only dark olive complexioned, bearing no real resemblance to African negroes. Seen walking from you, their physical appearance is rather commanding. They are straight as arrows, and flexible in their motions. The skin is brown and smooth, and the hair straight, black, and glossy. Their foreheads are low, eyes full and far apart, nose broad, mouth wide, and filled with large, white teeth. When sporting, using the boomerang, or throwing the spear, their attitudes are exceedingly graceful. Many of the men not only have sinewy and finely-chiseled limbs, but long beards that would naturally excite the envy of smirking aristocrats.

Sir Thomas L. Mitchell says, "They are a fine race of men. Their bodies individually, as well as the groups which they formed, would have delighted the eye of an artist. Is it fancy? but I am far more pleased in seeing the naked body of the black fellow than that of the white man. When I was in Paris, I was often in the public baths, and how few well-made men did I see!"

Dr. Leichhardt, when visiting Australia, gave this description: "The proportions of the body in the women and the men are as perfect as those of the Caucasian race; and the artist would find an inexhaustible source of observation and study among the black tribes."

These aborigines, residue of a very ancient race, number little over a thousand now in the colony of Victoria, and probably not many over a hundred thousand in the entire country. The fittest survives. Such is the logic of law.

THEOLOGICAL AND SOCIAL CHARACTERISTICS.

Religion is innate, and in some form universal. Theology is man-made, stinging the bosom that hugs it. Belief affects the moral conduct.

Ethnologists and Australian residents differ in their estimates of the native character. Certain missionaries, pronouncing them the lowest specimens of humanity, declare that they have "no conception of Jehovah, innate depravity, justification by faith, nor pardon through a sacrificial redemption." This is quite likely; all of which, putting the evangelical construction upon these terms, is quite to the credit of these "heathen" aborigines.

It is the united testimony of thoughtful, honorable men, however, that aboriginal children are noted for retention of memory, quickness of perception, and readiness to acquire the usual elements of education. This was demonstrated by the experimental school at the Merri-Merri. And, a few years since, an aboriginal boy in the Normal School of Sydney carried off the prize from all his white companions. They are trusting and affectionate among themselves. Respect to age is rigidly enforced. Without the hollow fashions and jealousies, without the conventional decorum and restraints, of civilized society, they sing and gambol in the evening-time as though life were a continuous carnival. Suicide is unknown among them. Some of them tattoo themselves. The women use ochre, and other colored ingredients, to paint their faces. What of it? English, French, and American women quite generally paint and powder. What a merciless tyrant is fashion!

TESTIMONIES IN FAVOR OF THE WILD AUSTRALIANS.

These inhabitants, evidently a cross between the African and the Malay, exhibit some excellent traits of character. Archbishop Polding, of New South Wales, said to the Sydney Legislature, " I have no reason to think that the primitive natives, uncontaminated with modern civilizations, are much lower than ourselves, in many respects. The missionary Ridley, noted for his candor, declared that in mental acumen, and in quickness of sight and hearing, they surpass most white people."

Mr. Batman, not inaptly denominated the William Penn of the colony, finished an interesting account of the original inhabitants, many years since, in these words: "They certainly appear to me to be the most superior race of natives which I have ever seen." This is an extreme view: the Maoris of New Zealand, and certain other races in the Pacific islands, are vastly their superiors. European interference here, as elsewhere, has proved a destructive curse to the original inhabitants.

Essayists of materialistic tendencies have strangely, though doubtless undesignedly, underrated the intelligence, the moral and religious position, of the Australian tribes. Mr. Whitman, writing in "The Boston Radical" upon ideas relating to immortality, says, —

"The intellectual plane of the Hottentots, Andamanas, *many* of the Australians and Tasmanians, and some of the Esquimaux, is but little, if any, better than that of the ape-like Bushmen just described. It has been said that the Australian savages can not count their own fingers, not even those of one hand."

If this writer had ever conversed with old colonial residents, and read the carefully-written works of Mitchell, Sturt, Leichhardt, and Gov. Gray; or if he were conversant with the history of William Buckley, who lived with the Australian natives thirty-two years, never seeing, during this time, a white man's face, — he would not have written thus disparagingly, and unjustly too, of these aborigines. Long acquaintance and study led Sir Thomas Mitchell to exclaim, "They are as apt and intelligent as any other race of men I am acquainted with." Mr. Burke bears this testimony before the Committee of Council in 1858: "I believe," says he, "the intelligence of the aborigines has been much misunderstood. The introduction of civilization has not tended to develop their character advantageously; but, on the contrary, they have suffered a moral and physical degradation, which has re-acted upon their intellectual powers."

CLOTHING. — COOKING. — HOMES.

Tacitus informs us that the ancient Germanic tribes spent "whole days before the fire altogether naked." The old Caledonians of Scotland were described by the Romans on this wise: "They live in tents, without shoes, and naked." Gov. Hunter thus mentions his glance at the natives of Jervis Bay, New South Wales, Australia, in 1789: "They were all perfectly naked, except one young fellow, who had a bunch of grass fastened round his waist, which came up behind like the tail of a kangaroo."

The climate being temperate or tropical, they require but little clothing. In the colder portion of the season, they wear rugs made of opossum and kangaroo skins. They are not given to finery. The feathers of the emu, swan, cockatoo, &c., are their ornaments upon important occasions. Some tattoo themselves. This custom, prevailing quite generally among uncivilized nations inhabiting warm countries, owes its origin probably to a want of mental resources, and more attractive employment of time, together with a love of ornament. They bore the cartilage of the nose to suspend bones and shells. American ladies prefer having the ears bored. The Chinese compress their feet, French women their waists.

Nutrition was abundant till the invasions of the Europeans. They pitched their kangaroo meat upon live coals, steamed their fish, and baked their turtles in the shell. Hunting wild honey was a favorite pursuit. The mysnong-root, the ends of tender grass-bulbs, the tops of certain palms, and various wild berries, also constituted articles of diet. Their dwelling-places, though unsubstantial, were sufficiently comfortable for such a fine, warm climate. Sticks, reeds, boughs, and blankets, by the side of a rock or tree, with opossum rugs for breakwinds, were about all they desired. These homes, though comparatively transient, were made musical and happy in early night-time with the relation of droll stories, the appearance of weird apparitions, the song, and the dance. The learned Dr. Lambie, visiting and spending a long time either with, or in the vicinity of, the natives, gives this interesting description: "In some places, large, well-constructed habitations, shaped in the form of a span-roof, thatched with reeds, pleasantly situated on the verge of a lake, though quite unique, were highly creditable to their industry and skill." They are very warm-hearted in their natures, and kind to their aged; they seldom have but one wife at the same time; they will always generously divide with each other, and especially with Europeans who visit them. "These Australians drank only water," says Mr. Thomas, "till white men introduced their poisonous liquors; and imported private diseases also, that are now rapidly sweeping them off from the face of the earth." Mr. Protector Robinson reported officially, that "nine-tenths of the mischief charged to the aborigines is the result of the white men's interference with the native women."

RELIGIOUS NOTIONS AND CUSTOMS.

Worship is natural to all grades of humanity. There have been found, among the aborigines in portions of Australia, remnants of ancient faiths and traditional mythologies. Caves have been opened along the coast, on the walls of which were drawn unique and telling figures. The bottoms were handsomely paved. Mystic circles have been noticed on the tops of hills, the stones of which were arranged after the Druidical fashion. Enough has been discovered to indicate their connection with the civilizations of the most early Asiatic races.

Though probably dimly conscious of an indivisible deific Presence, they evidently adored the starry hosts, — believed in a multiplicity of gods, and in some sort of a future existence. "Go down, black fellow; come up, white man!" is at present a common saying among them. That critical ethnologist, Strzelecki, says in his exhaustive volume, " The native Australians, recognizing a God, whose duty it is to supply them with all the necessaries of life, regard themselves as his servants. They believe in immortality, and locate their heaven in the stars: they do not dread God, but reserve all their fears for the evil spirit. To this spirit, the ' Debble,' they render a sort of worship."

Upon each returning November, the Australian spring-time, these natives hold the grand festival of the Pleiades, called the "Corroboree." It was a matter of individual regret that I could not have personally witnessed this native anniversary. Those in Northern and North-eastern Australia are far the most interesting. These "corroborees," celebrated only in the spring, when this cluster of stars shines the most brilliantly, are evidently a kind of worship paid to the Pleiades " as a constellation announcing the spring season." Their monthly festivals and dances are in honor of the moon. An intelligent native said to me in Sandhurst, "The Pleiades are the children of the moon, and very good to us black people." The remark reminded me of a line in that Biblical drama, the Book of Job, —

"The sweet influences of the Pleiades."

These, called by the Romans " Vergiliæ," the stars of spring, appear above the horizon at evening-time in November, and are visible in these regions all night. The prophets of the tribes believe that these stars rule natural causes. Some of their festivals are connected with the worship of their dead ancestors. These last three days.

FROM WHENCE THESE NATIVES?

Their origin is involved in impenetrable obscurity; and those who have attempted to trace their migrations, or detect the links which connect them to the primitive races, have failed of satisfying even themselves. The structure of the language is said to be the most nearly identified with the

Sanscrit; others choose to connect it with the nomadic Tartars. In physical type they resemble the Malays, and yet there is not a Malay word in their language. They have religious mysteries, and a fearful method of initiation. Some of the tribes practice, like Jews and Mohammedans, the rite of circumcision. They wear charms upon their persons; and certain of the old chiefs, looking into rock-crystals, profess to see the future. They find the bodies of murdered men by watching the trail of beetles. Mourning paint to be used for the face is invariably white. Young mothers used to very frequently name their children after flowers. A surname was sometimes added, descriptive of personal peculiarities. When a child is named after another person, and this person dies, the name dies also. The dead are never spoken of by name, nor referred to only by implication. They refrain from touching a dead body, as did the Jews and ancient Phœnicians. That a bond of brotherhood exists among the dark races of Australia and the Indian seas, is indisputable; but whence they originally sprang, and by what circumstances they became scattered over thousands of miles, through seventy degrees of latitude, remains a problem to be solved. Doubtless the Australian country was peopled long before Abraham went down into Egypt, or before the walls of ancient Nineveh and Thebes were raised to their proud position.

THE NATIVE'S BELIEF IN SPIRITS.

Spirit is the underlying cause of all motion, energy, and moral activity. In the aboriginal "ceremonies, superstitions, and beliefs, there may be traced," says Mr. Parker, "relics of sun-worship, serpent-worship, and the worship of ancestral spirits whom they profess to frequently see." They believe that one class of spirits dwell in the air, another in the mountain, and others still wander about among the tall trees. These natives seldom quit a camp-fire at night, for fear of encountering malignant spirits. Mr. Benwick, among other marvels, writes this: "A spirit appeared to a *lubra*, — black woman, — announcing her speedy death. She related the occurrence the next day, with serious forebodings. Two days after seeing the apparition she died. Believing in demoniacal possession, the mediumistic 'medicine-men' of the tribe 'exorcise the evil spirits,' something as did Jesus and the apostles in New-Testament times. This class of men also alleviate pain, remove disease, and heal the sick, by charms and magnetic manipulations. They dance within the inclosures of mystic rings, fall in the trance, and describe the marvelous visions beheld." The Rev. Mr. Ridley gives the following account of a "corroboree:" "At Burndtha, on the Barwon, I met a company of forty blacks engaging in a ceremony of some mystical purpose. A chorus of twenty, old and young, were singing, and beating time with boomerangs. A dozen or more were looking on. Suddenly, from under a sheet of bark, darted a man, with his body whitened by pipe-clay, his face painted yellow, and a tuft of feathers fastened upon the top of his head. He stood twenty minutes gazing upwards. One of the aborigines, who stood by, said he was looking for the spirits of dead men. At length they came, proving to be evil spirits, and a brisk conflict followed. Others of the party joined in this warfare with the 'powers in the air,' driving the ghosts away." They have a singular ceremony, called *Ye pene amie gai*, or dance of separate spirits. Holding branches in their hands, they dance in measured tread, and sing, till they fall prostrate in a sort of ecstatic trance. While in this condition, they hold converse with spirits, and utter prophecies.

DECLINE AND DESTINY.

Nominally the aged men are their chiefs, exercising the principal influence in the tribes. "Civilization" is a very indefinite term. Australian aborigines, believing it to consist in being and doing like white men, engage in smoking, swearing, tricking, drinking, and gambling. The Rev. J.

C. S. Handt, Lutheran missionary, bears this testimony: "A principal cause of their decrease is the prostitution of their wives to the Europeans. This base intercourse not only retards the procreation of their own race, but almost always tends to the destruction of the offspring brought into existence by its means." Mr. Cunningham, well known in England and the English colonies of the Pacific, wrote thus: "Personal prostitution, among those associating with the whites, is carried on to a great extent, the husbands disposing of the favor of their wives to the convict servants, for a slice of bread, or a pipe of tobacco. The children produced by this intercourse are generally sacrificed."

Infanticide is very prevalent. Tradition says it did *not* exist in the past. At present half-caste infants appear to be the most exposed to this fate. Chiefs living and roaming back in the mountains, or interior districts, acknowledge that they cannot stop the murderous practice. When the parties are reproved for the unnatural crime, they at once respond, "We have no country now, no good children now, and nothing to keep them on." A glance at the journals reveals the fact that infanticide is not uncommon in Victoria; while fœticide is a quite common practice in the most aristocratic families. It is *murder* nevertheless.

Without hope, without seeming ambition, the remaining Australian natives have sunk down into a state of stupid listlessness. They know they are declining, and are conscious of their destiny. It seems an inflexible law of nature, that aboriginal races must, in every instance, either perish, or be amalgamated with the general population of the country. In Tasmania, originally known as Van Diemen's Land, there is not a native left. The bell of fate has tolled; and the last man of his race, putting down his rude pilgrim staff, has gone on to the shadowy land of immortality.

CHAPTER VI.

NEW ZEALAND.

THE steamer "Albion" was five days from Melbourne to The Bluffs, a small, rough-looking town on the west coast of New Zealand. Twelve hours more brought us to Port Chalmers, where, after clasping the fraternal hands of several friends who came to welcome us, a new railway dropped us down, in less than half an hour, at Dunedin, a city of over nineteen thousand inhabitants, sitting like a young queen, overshadowed with mountains, and crystal waters rippling at her feet.

The magnetic atmosphere of Otago differs materially from that of Victoria. It is Scottish; and, though sterner, is morally superior.

Constantly summering, and wintering too, under the Southern Cross, the evergreen foliage of New Zealand — the Britain of the south — literally charms me. The scenery seems a blending of Swiss with the Scottish Highlands. As I see the clear waters, and the fern-clad hillsides, from the windows of "mine host," — Mr. Redmayne, — this sunny February morning, they remind me not a little of deeply wooded isles reposing under Ionian skies, rough, rugged, and yet inviting, in some respects, as the gardens of the Hesperides. God be praised for every hill and valley, and tree and flower!

March in New Zealand corresponds to September in England: accordingly, it is now approaching autumn-time, and the leaves are falling from the elm and the oak, and other trees imported from the northern latitudes of Europe. The indigenous trees, whether ornamental or valuable for building purposes, retain their native verdure throughout the year. When these islands were discovered by the Dutch navigator, Tasman, 1642, they were inhabited by a bold, athletic, dark-skinned race, supposed, while closely related to the Hawaiians, to have descended from the Malays; others say from the Central Americans. They are called *Maoris;* the word meaning "primitive inhabitants." In Capt. Cook's time, and after, some of the tribes were cannibals. These natives, though superior, on the whole, to most aborigines, are fading away. They understand their destiny. Wellington, though not as large as Dunedin, Auckland, or Christchurch, is the seat of government. There are four of these *Maoris* in the General Assembly. Britain has set Columbia a good example in this matter. May we not hope to see, at no distant day, both Indians and women in our American Congress?

New Zealand is nearly on the opposite side of the globe from Great Britain, the precise antipodes being a small island seven hundred miles to the south-east. The two islands designated as the North and the Middle, separated by Cook's Straits, are over a thousand miles in length, volcanic in formation, and contain about sixty million acres. Seen from the ocean, the land is rough and barren; and yet the country has fine plains, open valleys, beautiful springs and rivers, and is unsurpassed in value for agricultural purposes. I have met wool-buyers here from New York and the New-England States. Having a seaboard extent of some four thousand miles, with several splendid harbors, this country is destined to occupy an important position in trade and commerce. Auckland, Christchurch, and Dunedin are the three largest cities.

CLIMATE OF NEW ZEALAND.

Though one of the finest in the world, the climate is far warmer and more genial on the western than on the eastern coast of this group. The average rain-fall is twenty-nine inches. The atmosphere is light and buoyant; while the winds are continually freshened by traversing an immense expanse of ocean. Not a flake of snow is seen in the northern island of this group, save in the highlands. At an elevation of six thousand feet, however, the snow is perpetual. These islands, unlike many in the South Pacific, are eminently adapted for agricultural and pastoral pursuits. The sunny valley of the Taieri, the undulating plains, the neatly tilled fields in the rural districts, with millions of choice yet unoccupied acres, incline one to ask, "Why do tens of thousands remain in Britain to beg or starve? England has colonies and provinces enough to supply multitudes with homes, thus feeding her over-crowded population. Why do they not emigrate?"

It is contended by the "old identities," —the first settlers, — that Anglo-Saxons can work, and expose themselves to the climate of New Zealand, without injury, more days in the year, and more hours in the day, than in any other country. The mountains abound in wild swine, descendants of those let loose by the navigator Capt. Cook, a hundred years ago. There are also wild cattle and goats in the woodlands, called the "bush." English deer, hare, grouse, pheasants, sparrows, larks, and other singing birds, have been introduced into the country by acclimatization societies. These in time will furnish scope for English field-sports amid scenery resembling that of Northern Italy or the Highlands of Scotland. Gold interests, wool-raising, and rich agricultural districts, with superior commercial advantages, must ultimately make New Zealand a great country.

The whole population of these islands is about two hundred and seventy thousand, of which some seventy thousand are the residents of Otago province. There are over forty thousand *Maoris*. The gold-fields are the source of its permanent wealth. Dunedin, a slim settlement twenty years ago, is now a thriving city of nearly twenty thousand. The magnetic element is cold and stolid, substantial and solid.

BOTANIZING IN FERN-FIELDS.

Cordially invited, Dr. Dunn and the writer accompanied the Dunedin "Botanical Club" on excursions to gather ferns in the gullies and up on the mountain-sides. Though fatiguing, it was thrillingly interesting; and the more so, because — as in Ireland — there are neither frogs, toads, nor serpents. How is this, since no St. Patrick banished them? Fuchser was a German botanist; and the small, yet beautiful flowering plant in America, named after him, is a native tree in these islands, with a trunk from a few to eighteen inches in diameter. Tramping over the hills, one is continually reminded of extinct volcanoes and the carbonaceous period. Some of the tree-ferns are over one foot in diameter. They grow straight and erect as chiseled pillars, while their long, arching, thick-ribbed leaves spread out like roofs of daintiest beauty, through which sun-rays can scarcely gleam. The birds we saw on the mountains were few, but exceedingly tame. These natives, the *Maoris*, neither shoot nor otherwise harm them. What a lesson to Christian sportsmen! The kiwi is the last living representative of the New Zealand wingless birds. These wild birds, so called, will sometimes take crumbs from the hand, and peck at the nails in your boot-heels when sitting down to rest in a thicket. The moa, a gigantic wingless bird, corresponding to the giraffe in the animal kingdom, has long been extinct. The bones are valuable to naturalists. Several skeletons of this bird may be seen in the Christchurch Museum, nine, ten, and even twelve feet high. The flesh was eaten by the Maoris; the feathers were used as ornaments, and their skulls for holding tattooing-powders.

MAGNIFICENT SCENERY AND MINERAL SPRINGS.

Among the natural wonders of this island group, are the geysers, or boiling lakes. They are said to far surpass those of Iceland. Columns of steam, rising from these volcano-heated springs, may be seen above the white cliffs while sailing along the coast. Approaching them, the roar seems like mighty engines madly working in the bowels of the earth. And, what is singular, no two throw up water of exactly the same character. Some are clear as crystal, others are dark-hued and muddy; some are impregnated with acids, some taste of soda, many contain sulphur, and one is salt as the briny ocean; but they are all intensely hot and boiling. The natives make use of them for all kinds of skin diseases and rheumatic complaints. Not far distant from these springs, on the North Island, are the Tarata Falls, fringed with weird shrubbery and incrusted boughs. The sprays and glassy sheets, pouring over molded alabaster, are strikingly beautiful. Below are delightful baths of different temperatures. The baths of the ancient Romans, so famous in history, could not have surpassed these adjacent to the boiling lakes. The crystallized terraces are absolutely magnificent. Te Roto Wanapanapa is a strange-looking greasy lake of yellowish-green water, clear, cold, and deep. There are hot, muddy springs close by, throwing up a gray-colored, greasy clay, which the roaming Maoris call *Kaikai*, and eat with avidity. The prettiest hot spring is Nawharua, called the Moss Spring. It is used for cooking purposes. The quantity of sulphur around some of these lakes is enormous; and the mineral impregnations give the waters all kinds of colors. Some of the terraces are pink, some purple, and others white or orange, caused by crystallizations. Names written on them are soon coated over, becoming permanent; while fern-leaves, flowers, and the fine swinging twigs, seem to have been converted into stalactite-shaped crystals of silver and gold. No painter can put this scenery upon canvas. A Walter Scott or Bulwer-Lytton could hardly do the subject justice. The prince of all romancers, Dumas, would fail.

AKAROA. — ITS FRUITS.

Invited by Mr. W. D. Meers, one of Nature's noblemen, formerly of London, to lecture in Christchurch, Canterbury, the latter part of February, I shipped aboard " The Beautiful Star." The passage of nearly four days — which should have been less than two — was rough and stormy, and the accommodations shabbily miserable.

On our way up the coast, the captain put into Akaroa Harbor, at the head of which is a quaint village, originally settled by the French. The harbor is really a gem, set between two mountainous ridges, and extensive enough to hold the navy of the world. Afar up this harbor, there juts from its blue depths a sunny isle, which the Maoris consider one of the habitations of the " dead." They declare that apparitions walk this ghost-isle by night; giving it, to them, a sort of sacredness. The quiet village of Akaroa is famous only for its fruits. The orchards and gardens were burdened with figs, peaches, apricots, apples, pears, and plums.

Walking up Main Street, fringed with white clover in blossom, and gazing at a unique, old-fashioned cottage partly embowered in ornamental trees, a voice rung out, " Would you like some fruit, sir?" Thanks. ".Walk in, *walk in*, sir." We did so, finding this gentleman's fruits most delicious. Turning to leave, the kind-hearted old Frenchman said, " Fill your pockets, sir; you'll relish it on the steamer." Urging was unnecessary. Surely there are benevolent men everywhere, — great, generous-hearted souls, away even on the south-east coast of New Zealand.

Mr. Meers successfully engineered this first course of Spiritualist lectures, given in Odd-Fellows Hall. The meetings increased in interest to the end. The first families of the city were in attendance. Mr. Hart, owning extensive coalfields, occupied the chair three of the evenings. The daily journals reported the lectures fairly and generously.

CHRISTCHURCH CITY.

Every street, in this city of some fifteen thousand inhabitants, is named after an English bishop. The climate is warm, dry, and inviting. Canterbury Plains, on which it is situated, are one hundred and fifty miles in length, and from forty to fifty in width. These fertile, undulating plains, a very paradise for agriculturists, reminded me of our own broad western prairies, that laugh with golden grains when tickled with spade and plow. The harvests in this February month had just been gathered, and rumbling threshing-machines were separating the chaff from the wheat. Half circling Christchurch, runs a willow-shaded stream, clear as a crystal. In the city proper, are five hundred Artesian wells, with an average depth of eighty feet. There are also six huge tanks within the city limits, ever full and bubbling, as a safety against fires. Each tank holds twenty thousand gallons. Here, too, is the choicest, and by far the most extensive museum in the colony. Dr. Haast, the presiding genius, is a scholar, a liberalist, thoroughly up in geology and biological studies, and predisposed in favor of Spiritualism. He attended our lectures. The museum is a stately building, and has the finest *moa* skeletons in New Zealand.

The gardens in and about the city at this season, though well cared for, and English-looking, were not rich in loquats, scarlet pomegranates, and golden oranges; neither were they arrayed in the gorgeous blossoms of the tropics, but were full of sweet, common flowers, such as we have seen in American cities, and the Kew Gardens of London.

RANGIORA.

Though mine is a missionary work, it is not for the nature-children of New Zealand, the Maoris, but for the self-righteous, who while crying, "Lord, Lord!" stone the prophets, persecute their peers, and piously thank God that they are " not like other men."

While in the vicinity of Canterbury, I visited and lectured in Rangiora, a stirring city of several thousand. Mr. R. Schmidt and his estimable companion are the only avowed Spiritualists. Our first introduction to this family was in Christchurch. Their harmonious home, just out of the city, is a little paradise. Those bending fruit-trees, beds of flowers, oddly-shaped cabbage-trees, winding walks, and a deep, clear spring bubbling up in the lawn, arched with weeping willows, are things of beauty not to be forgotten. This home we termed the Pilgrim's Rest. Here, too, I found copies of " Daybreak," and "Medium and Human Nature," published by James Burns. Thus does this enthusiastic worker and editor preach the " gospel to the ends of earth."

Though this portion of New Zealand had been settled only about twenty-one years, it seemed like an old country. Along the line of the railway were eucalypts, poplar, and elm trees, with handsome fields of white and red clover thickly dotted with grazing herds.

Tussock grass — a wild native grass — covers much of the uncultivated upland country. It is capable of making good paper. Cows feeding upon it give to dairymen a superior quality of butter; but, added our German railway informant, the " water in this part of the country contains too much lime to make good beer."

FIGURES.

At the close of 1871 the population of New Zealand was 156,431 males, and 110,555 females. The excess in number of men over women is 45,876. The number of letters received in the colony in 1871 was 3,291,990, and the number dispatched was 2,784,707. The number of newspapers received was 2,308,633, and the number dispatched was 1,871,150. The postal revenue is very large. Government has a system of telegraphing money-orders. It is admirable, and Americans should adopt the method. This island colony in the southern seas owns three hundred and eighteen sailing-vessels, and fifty-three steamboats. The people have advanced more rapidly in mechanics than matters moral and spiritual. A Dunedin company is constructing a submarine boat, to extract gold from the deep river-beds of Otago. An American constitutes the backbone of the enterprise.

My countrymen are more highly esteemed in New Zealand than in Australia.

WINES AT FUNERALS.

Officiating at a funeral in Dunedin, New Zealand, there were wines put upon the same table with the encoffined corpse. After I had spoken the words of consolation, the sectarian neighbors present, and a portion of the mourners, "imbibed." This is quite common, I am told, at Christian burials. Think of it, — wines at births, and wines at funerals! Think of it, O ye priests! who, guzzling wines, beers, and brandies, solemnly preach that "no drunkard can enter the kingdom of heaven"! Is it not to the silly and stupid custom of "entertaining" by drink that Hamlet alludes, when he says to Horatio, "It is a custom more honored in the breach than the observance"? The peerless Shakspeare makes Cassio to say, "Oh that men should put an enemy in their mouths to steal away their brains! that we should with joy, pleasure, revel, and applause, transform ourselves into *beasts!*"

During the late English elections, overthrowing the reigning Gladstone party, both the Scriptures and liquors were used at public gatherings for political purposes. Flags and banners bore this inscription: "*Beer and the Bible,* — *a national beverage and a national Church!*" Chinese, Persians, Arabs, "heathens of the East," often taunt and scourge Christians for their habitual drunkenness. One of Buddha's commandments was, "Drink no liquors, neither wines; but walk steadily in the path of purity." Mohammed said,

"O true believers! surely wines and games are an abomination, a snare of Satan." The heathen (?) of Asia have wines neither upon their sideboards, nor at their funerals.

CANNIBALISM.

As one stimulus leads to another, why should not meat-eating open the way to cannibalism? If, according to the unphilosophical epicure, flesh is a better food than vegetables, grains, and fruits, and higher, too, in the scale of sustenance, why not subsist upon it altogether? And so, if *human* flesh is still higher, more readily assimilating with the juices and forces of the system, because magnetically humanized, why not eat *that* also? The Maori cannibals of New Zealand did *this* very thing. When the giant-like moa-birds failed to supply necessary meat, the natives resorted to cannibalism; eating, first, enemies slain in battle. *Animal food* they must and *would* have.

The Rev. Mr. Baker said to me, while at a dinner-party given by the Rev. Dr. Lang, Sydney, "I have visited one hundred and ten of the South-Sea Islands, and am perfectly acquainted with their manners, customs, regulations, and religious notions. They believe in one or more gods, and in an existence hereafter. Those on the Isle of Lifu, Loyalty Group, Western Polynesia, believe that the good spirits of their ancestors — whom they sometimes see as apparitions — dwell on the sunny side of the island, and the bad spirits among the lagoons on the other. They are dark complexioned, and capable of a high civilization. Some of these islanders yet continue their cannibal practices." This clergyman personally knew one old chief who had helped to eat and digest thirty human beings. They generally bake them. It is considered an honor to drink the blood, and feast upon certain parts of the bodies, of those slain on their battle-fields.

MAN-EATING UNNATURAL.

Animals, only in exceptional cases, devour each other. It was not innate barbarism, nor a monstrous heathenism, that drove the South-Sea Islanders to eat their fellows. It may be accounted for in the extermination of the moa-birds and the native rats, depriving them of flesh-food. Europeans, when shipwrecked and at the point of starvation, have laid hold of and greedily devoured their companions. History relates many occurrences of this kind. Before casting too many stones at those "vile savages," it were well to glance at antiquity. Donovan, in Lardner's Cyclopedia, assures us that "our own ancestors were of the number of these cannibal epicures." Diodorus Siculus charges the Britons with being *anthropophagi*; and St. Jerome, living in the fifth century of the Christian era, accuses the British tribes, not only of a partiality for human flesh, but a "fastidious taste for certain delicate parts of it." Gibbon brings the same accusation against the Caledonians. Allied by a common bond of sympathy, war in Christian nations, and cannibalism among the native islanders of the Pacific, must perish together.

THEOLOGICAL CANNIBALISM.

Did you ever attend the Sunday services of the Ritualists? What a display of millinery! — the alb, girdle, stole, maniple, and chasuble; referring, it is said, to the trial and death-scene of Jesus! After the waving of the incense, comes the administration of the eucharist, which eucharistic elements are declared to be the "veritable flesh and blood of Jesus Christ."

The Rev. Mr. Bailey, the English clergyman of Christchurch, New Zealand, says that the "priests of a certain order offer the sacrifice; and such mysterious authority do they wield, that the *real body and blood* become infused into the bread and wine upon the altar." These are the teachings of the "Prayer-Book." At the words; "THIS IS MY

BODY, THIS IS MY BLOOD," you must believe that the bread and wine become the real body and blood, with the soul and the Godhead, of Jesus Christ. . . . Except " ye eat my *flesh*, and drink my *blood*, there is no life in you." 'Mid gorgeous vestments, bursts of music, and clouds of incense curling above the altar, the priest asks the members of the church present to eat the *miracle-made flesh*, and drink the *blood* of Jesus the son of Joseph, called, in his time, Joshua the Galilean. If this bread *is* made "flesh," as the clergy affirm, eating is cannibalism! There are few churchal practices more opposed to the genius of the nineteenth century, than these little select Sunday parties denominated the "Lord's Supper." Open wide your church-doors, O Christians! and spreading out, with liberal hands, good coarse unleavened bread, fresh fruits, and pure cold water, invite in "the poor, the halt, and the blind;" and then converse of the Nazarene, his benevolence, his self-denial, his devotion to principle, and his martyrdom upon Calvary!

THE MAORI RACES.

The original inhabitants of an island or country must naturally interest all thoughtful persons given to ethnological studies. According to Tasman, Cook, D'Surville, and other navigators, New Zealand, when discovered, was thickly inhabited by a most interesting people, — one hundred thousand or more in number. In color they were of a yellow brown or olive. Those that I have seen on camp-grounds, or strolling along the streets, were of a light copper hue. Blood, in many of them, is strangely mixed with that of Europeans. In hight they are above middle stature, erect, well proportioned, and muscular. Their countenances are open, eyes dark, foreheads finely developed, noses large, broad at the base, and often aquiline, and their hair black, waving, and often inclined to curl. Some of them have as fine, heavy beards as Americans. Their hair never falls off from their heads, but gradually turns gray. The old natives affirm that their ancestors lived to be very aged, and then died by slowly wasting away, as a lamp goes out for lack of oil.

THEIR HOME MATTERS.

These Maoris, as relics demonstrate, were certainly, in the past, more than semi-civilized. Those yet living are the degenerate specimens of a nobler ancestry. In social life they were industrious, good-natured, temperate, and cleanly. They dwelt together in large fenced villages. Rising early, the men went to their land-cultivations or sea-fishing, and the women to cooking or basket-making. Their house-building, and architectural conceptions generally, were infinitely superior to those of the Australian aborigines. They excelled in some few manufactures, especially in weaving mats and garments from *phormium*, — New-Zealand flax. This plant, growing spontaneous, reminds one of the wide green flag-leaves seen in American marshes. The fiber is wonderfully tough ; and the mats and rude dresses, made from it by the natives, were both useful and ornamental. This flax is now being utilized for the English market.

Iron was unknown to the New-Zealanders when Capt. Cook landed upon the island. Their stone axes of various sizes, used for felling trees, were made of green jade, basalt, or hard gray stone. For water-vessels, they used the ripened rinds of gourds. Oil they kept in calabashes similar to those we saw in the Sandwich Islands. Their musical instruments, such as the flute, were made from human bones, or the hollow stems of wood. They did not buy and sell, but dealt in exchanges and gifts. Priests generally named the children. They practiced polygamy. As a religious animal, man is polygamic and promiscuous; as a spiritual being, he is monogamic in marriage, and chaste in marital conduct; and as an angel he is a celibate. The embryo angel is within. Men may become angelic on earth. This is the resurrection with God's " will done on earth as in heaven."

The chiefs of these tribes were known by their tattooing, dress, insignia, and ornaments. The eldest child was the favorite one, ruling the others. A species of slavery existed among them. Slaves could never reach the rank of patricians. When these Maoris met, they did not shake hands, but affectionately rubbed their noses together. This is their present practice. While some American women carry poodles for pets, these natives carry little pigs. They are very hospitable to strangers. Cannibalism was unknown in their earlier traditional times. Their decline commenced with the advent of the missionaries. The "Wanganui Herald," in an able editorial upon the "decline of the native race," says, —

"Let one get into conversation with any of the old settlers, principally whalers, whose recollections date back some forty years, and he will be astonished to learn how these tribes have disappeared off the face of the earth, and how the present representatives of these departed races, noble specimens of civilized savages as some of them are, bear comparison in stature, appearance, mental qualifications, or social influence among their respective tribes, with their departed ancestors. It is almost saddening to watch the gradual though certain diminution among those once powerful *hapus;* and it is no less humiliating to have to acknowledge, that in the majority of instances, death and disease can be unerringly traced to their intercourse with the less civilized *pakeha,* the white man. In Otaki, the centre of missionary influence on this part of the coast, will be found the greatest immorality, the most degraded mental and physical condition, and consequently the most rapid and certain decline, among the natives as a people. . . . Yearly statistics unerringly state, that, so far from the natives being benefited by their religious, political, and social intercourse with ourselves, the reverse is the case. Disease and death are on the increase; and crimes, often of a heinous nature, are committed more frequently in proportion to the progress of their acquaintance with our manners and our customs, our habits and our views, our treachery and our falsehood. This seems an appalling picture, but nevertheless it is a true bill."

TATTOOING.

The term "tattoo," of Oceanic origin, relates to those indelible devices pricked into the skins of natives. The

New-Zealanders used originally the wing-bone of a bird, sharpened to a point. This they dip into the juice of a tree, producing the desired color. The tattoo-artists hold a high social position. The process is painful and tedious. Chiefs are very thoroughly as well as weirdly tattooed. Besides being ornamental, the operation is regarded with religious veneration; the one thus decorated being placed under the protecting care of some spirit. The god of the tattoo is called Tiki. The practice is ancient. Herodotus informs us that "both in Thrace and Lybia the natives were accustomed to puncture and color their faces, and various parts of their bodies."

WHENCE CAME THESE MAORIS?

The native population may be classed into several divisions, distinguishable by peculiarities of dialect, physiognomy, and disposition. These divisions are dimly traceable to the crews of different canoes finding their way to these islands. Evidently they came from different Polynesian groups. They certainly did not come from Australia, as their color, habits, religion, and language demonstrate; neither are they the descendants of the Sandwich Islanders, as some have contended. Among substantial reasons to the contrary, the following may be mentioned: The New-Zealanders carry their burdens on their backs, much like our North-American Indians; while the Sandwich-Islanders carry theirs on a balance-pole, something like the Chinese. Further, these New-Zealand Maoris have no words for swearing, no temples for religious worship, no idols, no refuge-cities; nor did they ever practice circumcision. Many of their taboos, *tabu*, were utterly unlike those of the Hawaiians. But, affirmatively, the carvings of the Maoris agree wonderfully with those of the ancient inhabitants of Central America. Like those Central-Americans, these aborigines obtain fire by friction; they steep kernels of *Karaka* for food; and have religious as well as many other customs resembling those remote nations, as late discoveries at Uxmel and Palenque plainly show.

THE MAORIS' RELIGION.

Men, civilized and savage alike, are naturally religious. The principle is God-implanted. These New-Zealand Maoris believed in a plurality of invisible gods, and a future existence, although the *tapu* took the place of religious observances. They had priests and "sorcerers," and held intercourse with their "ancestral dead." They were troubled with demons. The heads of the chiefs were tabooed (*tapu*), no one being allowed to touch them, or hardly allude to them, under fearful penalties. They believed in charms, and wore them. Death, to them, was the passage to the *Reinga*, the unseen world, or the place of departed spirits. They prayed to their gods for aid and direction. They did not fear to die, yet preferred living in their mortal bodies. They believed that individuals occupied different apartments in *Reinga*, according as their earthly lives had been good or ill. Messages were frequently given to dying persons to bear away to deceased relatives in this shadow-land of souls. All of their funeral wails over their recent dead ended with, "Go, go, dear one, away to thy people!" It is a singular coincidence that the Fijians, Tahitians, Tongans, and Samoans, as well as the New-Zealanders, considered the place of departure of the spirits, on their journey to the unseen world, as the western extremities of their islands.

Burning *Kauri* gum for a kind of incense at funerals and festivals, they considered the trees pointing skyward as symbolizing life in a higher, better state of existence. This resinous substance, *Kauri*, — imported for making varnish, — is not obtained in the present living *Kauri* pine-forests, but only in the Auckland province of the north island, where such trees originally grew; yet of such ancient forests no other trace remains than the resin now found deep in the soil.

MAORI SPIRITUALISM.

Relation to, and communion with, a world of spirits are beliefs almost, if not completely universal. The native tribes and clans of these islands are not only aware of holding intercourse with the so-called dead, but they understand the abuse, often using their mediumistic privileges for selfish ends. During their wars with the English, they were uniformly made acquainted by vision, clairvoyance, or clairaudience, with the movements of the British troops, before action in battle. Not a plan of her Majesty's officers could be kept from them. The leading chief of the *Han Hans* was a noted medium and medicine-man. He distinctly said that the "spirits of the dead" guided him to his victories. The Maoris in the north island still own much territory, have their king, believe in communicating spirit intelligences, and hold but little intercourse with *pakeha*, the white man.

The medium-priest in a tribe is called *Tohunga*. They meet in close apartments, and chant their songs till the flickering fire fades away, when the *Tohunga* goes into his ecstatic state, and the spirit controlling tenders counsel, describes his new habitation in spirit-life, gives the names of those whom he has met, and bears messages in return to kindred in the higher life. That these *Maoris* of New Zealand talk with immortals, no intelligent man having lived among them disputes. Are they Spiritualists, then, or *Spiritists*? Spiritualism is the synonym of the harmonial philosophy. Spiritism is the bare *fact* of spirit-converse.

TOHUNGA, AND VOICES OF THE DEAD.

The racy writer of "Old New Zealand,"* treating of spiritual experiences among the Maoris, says in substance, "A popular young chief, something of a scholar, and register of births and deaths, had been killed in battle; and, at the request of friends, the *Tohunga* had promised to evoke,

---

* Old New Zealand, by the Pakeha, p. 157-161.

on a certain night, his spirit. The appointed time came.
Fires were lit. The *Tohunga* repaired to the darkest corner
of the room. All was silence, save the sobbing of the sisters
of the deceased warrior-chief. There were thirty of us, sitting on the rush-strewn floor, the door shut, and the fire now
burning down to embers. Suddenly there came a voice out
from the partial darkness, '*Salutation, salutation to my
family, to my tribe, to you, pakeha, my friend!*' Our feelings were taken by storm. The oldest sister screamed, and
rushed with extended arms in the direction from whence the
voice came. Her brother, seizing, restrained her by main
force. Others exclaimed, 'Is it you? is it you? *truly* it is
you! *aue! aue!*' and fell quite insensible upon the floor.
The older women, and some of the aged men, were not moved
in the slightest degree, though believing it to be the spirit
of the chief.

"Reflecting upon the novelty of the scene, the 'darkness
visible,' and the deep interest manifest, the spirit spoke
again, 'Speak to me, my family; speak to me, my tribe;
speak to me, the pakeha!' At last the silence gave way,
and the brother spoke: 'How is it with you? is it well
with you in *that* country?' The answer came, though not
in the voice of the Tohunga-medium, but in strange, sepulchral sounds: "*It is well with me: my place is a good
place. I have seen our friends: they are all with me!*" A
woman from another part of the room now anxiously cried
out, 'Have you seen my sister?'—'Yes, I have seen her: she
is happy in our beautiful country.'—'Tell her my love so
great for her will never cease.'—'Yes, I will bear the message.' Here the native woman burst into tears, and my
own bosom swelled in sympathy.

"The spirit speaking again, giving directions about property
and keepsakes, I thought I would more thoroughly test the
genuineness of all this; and I said, 'We can not find your
book with the registered names; where have you concealed
it?' The answer came instantly, 'I concealed it between the

tahuhu of my house, and the thatch; straight over you, as you go in at the door.' The brother rushed out to see. All was silence. In five minutes he came hurriedly back, with the *book in his hand!* It astonished me.

"It was now late; and the spirit suddenly said, '*Farewell, my family, farewell, my tribe: I go.*' Those present breathed an impressive farewell; when the spirit cried out again, from high in the air, 'Farewell!'

"This, though seemingly tragical, is in every respect literally true. But what was it? ventriloquism, the Devil, or what?"

This last paragraph is simply a sop thrown out to please the orthodox. It might be paralleled thus: Peter, James, and John heard the spirits of Moses and Elias "talking with Jesus" upon the Mount of Transfiguration. "But what was it? — ventriloquism, the Devil, or what?"

Spiritualism is as common in the isles of the ocean to-day as it was in Palestine when the Nazarene there lived, eighteen centuries since. Dillon, commanding the East India Company's surveying ship "Research," visited the island of Vanikovo, — lat. 11° 40′ south, long. 166° 40′ east, — for the purpose of inquiring into the fate of the French expedition under La Pérouse. At this island, where Dillon remained twenty-three days, he tells us there were *large houses set apart for the use of disembodied spirits*. Markham, in "The Cruise of 'The Rosario' in the South Seas in 1871," refers to the fact as related by Dillon.

STATUS OF SPIRITUALISM IN DUNEDIN.

Conscious of a necessity for unity of action, the liberalists of this city organized a "Society for the Investigation of Spiritualism," selecting the following gentlemen for officers: Mr. Redmayne, president; Mr. Wilson, secretary; Mr. Beverly, treasurer, and Messrs. Logan, Stout, and Carrick, a committee.

Mr. Beverly, born in Dundee, is a botanist, a mathematician, and a solid thinker. It is believed that he knows more about the geometrical and astronomical purposes of the great pyramid *Ghizeh* than any other living man. He has done much for the Dunedin Museum, corresponded with Prof. De Morgan, of London, invented a singular thermometer, solved heretofore unsolved mathematical problems, and "squared the circle;" which, if I understand it, is to find the ratio between the diameter and the circumference, or to find the side of a square which is equal to a given circle.

Our lectures were largely attended by the more thinking class of the citizens. Dr. Dunn had a most successful run of practice in the city, to the great horror of "professors" and the medical fraternity. His trances puzzled, and correct clairvoyant examinations maddened them. The newspaper correspondence, brisk on both sides, was personal and emphatically base on the part of the "profession," touching the "official sheepskin." While away from the city, laboring in Christchurch, the doctor filled our lecture-hours in the theatre most acceptably to the listening people. And, further, he reviewed several clergymen, in their united attacks upon Spiritualism, in a most able and eloquent manner. I felt proud of his efforts. Both "The Times" and "The Star"— daily papers — reported us both quite fully and impartially. The theatre was crowded to the conclusion of our stay. Seed was sown, that, under the watch-care of angels, must produce a bountiful harvest.

TASTES AND TRIUMPHS.

The New-Zealand mind is naturally skeptical. And some of the Spiritualists tread upon the very border-lands of materialism. Their motto is, demolition, — "Down with the Christian religion!" Newly-fledged, marvel-hunting Spiritualists here, as in America, requiring a "sign" daily, as did the Jews, are not generally pleased with the practical "cross-bearing power of Spiritualism." The majority prefer a combative, frisky sensationalism to the historic, philosophic, and pathetic style of lectures. The two methods of public utterance are the solid and the sensational. Each fills a necessary niche: the one is enduring, the other ephemeral. Straws, touched by a torch, flash and flame; but it is the clear, glistening anthracite that warms the apartment, and gives permanent comfort.

THE CHALLENGE.

Previous to our reaching Dunedin, and after, cringing sectarists, half frightened at the tottering condition of their creeds, kept up a continual attack upon Spiritualism, in the daily journals, over fictitious signatures; cowardly business at best, and infernal when descending to personalities.

To test the mettle of the clergy, and put a veto upon so much anonymous scribbling by churchly pettifoggers, I expressed the desire publicly, to meet the clergy in a four-days' oral discussion upon these propositions: —

1. *Resolved*, That Spiritualism is true, and King James's Version supports it.
2. *Resolved*, That the system of faith denominated "evangelical theology" is true, and King James's Version supports it.

None of the clergy could summon sufficient courage to enter the arena. They lacked confidence in their doctrines, or their ability to defend them. They felt the ground trembling under their feet. Old dogmas are dying. Orthodox churches are the churches of the tombs. All that the clergy can say is, "Come and see where our Lord lay;" while Spiritualists exclaim, "*He is not there, but risen.*" Angels and spirits are with us; and the golden future is musical with promised beauties and beatitudes.

DUNEDIN PRESBYTERIANISM.

Original sin, total depravity, Trinity, vicarious atonement, and endless hell-torments, are the leading dogmas of Calvinism. Presbyterians are Calvinists. These quotations are from their published sermons: —

"The happiness of the elect in heaven will, in part, consist in witnessing the torments of the damned in hell; and among these, it may be, their own children, parents, husbands, wives, and friends on earth." *

"When the damned have drunken down whole draughts of brimstone one day, they must do the same another day. The eye shall be tormented with the sight of the Devil, the ears with the hideous yellings and outcries of the *damned* in *flames;* the nostrils shall be smothered, as it were, with *brimstone;* the tongue, the hand, the foot, and every part, shall *fry* in *flames.*" †

"The God that holds you over the pit of hell much in the same way as one holds a spider, or some loathsome insect, over the fire, abhors you, and is dreadfully provoked; his wrath towards you burns like fire; he looks upon you as worthy of nothing else than to be cast into the fire." ‡

"The rich man, tormented in hell, 'lifted up his eyes,' and saw Lazarus in Abraham's bosom; and to his entreaties for succor and intercession, Abraham had replied, 'Between us and you there is a great gulf fixed.' . . . Water boils at two hundred and twelve degrees Fahrenheit, but it requires two thousand and six hundred degrees to melt rocks. This, therefore, was the *minimum* of the heat of hell; whose *frontiers*, therefore, lie twenty-one miles below the *surface* of the *earth.* . . . In these eternal fires every limb and member of our bodies, every nerve and muscle and tendon, every part of us, in fire, over which the sense of feeling predominated, would be for ever racked and tortured, and yet never consumed." §

Mr. Logan, feeding upon these sulphurous husks, longed for fresh pasturage, and accordingly attended our lectures upon Spiritualism. Other patrons of churches did the same. The theological waters were troubled. Action must be taken. The following was an ominous mutter: —

DUNEDIN, March 19, 1873.

MR. JOHN LOGAN. *Dear Sir*, — I am directed to summon you to appear before the session at a meeting to be held in the front vestry of the church on Monday, the 10th instant, at half-past seven (7.30) in the evening, to answer the following charges made against you; viz., That you appeared on the platform of the theater at a public lecture, delivered by Mr. Peebles, on the evening of the Lord's Day, 2d February last,

---

* Emmons's Sermons, xvi.
† Rev. Ambrose's Discourse on Doomsday.
‡ Presbyterian Tract Publication, p. 9.
§ Rev. Walworth's Sermon on Rich Man and Lazarus.

when certain doctrines were propounded, as reported in the papers, contrary to the doctrines of this church.

That, being waited on by a committee appointed by the session, to remonstrate with you, and express its strong disapproval of your conduct, you avowed your right to appear where you did on Saturday or Sunday, and refused to abstain from such conduct in the future. . . . .

I am, &c.,
JOHN BOVIE,
Session Clerk, Knox Church.

This gentleman, Mr. Logan, was a most exemplary man, a faithful officer in the church, and a clerk to the superintendent of Otago, his family occupying a high social position. And yet he was arraigned, tried, convicted, and excommunicated by presbytery and synod! And why? was it crime? No. Vicious misdemeanor? No. For unchristian habits? No. For immorality of any kind? *No.* This was the only cause, — encouraging the investigation of Spiritualism; a subject that takes hold upon immortality, upon the soul's holiest affections, and upon the ministrations of angels and spirits, of which Jesus Christ stands as the great exponent of the ages. Let this disgraceful decision of the Dunedin Presbytery go down to posterity.

RACIAL INFLUENCES.

Is it not true, ethnologically speaking, that the children of settlers partake of the nature of the original inhabitants of a country? Is there any reason for it? Deer and foxes certainly leave the scent of their footsteps along their " runs." Aboriginal men impart a characteristic aroma to the soil their naked feet press, and the atmosphere they breathe. Seemingly minute causes produce mighty effects. People born in the western portions of America become tall, wiry, angular, and active, like the Indians. In South Africa, children born of European colonists are not only more rounded in features, and sluggishly heavy, but they are inclined to be indolent, like the Hottentots. This theory finds considerable confirmation, in my mind, from studying the *physique* of the youth in Australia and New Zealand. Pursuing the ethnological thought, it must be admitted that the young men, especially in the mining portions of these countries, have a want of application and concentration of effort peculiar to the natives. They are not only excitable, restless, and roaming, but there is in them a sort of wild dash, and waywardness of will. Of the "swells" occasionally seen, they may be described as appearances with perfumery around them.

Most of the aristocratic ladies in Australia and New Zealand have more of the coarseness of Rubens's beauties, than the delicacy and refinement of those noble women mentioned by the Roman senator. Neither paint nor powder can make up for inferior quality of outline. "Beauty" is a word of indefinite meaning. It cannot be expected that "Bushwomen," traversing the gum-fields of Kangaroo-land, or the fern-gullies of Moa-land, can equal, in refinement, women frequenting the drawing-rooms of more cultivated countries. Their roughness reminds one of the Swiss peasants on the banks of Lake Leman, or the stamping tread of the hardy Tyrolese mountaineers. There are few Byronic dreamers or simpering sentimentalits, gracing or disgracing — as you please — the English colonies of the Pacific. Pursuing their own line of tactics, they take their "rights," and attend to their daily duties. To be personal, I have seldom found better women, or nobler, honorable men. This is especially true as referring to leading Spiritualists.

Long shall we remember the personal kindnesses of Messrs. Beverly, Logan, Redmayne, Stout, Reid, Carrick, Allan, and others. Upon our departure the friends presented us beautifully illuminated scrolls. For these testimonials, they have our heartfelt thanks. Peace, peace be unto you, O New Zealand, "Britain of the Southern Pacific!"

"The landscape sinks beneath the billow's swell :
Farewell, ye isles! and once again, farewell!"

CHAPTER VII.

FROM NEW ZEALAND TO CHINA.

THERE is no line of steamers from New Zealand or Australia direct to China. A sailer was the only alternative. Ours proved to be the bark "Harriet Armitage," well fitted, and freighted with one hundred and seven Chinamen booked for Hong Kong. Having gathered their glittering piles in the gold-fields of the south seas, they had turned their faces toward their native land to enjoy their gains, and be buried with their fathers.

On the twenty-seventh day of March, 1873, we shipped for China, a distance of some seven thousand miles. Messrs. Beverly, Redmayne, Allan, Logan, and others, knowing our tastes, prepared for us flowers, fruits, jams, honey, and other delicacies so enjoyable during a long voyage through the tropics, and under the burning skies of the equator.

TIME: WHAT IS IT?

Our captain, often crusty, is a man of moods. The doctor and our invisible intelligences are my only soul-companions. No library, no daily journals: time drags. And what *is* time? A series of conscious impressions daguerreotyped upon the spiritual sensorium. And, considered with reference to the primal God-principle, *all* are equally aged. Each is pivoted in the centre of eternity. Causes are before effects; so are souls before bodies. To affirm that bodies make souls, is only paralleled by the position that ignorance is the source of knowledge; that matter may produce spirit, and nonentity reality. In dream and trance, memory sometimes so dispels slumber that the conscious soul recovers recollections of pre-existence, of its descent and destiny,

TOO TRUSTING, OR NOT?

If, as Lord Bacon said, "reading makes the full man, talking the ready man, and writing the exact man," travel makes the *doubting* man. The past eight months' experiences in the colonies and islands of the Pacific have cooled my ardor as to the immediate approach of any world's millenium. I can but think of these lines in the "Songs of the Sierras:"—

> "For I am older, by a score,
> Than many born long, long before,
> If sorrows be the sum of life."

The play of Hector and Achilles is being constantly reacted in my presence. Though there are tropical sunsets, and gorgeous skies, seen on this sapphire-crowned ocean, "my" and "mine" are the rallying-words. Men are exceedingly intriguing and scheming. Why, there are men mean enough, on this Polynesian part of the globe, to steal cocoanuts from a blind savage, or the sandals from the feet of Jesus! It saddens my soul.

Reviewing the fading years of half a century, I am certain of having believed too much, trusted too much, and confided too much in others. And yet is it noble or wise to write upon every human forehead, "*Cave hominem*,"— beware of man? Is there not a golden mean? Are not the extremes of distrust and suspicion a long way from a just estimate of human nature? And may not the constant exercise of harrowing fears and doubts be hindrances, rather than helps to the soul's unfoldment?

MEN IN AND OF THE WORLD.

It quite shocked me, a few hours since, to hear a man say, "Well, the only two principles insuring success in this age are, to look out for one's *self* first, and, secondly, to consider every man a rogue till proved honest." Are not such words revelators, — voiced echoes out of a grasping, cankering selfishness? Is not a man-distruster a bad man-helper? Did ever a libertine believe in the virtue of woman? Or did ever a thief like Ahab fail to keep his locks and keys bright? The sordid, selfish man, the petty village lawyer, knows no other text than this : " To them that are under the law I became as under the law, and to them that are without law, as without law;" adding, not as Paul did, " that I might gain *them*," but, " that I might gain their *fees*." In this money-worshiping, transition state of society, men seem to be drifting into a set of repulsive atoms, each seeking his own gain and welfare to the neglect of the common weal. This "getting-on system," with the "survival of the fittest" and the "Devil take the hindmost," is well expressed in the abominable lines, —

> " As I walked by myself, I said to myself,
> And the selfsame self said to me,
> *Look out for thyself: take care of thyself*,
> For nobody cares for thee."

Let us deepen the thought, and widen the vision, of existence! Essential spirit infills and spans all space. The "image of God" — the divine spark — is within; and human nature, therefore, sounded to its depths, is good. If there is not a charity that "believeth all things," there *is* a charity that "hopeth all things;" and, further, there is in the world tender sympathy, genuine friendship, manly honesty, generous benevolence, unselfish love; and there are beautiful characters too: the angels affirm it. Cunning, shrewd, and selfish men, who can not discover it, are comparable to blind men who can not see the sun. Be it mine still to seek the good of *others* first, and to believe every man *honest* till proven to the contrary. If the practice of such principles produce failure, let "*failure*" be carved on my tombstone.

TRUCKLING TRIMMERS.

He who removes a thorn, and plants a rose, who brushes away a falling tear, plucks a scale from a theologian's eye, or transforms a bit of chaos into *kosmos*, is a benefactor of his race. Turn over the picture. Do not the angels weep o'er the platitudes of truckling, two-faced, many-sided hypocrites, standing in market-places, in pulpits, and upon public rostrums, with no higher aims than gold, or a stamping, sensational applause? Oh for men of principle! Policy-men fatten to-day, to faint in the to-morrow of eternity. It was a childish weakness in Peter to deny "knowing the man." Erasmus was too much of a trimmer. Luther was a reformer that made Rome tremble. The waters of a dashing cascade are sweet and fresh. A good, screaming fanatic, with sling and stone, will always floor the greatest giants, though armed with the newest devices of controversy. I sympathize deeply with fanatics. They generally have something to say, and are brave enough to say it. They keep the mental world in motion. John the Baptist was a fanatic. Fanaticism is not coarse, brawling, blatant, overbearing egotism, but earnest enthusiasm, steady, stirring self-denial, coupled with a conviction of some living truth as a potent spiritual force. These fanatics, these resurrected souls, preach of heaven on earth, sing of Utopia to-day, and often die early, as did Keats.

"Thy leaf has perished in the green."

CANNIBALISM AND COMMUNISM.

Passing an art-gallery in Dunedin, a friend pointed me to a photograph of an old, tattooed Maori, who had assisted in baking and eating seventeen human bodies since his remembrance. Cannibal eats cannibal, and clinging, parasitic souls feast upon the magnetic life of other souls. Such is selfishness, — the devouring, corroding selfishness of the world! And yet who has not pictured and prayed for the prophets' realization of "Zion"? or who has not dreamed of that golden age where love shall be law, where the only rivalry shall be in doing the most good to others, where harmonial souls shall breathe benedictions of peace and good-will, and where a competitive, clutching self-appropriativeness shall have become a half-forgotten tradition? May we not still hope that, before the sunset of this century, co-operative leagues, and communistic fraternities, may dot the land, as cities of light set upon a thousand hills.

PLATO'S REPUBLIC.

The most eminent philosophers and sages of antiquity, when mediumistically illumined by heavenly wisdom, either conceived or wrote of a coming communism, — a state of society where every one would be respected according to his worth, where individual happiness would be sought in seeking the happiness of all, and where the isolated family would widen out into co-operative combinations, and these into spiritual families, with wisdom and love the governing powers.

Among the more prominent of this school was the Grecian Plato. This prince of philosophers, flourishing some time before the Christian era, defined a well-ordered, if not an ideally *perfect* state of social life, to be known as a "republic." Though treating largely of justice and charity, he considered absolute "communism of property" an indispensable condition. He lived unmarried, had no children, died a *celibate!*

SIR THOMAS MORE'S UTOPIA.

Looseness in the use of phraseology causes many fruitless discussions. "Socialism" and "communism" are not interchangeable terms. Communism proper should never be confounded with " Red Republicanism," the " Paris Commune," or any form of "loose socialism." They are as unlike as Christ and Belial. Socialism implies co-operation, or any form of association which does not involve the abolition of private property; while communism in the absolute is that unselfish apostolic system which " *holds all things in common.*"

Sir T. More, at one time privy councilor to Henry VIII., and afterwards lord high chancelor, published his Utopian theories in 1516, creating a deal of excitement because of his scholarship and high social position. This distinguished personage painted his conceptions of a commonwealth, or true state of society, as a " *Happy Island*," based socially upon the Utopian idea of equality of rights and the communism of property. He says,—

" Thus have I described to you, as particularly as I could, the constitution of that commonwealth, Utopia, which I do not only think to be the best in the world, but to be, indeed, the only commonwealth that truly deserves the name. In all other places it is visible, that, whereas people talk of a *commonwealth*, every man only seeks his *own* wealth; but in Utopia, where no man has any property, all men do zealously pursue the good of the public, . . . for every man has a right to every thing. There is no unequal distribution; no man is poor, nor in any necessity; and, though no man has any thing, yet they are all rich; for what can make a man so rich as to lead a serene and cheerful life, free from anxieties, neither apprehending want himself, nor vexed with the endless complaints of others?"

Respecting labor, he speaks as follows:—

" They do not wear themselves out with perpetual toil from morning till night, as if they were beasts of burden; which, as it is indeed a heavy slavery, so it is the common course of life of all tradesmen everywhere except among the Utopians; but they, dividing the day and night into twenty-four hours, appoint eight hours of these for work, and the remainder for rest and individual improvement. Each seeks another's good; and, as to the studies and employments of women, all living in Utopia learn some trade. Industry is honorable: men and women go in large numbers to hear lectures of one sort or another, according to the variety of their inclinations. Women are sometimes made priests, . . .

and a peace that the world knows not of crowns the days of the happy dwellers upon this island."

ST. SIMON AND FOURIER.

No man could be a socialist or communist, without being moved by a welfare for his fellow-men. It was to Horace Greeley's credit that he took such a deep interest in the North American phalanx. Socialism in Europe, promoted not *by* the poor, but *for* the poor, has generally been espoused by men of generous impulses and honorable enthusiasm. Fourier's great idea was to make labor attractive. He thought, that, by rightly grouping people together for work, all the natural passions would fall into harmony, and become utilized for human good. The movement gained but little footing in France. St. Simon, dying in 1825 at the age of sixty-five, had already become quite an author. He contended in his books that all social institutions ought to aim at the amelioration, physical, mental, and moral, of the poorer classes; that privileges of birth should be abolished, and the state be the ultimate owner of all lands, all public works, and all realized property. Associative effort was to be among the prominent teachings of science, the Church, and the State; while the natural inequalities of men, as primal gradations, were to be made basic pillars in this Simonian order of social life. St. Simon was eccentric, and aflame with humanitarian sentiments. He was far more imaginative than practical. Suffice it, that, while many of the ideas put forth were rational, the plan, though eagerly seized by a few trusting disciples, proved a speedy failure.

ROBERT OWEN.

This philanthropist and great social reformer, while showing at New Lanark, Scotland, that he was a clear-headed business-man, proved himself at the same time a genuine humanitarian. If a dreamer, he dreamed grand and golden dreams; and, what was more praiseworthy, sought to realize them. As the friend of man, he frequently said to English society, "If you want the poorer classes to become better men, place them in better circumstances; raise the wages of laborers, diminish their hours of hard work, increase their food, improve their dwellings, expand their range of thought; let science serve them, culture refine them; and, above *all*, help them to help themselves." Though emperors and kings had listened to Mr. Owen, and though distinguished statesmen had been his associates, he never forgot the crowning ideal principle of his life, — *communism!*

Rising from the miry plains of selfishness, to the mountain-tops of equality and "good-will to men," it may be clearly seen that communism is the voice of God through Nature. Light and air, rain and sunshine, are common. The prince and the pauper child, at the hour of birth, are equal and common. Death is common to king and subject. And the laws of the universe are common.

A disorderly, anti-law, anti-marriage "Paris *commune*" aside, Mr. Owen meant by communism that state of society in which the common fruits of industry, and the common results of science, intellect, and a sincere benevolence, should be so diffused that poverty would be unknown, and crime quite impossible. Though a theist, contending that "theology was a mental disease," though loathing pious cant and churchal superstitions, he was nevertheless a religious man in the best sense of the term. Non-immortality did not satisfy the wants of his great, manly soul. Investigating the Spiritual manifestations, in the later years of his life, he became a believer in a future existence. He died, or, rather, went up one step higher, a Spiritualist. Robert Dale Owen is the worthy son of such a sire.

Many are the pleasant hours that I've whiled away listening to Elder Frederic W. Evans's descriptions of memorable occurrences transpiring in the life of the large-hearted Robert Owen. It may not be generally known that Elder Frederic, one of the prominent Shaker elders at Mount Lebanon,

N.Y., was one of the Harmonial brotherhood, settling with Mr. Owen upon the thirty thousand acres purchased of the Rappites in New Harmony, Ind. This great and good man, a communist and Spiritualist to the last, passed to the world of spirits Nov. 17, 1858.

> "They made him a grave too cold and damp
> For a soul so warm and true."

Looking with thoughtful, cosmopolitan eye at the state of society in different countries; considering the poverty of Pekin, the beggary in Constantinople, the infanticide in Paris, the political corruption in New York, and the fifty thousand thieves, one hundred thousand prostitutes, and one hundred and sixty-five thousand paupers, of London, — is it strange that noble souls in all lands yearn for social reconstruction? Are not mediæval methods already dead? Are not present political and social systems falling to pieces? What mean these panics, strikes, internationales, trades'-unions, and co-operative fraternities? Does not Whittier, writing of recurring cycles, say, —

> "The new is old, the old is new"?

JESUS THE SYRIAN COMMUNIST.

Oh, the moral altitudes attained by those great practical communists of the past, Jesus and the apostles! The Nazarene, gifted with the intellect of man, and the love of woman, loathed that reform which talked platitudes of well-meaning, and did no work. His promise was "to him that *doeth* the will of my Father." The present "landshark" talk about the sacredness of private property constituted no part of Jesus' teaching. The apostles, imbibing his spirit, pronounced woes upon the selfishly rich. "Go to, now," says St. James, " ye rich men, weep and howl for your miseries that shall come upon you; . . . your gold and silver is cankered, and the rust of them shall be a witness against you." Few need to be reminded of the "gift of tongues," and the other rich spiritual gifts showered upon trusting hearts on the "Day of Pentecost." The power was so marvelous that "three thousand souls" were moved to repentance. And of these it is recorded, "All that believed were together, and had all things in common, and sold their possessions and goods, and parted them to all men, as every man had need." On this auspicious day the Jewish Apostolic Church, or genuine Christian church, under the inspiration and baptism of the *Christ-spirit*, began to exist. The communism was absolute. These newly baptized souls, full of fervor, were willing to surrender selfish ownership for the common good. Their principles were peace, purity, and "all things in common," constituting the millennial church, the church of the ages. "*Ekklesia*," translated "*church*," means, literally, "assembly." As understood apostolically, it implied a sympathizing assembly, convened and welded for a heavenly purpose. "Now there were in the church (*ekklesia*, assembly) that was at Antioch certain prophets" (Acts xiii. 1). These prophets, apostles, "women of Samaria," and believers generally, quickened by the Christ-principle, constituted themselves into spiritual families, brotherhoods, and communities holding "all things in common." "But," says one, "men naturally like to have their own." Granted; and so *some* men naturally like to have their neighbors'! Thieves are of this kind. But it is no more natural for thieves on a low physical plane to steal, and misers to clutch and hoard, than for the philanthropic and spiritually-minded to adopt a broad, fraternal communism. The angelic in the heavens are certainly communists. And I have yet to learn that spirits put patches of the summer-land into market, loan money, or speculate in corner-lots. When men pray, "Thy will be done on earth," why do they not go to work, and *do* it? Jesus came centuries ago. When is salvation coming?

THE CHINESE PRAYING FOR WIND.

Our crew of Chinamen is a source of fruitful study. They have books aboard, and read them, when not playing at chance-games. Their heads are all shaven, save the pig-tail tuft. Rising in the morning, they clean their tongues by scraping them, and then sip their black tea.

In the latitude of the trade-winds, we were sorely vexed with calms. It had been a dead calm under a scorching sun for five days. As Nature hates a vacuum, so do sailors a calm. Was there a remedy? On the sixth day, Sunday morning, at sunrise, there came on deck a dozen or more serious-visaged China passengers, with dishes of rice, bowls of tea, different colored paper, slim, dry incense-reeds, slender, red-topped wax-candles, and matches. "What's up?" inquired Dr. Dunn. Just informed by the "mate," our reply was, "The Chinamen are going to pray for wind." Among the number who had come forward, was the Chinese doctor, and another grave-looking, shaven-headed individual, evidently endowed with some priestly function. Putting themselves in position, they touched matches to the paper, throwing it overboard while in flames; then, lighting their reeds and candles, they went through with certain pantomimic incantations, becoming their method of prayer, ending by throwing the rice and tea into the ocean. Result, a fine breeze soon from the right quarter. "There!" exclaimed our exultant Celestials, "the wind-god has heard us!" Why not just as rational for Chinamen to thus pray for wind, as for Christians bowing over cushioned pulpits to pray in their way for "rain," for the "staying of the grasshopper devastation," or the "recovery of the Prince of Wales"? True prayer is not lip-pleading, but silent aspiration. It affects suppliants, and inclines angels to listen, but does not change the deific laws of the universe.

THE SCIENCE OF SAILING.

Navigation has reached a wonderful degree of perfection. How soon will aëronauts sail through the atmosphere in safety? Air-ships are sure to prove successes. The principle is perfectly understood in spirit-life.

Our captain brings out his "sea-Bibles" each day, — the sextant, quadrant, and chronometer, for observations; the thermometer, indicating the temperature; the hygrometer, to show the degree of moisture in the air; and the barometer, to mark its weight. *These*, locating positions, foretell approaching weather with great exactness. What a perfect system of circulation! — the aërial wind-currents, and the briny currents of the ocean. It is thrillingly interesting to watch storms at sea. By the way, the typhoons of the China Seas and the cyclones of the Indian Ocean have their fixed laws. When courses of steady winds are obstructed by islands, towering mountains, or other causes, producing whirling tempests termed typhoons, the wind takes a rotary motion, while the storm itself has a progressive motion. These spiral storms, following the law of gyration, sometimes move at the rate of fifty miles per hour. The typhoons prevail in the China Seas from June to October. Sailors dread these storms, and also the "pirate-junks" of Chinamen. The approach of a typhoon is indicated by rolling, uneven swells, the rapid sinking of the barometer, and reddish, hazy clouds deepening into purple and black. "No rules can be relied upon," says Capt. R. Mailler, "for the management of a vessel during these terrific tempests." "Give us sea-room," however, is the sailor's cry.

THE NORTH STAR AND SOUTHERN CROSS.

We are nearly under the equator.

The stars, luminous lamps of heaven, are out each evening on parade. The nights are gorgeous. I sometimes picture the constellations as star-ships sailing on the ether-ocean of infinity. The clouds, white and crimson, are the coral-reefs, and the winds the breathings of God.

Nearing the equator, on the voyage to Australia, I was thrilled with delight when catching the first glimpse of the Southern Cross glittering, in a peerless beauty all its own, just above the horizon in the south-west path of the Milky Way. Seeing churchmen thought of Calvary; while scholars, more conversant with antiquity, talked of Oriental phallism. Getting near the equatorial circle again from the south, on this route northward to China, the cross was seen to be nightly receding; and, at the same time, the Great Dipper was looming up from nearly the opposite direction. Two of its stars point to the North Star, not yet in sight. Most gladly shall I welcome the appearance again of the " pole-star," as it points in the direction of home and friends.

I never tire, in these clear, tropical regions, of gazing at those mighty orbs, sailing through the ether-ocean of space, shedding their tremulous beams upon the restless waters.

> "I sit on the deck, and watch the light fade
> Still fainter and fainter away in the west,
> And dream I can catch, through the mantling shade,
> A glimpse of the beautiful isles of the blest."

See! there is Orion, there Andromeda, there Sirius, brightest of the so-called fixed stars; and there are the Pleiades, Alcyon excelling in magnificence, and of which Homer sung nine hundred years B. C. Turn back in thought to the Chaldean shepherds who watched the waning moon from the plains of Shinar; study the astronomical observations recorded in the East three thousand years ago, — and ask yourself, O modern! how much the intervening decades have added to the literature or general knowledge of the ancients.

THE LOST DAY.

Since sailing upon the Pacific westward, the question has been sprung, "Where does day begin?" The general answer was, "Here, there, or at that place where the sunbeams first strike the earth during the twenty-four hours." The geographical and nautical answer is, "Day begins at the degree of longitude 180 east or west." Every schoolboy knows, that, traveling round the world from east to west, a day is literally lost, and for the reason that there is a difference of one hour for every fifteen degrees of longitude in each day. Accordingly, journeying westward, a certain length of time is added to each day; and, making the world's circuit, — as many are doing at present, — would amount to an entire day. This is a puzzler to strict observers of "sabbath days." When crossing the meridian 180°, before reaching Auckland, New Zealand, our captain dropped from his reckonings the day we had lost; and Sunday was this *very* lost day! How queer, going to bed Saturday night, and getting up on Monday morning! Invited by our fellow-passengers on "The Nevada," I lectured upon Spiritualism.

But what a babyish notion, — this stress laid upon Sunday, or Saturday, or any day, as especially " holy "! Considering the revolutions of our earth upon its axis, it is absolutely impossible for all its inhabitants to keep the "Christian sabbath" at the same time. If a party of Second Adventists, Seventh-Day Baptists, and Israelites should sail from San Francisco on Friday (the Mohammedan's sacred day of rest), circling the world, they would all be converts, willing or not, when reaching New York, keeping or observing the Christian's Sunday! To a Spiritualist, all lands are equally holy, and all days are equally sacred. The observance, however, of one day in the seven for rest, recreation, and spiritual improvement, is eminently profitable.

SPIRITUALISM IN THE FIJIS.

This group of Pacific islands, numbering over two hundred, sighted by Capt. Cook, and discovered by the navigator Tasman, has recently become somewhat famous with

Englishmen, because of its cotton-planting advantages. The climate is tropical. Naviti Levu is the most populous of the isles; and Thakombau, a native six feet high, and kingly in bearing, is the most influential of the chiefs. Levuka, though having few natural advantages, is the principal commercial mart. Cotton, sugar, and coffee planters do well. Cocoanuts are abundant, and some wool is exported. The ramie plant, or China-grass, samples of which I remember to have seen in New Orleans, grows finely in these islands. Cannibalism was practiced here till 1854. What Americans there are here, were originally from the Southern States. White men are in possession of three hundred and fifty thousand acres of these cotton and coffee growing lands.

In a recent copy of "The Fiji Times," I find a labored article under this heading: "*Spiritualism in Fiji*." The writer, after speaking of the natives as "low and depraved in the moral scale," assures us that, "low and brutal" as they are, they "believe in a future state of existence, in apparitions, and the efficacy of charms;" their "prophets profess to talk with the dead; and they cure by striking the diseased part with the hand." This writer, treating of Spiritualism among the European residents, says, "There is a deep interest, among the more thoughtful of our citizens, upon this important subject. . . . Those who believe, affirm that the phenomena throw new light upon the Scriptures, as well as demonstrate immortality." There is a "want among us," he further says, "of a good test medium."

The Fijis must soon fall into the hands of the English.

LONGINGS FOR THE LAND.

And still a prisoner on this ocean clipper, — a vault, a charnel-house; oh, how monotonous! Nearly two months now at sea, utterly oblivious to all the doings and rushing activities of land-life; and yet a long distance from Hong Kong! Each returning day brings fair skies or dripping clouds, surging waves or dead calms, finny tribes, sailing sea-birds, chattering Chinamen, and stale, ship-scented food. Sea-birds, weary with flight, light in the rigging. The sailors pet them. Oh for the wings of — well, any thing that would drop me down upon *terra firma!* I term this, cabalistically, " concession " route. The luckless position is not without rich lessons; the blue, unfathomed depths beneath, and the infinite expanse above, kindling the fires of the ideal, incite me to self-examination, to meditation, and hopeful conceptions of a social state to be ultimately realized by all nations, — a peaceful state rivaling in moral excellence the Eden of the poets, and the Zion of the prophets. But to contemplation.

AN ECLIPSE AT SEA.

May 14. — Forty-seven days from New Zealand, and no land seen since the seventh day out. Any thing for a change! — a calm, a storm, rainbows, lightning, sea-birds on the yard-arms, whales spouting, sharks following the ship, one of which Dr. Dunn and the sailors caught; and now an eclipse. Last night, in long. 134°, 22' east, and lat. 16°, 11' north, the moon rose at seven o'clock full and fair. Soon a dark shadow was seen creeping slowly over the eastern limb. Our China passengers were quite frightened. The coolies are ignorant and superstitious. At nine o'clock the scene was absolutely magnificent, — the shadow-draped moon in the east; at the right, in the south-west, the Southern Cross; at the left, and nearly opposite the cross, the North Star; while rushing planets poured their shimmering beams down through abysmal spaces into the mirror-polished ocean. The grandeur of the scene can never fade from my memory.

CHAPTER VIII.

A SERIES OF SÉANCES UPON THE OCEAN.

AMONG the beautiful thoughts of that celebrated German philosopher, Kant, are these : —

"The day will come when it will be proved that the human soul is already, during its life on earth, in a close and indissoluble connection with a world of spirits; *that their world influences ours, and impresses it profoundly;* and that we often remain unconscious of it as long as every thing goes right with us."

Mediums, necessarily sensitive, are as well aware of this connection referred to by Kant, as thinkers are conscious that sound, healthy bodies, and clear, well-balanced minds, are requisites for the reception of high spiritual inspirations. Mediumship, a powerful mental stimulant, is largely fashioned by the controlling spirit-intelligences. Therefore, studying a medium's tastes and tendencies, through a term of years, is comprehending the characteristics and purposes of such spirits as influence and minister to the medium, or psychological subject.

DELICACY OF CONDITIONS.

It is becoming definitely understood that Spiritualism in its phenomenal aspects is a science controlled by laws as fixed and absolute as those that govern the motions of physical bodies. All of Nature's forces are exceedingly subtle. Therefore, in every branch of research, compliance with conditions is indispensable; and these conditions must be thought out and experimented upon, until they can be formulated. Then they are ready for future service.

Physicists understand the delicacy of the conditions they impose. It is said that Dr. Kane, while wintering in the extreme polar regions, discovered that three thermometers, agreeing at medium temperatures, disagreed materially at very *low* temperatures, though suspended near together. Approaching them suddenly from the windward side affected them. Also a breath, and even the electric emanations of the body, would cause fluctuations, and accordingly incorrect readings. The common surveyor, using a delicately balanced compass, need not be informed that bodies of iron and steel affect his needle. The presence of a pocket-knife sometimes vitiates results. Sea-captains, using mercury for an artificial horizon in sextant observations, know that a footfall, a loud word, or a quick motion of the body, causes an oscillation of the quicksilver, and necessarily incorrect calculations. Alpine travelers tell us, that, on ascending Mont Blanc, strata of snow are held in such wonderful poise that a violent exclamation would precipitate a thousand tons down the declivity. Returning, a few years since, from Pompeii and Herculaneum to the Museum in Naples, I there saw vast rolls of calcined papyri covered with legible writing, though nearly two thousand years buried; and a quiet gentleman, with repressed breath and dexterous fingers, identifying, lifting, or unrolling those long-interred evidences of literary wealth and historic record. A breath might have reduced these charred leaflets to an impalpable powder. Success lay only in the most delicate manipulations. If compliance with conditions are so indispensable, then, in dealing with physical bodies, with *known* phenomena, — how much more so when investigating partially unknown phenomena, involving the laws of psychic force, and the momentous subject of spiritual manifestations! Mediums, sensitive and highly impressional, are in circles infinitely more susceptible than Kane's thermometers. A harsh word, a disagreeable odor, the sudden opening of a door, the introduction of a certain individual into the séance, — *these*, and other disturbing causes, may destroy all the conditions necessary for the influx of thoughts and ideas from that ethereal world of spirits.

TEACHINGS OF SPIRITS.

The following communications, and many others through the unconscious mediumship of Dr. E. C. Dunn, were received during four-o'clock sittings in our stateroom when the conditions of the treacherous ocean would permit. They were generally given in answer to questions; though, for want of space, the inquiries are usually omitted.

The spirit Aaron Knight, controlling one afternoon, coolly remarked, "I see that my years of labor with you have not produced a very luxuriant harvest."

"How so, Mr. Knight?"

"Well, approaching your sphere a while since, I heard you remark that you had only a slight, or, rather, no positive knowledge, of spirit-life and its peculiar conditions."

"True; but I referred to daily objective knowledge."

"Metaphysical terms are of little avail. You have heard my voice frequently for years. You have felt our magnetism upon your brain. You have inhaled the fragrance of spirit-flowers. You have had things borne to you through the atmosphere. You have been made spasmodic when alone, by our electric touch. You have seen spirit-forms improvised, and then vanish from sight. *These*, with such confirmatory witnesses as consciousness, intuition, and reason, ought to have given you *positive knowledge*."

"Well, let *that* pass. Do you hear all I say?"

"No, not necessarily; but then I could, if desirable, know all you said; and, further, could know your very thoughts, inasmuch as they produce a reflex action readable by your attending circle. And, what is still more recondite, the effects of your thoughts, aims, and plans are spiritually photographed in the sphere you will inhabit when released from mortality. You have no secrets. It would be well if all men thoroughly understood this."

"Are you now within this stateroom?"

"I am, and others also. We have so fixed the atmosphere, that, if not congenial, it is endurable."

But some clairvoyants tell us that spirits seldom return to earth, to dwell in our midst even for a moment.

"Can you conceive or imagine any thing that clairvoyants and psychological sensitives have not taught? The truth is, millions of spirits have never got away from the earth, spiritually speaking. Their past tendencies, present desires, and undone work, chain, mentally hold them near to your earth. Those more advanced, who have passed to the heavenly abodes of the divine life, can return at will; while very ancient spirits seldom visit earth, and then only for the holiest purposes."

SÉANCE II.

How long a time has man inhabited the earth?

"Time — indefinite term! Nations of antiquity reckoned time by the revolutions of constellations, by the disappearance and return of comets, by the sun and moon; and others less ancient by kingly dynasties. It is difficult to even approximate the period when man first appeared on earth. The most ancient spirits with whom I have conversed upon the subject tell me it was millions of years in the past. Three times, at least, the earth has been nearly submerged in water, destroying the people. The whole surface has been repeatedly changed and modified by fire and flood, heat and cold. Fossilized elephants and other tropical animals are often unearthed in the frigid zones, proving that those ice-belted regions were once tropical and even equatorial in temperature.

"*Present man*, with the shattered remnants of his primeval civilization, originated in the southern zones more than fifty thousand years since. There are traditions and legends extending back full forty thousand years. Types are permanent. Vegetation there was perennial. Fruits grew spontaneous. Tilling the earth was unnecessary. To reach up, pluck, and eat, was the only requisite. From Southern Asia there were radiations east, west, and north, peopling foreign lands. After a series of centuries, the Northmen, increased in numbers, and warlike, swept down into Central and Southern Asia. Wars crimsoned hills and mountains. The conquerors drove their vanquished foes into that country now known as Hindostan. They were hunters and herdsmen, leading roving lives. Peoples making a second descent from the rich table-lands of Asia into India gathered into communities, establishing petty kingly governments. These were denominated Aryans."

SÉANCE III.

... " Be punctual to the appointed time of meeting us. Remember that our avocations and appointments are quite as important as yours. . . . Prophecies are often fulfilled by the prophets. I remember of saying to you, in my earliest conversations, that the medium and yourself would be mutual helps, traveling together, even to making the circuit of the globe. . . . Preceding him to spirit-life, you will impress and entrance him with perfect ease because of your earthly associations social and spiritual." . . .

Could you go directly through our globe?

" Possibly; although, from having no desire, I have never made the attempt."

If you were to go, when leaving the medium, to my home in Hammonton, America, would you take the short cut straight through the earth?

" No: I should pass above the surface of sea and land. This would be the more feasible route. Solid matter, so called, forms little or no obstruction to the movements of spirits. But gross matter, remember, is interpermeated with etherealized spirit-substance; and then, there might be emanations from spirit-strata and various entities, preventing or at least impeding the passage. The walls of a room may be so surcharged with magnetism and spirit-auras that a spirit can not pass them. There are gradations of spirit-substance as of matter. When you are in your library-room, we fix an atmosphere about you, and so infill the walls of your study-room with our positive magnetic spheres that intruding spirits can not enter."

SÉANCE IV.

. . . " If angel lips are portals to the palace of wisdom, angelic beings are modest and unassuming. Whenever you hear a spirit talk about himself, — what mighty things he did on earth, and what he has done in the supernal spheres, — put it down that the brother is but a pupil in the primary department of immortality. High and pure spirits are disinclined to even give their names. And there is nothing more repellant to an exalted spirit, than to refer to himself. In a congress of spirits, I once heard a spirit of sage-like appearance say he had sometimes thought that loss of memory would be a great blessing, thus forgetting *self*. Selfishness is the root of all the cankering vices of the age.

. . . A mortal, reaching the better land of immortality, gravitates, or seeks the plane of his choice, something as the immigrant in a new country looks for highlands or lowlands, cultivated fields or heavy-timbered forests; but a spirit, owing to the condition of the spiritual body and other considerations, can not become a permanent resident of a higher plane than he is spiritually prepared for. . . . The desires, or, rather, the demands of the carnal nature, such as gluttony, and sexual intercourse, do not obtain in the spiritual world. These fleshly and animal appetites are laid aside at death. And yet low, undeveloped spirits, from force of habit, vividness of memory, or downward tendencies acquired on earth, may enjoy the sight of lasciviousness; or, for some scheming wicked purpose, may psychologically lead mediums into debauchery and the 'unfruitful works of darkness.' Low, selfish, disorderly spirits are at the bottom of the 'free-lust movement,' known by the more attractive term, 'social freedom.' This scum, now floating upon the peaceful stream of spirit-communion, will ere long settle away into merited oblivion."

SÉANCE V.

You speak of conditions and employments in the spirit-world: I wish you would be more minute in your descriptions.

"Hoping to enlighten, I will try. The spirit-world, real and substantial, is the counterpart of your world. The earthly life is rudimentary and preparatory. The wise of earth ripen up, while in their bodies, for higher planes of existence. As to 'discreet degrees,' referred to by the admirers of the Swedish seer, they do not exist *per se*. The phrase 'discreet degrees' should give place to 'states' and 'conditions' of being. Logically understood, the spirit-world is *all* space, because essential spirit fills all immensity. Inhabitants leaving your earth by death occupy the atmosphere immediately surrounding it, — *many* of them, at least, for ages. They can in time occupy other places and spheres. The difficulty in passing to remote spaces and regions is at the medial points of conjunction between different planets and systems. Each planet, and system of planets, have their physical, gaseous, ethereal, electrical, and spiritual atmospheres. In these atmospheres abound the centripetal and centrifugal forces; and these forces hold a similar relation to spiritual beings that the physical forces do to human beings. Therefore they encounter kindred difficulties in passing and repassing the aural atmospheres, and different strata, of the interstellar spaces, that mortals do in exploring pathless oceans, or aëronauts in their air-ship expeditions.

"In the belts that encircle your earth, the grosser lie the

nearest to it. The more refined extend outward into the ethereal regions. Coarse spiritual natures inhabit the outer surfaces of the inner belts; while the more refined and spiritual of earth pass on, by virtue of their refinement and purity, to remote and those more beautiful belts in astral spaces. The lower spheral belts, partaking of the earthliness of the earth, and embodying the grosser of the spiritual elements, abound in things similar to earth-life, such as lawns and lowlands, fields and swamps, insects and animals. The inhabitants are likened unto these conditions. Here the worldly and the sordid have taken up their abodes. Awakening to consciousness, from the event termed death, they found they had entered the new plane of existence mentally and morally as they had left mortality. This realization was at first exceedingly gratifying. Activity is natural to all spheres. In this first spheral zone, the selfish find a satisfaction in the gratification of their desires and tendencies. Those who loved sport, and low theatrical amusements, here find means for their enjoyment. Misers seek and clutch money. Greedy landholders find broad acres. Speculators traffic in spiritual estates. Gamblers engage in games of chance; and here, too, deceivers and tricksters ply their wily arts during long periods of time. It is their choice. They prefer these groveling planes, because satisfying their desires in connection with the influences they are able to exert over the mediumistic of earth. . . . It should be remembered, then, that shrewd, scheming spirits of the lower spheres cast a powerful psychological influence upon earth's inhabitants; and that miserly fathers, influencing, often intensify the selfishness of their sons by pointing out rich mineral beds, and otherwise aiding them in earthly speculations, which, eventually culminating in hoarded wealth, must be followed ultimately by remorse and deepest suffering."

SÉANCE VI.

What have you been doing in spirit-life to-day, friend Knight?

"Accompanied by a sympathizing band of philanthropists, I have been teaching the truly repentant how to make reparation for wrongs done on earth; the ignorant and superstitious, how to rise out of their darkened spiritual conditions. . . . There are no arbitrary barriers to coarser, undeveloped spirits passing to the outer and higher zones of perpetual joy. It is only a law of adaptation that attracts, *chains*, them to the plane of their own preferences. Clairvoyants who speak of a summer-land only in spirit-existence, convey an erroneous idea. There are summer-land surfaces on the outer belts, freighted and dotted with magnificent forests, fountains, fields, fruits, gardens, and flowers, of the exquisite beauty of which mortals have no conception; and there are dark winter-lands too, corresponding to the cold, selfish, and perverted natures of those dwelling on earth.

"The lower, grosser planes of spirit-existence necessitate animal life; not the individualized spirits of *your* animals, but the legitimate productions of the sphere in which they exist; something as the birds and animals of your physical earth are *its* natural productions. As you pass outward and upward through almost measureless spaces, you find less of animal life, till in the celestial spheres there are no animal forms whatever. This might suggest a question relating to the unhappiness of certain spirits if deprived of pet animals. If unhappy for this reason, it would only prove that they were yet clogged and tainted with earthly tastes and tendencies. Angelic affections do not flow out to animals. This explanation harmonizes the seemingly different statements of clairvoyants; and, more particularly, those who pass out of their bodies, traversing spirit-spheres. Some while thus disinthralled, save by the silken cord of magnetic life, beheld animals of a low type, others of a high type, and others still none whatever. Briefly stated, they described such conditions and localities as they had explored. In all the planes and states of infinity, there's a marvelous adaptation of means to ends. If discord is the child of the hells, order reigns in the heavens. . . . Grossness of condition, referring not alone to the spiritual body, holds a direct relation to the mind, *alias*, the inner spiritual nature, and the influences proceeding therefrom. Coarse, selfish organizations in spirit-life eliminate coarse auras and influences, tending to deception and vice; while those in high celestial spheres, having more refined spiritual bodies, and more intellectual and spiritual natures, generate conditions of harmony and purity. These revel in the golden sunlight of perpetual love and happiness. The life that each leads on earth prepares him for the sphere of his own moral likeness. These spheres — heavens and hells — were vaguely described by the seers of antiquity. All modern theological doctrines are but the shadows that the ancient cast."

"These spheres, or zoe-ether zones, related to, sail *with*, the earth in her revolutions through space. Some spirits take up their immediate abode just above their former homes, casting upon them a powerful psychological influence. Miserly spirits linger about their vaults; and others, disorderly, and maliciously inclined, cling to their previous localities, producing magnetic conditions suitable for haunting houses, for producing obsessions, insanity, and nervous diseases."

SÉANCE VII.

"Remember that in the lower spheres are found the counterparts of your earth, — its follies and vices, its labors and pursuits, prompted by natural desires; and spirits here, as mortals with you, are subject to disappointments and failures; while in the heavens love, — *love* devoid of all selfishness, is the motive that inspires action. Here harmonial spirits reap a rich reward in leading the aspirational into the paths of purity, in laboring unselfishly for the good of others, and in pointing those who will listen to the "tree of life," that ever buds, blossoms, and bears immortal fruitage. *This* is to them satisfaction, true rest, heaven! Considering the condition of those in the lower spheres of moral darkness, you see that it is infinitely preferable for mortals to prepare, while on earth, for the higher life, that at death, so called, they may avoid the planes of pride, passion, and perversions, that, with their seeming gains and joys, bring to their possessors, in the end, mental grief and deepest despair.

"Passing from this first spheral belt outward, we pass different gradations of indulgence, vice, and discontent, — outward and upward, till we reach etherealized planes of spirituality, where resurrected souls have no desire to engage in activities beneath themselves. These heavenly inhabitants have become baptized into a celestial life of love, with desires only for the cultivation of the spiritual; quite forgetting the things beneath, and seeking the ideal of perfection, which must ever lie in the infinite beyond.

"The intermediate spheres between the two just described abound in all the employments and associations conceivable. There is the scholarly plane, where all else is sacrificed to intellectual research; the musical, and the poetic; and the inventive, where all things are made subservient to the genius of mechanism, thus sacrificing much that is higher and more divinely beautiful. And there, too, is the domestic plane, where abound the attractions of family and family associations, with the narrow and selfish love for one's own offspring. Family love, as opposed to universal love, is a serious impediment to unfoldment of the soul. Complete happiness is attained by sacrificing present ease, by forgetfulness of self, in labor for others' good. Those thus toiling mold angels from their own forms.

"In the more exalted states of existence, it is considered that an equalizing and harmonizing of the mental and moral faculties indicate an approach to the Christ-sphere of immortality, where we have the highest form of the perfected spiritual being. In advancing from this high moral stand-point to diviner altitudes, extending above and still beyond, souls are intromitted into the sphere of virgin purity and love; the sphere of spiritual balance, properly denominated the holy; the Christ-sphere of angelic purity, where the spiritual brain-organs, subjecting and over-arching, crown all the others with a matchless glory."

CHAPTER IX.

CHINA.

"When thou haply seest
Some rare, noteworthy object in thy travels,
Wish me partaker of thy happiness." — SHAKSPEARE.

ON Chinese soil at last! Hong Kong, a rough border-island of the Flowery Land, has been under British control since 1842. It is properly an English colony, though the people are mostly Chinamen. The sweeping distance we traversed from the southern portion of New Zealand to China was nearly seven thousand miles, meeting necessarily with islands, coral shoals, calms, tempests, burning equatorial suns, — *many* bitter experiences! The passage occupied over two months.

I became heart-sick of hearing the guttural gabble, and of looking at our China passengers, with their inevitable cues dangling from their crowns, their shaven heads, almond-shaped eyes, flat noses, high cheek-bones, saffron-colored complexions, and sack-like clothing loosely, awkwardly hung around them. Being from different portions of China, they had among themselves one serious fight, using clubs, bits of wood, and marline-pins, the blood flowing freely for a few moments. While censuring, I must not forget that these are *coolies*, — the poorer classes.

Steaming up the harbor, and landing at Hong Kong, we leaped into a " sam-pan," -- a small Chinese skiff, partially roofed with bamboo. There were seven residents in this junk-shaped boat, — the youngest, a child, strapped to the mother's back, Indian fashion. Both grandmother and mother aided in rowing the "sam-pan." These families know no other homes.

Hong Kong, in the Chinese language, means "Incense Harbor;" referring to the junks and proas, that here discharge their cargoes of fragrant spices.

THE FIRST OUTLOOK.

The city is crowded. The country presents every conceivable shade of landscape, — rich valleys, alluvial plains, high table-lands, and magnificent mountains. Stretching along the coast-cities, canals, to quite an extent, take the place of roads. Instead of locks, they have what are termed "mud-slides," using cables of bamboo, and windlasses. Men, instead of machinery, turn them. Multitudes are born, eat, sleep, live, and *die* in these boats. Every thing looks un-American. The people are mainly agricultural, cultivating almost every available foot of the soil. Every object seen indicates an overburdened population. The canals swarm with boats, the shops with artisans, the roads with pedestrians, and the fields with hard-toiling workmen. It is work or starve in China.

The empire proper has eighteen provinces, each of which is divided into about ten divisions called *Fu;* and these are still further divided into *Hien*. Politically speaking, these correspond somewhat to our districts, counties, towns, only they are much larger than with us in America. The empire contains five millions of square miles. Each provincial capital averages about one million of inhabitants. The great Chinese Empire numbers nearly five hundred millions, — *one-third* of the whole human race. It has one thousand seven hundred walled cities.

CHINA'S PAST HISTORY.

Humiliating as it may be to Europe, it is true, that, for a period of nearly three thousand years, China existed in almost complete isolation from other portions of the globe. This made her arrogant and egotistic. During those mediæval times known as the "dark ages," the very existence of China was unknown to Europeans. The Chinese themselves knew nothing of the term "China." Speaking of their country, they denominated it *Chung Kwoh*, the Middle Kingdom, or *Chung-Hwo-Kwoh*, the Middle Flowery Kingdom; because they consider themselves as occupying the middle of the globe, and as being the centers of civilization and intelligence. They further believe that their empire, once proud and world-commanding, was established by the "law of Heaven" over forty thousand years ago, and is destined to stand for ever. Owing to national conceit, Western nations call them "Celestials."

The almost measureless antiquity of China is not denied. The point in dispute is as to the boundary-line between the genuinely historic and the mythological. Of this, Chinese scholars are certainly the best judges. Meadows, in his elaborate work upon the Chinese, puts the reign of Fuh-hi B. C. 3327. The reign of the *Chow* dynasties began about one thousand years before Christ, during which Lau-tsze and Confucius lived. Though Lau-tsze was the oldest, born B. C. 604, they were cotemporaries. Both of these philosophers, referring to the wise who lived before them, term them "the ancients."

Herodotus and Ptolemy, treating of this quite unknown country, referred to these isolated people living in the northeast of Asia as "inventive and prosperous." Marcellinus the Roman writer, Virgil, Pliny, Tacitus, and other historians, mention these olive-colored people under the name of Seres, dwelling in the land of Serica. They speak of them as "rich in silks" and the "luxuries of life," besides being cumbered with "much useless lore."

The "Chinese annals" give their nationality an antiquity so marvelously vast, that sectarists sneer. This is a too common argument with the ignorant and the impudent. A learned Chinaman, *Le Can*, assured me that Confucian scholars put their reliable historic records relating to the creation back full forty-four thousand years ago. The candid and scholarly John Williams, in his "Observations on Comets," admits the accuracy of the Chinese chronological computations. In his investigations he shows, from the "records in the Shu-King, one of the oldest historical documents of the empire, that the star *Cor Hydræ* culminating at sunset on the day of the vernal equinox, in the time of *Tau*, the sun must have been in Taurus, then the equinoctial point. By a simple calculation, *Tau* can be shown to have lived four thousand one hundred and seventy-six years ago, or two thousand three hundred B. C.; just after the dispersion from Babel, according to the common chronology." . . . Dr. Hales long ago pointed out the agreements of the Egyptians and Chinese with the Babylonian or Chaldean astronomical observations.

THE ANCIENT NAMES OF CHINA.

The primitive inhabitants of Southern Asia, speaking of the people now known as the Chinese, used the terms, Jin, Chin, Sin, and Sinistæ; referring, evidently, to the Tsin dynasty, which took absolute control of the northern portion of the country about 770 B.C. Being ambitious and powerful, this Tsin family wielded the scepter over the whole empire as early as 250 B.C. This period, and several hundred years previous, was famed for its literary men. The prominence of Tsin, and the dimmed records of travelers, confirm the view taken by learned commentators, that the Chinese were referred to in the forty-ninth chapter of Isaiah, — "Behold, thou shalt come from afar, . . . and those from the land of *Sinim*." Classic writers described the country under the names, Sinæ, Seres, Serica. An Alexandrine monk, writing in the sixth century, called it Tzinistæ, which much resembles the Persian appellation, Chinistan. The Turks and Russians knew it as Khitai. The Khitans were of Nanchu lineage, and related to the present imperial family. In the tenth century they completely conquered the adjoining provinces. From about this period, or before, strange as it may seem, Europe became utterly oblivious of any such great civilized nation in the East. But in the year 1245, John of Plano Carpini, a native of Umbria, and another Franciscan monk, wandering along the Mongolian desert, found their way into Eastern Asia; and, returning from their mission, told of a highly-civilized people living in the extreme East, upon the shores of the ocean. To this country, so unexpectedly found, they gave the name of Cathay. One of these monks describes them thus: —

"The Cathayans are a Pagan people, who have a written character of their own. They are learned in many things. They worship the one God, and have sacred scriptures. . . . They have no beard, and in their features are very much like the Mongols, but not so broad in the face. They have a peculiar language. Better craftsmen, in all the arts practiced by mankind, are not to be found on the face of the earth. Their country, also, is very rich in corn, in wine, gold, silver, and in silk, and in all other things that tend to human maintenance."

EARLY EFFORTS TO CHRISTIANIZE THE CHINESE.

Portuguese missionaries reaching China by doubling the Cape of Good Hope, near the close of the fifteenth century, despaired of converting self-willed Chinamen to Christianity; because, said these Romish zealots, "They have a God of their own. Burning incense, they worship their ancestors. They also hold converse with spirits, using the black art, and think that the original tendency of man's heart is to do right."

De Rubruquis, an intelligent monk, was the first to identify, in 1253, Cathay with the ancient *Seres* or *Sinim*. In 1295 Friar John went on a mission to China. Writing to Rome, he says, —

"I have bought gradually one hundred and fifty boys, the children of Pagan parents, who had never learned any religion. These I have baptized, and taught Greek and Latin after our manner; also I have written out psalters for them, with thirty hymnaries and two breviaries. . . . And I have a place in court, and a regular entrance, and seat assigned me as legate of our Lord the Pope; and the Cham honors me above all other prelates, whatever be their titles."

All early travelers to this Asian country were stars of the second magnitude, however, compared to the Venetian, Marco Polo; and yet for a long time he was counted a romancer. This injustice ultimately died away; and this gentleman's veracity, and correctness of observation, shine brilliantly to-day under the recovery of much lost and forgotten knowledge. His descriptions of cities, libraries, civilization, and the general refinement of the people, read to Western nations like fairy-tales. He was the great traveler of his age.

Hon. Anson Burlingame, head of the Chinese embassy to our and other countries, said, in his speech delivered in New York, June, 1868, —

"China is a land of scholars and of schools; a land of books, from the smallest pamphlet up to voluminous encyclopedias. It is a land where privileges are common. It is a land without caste; for they destroyed their feudal system over two thousand years ago, and they built up their grand structure of civilization on the great idea that the people are the source of power. This idea was uttered by Mencius between two and three thousand years since, and it was old when he uttered it. . . . They make scholarship a test of merit."

HONG KONG TO CANTON.

If not original, the Chinese are certainly unique. Hong Kong has a population of one hundred and twenty-five thousand, about four thousand of whom are Europeans and Americans. The buildings are roofed with tiles. The streets, narrow and dirty, swarm like beehives. All nationalities dress to suit themselves. Nearly every Chinaman has an umbrella over his head, and a fan in his hand. They are compelled by law to carry a hand-lamp, if traversing the streets after seven o'clock. Only a portion of the women — the better classes — have small feet. These, in walking, simply waddle as though lame. They think it graceful.

After visiting the Chinese temples, hospitals, foundling institutions, and riding upon men's shoulders in sedan-chairs, — a method of locomotion to us as distasteful as unnatural, — we took the steamer for Canton. The native name is *Yang-Ching*, meaning "the city of rams;" but from subsequent mythological circumstances connected with the wise men of the past, and their communion with the gods, it now signifies "the city of genii." Thronging with a population of over a million, it numbers less than two hundred foreigners. The city is situated on the Pearl River, up the country some ninety miles from Hong Kong. The river, wide, muddy, and moderate, reminding one of the lazy Missouri, flows into the bay at Hong Kong, just under the shadow of Victoria Peak, a mountainous point, towering up nearly two thousand feet above the level of the sea. The flat lands all along this river were covered with rice-fields, banana plantations, ly-chee trees laden with ripening fruit, peach-orchards full of promise, and banyan shrubbery, more ornamental in this latitude than useful. Odd-looking villages, lying a little distance away, dotted the river valley. These are more noted for compactness and bustle, than cultivation or beauty. The most important of these minor cities, commercially considered, is *Whampoa*, — virtually the port of Canton, — being just at the head of navigation for heavily-laden vessels. Seen from the steamer, agriculture and architecture seemed decidedly primitive. The buildings were generally one story high, and covered with tiles, — no glass in the windows, nor gardens in front of them. Back in the fields, men and women were plowing their half-submerged rice-lands with water-buffaloes. These huge, hairless creatures are considerably larger than our wild droves of the West. Butter made from their milk is white as lard. These buffalo-cows, with others, and goats also, are driven to the door to be milked, thus avoiding the city pests of impure milk.

CANTON WITHIN THE WALLS.

Approach to this, the wealthiest and most elegant city of China, seemed almost impossible, from the wilderness of skiffs, "sam-pans," and junks plying the muddy waters. These junks, clumsily modeled, yet richly decorated, have bamboo sails, and are better adapted to inland harbor and river purposes than European-rigged vessels. Full two hundred thousand Cantonese live, traffic, eat, sleep, and die on these river-boats. Their sam-pans, though floating property, are their real estate. The smallest children have bamboo-blocks tied to their bodies, so that, should they tumble overboard, they could be easily rescued. Landing, and presenting letters of introduction from the Rev. Dr. Eitel, and our gentlemanly and kind-hearted consul Mr. Bailey, appointed to Hong Kong from Cincinnati, and, by the way, a distant relation, his maternal grandparent being a Peebles, we were made the recipients of the Rev. Dr. Kerr's hospitalities.

The streets of Canton, irregularly laid out, are from five to seven and ten feet wide, and generally covered in with fluttering matting and bamboo-reeds, giving them a dull, shadowy appearance. Broad avenues are yet to be dreamed of by Chinamen. Wheeled carriages out of the question, sedan-chairs carried by coolies are the only means of transportation. It pained me to see that the shoulders of some of these poor burden-bearers were calloused and scarred. The principal streets, with such lofty names as "Pure Pearl," "Just Balance," "Unblemished Rectitude Street," &c., have banners and gaudily painted signs dangling in front of their bazaars, presenting an aspect at once gay and gorgeous. China has a million of temples. The emperor's temple is magnificent. Only imperial buildings have yellow tiles. Canton's guardian god sits majestically in the city temple. The Confucian temples have images of Confucius. There are few places more frequented that the Temple of the Five Genii. In this, and the Temple of Horrors, daily congregate magicians, diviners, and fortune-tellers, spiritual quacks. Sam-un-Kung is a Tauist temple; while Hok-hoi-tong is a hall to encourage literary men by granting prizes for the best compositions. There are a hundred and twenty-five temples in Canton.

The viceroy, the highest civil officer, is appointed from Pekin for the term of three years. Chinese lawyers have no fees; and yet, when gaining the suit through marked ability, they accept presents.

The native dispensary, located in the eighteenth ward, employs three Chinese physicians, besides providing support for widows, coffins for the poor, and funds for the support of free schools. Penalties for treason are rigidly severe. During nine months of the provincial rebellion, in 1855, fifty thousand rebels were beheaded on the "execution-grounds," in the southern suburbs of Canton.

China had homes for the aged, asylums for the blind, foundling hospitals, and retreats for lame and worn-out animals, long before missionary feet touched their soil. Streets leading from the city of Canton into the country should, after a few miles out, be called paths. Poorly paved, if at all, they range from three to seven feet wide. Canals are really the thoroughfares of the country.

CHINESE AS THEY WERE AND ARE.

Cycles are certainties, pertaining alike to individuals and nations. China had her noonday of prosperity many thousands of years ago. To-day, and for centuries, she has been in a galloping decline. In that indefinite period known as antiquity, she rightly considered herself the superior race, the center of civilization and learning. It must not be forgotten by Americans that the Chinese were adepts in astronomy and medicine over two thousand years since; that they employed the magnetic needle when Europe was smothering under the pall of the dark ages; that printing, originating with, was used by them for centuries before known in the West; that they discovered electro-magnetism, the curse gunpowder, and that they have excelled in silks, chinawares, and porcelains from time immemorial. It should be further borne in mind that the Chinese inoculated for the small-pox nearly three thousand years before the Christian era, putting the virus in the nostril instead of the arm; and that a medical work published prior to Christ's time, during the Hau dynasty, treats in part of the circulation of the blood.

Chinese scholars are proud of their past. They admit that "Western barbarians" excel them, at present, in science and the mechanical arts; but they claim the pre-eminence in literature, metaphysics, and the mysterious sciences, such as ontology, geomancy, physiognomy, divination, and necromancy, or methods of conversing with the dead.

During the tedious voyage from New Zealand with a crew of Chinese, I was surprised one day to see a young coolie perusing a fine old Chinese volume, thickly embellished with pictures and plates of the human form, the human brain laid open, the curves and facial features indicating character delicately marked, and the fortune-lines of the hand clearly traced. Inquiring through the interpreter when written, and by whom, I ascertained that it was one of a series of volumes by an ancient sage, treating of reading character by the brain-organs, the facial angles, and the general contour of the person, *alias* a volume upon phrenology and physiognomy.

It can not be consistently alleged that Christian missionaries would be partial to, or inclined to overrate, the virtues and intellectual altitudes of the "heathen" they were sent to save. And yet the Rev. J. L. Nevius, ten years a missionary in China, says in his work entitled "China and the Chinese," "China may well point with pride to her authentic history, reaching back through more than thirty centuries; to her extensive literature, containing many works of sterling and permanent value; to her thoroughly elaborated language, possessed of a remarkable power of expression; to her list of scholars, and her proficiency in belles-lettres.

"If these," says Dr. Nevius, "do not constitute evidences of intellectuality, it would be difficult to say where such evidences might be found." Further, China has given a literature to nearly forty millions of Japanese, and also to the inhabitants of Corea and Manchuria. If the Japanese surpass the Chinese in skill and impulsive action, the Chinese excel them in intellectuality and morality. The better classes of Japan use the Chinese classics, much as we do, in our collegiate courses, those of Greece and Rome.

For centuries the Chinese have been traversing the downward segment of their national cycle. Compared with Americans, they seem dull and phlegmatic. Though their bodies are healthy, they lack energy, muscular force, and mental activity. To see a Chinaman in a hurry would be a marvel. They walk their narrow streets moderately, seldom getting excited about any thing. Gymnasiums, and vigorous athletic exercises, are quite unknown among them. They have the appearance of being timid; and yet they are persistent in accomplishing what they undertake. Most of these Chinese labor sixteen hours a day. Their industry is proverbial.

THE CHINESE COOLIE TRADE.

Portugal and Spain, Christian (?) nations, commenced the coolie traffic some forty years since. Labor in China was exceedingly cheap. Europeans were quick to discover this. Accordingly, a Spaniard from Peru, while at Macao, China, seeking a cargo, conceived the idea of securing under some pretense a crew of coolies to work in Peru. This he did under the false promise of conveying them to the island of Java, to return in a few years well paid for their services. But they were landed in Callao, South America, never again to see their native land. They complained bitterly of the deception; but no number of Chinese complaints could avail in court against a Spaniard's oath. The reported industry of these Chinamen reaching the ears of Cuban planters, ships were sent out bringing cargoes of them to labor on their plantations. But when those who first went out with the Spanish captain on the "Don Pedro," and those who afterwards sailed for Cuba, and other islands in the west, did not return to their homes and families; and when rumors returned that these Chinese labor-emigrants had been enslaved, or slain for insubordination, — no more would ship for that land afar over the waters. Then commenced that wretched system of buying, kidnapping, and chaining, which disgraced our common civilization. Ship-owners and traders, sailing into Chinese ports, organized bands of thieves to steal and kidnap coolies by thousands. And these poor Chinamen seized in rice-fields, and boys in schoolrooms, were gagged, and dragged by force down into the ill-aired holds of vessels, to be borne away, the veriest slaves, to toil in the guano-islands, or other portions of the distant West. And all this under the flag of European civilization! Guilty of theft, and red-handed, wholesale murder, these Christian nations have the cool impudence to send missionaries to heathen Chinamen!

Kidnapping is still quite a business in the South-Sea Islands. A little prior to our reaching Australia, the brig "Carl," owned by Dr. J. P. Murray, sailed under the British flag from Melbourne towards Fiji, for the ostensible purpose of pearl-fishing; but really engaged in man-stealing in the southern sea. This was afterwards proved in the court of justice that arraigned Mr. Mount. Dr. Murray, now professedly pious and prayerful, was guilty of deception, of stealing natives, and downright murder. Some of the wounded Bougainville natives were *thrown overboard alive.* Is it strange that missionaries find it so difficult to convert South-Sea Islanders to Christianity?

AMERICA LONG KNOWN TO THE CHINESE.

A scholarly writer in the "North China Herald" assures us that a "superstition" in the provinces of Honan and Hupee declares that America and China are to be sympathetically, if not politically and religiously united. This is based upon the testimony of Chinese visionists, who in their ecstatic state see "an immense bridge over to the United States." These clairvoyant visionists further teach that the "Chinese and American nations were once brothers." The mandarins say they have books under the name of *Fusang*, written long ago, that describe America and Occidental scenery with a marvelous precision. Chinamen returning from California tell their relatives that they found races in America — the Indians — who could talk some of their own language. These notions, with the admiration that China had for Mr. Burlingame, give them a strong predilection in favor of America, as well as constitute the *animus* of their emigration to our shores.

The French ethnologist Baillet, in a letter to the Royal Society of Antiquarians, makes certain statements, current among the Ting-chause scholars of China, of which the following is the substance: —

"There was a great family, called Tooloong, which lived in the land of Fukien, and became rich. When a mighty conqueror came from the north, and the emperor Hia was not able to protect his children, Tooloong and his family joined themselves with some barbarians, — Assyrians from the west, — and abandoned their homes in grief. They gave themselves into the hands of the gods. The great dragon watched them by night, and Su-wang-Shangty by day. For more than a thousand days, Tooloong wandered northward and eastward until the icicles grew on the skirts of his garments; still the gods said, 'Go on,' and Tooloong's heart was stout. Then they found a great bridge as white as the summer's cloud, and very strong. The barbarians hesitated, but Tooloong was brave. They all crossed over. On the other side was a new China, where no one lived. The trees were beautiful, and the beasts kind. Tooloong wondered. But they kept on till a land of flowers was seen in the distance. The barbarians said, 'Let us not go farther: it will burn us.' But Tooloong said, 'I stop not till the dragon-god stops.' So they entered the land of flowers. Here they were blessed. The gods were very kind. Toolong wanted dwellings and a pagoda. He built great cities in the flower country, and died. After a long period, some of his children tried to come back to China. But the great bridge was gone. So they all, with the exception of *Nung-yang*, were sent back to the flower-country by the gods. He, becoming immortal by death, flew over on a cloud, and told his kindred of the great things Tooloong had done."

The Americans, whom the Chinese hear of as living in a great country to the north and east, are believed, says M. Baillet, to be the descendants of Tooloong and the Assyrians that accompanied him.

And Mr. Conwell, a Chinese traveler and author, suggests that the "north and east" would very naturally refer to the direction of Behring's Straits; that the "bridge" might have been ice, or an isthmus covered with snow, since submerged; that the "flower-country" might be the land of Mexico; that the "pagoda, and blocks of stone dwellings," might relate to those wonderful structures, the ruins of which, at Palenque and Uxmal, astonish the antiquarian, as well as favorably compare with those of Upper Egypt and Syria. And what, if possible, is more singular, the images of gods manufactured at Bohea, near Ting-Chan, are the exact counterparts of the idol-gods found in Southern California and Mexico. A striking corroboration of the above hypothesis is furnished by Gen. Crook, in his discovery of ruins, while operating against the Apaches. And Capt. Manning, of the regular army, writes from New Mexico under date of July 14, 1874, touching the discovery of ancient ruins, and the remnants of a fading race, "This once walled, but now city of ruins, was originally discovered by a Spanish Jesuit, who published his wanderings in America in 1529. His account is quite correct. The demolished structures symbolize, in conception, those of the East. The language of the remnant of this people, so says an eminent archæologist visiting them last season, resembles the Chinese. And so do some of their minor customs; such as their reverence for the aged, and devotion to ancestors. The women are of the Celestial type, — almond eyes, protuberant bodies, and small feet. They dress much in Chinese fashion. Their religious ceremonials are formal, the priests wearing embroidered robes." Were not the Aztecs the racial link, connecting this fading race in New Mexico with the migrating Chinese and Assyrians of the Tooloong era?

COOLIES IN CALIFORNIA. — WHY THEY COME.

The first Chinamen reaching California in 1849 were not gold-hunters, but fugitives from Peruvian masters, hiding in ships *en route* from New York to San Francisco, *via* Callao. Others came, ere long, from China in vessels, as Chinese cooks and servants. Hearing of the gold-diggings, these, with those from Peru, hurried to the mining districts. Purses soon filled with the precious metal, they returned to their native country, *prodigies*, painting the Pacific coast a very paradise. The news flew. The lower classes, listening, became uneasy. While mandarins and Confucian scholars live in palatial buildings, rich in furniture, sofas, mirrors, and china dishes, the coolies live in houses built of bamboo-matting and mortar, with sliding doors for windows, and no chimneys, neither pulu upon which they may pillow their heads. Often a room in which a family lives is not over ten feet square. Their fires are kindled and kept burning outside their miserable dwellings. In this one room may be found scraps of red paper, as "tablets" to some guardian spirit, a kitchen-god, a few stools, and burning joss-sticks. Their daily dish is rice, pork, paste rolls, and pulse. Rice the great staple, they cook by steaming.

Most of the coolies come from the Canton district. Shipowners and brokers in Hong Kong send circulars up into the provinces, describing our country in glowing terms. And further, they urge coolies to arrange their affairs, social and financial, preparatory to embarking for America, where they may soon acquire fortunes, becoming rich as the mandarins.

CONSULTING KITCHEN-GODS AND SPIRITS.

The Chinese have been educated to believe that communications can be received from the inhabitants of the heavens and the hells, after complying with certain conditions. Dreams and visions are carefully noted. Trance is common in the higher circles of Chinese society. Considering it sacred, and connecting it with their ancestors in heaven, they conceal it, so far as is possible, from the searching, critical eyes of foreigners. A recent writer* says, "I wonder if the Spiritualists of this day in New England ever think that their belief is nothing new in theory or practice, or that it has been known and believed in China for more than twenty-three hundred years. Not only do the Chinese Spiritualists believe in the same agencies and same results which distinguish Spiritualists here, but they also practice all the methods adopted in this for spiritual manifestions, and a hundred others that do not seem to be known here. . . . During the stay of spirits in that nether world, the lower spheres, they can rap on furniture, pull the garments of the living, make noises in the air, play on musical instruments, show their footprints in the sand, and, taking possession of human beings, talk through them. In a thousand other ways they manifest their presence."

It is very common for coolies to consult trance-mediums of the cash-taking kind, touching the wish and will of their ancestors, before deciding to sail for the western world.

* R. H. Conwell's Travels in China, pp. 163, 164.

They also sacrifice to Buddha, and petition the attendance of guardian spirits during their absence from China.

THEIR HOME IDEALS.

These are, good health; happy families, several living contentedly under the same roof; gardens and fish-ponds, well stocked; tea fragrant, and grain abundant; the young Confucius of the family preparing for competitive examinations; ancestral tablets recording honored names; gilded halls for the wise elders; violin-shaped instruments with but a single string; plenty of holiday festivals, cheerful with music, showy silks, savory dishes, flowers, and hanging creepers; city walls and store-fronts glittering with quotations from favorite authors; the conscious presence of spirits; sacred books, treating of old sages, reverentially read: *all* these, with residences near Confucian, Buddhist, and Tauist temples, and Chinamen are supremely happy.

CHINESE CEMETERIES.

When approaching Whampoa, we had a fair view of a Chinese cemetery, the tombs in which were constructed much in the shape of the Greek Omega. They are built upon hillsides, and terraced up to the very summit. It is believed that tutelary gods protect the graves, and guide the spirits of the dead back at certain seasons to their earthly homes and ancestral altars. The captain of our steamer, pointing to this hill of bones and ashes, said, "I have seen on festal days, crowding about those graves, fifty thousand people." At the time of burial, they usually make an offering to hungry and unhappy spirits, believed to haunt burial-places. They clothe their dead bodies in several suits of garments for burial. Fashion demands this, which, if neglected by the children, is construed as a want of filial piety. White is the proper emblem of sorrow and mourning, — red of joy and gladness. Widows are required to wear mourning three years; while the widower is expected to mourn but one year, wearing a white girdle. The Chinese have not the least fear of death, and really mourn deeper and wail louder at their weddings than at their funerals. The aged procure their coffins before they die, decorating them with red silk and other costly material, keeping them in their houses as ornamental furniture. One monument in this cemetery, towering above the others, was erected to the memory of a "*literary man.*" Money, oftener than merit, puts up marble shafts in both Europe and America. They are useless expenditures in any country.

PAGODAS.

Who built them? and what the original purpose? There are several within the walls of Canton, and we passed a number crowning the hill-tops on the way up the Pearl River. These graceful towers, three, five, and nine storied, are built of brick or stone. The walls are some ten feet thick. Perfect in proportion, they range from seventy to two hundred feet high. Difficult of ascension, terraced with vines, and capped with verdure and tropical foliage, they constitute an interesting feature in Chinese landscapes. The one near Whampoa is only about six hundred years old. Many of them, however, are very ancient, antedating the introduction of Buddhism into China from India, 250 B.C. They originally symbolized aspiration, pointing toward the great Ruler of heaven. At the base, and up their rising stairways, the wise sat for meditation and self-examination. They were also used as outlooks in time of danger, and places of rest for traveling pilgrims. After the visits of Buddhist missionaries, they became the repositories of the ashes of Buddha and various relics. In some localities they are now falling into ruin. Everywhere and in every thing there seems a lack of enterprise.

CHAPTER X.

CHINESE RELIGIONS AND INSTITUTIONS.

"Chariots are vanity, horses are vanity : the thing remains, the man departs : a shadow leaves no trace behind.

"Station is vanity, office is vanity : when the tide of fortune is spent, the retributions of justice begin, and remorse is without bounds.

"It may be said of every thing in earth which affords happiness, after a little time the gratification passes away, and it is, after all, but emptiness.

"The conclusion of all is, that only one thing is real, and that is the effect of virtuous deeds leaving their lasting impress on our individual being."

CHINESE ESSAY.

CONFUCIAN TEMPLES.

CONFUCIANISM is not a religion, but rather a system of morals. The best scholars of China to-day are the Confucians and Tauists. Mandarins never attend services in missionary chapels : it is beneath their dignity to listen to the theological religions of Christian nations. They have no objections to Jesus, the Syrian sage, and would willingly give him a niche in the temples of their gods; but hypocritical, money-making, warlike Christians they despise. Visiting a Confucian temple, I saw a costly image of Confucius. There were also tablets of his most distinguished disciples and commentators. Students occupied rooms in rear of the building. The Chinese no more worship Confucius and hero-gods, than do Americans George Washington and Thomas Jefferson, or High-Churchmen the Bible and prayer-book.

Walking up the Highway of Science with Dr. J. G. Kerr, Secretary of the Medical Hospital in Canton, to the "Examination Hall," I was filled with wonder and admiration. The hall itself is about fourteen hundred feet in length, by six hundred and fifty wide. The principal entrance is at the "Gate of Equity; " and the first inscription over the avenue reads, "The opening heavens circulate literature." The examination of candidates for the Kü-yan, or second literary degree, is here held triennially. Connected with this mammoth hall are nine thousand five hundred and thirty-seven stalls, or rooms for the students on trial; and in rear of these rooms are other apartments for three thousand officials, — copyists, servants, policemen. Each candidate for a degree is put into a stall, with only pen, ink, and paper, and required to write an essay from a given text in the classics. One day and one night only are allowed for the production of the thesis. There is great competition; and there are thousands of strangers in the city during these examinations. The third degree is conferred only in Pekin.

WALLS IN THE EMPIRE.

In the declining years of the Mongolians and Chinese, man losing faith in man, reigning dynasties conceived the notion of constructing gigantic walls. For over three thousand years, therefore, the Chinese have been a wall-making people. Those around the old city of Canton, as they now stand, were built in 1380 A.D. The one inclosing the new city dates to A.D. 1568. The oldest of the walls surrounding Canton is thirty feet thick at the base, about thirty feet high, nearly seven miles in length, and four horses may travel upon the top abreast. A recent writer says, "It would bankrupt New York or Paris to build the walls of the city of Pekin. The great wall of China, the wall of the world, is forty feet high. The lower thirty feet are of granite or hewn limestone; and two modern carriages may pass each other on the summit. It has parapets the whole length, and frequent garrisons along the way, whether running through valleys, or over the crests of mountains. It would probably cost more now to build the great wall of China, through its extent of a thousand miles, than to build the sixty thousand miles of railroads in the United States. This wall, so effectual several thousand years since, is now an incumbrance." Borne in a sedan-chair, one hardly observes the gate that lets pilgrims inside the Canton walls. A sort of a cross-wall surrounds *Shameen*, the chief residence of foreign merchants. This wall was finished in 1862.

SIGHTS AND SCENES IN THE CITY.

Traversing the streets, the olfactories suffering more or less from contiguous meat-markets, gaping crowds would gather around us, commenting upon our dress, beard, and unshaven head, calling us in Chinese " red-haired men from the west." It is reported that they shout, " *Fan Kwai*," — foreign devils. Though this were true once, it is not now. They treated us with perfect respect.

Do they eat " rats, cats, and puppies," as the old geography-makers said ? If so, it is an exceptional custom practiced by paupers. I saw no cats, but did see a few dressed rats and dogs in the Canton markets. Missionaries are very apt to see in " heathen lands " what they search for. Dr. Kerr informed us that a very small portion of the poorer classes probably ate them, superstitiously connecting them with certain medical effects, upon the principle that "every part strengthens a part." The unjust reports that Chinamen ate " cats and puppies," put in circulation by sensationalists, were keenly parried by the fact that Europeans ate swine, shrimps, snails, frogs, horses, and water-serpents!

The Chinese are naturally, a rice-eating people ; and in the palmy ages of their old seers they subsisted entirely upon vegetables, grains, and fruit. Meat-eating, and the shaving of their heads, are modern customs; the one indicating the moral degeneracy, and the other subserviency to a foreign power. When the Tartars poured down from the north, conquering China, the shaving of the head, except the cue, was imposed as a token of subserviency to the new dynasty. It is now fashionable; the more foppish adding black silken braids to make their long, glossy cues more conspicuous. The women dress their heads doubtless, as they imagine, very artistically, combing the hair straight back, and then putting into it a profusion of tinselings, ornaments, and artificial flowers. The Chinese are naturally polite, the mandarins haughty. The women paint and powder much as they do in America.

The two sexes occupy different rooms at night, and also eat separately: chop-sticks take the place of knives and forks. During the first day after reaching Canton, we visited Buddhist temples, a Confucian temple, the Examination Hall, Chinese printing-offices, china-ware manufactories, embroidery shops, native schools, the execution grounds, and the "Temple of Horrors," where are exhibited the pictorial presentations of the ten punishments in hell. This temple is much frequented by tricksters and fortune-tellers. The schools half deafened us, because the scholars all study aloud at the same time; some literally screaming from behind their desks. It was Babel. Education in these primary schools consists principally of committing to memory things worth knowing in books; when well committed, the teacher explains the meaning, and the application to life.

In surgery Chinese physicians are far behind European; and for the reason they do not believe in amputations, or the use of the knife. They diagnose disease by touching the pulse. Some heal by "the laying-on of hands." They permit their patients the use of little or no water. Much sleep is among their recommendations. They use a vast number of remedies, some ridiculously superstitious and useless. They rely much upon diet, charms, faith, and the driving away of evil spirits. Some consider these Chinese physicians exceedingly skilful: others do not. They certainly are not scientific in the Western sense of the term. But *is* medicine a science? Dr. Kerr is doing an excellent work, and Chinamen have in him great faith. Speaking, at the breakfast-table, of the general intelligence of the Chinese, Mrs. Kerr remarked, " These Chinese are in some respects in advance of the Europeans and Americans: *all* they need is the Christian religion."

It must be remembered that Chinese literature is not only extensive, but absolutely *massive*. The Chinese dictionary is a work of one hundred and fifty volumes; the history of China is a work of three hundred and sixty volumes; while there are one hundred and twenty volumes in just the catalogue of the imperial library at Pekin. The learned Low Heang (120 B.C.) wrote several voluminous works entitled, " The Biography of Famous Women." Two thousand, and even one thousand years previous to Heang's time, women in the Mongolian countries were considered the equals of men. The greatest of these nations was governed by a queen, with a liberal sprinkling of mothers and sisters for officials. No traveler reading ancient literature, and studying old ruins, can deny the " fall of man."

When the French and English, under their national banners, entered the gates of Pekin in 1860, be it said to the lasting shame of that portion of the " allied army," the French, that they burned a very valuable library connected with the summer-palace of the emperor; and these Frenchmen are called Christians, and the Chinese "heathen."

Not only is Chinese literature, extensive as it is, free from all obscene allusions, but most of it is eminently suggestive and moral.

In one of their odes treating of " discontent," the voyage of life is graphically traced from babyish longings to youth, then to ambitious schemes, thence to family associations, to the possession of horses and vehicles, to thousands of fertile acres, to official stations, and finally to positions of rank. Still discontented, he aspires to be prime minister, then emperor; and then he calls for exemption from death, that he may rule empires and worlds. The following are the closing lines of this ethical ode: —

> "His numerous and foolish longings know no stopping-place;
> At last a coffin for ever hides him,
> And he passes away, still hugging his discontent."

In a Tauist work, treating of "rewards and punishments," I find these Emersonian teachings: —

"When you see the way of truth, enter it. What is not truth, avoid it. Watch not in false ways. Do not deceive yourself in committing sins in secret. Add to the store of your virtues, and thus increase your merits. Let your compassion extend to every object. Be loyal, dutiful, and affectionate. Reform yourself that you may reform others. Pity the desolate, compassionate the distressed. Honor the aged, be kind to the young. Have a care not to harm either plants or reptiles. Sympathize with the unfortunate, rejoice over the virtuous. Help those who are in difficulty, save those who are in distress. Regard the good fortune and losses of others as if they were your own. Do not make a display either of the faults of others, or of your own excellences. Suppress what is evil, give currency to what is good. Receive abuse without resentment; receive favors, as it were, with trembling. Dispense favors without asking a return. Give to others without after-regrets. There is no peace in wrong-doing. The effect follows the producing cause. If a person has been guilty of wicked deeds, and afterwards repents, receive him into confidence. Forget the past. To appropriate to one's self ill-gotten gains, is like allaying hunger with poisoned food. If desires to do right arise in the mind, divinities are present to aid and bless.

"As regards the virtuous man, all men honor him, Heaven protects him, happiness and fortune follow him, evil influences flee far from him, divine spirits attend him; whatever he does will prove successful, and he may aspire to being one of the genii of heaven."

LAU-TSZE, THE GREAT MAN

Circumstances, rather than merit, often weave the crown of fame. Confucius is often termed the sage of China. That he was treasury-keeper to the court of Chow, a gatherer of ancient wisdom, and a wise man, is admitted; but he was not original, as was the old philosopher Lau-tsze, who founded the Tauist sect or school of thinkers. Tauism is literally rationalism. Confucius spoke as a schoolmaster, quoting the ancients of almost forgotten dynasties as authority.

Lau-tsze, born 604 B.C., was a radical intuitionist. His great work is called the *Tau-teh-king*. " Tau" means "truth," or "doctrinal discourse." Most of his works are abstruse and metaphysical. He is represented to have descended from heaven, being begotten in a miraculous manner, as were Pythagoras and Jesus. At birth his hair was already white with age; and accordingly he was named what the word "Lau-tsze" implies, — "the immortal boy." In a poem aflame with rhapsody, addressed to this personage, these lines occur: —

> " Great and most excellent Tau,
> Thou who gavest instruction to Confucius in the east,
> And called into existence Buddha in the west,
> Director of kings, and parent of all sages,
> Originator of all religions, *mystery* of mysteries!"

Confucius, once visiting him, did not seem to comprehend his transcendental philosophy. Confucius's brain was a cistern; Lau-tsze's a living fountain. Seeing the hollowness of education, government, and society, he condemned it; and then, soaring into the regions of thought, he uttered truths, and lived them.

It is a matter of no little surprise to us that friend Stebbins, in his excellent compilation, "The Bible of the Ages," made no selections from the venerable philosopher Lau-tsze, who, though preceding Confucius by a few years, lived in the sixth century before Christ.

The following are gems gathered at random from the volume entitled "Tau-Teh-King:" —

" The wise produce without holding possession; act without presuming on the result; complete their work without assuming any position for themselves; and, since they assume no position, they never lose any."

"The sage has no special love. He puts himself last, and yet is first; he abandons himself, and yet is preserved. Is not this through his having no selfishness? When a work of merit is done, and reputation is coming, he gets out of the way. To produce, and have not; to act, and expect not, — this is sublime virtue."

"A man on tiptoe can not stand still; astride his neighbor he can not walk on. He who is self-displaying does not shine; he who is self-praising has no real merit. The unwise are full of ambitious desires, lusting for the stalled ox, or for sexual enjoyment. The wise conquer themselves, putting away all impurity, all excess, and all gayety."

"The sage, timid and reserved, blends in sympathy with all, for he thinks of them as his children. There is no greater misery than discontent; no greater sin than giving rein to lust. Tau, the spirit, is permanent, yet undefinable. Spirits, but from some source of spirituality, would be in danger of annihilation."

"The sage wears a coarse garment, and hides his jewels in his bosom. He grasps nothing, and therefore loses nothing. He does not copy others. He recompenses injury with kindness, and excels in forgetting himself."

After a long conference between Lau-tsze and Confucius, the latter said to his disciples, "I can tell how the runner may be snared, the swimmer may be hooked, and the flyer shot by the arrow. But there is the dragon: I can not tell how he mounts on the wing through the clouds, and rises to heaven. To-day I have seen Lau-tsze, and can only compare him to the dragon."

RECKONING TIME.

The Chinese profess to trace mystical relations between time and certain inherent principles in nature. Their year is composed of lunar months, beginning with the new-moon, that is, the first new-moon after the sun enters Aquarius, which occurs between the 21st of January and the 19th of February. This period marks the returning spring; and the first day of the new year is a universal holiday throughout China. In reckoning their time, especially if it relates to astrology, they use a sexagenary cycle, which confers meaning names upon years, months, days, and hours. The Swedenborgian theory of correspondences takes a wide range with Chinese scholars. They insist that the earth in organization bears a striking resemblance to man; having veins, arteries, magnetic currents, and a principle of life infilling the whole, which principle is denominated *fung-shwuy*.

CHINA-WOMEN AND SERVITUDE.

Women, though occupying a better position than in Mohammedan lands, are held in a sort of semi-subjection. Their often-expressed desire to be born men in the next state of existence, reveals their real condition. They paint excessively, are exceedingly polite, and desire to become the mothers of *male* children. In some localities women are virtually sold. And yet Chinese slavery is much less irksome than was African slavery in our country, inasmuch as it is not hereditary. When a coolie sells a daughter, he is supposed to convey no right to the services of unborn grandchildren.

Nearly all Europeans and Americans doing business in the cities and treaty-ports buy each a China girl as a "mistress," for from three to five hundred dollars, keeping the same till returning to their native country. This, though considered no disgrace by Europeans residing in China, gives the Chinese a bad opinion of "Christian" morals in the West. Leaving for their homes, some of these men make provision for their "kept women" and their children; others sell them; and others still turn them off upon the world's cold charities.

Matches being made by the parents, the luxury of courting or love-making is not among the fine arts of the Flowery Land. Betrothals take place at a very early age, and frequently the parties do not see each other till the day of marriage. Living together, they generally learn to love as husband and wife.

Though polygamy is permitted, the rule is one wife. Taking other wives, though not highly reputable, is excused when the first proves unfruitful. Ancestral worship is fundamental in the Chinese mind. Nothing can exceed their desire to have male children to visit their graves, and venerate their memories. Parents in some of the provinces have the power of life and death over their children. Sons obey their parents the same after as before their marriage. Children by the second, third, and other wives are legal, and have the same rights as those by the first. Sons, marrying, bring their wives to the father's house, having different rooms, yet forming one household. The first wife, queen of the shanty, may not only control, but legally beat the others to produce obedience. They are, in fact, her servants; and she claims the ownership and jurisdiction of their children.

The Rev. Dr. Eitel, of Hong Kong, gave us an interesting account of a childless couple connected with his church, who came to him begging consent for the husband to take a second wife, hoping to raise a son. The wife was far the most anxious of the two for this consummation. During the importuning, she quoted the Bible case of Abraham and Sarah. The doctor, after advising them to " submit to the will of God," suggested, that if they must have a son, looking forward to ancestral worship, they adopt some outcast child. The Christian woman replied, " This was not Abraham's course; and then, such children usually inherit bad temperaments and dispositions."

BUDDHIST TEMPLES AND BUDDHISM.

Buddha means the " enlightened; " as *Christos*, Christ, signifies " anointed."

Having read for years of Buddhism, and the older religions of Asia, my first visit to a Buddhist monastery, to witness the temple-services of the priests, was thrillingly interesting.

Stepping inside, and glancing at the brazen trinity of the " three precious ones," the lighted tapers and burning incense, the priests with shaven heads, long robes, — gray, black, and yellow, according to the order, — bowing their heads to the floor, then rising and re-bowing before their images, I mentally said, "Who are the thieves?" Nothing can be more patent than that Roman ritualism is stolen from the Buddhists, or that Buddhism is borrowed bodily from Roman Catholicism. Unfortunately for churchmen, *Sakamuni*, Gautama Buddha, the original founder of Buddhism, died in the year 543 B.C. One of the earlier Catholic missionaries, traveling in China, wrote and published that " there was no country where the Devil had so successfully counterfeited the true worship of the Holy Church as in China. . . . These Buddhist priests burn incense, hear confessions, and wear long, loose gowns resembling some of the fathers. They live in temples like so many monasteries, and they chant in the same manner as with us." The vesper services in this temple were conducted in the following order: the striking of a tom-tom, ringing of bells, intoning, chanting, genuflections, and marching up and down the gorgeously decorated edifice. The chanting was not only in good time, but really melodious. We had a social chat with these priests, Dr. Kerr interpreting. The abbot who led the service had a solemn visage, and finger-nails nearly an inch in length. Taking our departure, these priests joined each his *own* hands, and shook them vigorously, instead of shaking *ours*, — the sweaty, clammy, unclean hands of flesh-eating Christians (?)

The appearance of a superior Buddhist temple, exhibiting considerable architectural skill, is to an externalist truly grand and imposing. Symmetrical and well-proportioned, these structures, with their adjoining gardens, are admirably calculated to excite wonder and reverence. The tiled roofs are decorated with fretted-work, — unique figures of dragons, elephants, war-horses, and historical dramas; while their interiors are ornamented with Oriental carving-work, weird scrolls, mysterious inscriptions, and gilt sentences written over the heads of their divinities. Lotus-flowers adorn most of their altars. This lotus symbol is not understood, however, by the more ignorant of Buddhist worshipers.

Passing the gates of this temple, we saw on our right a number of pigs wallowing in the choicest food. An inscription upon the block by the inclosure read, "*Save life.*" All life, in the eyes of Buddhists, is sacred; one of their chief commandments being, "Thou shalt not take life." And yet travelers, — and among them a member of the "American Expedition to China and Japan," — after describing what they term their "sacred pigs," speak of the worship paid to this "sanctified pork." Saying nothing of the injustice done, such a blunder is almost unpardonable. The Rev. Dr. Eitel, a German clergyman of Hong Kong, in publishing a correction of this mistake, adds, "There is not a trace of porcine-worship to be found among Buddhists." Modern Buddhism, bearing but little relation to its ancient grandeur, exists to-day in a degenerate and dying state. This missionary, the Rev. Dr. Eitel, treating of ancient Buddhism in his "Three Lectures" delivered and published in Hong Kong, says (p. 37): —

"Ancient Buddhism knows of no sin-atoning power. It holds out to the troubled, guilty conscience no chance of obtaining forgiveness. A Buddha is *not* a Saviour. The only thing he can do for others is to show them the way of doing good and overcoming evil; to point out the path to Nirvana by his example; and to encourage others, by means of teaching and exhortation and warning, to follow his footsteps. *Do good*, and you will be saved: this is the long and short of the Buddhist religion."

CHINAMEN AS EMIGRANTS.

The written language of this vast empire, understood by the learned of Japan, Loo-Choo, Corea, Manchuria, and Cochin China, reaches and may influence more of the human race than any other in the world. The genius of emigration has touched, and become a kind of inspiration with, a portion of these Asiatics. Ubiquitous by nature, these Chinese are literally the Yankees of the East. For a long period, ingress and egress from the empire were governmental regulations. The policy was eventually changed; and Chinamen are now everywhere in the great cities of the world, and the out-of-the-way islands of the Pacific,—servants, agriculturists, artisans, as circumstances demand.

Every Chinese dealer, buyer and seller, has his own scales. They can not trust to others. They live cheap, except on feast-days, and keep their valuables in tall stone buildings called by Englishmen "pawn-shops." In detecting counterfeit coin they are experts, depending entirely upon the touch and the ring of the metal. While canals are very common, they have no railways, no telegraphic lines, and no insurance-offices. In money-making they excel, and yet they are not considered miserly.

It matters little what rival Irish laborers in America may say or do: Chinamen are certain to flock westward in increasing crowds. Competition in many directions, and ultimately an intermingling of blood, an intermixture of the whitish-pink and the olive-brown races,—beneficial perhaps to both the Orient and the Occident,—will be the result. There are no white men on earth. The three original colors were pink, copper, and black, corresponding to the equator, the tropics, and temperate zones. Already in Australia and the Pacific islands marriages are not uncommon between Englishwomen and wealthy Chinamen. This cross of blood and temperament produces handsome as well as very intelligent children. Is it a foreshadowing of their future social life in America?

MURDER OF THE INNOCENTS.

China is packed with people. Though ambitious crowds emigrate, the old hive continues crammed. The Tai-Ping war took off infatuated multitudes; and provincial rebellions result not uncommonly in a wholesale slaughter. Still the country swarms with over-population. This *fact* is father to much of the *infanticide*. Is there as rational an excuse for the prevailing fœticide of America? That infanticide prevails to an alarming extent in some of the poorer localities, is beyond dispute, while in others it is entirely unknown. Major Studer, our American consul in Singapore, though residing in this city of sixty thousand Chinamen, says there has not been a case of infanticide before the courts, nor has he as yet even heard of a child's being killed by the parents. Chinese women, like other mothers, naturally love their children; but the family is large, the means of support limited, and the country deluged with population. What must be done? A check of some kind seems indispensable. They do not destroy the first female infant. If the second born is a female, there comes a struggle between natural affection, and the nuisance of two female children, with no son to bear the name down to posterity, securing ancestral worship. If the third is a daughter, it seldom escapes strangling by the "woman-nurse" in attendance. There is a tacit understanding between the parties to this effect. The method of destruction is either by strangulation or drowning. True, there is a well-defined law against this crime; and the public sentiment of China is decidedly opposed to it. And what is equally encouraging, Chinese scholars write essays and books against the criminal practice. A popular tract has this heading: "*An Appeal to dissuade from drowning Female Children.*" In it I find these teachings: —

"Virtue and vice are connected with their appropriate results as the shadow follows the substance. The offending man meets with innumerable troubles and distresses. Suffering follows him. . . . Suppress what is evil. . . . Avoid displaying the faults of others, doing things in an underhanded manner, and *destroying children before or after birth.*"

Not mentioning other authorities, the Rev. Dr. Eitel, the German missionary in Hong Kong, assured us that the morals of Chinamen would compare very favorably with those of Europeans; that they were far more chaste, and upright every way, in the country than in the cities; and that, just so far as traders and foreigners generally exercised any influence, it was in tendency demoralizing.

CHINESE BENEVOLENT INSTITUTIONS.

Churchmen are inclined to boast of their charitable asylums and reform-institutions as proofs of the divinity of the Christian religion. When premises are assumed, erroneous conclusions quite naturally follow. Many hundreds certainly, and in all probability thousands, of years before the Christian era, China not only had her universities of learning, but her public charities and extensive benevolent institutions. And though China is, intellectually and nationally, in her dotage now, *these* have not ceased to exist. Not only every city, but every country village of any importance, has its free school and orphan-asylum. Some wealthy citizen leading the enterprise, others unite in raising funds, which are often increased from the government treasury.

"In Hang Chow," says the Rev. Mr. Nevius, "I found, in connection with a variety of benevolent institutions, an asylum for old men, which had about five hundred members." It was my good fortune to visit *one* foundling-hospital. By diligent inquiry I learned that there were many societies for the relief of aged widows, and also for cripples, but none for the insane, and for the plausible reason that it is among the marvels of the country to see or hear of an insane person.

Charity-schools are very common in China. And then there are numerous medical hospitals, where medicines are administered to the poor gratuitously. "There is a society in Suchow," writes the missionary Nevius, "for the suppression of the publication and sale of immoral books." The mandarins contributed largely to this establishment.

I was repeatedly informed by hunters and travelers that in the interior of the country the people were exceedingly hospitable, bringing tea and rice to the roadside to refresh the wanderer. Turanians and Semitics are proverbially less acquisitive than Europeans. Just in proportion, however, as they mingle with the Western civilizations, do they become scheming and mercenary. Heaven knows, I despise a grasping selfishness! There are individuals of Aryan descent mean and selfish enough to suck the moon from the sky, bag the golden sun, and, pocketing the stars, wait for a rise in fire-mist matter, hoping for a "bargain" at world-building. Selfishness breeds devils.

THE MOSAIC OF GIVE AND TAKE.

Scholastic Chinamen, given to egotism, think meaner of us than we possibly *can* of them. Their map of the world puts China in the center, and America in a small compass adrift on the border-lands of the globe. If we laugh at their shaven heads, thick-soled shoes, and sack trousers, they sneeringly smile at our shaven faces, short-cropped hair, stovepipe hats, gloved hands in summer-time, and tight-fitting pants half revealing the physiology of the organism. If we refer to the small feet of women among the Chinese nobility, they sarcastically point to the wasp-like waists, swinging hoops, uncouth chignons, and tawdry manners, of the Americans. And then, to walk arm in arm, man and woman, is considered by them exceedingly vulgar. Lecture the more intellectual upon the subject of morals, and they will push in your faces an old copy of "The New-York Herald," with flaring sub-headings of *poisonings, forgeries, murders, drunkenness, thieving, suicide, divorces, adulteries, fœticide,* &c. Chinamen and Japanese, attending school or traveling through America, see in the city hotels printed cards of warning, "*Valuables must be handed to the clerk to be locked in the safe.*" Sallying out into the streets, they see club-bearing policemen arresting disorderly and drunken men, and occasionally a drunken woman. These vices, and others so common in Christendom, they report to their countrymen when returning, and then make merry over the mock civilization of Christian nations.

CHINESE RELIGIONS AND INSTITUTIONS. 167

Cool and reflective, these Asiatic Chinese are not slow to forget that foreign Christian nations introduced opium into their empire, against the positive remonstrances of the Pekin government. Out of this opium-trade business, grew the first war, with a great slaughter of life. They also well understand that their countrymen have not been allowed to testify in the civil and criminal courts of America only under certain crippled conditions; and, further, they take a sort of demoniac satisfaction in reminding Western nations of their frequent drunkenness, their houses of prostitution, their city dancing-dens, their immodest pictures, and their publication of obscene books. On the whole, they think Christian nations not only terribly immoral, but downright hypocrites. Sir John Davis sensibly wrote thus to Englishmen: "The most commendable portion of the Chinese system is the general diffusion of elementary *moral education*, among even the lower classes. It is in the preference of moral to physical instruction that we might perhaps wisely take a leaf out of the Chinese books, and do something to reform this most immoral age of ours."

THE MANDARINS AND SCHOOLS.

Those known as mandarins are all scholars, having passed the prescribed examinations. The important offices of the empire are filled with mandarins only. They may be recognized by their costly costume, insignia, and train of attendants. Money does not, as in America, buy "honorable" positions. Bating the "blue-button" mandarins,—those who, because of some signal service rendered, have received a sort of "side honor,"—the others, the genuine, are often popular in consideration of their scholarly attainments and munificent gifts.

The court language is mandarin, being spoken by *all* officials; and although it is important as a written language, being spoken all over Northern China, it is nevertheless but one of the dialects of the empire. As the Latin may be read and spoken by the very learned of universities in all lands, so the written language of China may be understood by the *literati* of North-eastern Asia.

As a nation, China is eminently literary. The first degree conferred upon the scholar is A. B., "beautiful ability;" the second is A. M., literally "the advanced man;" while it is only after the most critical and rigid examination that students receive the crowning degree at the capital. Free "day-schools" for boys are common. Girls are neglected; and yet in some of the provinces there are free schools established for them also, with female teachers. Nearly *all* of even the poorer classes in this vast empire are versed, to some degree, in writing, reading, arithmetic, and memorized passages from the classics. Japan has a compulsory system of education, equally binding upon the children of both sexes. Religion in these lands is free. Church and State are unmeaning terms. Their great teachers, such as Lau-tsze, Confucius, and others, were moralists rather than religionists. Thousands of the truly learned are pantheists. Many of their statements are as transcendental as Emerson's. They believe in *Tau*, — the absolute Unity, manifest as duality in the positive and negative forces of the universe. There are three great systems of morals and religions in the country. Tauism savors of metaphysical pantheism; Confucianism, of practical morals; and Buddhism, of the old religions of India; and yet these different religionists frequently worship in the same temples. And why not? Is not this a lesson of tolerance to Christendom? "Heathen" may well say of Christians, "Behold how they love one another!"

GOD-WORSHIP AND GENERAL WARD.

Nearly every office and shop in China-lands has its image, its sacred altar, and its smoking incense as a "sweet-smelling savor." Rightly understood, however, worship in all Mongolian countries implies little more than respect paid to superiors. Besides ancestors, whose spirit-presences Chinamen evoke, scholars worship the god of letters, soldiers the god of war, business-men the god of wealth, medical men some Chinese Esculapius; and even gamblers have their altars and their gods, to whom they appeal, pleading for good luck. Lau-tsze and Confucius rank highest among their gods. The latter, generally called by them *the Ancient Teacher, the Perfect Sage*, is the most popular.

All these gods whom they worship were once men, famous and renowned as heroes or sages.

It will be remembered by Americans that John Ward, originally a Massachusetts sailor, and afterwards in league with Walker in the wild undertaking of conquering Nicaragua for slavery-extension purposes, took an active part in the Tai-ping rebellion, fighting on the side of the emperor, rather than in behalf of a more democratic government. The rebellion, calling to its aid many scholars, soon assumed gigantic proportions. These Tai-pings in their manifestoes indorsed the Christian religion, abolished slavery, encouraged education, and cautioned their soldiers against the inhuman treatment of prisoners. Victories attended them.

But the American Ward, introducing into the emperor's army European discipline and tactics, proved a martial success, and a help to the imperial cause. Still the rebellion continued. At first the French and English sympathized with the Tai-pings. But when the emperor, trembling for his throne, invited foreign assistance, the French and English, in consideration of *more* open ports, and other mammon-like interests in the line of finances, turned at once against the "Christianity" and promised constitutional government of the Tai-pings, in favor of the imperial reign, and co-operated with the Chinese army in the capture of cities held by the Tai-pings. Blood flowed in torrents.

During this Titanic struggle, in which a religio-spiritualism formed a powerful element, Ward married a mandarin's daughter, became immensely rich, and was promoted to the army position of general. But, while reconnoitering a rebel fort, a bullet from the enemy proved fatal. He closed his mortal career a few days thereafter, at Ningpo, and was interred in accordance with the Chinese method of burial. His body was afterwards removed to Soong-Kong, and then to the inclosure near the Confucian temple, where there is a tablet erected to his honor. Now deified, he is one of the warrior-gods of China. His widow and three children reside in a palatial mansion at Shanghai.

THE SPIRITUAL ASPECT OF THE TAI-PING REBELLION.

This daring movement originated with Hung-sew-tswen, born near Canton, — a clairvoyant seer from infancy. When a lad, he was considered strange and eccentric. Returning to his home, when a young man, from an unsuccessful examination, he was attacked with a severe sickness, during which he declared that he had been favored with supernatural manifestations and revelations. He felt that he had been washed from the impurities of his nature, and introduced into the presence of an august being, who exhorted him to live a virtuous life, and exterminate demons. This immortalized man, whom he often saw, of middle age and dignified mien, further instructed him how to act. Hung called this visitant his "elder brother." About this time he read the New Testament, and declared immediately thereafter that this imposing personage seen in his visions was Jesus Christ, the Sent-of-God. A scholarly friend of his, named *Le*, uniting with him, they commenced preaching, baptizing, and making converts. During their inflammatory discourses, persons would fall into the trance, speak in strange tongues, and utter alleged revelations and prophecies. They organized to protect themselves, and punish their persecutors. This led to war; the insurrection became formidable, and for a time successful. Multitudes perished by sword and famine; vacated fields, and burned cities yet in ruins, remain to tell the tale of war. The primal purpose was to overthrow the reigning dynasty, destroy the idols of the land, and establish a *quasi*-Christianity.

Hung-sew-tswen, now putting himself at the head of the new kingdom, was styled *Tai-ping tien Kwóh,* assuming the title, " Son of Heaven." He professed to have direct communications from God, and spoke very familiarly of Jesus as his brother. He continually read the Old Testament, and observed religious worship in his camp. He assured missionaries that his revelations were as authoritative as those of the Bible, and he could prove it by his divine gifts. He further declared that spirits aided him in his victories. Loyal Chinamen called him and his soldiers, "long-haired rebels." Successes corrupting his leading officers, with envies and jealousies in different camps, the emperor's armies aided by Gen. Ward and the English and French in combination, the Tai-ping rebellion was put down. The struggle continued fourteen years. The leading spirit of the rebellious host committed suicide. Those caught by the government officials were tortured and massacred. Hung-sew-tswen's teachings continued to produce their legitimate results. His admirers believed him to have been God-inspired for a purpose, as was Moses of Hebrew memory.

TEA.

Of tea-cultivation and the tea-districts I have little to say, and because everybody *does* who is privileged to put a foot down in China. Suffice it that the Chinese themselves, though great tea-drinkers, do not drink " *green tea.*" Further, in preparing tea, they steam it a long time, in preference to boiling. There is a delicious, invigorating freshness to the black tea, when thus prepared by the people who cultivate the shrub. They use their best teas themselves.

Stepping into their silk-shops, or bazaars of any kind, they present you a cup of tea instead of a glass of intoxicating liquor. Why should *Americans* drink tea? Why should so much pure crystal water be spoiled by putting into it tea, coffee, and other Eastern drugs? Why import either Asiatic herbs or religions?

The spirit of progress, which flashes up in the political heavens of the West, has touched with intellectual intensity our antipodal kinsmen of the East. Commerce, whitening all seas, is a great civilizer. "Transition" is the great word now in China and Japan. Europeans and Americans are not only flocking into the original "five treaty-ports" of China, but are exploring the interior and the highlands of the Mongolian regions. The central government, in admitting foreign ministers to Pekin, in sending an embassy to Western nations, in establishing a university and schools with European teachers, and treating other nations with the respect becoming the fraternity of humanity, is taking a step in the right direction. Bating a national egotism, and a certain innate reserve, I place a much higher estimate upon the China races, intellectual and moral, since seeing the better classes in their native country.

Mandarins and officials, so far as I heard, spoke in great commendation of the Hon. Mr. Burlingame, our former minister to the capital. It may not be generally known, even in America, that he was a Spiritualist. This writer in the Atlantic Monthly, however, must have known it: —

"As an example of the influence of a single man, attained over an alien race, whose civilization is widely different, whose religious belief is totally opposite, whose language he could not read nor write nor speak, Mr. Burlingame's career in China will always be regarded as an extraordinary event, not to be accounted for except by conceding to him a peculiar power of influencing those with whom he came in contact; a power growing out of a mysterious gift, partly intellectual, partly spiritual, largely physical; a power whose laws are unknown, whose origin can not be traced, and whose limits can not be assigned; a power which we designate as magnetism."

When the Chinese government received official notice of Minister Burlingame's death, they gave him a tablet in a Pekin temple, thus preparing the way to deification.

CHINESE SPIRITUALISM.

Conversing with consuls, missionaries, the older European residents, and the Chinese themselves, concerning their belief about gods and demons, genii and spirits, with the relations they sustain to mortals, the inquiry arises, " Where shall I commence? what say first?" The Rev. Dr. MacGowan, returning to America, said when lecturing in Chicago, " China is a nation of Spiritists." Dr. Damon reiterated the same thing to me in Honolulu. Mr. Bailey, our Hong-Kong consul, assured me that the lower classes were very superstitious; that the *Fung-shwuy* was a mystery; and that they all believed in the presence of their ancestors, and their power to hold converse with them." A delineation of the *Fung-shwuy* in its relations to the selection of burial-places, to the ethereal principles of the universe, to atmospheres, emanations, and vitalizing forces under the influence of gods and spirits, would require a chapter rather than a passing paragraph. When foreigners look at the sky, or at a beautiful landscape in the distance, Chinese bystanders are sure to remark, " They are looking at the *Fung-shwuy*."

These Orientals have their trance mediums, mostly females; their writing mediums, using a pointed, pen-like stick, and a table sprinkled with white sand; their personating mediums, giving excellent tests; their seers, who professedly reveal the future; and their clairvoyants, who, to express their meaning in English, " see in the dark." It may be affirmed without dispute, that Spiritism in some form is an almost *universal belief* throughout the Chinese Empire. It seems natural to the Turanian and Semitic races. In making this broad affirmation, I use the term "Spiritism" in preference to "Spiritualism," because the latter implies not only phenomena, but philosophy, religion, and the practice of true living.

WHAT MISSIONARIES SAY OF THEIR SPIRIT-INTERCOURSE.

Hear their testimonies: —

"There is no driving out of these Chinese," says Father Gonzalo, "the cursed belief that the spirits of their ancestors are about them, availing themselves of every opportunity to give advice and counsel."

"They burn incense, beat a drum to call the attention of the desired spirit," writes Padra De Mac, "and then, by idolatrous methods, one of which is a spasmodic ecstasy, they get responses from the dead. . . . They have great fear of the evil spirits that inhabit forests."

In two volumes entitled "Social Life Among the Chinese," by the Rev. J. Doolittle, the author informs us that "they have invented several ways by which they find out the pleasure of gods and spirits. One of the most common of their utensils is the *Ka-pue*, a piece of bamboo-root, bean-shaped, and divided in the center, to indicate the positive and the negative. The incense lighted, the *Ka-pue* properly manipulated before the symbol-god, the pieces are tossed from the medium's hand, indicating the will of the spirit by the way they fall." . . . The following manifestation is more mental: "The professional takes in the hand a stick of lighted incense to expel all defiling influences; prayers of some kind are repeated, the fingers are interlaced, and the medium's eyes are shut, giving unmistakable evidence of being possessed by some supernatural and spiritual power. The body sways back and forward; the incense falls, and the person begins to step about, assuming the walk and peculiar attitude of the spirit. This is considered infallible proof that the divinity has entered the body of the medium. Sometimes the god, using the mouth of the medium, gives the supplicant a sound scolding for invoking his aid to obtain unlawful or unworthy ends." . . . Another "method of obtaining communications, is for the applicant to make his wishes known to a person belonging to a society or company established for facilitating such consultations. Upon these occasions, the means employed consist in the use of a willow or bamboo pen, placed upon the top of the hand over a table of white sand; the arm becomes tremulous, and the writing is produced. And still another course is " for the female medium to sit by a table on which are two lighted candles, and three sticks of burning incense. After inquiring the names of the deceased, and the time of their death, she bows her head upon the table with the face concealed. Soon lifting it, the eyes closed, the countenance changed, the silence profound, she is supposed to be possessed by the spirit of the dead individual, and begins to address the applicant; in other words, the dead has come into her body, using her organs of speech to communicate with the living. . . . Sometimes these mediums profess to be possessed by some specified god of great healing powers, and in this condition they prescribe for the sick. It is believed that the god or spirit invoked actually casts himself into the medium, and dictates the medicine."

Rev. Mr. Nevius in his work, " China and the Chinese," declares that " volumes might be written upon the gods, genii, and familiar spirits supposed to be continually in communication with the people. The Chinese have a large number of books upon this subject, among the most noted of which is the *Liau-chai-che-i*, a large work of sixteen volumes. . . . Tu Sien signifies a spirit in the body. And there are a class of familiar spirits supposed to dwell in the bodies of certain Chinese who became the mediums of communication with the unseen world. Individuals said to be possessed by these spirits are visited by multitudes, particularly those who have recently lost relatives by death, and wish to converse with them. . . . Remarkable disclosures and revelations are believed to be made by the involuntary movements of a bamboo pencil, and through those that claim to see in the dark. Persons considering themselves endowed with superior intelligence are firm believers in those and other modes of consulting spirits."

It was my privilege to see these coolie Chinamen conversing with their spirit-ancestors in several temples. Their methods are numerous; and the prevalence of this belief among them astonished me. It is almost universal; and yet with the lower classes it has degenerated into absurd superstitions.

SPIRITISM VERY OLD IN CHINA.

"The practice of divination," writes Sir John Barrows, "with many strange methods of summoning the dead to instruct the living, and reveal the future, is of very ancient origin, as is proven by Chinese manuscripts antedating the revelations of Scripture." The "eight diagrams, with directions for devination, were invented," says the Rev. Mr. Nevius, "by the Emperor *Fuhi*, probably nearly 3000 B.C. About 1100 B.C., Wen-Wang, the Literary Prince, and his son *Chow-Kung*, further developed the system with explanations." The Yih-King is a sort of an encyclopedia of spiritual marvels and manifestations. It was denominated in the time of Confucius, the "Book of Changes."

Gliddon writes, "The emperor of China, Yao, who reigned about 2337 years B.C., in order to suppress false prophecies, miracles, magic, and revelation, commanded his two ministers of astronomy and religion to cut asunder all communications between sky and earth, so that, as the chronicle expresses it, there should be no more of what is called 'this lifting up and coming down.'"

This missionary, Mr. Nevius, further assures us that in the "latter part of the *Chan* dynasty, which continued to 249 B.C., *Kwei-Kuh-Sien-sz* applied the Yih-King to the use of soothsaying, and is regarded as among the fathers of *augurs*. During the past and the preceding dynasty, many books have been written upon this subject, among the most noted of which is the *Poh-shi-ching-tsung*, a work of six volumes on the "Source of True Divination." Here are a few passages from the preface:—

"The secret of augury consists in communication with the gods. The interpretations of the transformations are deep and mysterious. The theory of the science is most intricate, the practice of it most important. The sacred classic says, 'That which is true gives indications of the future.' To know the condition of the dead, and hold with them intelligent intercourse as did the ancients, produces a most salutary influence upon the parties. . . . But when from intoxication or feasting or licentious pleasures they proceed to invoke the gods, what infatuation to suppose that their prayers will move them! Often when no response is given, or the interpretation is not verified, they lay the blame at the door of the augur, forgetting that their failure is due to their *want of sincerity*. . . . It is the great fault of augurs, too, that, from a desire of gain, they use the art of divination as a trap to insnare the people," &c.

Naturally undemonstrative and secretive, the higher classes of Chinamen seek to conceal their full knowledge of spirit intercourse from foreigners, and from the inferior castes of their own countrymen, thinking them not sufficiently intelligent to rightly use it. The lower orders, superstitious and money-grasping, often prostitute their mediumistic gifts to gain and fortune-telling. These clairvoyant fortune-tellers, surpassing wandering gypsies in "hitting" the *past*, infest the temples, streets, and roadsides, promising to find lost property, discover precious metals, and reveal the hidden future. What good thing is not abused? Liberty lives, though license prowls abroad in night-time. Christianity wore the laurels it wove, though Peter denied and Judas betrayed. Spirit-communion is a reality, and, wisely used, a mighty redemptive power, as well as a positive demonstration of a future existence.

CHAPTER XI.

COCHIN CHINA TO SINGAPORE.

ABOARD "The Irrawaddy," a magnificent French steamer, the sea calm and smooth as polished glass, richly did I enjoy sailing down the coast of Cochin China to Anam.

THE ANAMITES.

Though the French are wretched colonists, they have made a success at Saigon, Anam, the southern part of Cochin China. The city, numbering several thousand inhabitants, has a naval station, situated up the lazy, serpentine Saigon River, some fifty miles from the beautiful bay.

Three miles from this French town, where we land facing bristling soldiery, is the old China city itself, claiming from seventy to a hundred thousand. During the latter part of the Bourbon reign, the Jesuit missionaries from France had difficulty with the Anamites in this portion of Cochin China, whose king resides up the River Hue, in an old walled city. France, in accordance with her usual policy, sided with the priests, sending a fleet to adjust a settlement, and enforce claims. The king was frightened. Demands were made, and a fine slice of territory was ceded to the French. This occurred during the reign of Louis XVI., noblest of all the Bourbon rulers.

The Anamites — evidently a mixture, afar in the past, of Malays and Chinese — are small in stature, and slovenly in appearance; chewing the betel-nut, which colors their lips, teeth, and tongue a dark, inky brown. Women are more excessive chewers than the men. Though a subject of discussion by our party, it was decided by a slight majority that their sooty, shriveled mouths excelled American tobacco-chewers in *nastiness!*

These women wear rings on their toes, ankles, wrists, and generally one in the nose. They sling the nude young child astride the hip, throwing the right arm around it as a protection. Their complexion is a dark olive or copper. Those residing back on the highlands, and in the interior, away from French civilization, are not only physically larger, but superior mentally and morally. History writes these people down as the original Chinese, — bold, brave, and unconquered by the Tartars. They do not shave their heads, nor wear clothing save around their loins.

The principal language spoken is French. The religion of the natives is Buddhism. The Bonzes are very courteous, allowing foreigners to inspect every thing in their temples. We are only a few degrees north of the equator. Intensely hot, it is the paradise of gnats and mosquitoes. Fahrenheit, 88°.

The country along the Saigon River is low, flat, and densely wooded, but excellent for rice-culture, the gum of lacquer, cinnamon, and many of the precious woods. The highlands afar back from the valley abound in fertile fields. Tropical fruits burden the markets. The city and valley-lands are unhealthy. This is acknowledged by the French. On account of the heat, business is suspended in the French part of the city from ten o'clock, A.M., till five o'clock, P.M.

FRENCH FASHION AND AMERICAN INDEPENDENCE.

The French are reported polite and fashionable. But what *is* fashion? How far is it authoritative? and who are subjects of the fickle goddess? Sitting at the table aboard our steamer, the doctor was reminded, and I was twice asked, by the *garçon*, to appear in certain suits at certain times of the day, — say the *dinner*-hour. It was a piece of impertinence; and I sent the following note to the navy officer in command of the steamer: —

COMMANDER OF "IRRAWADDY." *Sir*, — It is, in my estimation, nobler to be a man, maintaining true moral independence, than to be a Frenchman or an American. And as the two legitimate purposes of clothing are to cover the body, and conduce to its comfort, will you have the kindness to instruct your servants to give neither myself nor Dr. Dunn further annoyance by suggesting what hour we dress for the day, or in what style of dress we appear at the dining-table? *Fashion*, a heartless tyrant, has no international standard; and, if it had, I should be guided entirely by my own judgment and good sense of propriety.
Respectfully thine,
J. M. PEEBLES.

The reply, prompt and gentlemanly, saved us from future annoyances.

Society is like a light honeycomb, pretty but empty, while fashion is the ruling queen of the nations. Rich and poor, the stupid and the intelligent alike, fawn around, and bow down to this stupid goddess. And if any individual, man or woman, conscious of that moral independence inherent in the God-given nature, refuses allegiance to, or rises to overthrow the mandates of fashion, a pig-headed public raises the cry at once, "He's eccentric!" "He does it to attract attention!" And the poor soul, finding no moral support, is often whipped back into the popular rut, to sheepishly trot along with the dawdling multitude. Down in my soul's depths I detest, despise, loathe, and *hate* this cringing worship paid at the shrine of fashion; and be it known to France in particular, that I will shave or not, wear my hair long or short, and dress precisely as I please, regardless of fashionable dandies or dictatorial aristocrats.

SINGAPORE.

Sing of Cuba, queen of the Antilles, if you choose; but I'll sing of Singapore and its spice-fields, Singapore and its waters of crystal and sapphire. The word, literally *Singapura*, from the Sanscrit *singa*, touching, and *pura*, city, implies the ancient "touching-city" for commercial traders between China and the countries west.

Nestling down to within some seventy miles of the equator, one would naturally suppose, though embosomed in flowers and fadeless foliage, that Americans from the Northern States could not here live; and yet they do. The green isles, the sea-breezes, the atmospheric moisture from frequent showers, and the financial facilities for traffic, reveal the reasons. There are really no seasons here,—not even the wet and dry of California and Asia Minor; but a perpetual summer, with a remarkable equableness of temperature, crowns the year. All this said, nevertheless the climate must be enervating.

Just before reaching this unique city of 150,000, made up of Chinamen, indigenous Malays, Klings from Madras, Burmese, Siamese, Parsees, and Arabs, we crossed the 180th meridian west from New York, being almost directly opposite our home in New Jersey; and yet, though feet to feet with Americans, we did not fall off into space, nor did the law of gravitation cease to fasten us to Mother Earth. Making into the harbor, the steamer passed between a large island covered with palms, and a cluster of little islets putting up from coral depths. At the feet of these were glittering white sands, while their summits were crowned with rich green jungles. Others had been cleared, their sides serried something like potato-fields, and planted with pineapples.

The isle of Singapore is owned by the English. While there are about five hundred Europeans in the city, mostly English, it seems a general landing-place for the waifs of the world. Races are terribly mixed. This is a famous mart for articles in the line of jewelry. Their coral, sea-shells, precious stones, tiger's claws, birds-of-paradise, Chinese porcelain, and carvings in sandal-wood, are exceedingly beautiful. Many Oriental imitations are sold by these natives for the genuine. A daily-expected steamer, bound for India in the opium-trade, detained us over two weeks. It is at present (June 22) the season of the monsoons in this latitude. Junks are turning Chinaward.

NATURAL BEAUTY OF THE MALAY LANDS.

In these Eastern archipelagoes and oceans, Nature puts human language to shame when it attempts a description of her luxuriance. These islands of loveliness, comparable to emeralds set in seas of silver, or gems glittering upon the bosom of hushed waters, their foliage reaching to the shimmering edge, where they dip their broad leaves in heaving waves; *these Indies*, the lotus-lands of the East, considering the geological formations, the Oriental vegetation, the magnificent forests musical with birds of gaudiest plumage, the cocoanut-palm (prince of palms for beauty and nobility), the groves of spices, where one eternal summer gilds hill and dale, — *all* these conspire to constitute the loveliest region on earth. It is not strange that certain theologians, ethnologically inclined, have fixed the Adamic paradise in the Malay Archipelago. Other islands have their charms, but these bear away the palm. Perfumed isles and aromatic airs are no fabled dreams. Stepping out under brilliant skies in evening-time, when the land-breezes were coming in, I have been literally fanned by soft winds laden with most delicious perfumes.

The Malays proper inhabit the Malay Peninsula and nearly all the coast-regions of Borneo, Sumatra, Celebes, and many of the smaller islands.

In this equatorial latitude, and the islands adjoining it, Alfred R. Russell, the distinguished naturalist and Spiritualist, spent eight years collecting an immense cabinet of plants, insects, birds, and animals.

Though the Malay Peninsula abounds in bananas, mangoes, mangosteens, gambier, nutmeg, pepper, bamboo-groves, gutta-percha forests, pine-apple plantations, tapioca uplands, clove and cinnamon gardens, it has its drawbacks in the way of insects, lizards, serpents, and tigers. Mosquitoes sing the same bloodthirsty tunes as in America. Though tarrying at the best hotel, our rooms are infested with flies, beetles, fleas, and slimy lizards, crawling upon the walls and ceiling. The other morning, upon rising, and lifting my pillow, out darted from under it a wretchedly ugly lizard! All poesy lands have their prose sides.

THE MALAYS AN OLD RACE.

Though the Malay Peninsula was unknown to Europeans till the arrival of the Portuguese in India about the year 1500, the race for weary ages possessed the knowledge of letters, worked metals, domesticated and utilized animals, cultivated fields, and led the commerce of the Pacific Ocean. Their language crops out not only in very remote islands to the east, but according to the English ethnologist, Mr. Brace, "in Madagascar, three thousand miles distant, the Malay words form one-seventh of the vocabulary of the islanders."

Dr. Prichard regarded it as settled that there was a Malay-Polynesian race, which, at a period before the influx of Hindooism, existed nearly in the state of the present New Zealanders.

Marsden declares that the main portion of the old " Malay is original, and not traceable to any foreign source." *Humboldt* considered the Malay-Polynesian languages to have been " primitively monosyllabic, with marked resemblances to the Chinese."

Crawford, who has made the Malays a study, says, after speaking of the "immemorial antiquity of their language," that the art of converting iron into steel has been immemorially known to the more civilized nations of the Malay Archipelago. There are Sanscrit inscriptions in Java, and some of the other Malay-peopled islands. The Malay annals, a blending of fact and fable, date back nominally to the reign of Alexander the Great. Among relics found, while excavating in some of these islands, are very ancient Chinese coins.

MALAY FEATURES, DRESS, AND DISPOSITION.

Standing upon the steamer before landing in Singapore, you see a motley crowd dressed in every possible costume, from the simple white hip-rag of the nearly naked Kling, the silken attire of the well-to-do Malay, and the everlasting blue of Chinamen, to the flowing dress of the Mohammedan Hadjee. Wealthy Chinamen dress, however, in fine style, having on these islands their carriages, and scores of servants.

The Chinese coolies carry every thing, from pails of water to cook-shops, on balancing shoulder-sticks; while the Klings, from Madras and the Coromandel coast, and the Malays also, carry their cakes, fruits, and wares in trays upon their heads.

The Chinese in these islands are not permitted to be policemen because of their belonging to secret societies among themselves. These coolies are frequently brought into the criminal courts; but a Malay seldom appears as a culprit. The Malayan costume consists of a *baju*, or jacket, a pair of short trousers, with a *sarong*, i.e., a piece of silk, wide at the top as at the bottom, gathered close around the waist. In addition to the *sarong*, the women wear a loose, sash-like garment thrown over the shoulders, called a *kabia*, which, to say the least, is cool and comfortable.

In complexion they are fairer than the men, — a handsome light olive. In married life they are noted for chastity, and the love of family. Owing to the comeliness of their features, their delicate hands, drooping lashes, fair faces, lustrous eyes, and ruby lips, many Europeans are charmed with them; and who, if they do not, *ought*, by every principle of justice, to marry them.

Though a degenerate race at present, they are naturally

proud, frank, generous, true to their friends, and affectionate in disposition. In *physique* they are well-proportioned. They step with an independent gait. They are *not* industrious. They have no acquisitiveness. In an ungenial clime, among selfish worldlings, they would starve. They exemplify the command, "Take no thought for the morrow." Some of them are endowed with rather a high order of intellect. Their foreheads, though full, are larger in the perceptive than the reflective range.

The Malay nobility, usually exceedingly wealthy, are called *Rajahs*. These, with the *Maha Rajahs*, a rank higher, are now educating their children in Europe. The Rajah of Johore has eighty thousand subjects. His position is nearly equal to that of a petty king in Continental Europe.

WHENCE THE MALAY RACE?

America, young and ambitious, is not *all* of the world. Who were the mound-builders of the West? From whence the aboriginal red Indians? Before the American Continent had been pressed by human feet, Asian civilizations had flourished and died. Saying nothing of theories pre-historic, there are solid reasons for believing that the Malays were originally a composite of Central Africans and Mongolians. In fact, both tradition and inscription unite in teaching, that, long ere the Pyramids reared their mighty forms, the Malays were conquered by powerful kings from the north. Twice brought under the yoke of foreign rulers from the north and north-east, they inherited from that nationality now known as the Chinese. Each invasion necessarily left the racial effect upon the posterity.

Do not shrug the shoulders at the mention of Africa. Neither Congo nor Congo negroes constitute *all* of Africa. And, further, all Ethiopians did not originally have thick lips, a flat nose, and short, knotty hair. Cushite history proves this. The color, however, was always dark, or jet black. There is a lingering Aryan element in Central Africa. The New Guineans, set down by all ethnological writers as Malayans, have curly, crispy hair; it is also long and bushy, and of it they are very proud. Whenever the negro element comes in collision with the Mongolian or Malay race, in its advanced stages, as in Asia, and more recently some of the Philippine Islands, it melts away much as do wild animals before civilization.

HOW CAME THE MALAYS INTO NATIONAL POSITION?

Subjective thinkers, as well as geologists, care little for Jewish records, Usher's, or any other theologian's calculations. Ruins, monuments, inscriptions, and lingual roots.— these determine eras of civilization and the colonization of races.

Eastern traditions state that many, *very* many thousands of years since, when a traveler entered a distant country, having a different colored skin, he was supposed by the more superstitious to have been dropped from a star, to people a new portion of the earth; and accordingly the tribe that he visited gave him several wives, and sent him adrift to replenish and populate. But to approach the historical, with inferences from monumental ruins, inscriptions, and suggestions from attending unseen intelligences, some eight thousand years since the Malay Peninsula, and a vast tract of country north of it, was the great half-way halting-ground between the Central Africans of the west, and the Chinese or more northern Mongolians of the east. On these rich table-lands, abounding in wild grasses, grains, and fruits, intercrossing caravans with their merchandise rested and recruited. Settlements commenced, intermarriages followed, villages, then cities; and finally an opulent kingdom was the result. Becoming proud and depredatory, this kingdom warred with, and was conquered by, Tartar hordes and Mongolians; getting, among other consequences, a fervid infusion of Northern blood through the lax social relations then prevailing.

After the lapse of a few hundred years, they were again conquered by the Chinese and their allies, the conquerors in considerable numbers remaining in the country, softening the skin to a light copper, and straightening the hair, through intermixture in their social relationships. These causes, with various climatic conditions, constituted the Malay race, which about six thousand years ago were in their palmy periods. Their language, ever flexible, shows plainly that it has been acted upon both by the monosyllabic Chinese and the Sanscrit. The very word "Malay" is Sanscrit.

Inheriting Mongolian energy, and naturally sailors, these Malayans began at a very early period to emigrate, and colonize islands to the south and east. The north-east monsoons would take them first to Sumatra; and then, considering the oceanic currents and prevailing winds, they would gradually drift southward and to the east. Evidently the mound-builders, and the descendants of *these*, the North-American Indians, were largely Malayan in origin. This long-unsolved problem admits of ethnic demonstration.

THE MALAYANS AMERICA-WARD.

While cruising across the Pacific, Capt. Blythen pointed out to us, on his North and South Pacific charts, *sixty islands* reported and located by navigators some two hundred years since, that have sunk from human sight. Some of these were said to have been inhabited. Cataclysms and convulsions were ever common along the volcanic zones of the tropics. A vast continent, something like the New Atlantis spoken of by Plato, was submerged in the Pacific, save the mountainous peaks, several thousands of years ago. Such of the aborigines as survived, upon the mountain-summits and high lands, intermingled maritally with roving, eastward-bound Malays. They crossed from island to island in crafts corresponding somewhat to their present *prahus*. Traversing the island-dotted waters through Polynesia, they reached the western coast of South America. Their continental course during the succeeding centuries was northward, through Mexico, to the great chain of northern lakes. Ruins, symbols, and the crumbling pottery of the last of the mound-builders and Mexicans, are almost identical with ruins, carvings, and old roads in Malay-peopled lands.

The acute ethnological writer, D'Eichtal, declares that "the Polynesian is an original civilization, and apparently the earliest in the world; that it spread to the east and the west from its focus in Polynesia, *or in a continent situated in the same region, but now submerged;* that it reached America on the one side, and Africa on the other, where it embraced the Fulahs and Copts." He further suggests " that a germ from the Polynesian cradle, falling into the valley of the Nile, originated the ancient Egyptian civilization."

CUSTOMS COMMON TO MALAYS AND INDIANS.

The Rev. Mr. Keasbury, thirty years in the East, and one of the best Malay scholars in the world, has, in keeping with another gentleman, a list of words found both in the Malay and the original dialects of the American continent. But we have no space to adduce the argument from the similarity of language. Since starting upon this tour, I have seen no Pacific Islanders, no people anywhere, that in general features, color of skin and hair, carriage in walking, method in sitting, and government by chiefs and sub-chiefs, so closely resembled our better Indian tribes of the West and South-west.

Traveling out into the country from Johore, and also up the Peninsula (starting in at the Wellsley Province, opposite Penang), where monkeys and the ruder of the Malays inhabit alike fields and forests, I either observed, or learned from others, that these degenerate Malays, instead of shaving the beard, pluck it out, as do the Indians of America.

Walking in streets and forest-paths, the woman strides along in advance, the man following to ward off beasts of prey. So with the Indians. In this country, by the way, tigers, stealing up behind, pounce upon the victim, the forepaw striking the back of the neck. Deaths by tigers are frequent.

The Malays generally bury their dead in a sitting position, interring with them implements of war, and food, as do some of our Indian tribes.

The Malay women, back in the mountainous districts, perform all the hard labor, while the men hunt and fish. So with our Indians.

The Malayan-dyaks of Borneo, and others of the more warlike tribes, put showy feathers in their hair, and take a portion of the scalp from the head of the slain enemy as a trophy; and so with our Indians.

They wear their black hair loose and long, paint their faces in war-time, use the bow and arrow, are fond of tinsel jewelry, and never forget an injury, — *all* of which traits characterize American Indians. The above comparisons refer to the rustic tribes, however, rather than the higher classes of Malays.

THE "FALL OF MAN."

Under the droll drapery of Æsop's Fables nestle lessons sunny with moral beauty; so concealed in the Mosaic myth, "Adam's fall," there is a germ of truth. All through the East are moss-wreathed ruins, telling of golden ages and higher civilizations.

"In the province of Kedu," writes A. R. Wallace, "is the great temple of Borobodo. It is built upon a hill, and consists of a central dome, and seven ranges of terraced walls covering the slopes of the hills, forming open galleries. Around the magnificent central dome is a triple circle of seventy-two towers; and the whole building is six hundred and twenty feet square, and about one hundred feet high. In the terraced walls are niches containing four hundred figures larger than life; and both sides of all the terraced walls are covered with bas-reliefs carved in hard stone, occupying an extent of nearly three miles in length. The Great Pyramid of Egypt sinks into insignificance," says Mr. Wallace, "when compared with this sculptured hill-temple in the interior of Java." There are other templed ruins and inscriptions, remember, in Malay-peopled countries and islands, long antedating this. Who were the projectors? — who the constructors? Ask the Malays: echo! Appeal to history: it is silent as the chambers of death.

THE RELIGION OF THE MALAYS.

In the thirteenth century, Mohammedan missionaries converted the Malays in the Straits of Malacca to Islamism, using persuasion instead of the sword. Their original religion, however, was entirely different. John Cameron, F.R.G.S., assures us that "such Malays as have embraced none of the more modern religions believe in some divine personality, corresponding to God; and a future life, where good men enjoy ecstatic bliss, and the wicked suffer purgatorial punishments." But "their religion," he adds, "is strangely mixed up with *demonology*. They believe that every person is attended by a good and a bad angel; the latter leading to sickness, danger, and sin, while the good angel seeks the individual's health and happiness." In their "lives, they are influenced more by fear than hope." They propitiate the wicked angel and the evil spirits. It is only at death that they ask the especial care of their good angel. They stand in no fear of the transition. Some of their ruins indicate a relationship theologically to the sun and serpent worshipers.

MALAY HOSPITALITY. — THE "ORANG-UTAN."

"The higher classes of Malays," writes Mr. Wallace, "are exceedingly polite, and have all the quiet ease of the best-bred Europeans." To this I will add, they are very kind, warm-hearted, and hospitable. Calling at a Malacca-Malay's palm-thatched dwelling, we were at once treated to tea, fruit, cocoanut-milk, and durians. This latter fruit is quite generally considered the choicest and most luscious fruit in the world; and yet, like tomatoes, one must cultivate a taste for it. The odor of the shell is truly disgusting. The eatable substance is of a yellowish creamy consistence, tasting like a mixture of mashed beech-nuts, bananas, onions, strawberries, pumpkin-seeds, and sweet apples.

The children three, five, and seven years of age, playing about, perfectly nude, were quite shy of us. Though absolute nakedness in this climate is comfortable, the custom is quite too Adamic. These Mohammedan Malays circumcise between the years of eleven and fifteen; and old and young strictly abstain from opium and liquors of all kinds. Mr. Hewick, Chief of Police in the Wellsley Provinces, accompanying us into the country to see Malay life, amused us, when returning, by sending a baboon species of the monkey up a smooth, limbless cocoanut-tree to pick some fruit. The ingenious method the cunning brute devised to twist the nuts from the tree showed a striking intelligence.

In the Malay language "*muniet*" is the term for monkey, "*karra*" for baboon, and "*orang*" for man. "*Orang-laut*" implies sea-people, or seafaring men; "*orang-gunung*" is defined mountaineer, or a rustic, uncultivated man; while "*orang-utan*" signifies literally a man of the forest, or the aboriginal people. The famous "man-like ape," to which Darwinian sympathizers give this name, is never so called by the natives, but is known among all Malay-speaking races under the name of "*mias.*" How easily words mislead, especially when an extreme theory is to be maintained!

CHAPTER XII.

MALACCA TO INDIA.

THE little kingdom of Johore lies just across the straits from the isle of Singapore. Accompanied by our American Consul, Major Studer, a gentleman ever alive to the commercial relations of America, we called to see his majesty, the Maha-Rajah; who, if he does not sit

> "High on a throne of royal state, which far
> Outshone the wealth of Ormus and of Ind,"

has a fine palatial mansion, constructed in truly Oriental style. His "royalty" was absent, which left the secretary to do the etiquette of the palace. The drive across the island of Singapore, with the exception of the poor, vicious horses, was richly enjoyable. The Britains are famous in all foreign lands for excellent thoroughfares and an effective police. The Dutch are too rigid in their measures.

This excellent road above referred to is dotted and lined with bungalows, plantations laid out in exquisite taste, bamboo-hedges, and fan-palms, quite as useful as ornamental, called "the traveler's fountain." The out-jutting stems of these broad palm-leaves, collecting the night-dews, tender their cups of crystal water the following day to the weary, thirsting traveler. Surely God's living providence is everywhere manifest.

JOHORE.

Reaching this unique city of five thousand, we became the guests of James Meldrum, many years in the country, and owner of the largest steam saw-mills in Asia, employing five hundred men. His *bungalow*, situated upon a shady eminence, spans an extensive arc of enchanting scenery. "Bungalows," by the way, a *term* applied to all kinds of Eastern dwelling-houses having lofty ceilings and broad verandas, are built with reference to ventilation and coolness.

Mr. Meldrum saws the famous *teak*, as well as cedars, mahoganies, maraboos, kranjees, chungals, rosewood, sandalwoods, camphor-woods, &c. A report before me says, —

"The Johore forests cover an extent of about ten thousand square miles, and contain upwards of one hundred different kinds of timber-trees. These forests are being opened up by his highness the Maha-Rajah of Johore, K.C.S.I., K.C.C.I., &c., who is constructing a wooden railway into the interior. It will pass through dense virgin forests abounding in all the various kinds of timber-trees known in the Straits."

The Malay *Maha-Rajah* of Johore, being a strict Mohammedan, uses no wines, no liquors of any kind; and, further, he will permit the existence of no "house of ill-fame" in his dominion. Just previous to our arrival, he had broken up a den of prostitution established in New Johore by some Catholic Chinamen. Jesuit missionaries had converted these Chinese from Confucianism to Christianity! Is it strange that Mohammedans think Christians very immoral?

The Malays of these regions never, — no, *never*, drink intoxicating liquors of any kind. Such practices are forbidden by the Koran. Would not an infusion of Islamism into Christianity improve it, at least practically? The Arabian prophet taught no scape-goat atonement, no salvation through another's merits. Neither do Mohammedans in their mosques have "infidels" to *fan* them while they worship. Not so with Christians. In the Singapore English Church, built by convict-labor, sixteen "heathen" natives stand out under a scorching noonday sun on the "Lord's Day," pulling *punkas* to fan these ritualistic English Christians, while they drawlingly "worship God," saying, very sensibly, "*Have mercy upon us miserable sinners.*"

During this trip over to Johore, we saw monkeys leaping on trees, birds of rich plumage, a young elephant, a huge, slimy boa-constrictor just killed by the wayside, and the fresh skin of a tiger, which, while covering the ravenous brute, had concealed the remnants of many a man. In his stomach was found part of a breastbone, and several human hands. Government pays a handsome bounty upon tiger-killing.

A JUNGLE. — TIGERS.

What American has not read of the East-India jungles? Permit the pen to paint one. A jungle is a heavy forest of gigantic trees with a compact foliage of dark-green leaves. Under these grow up another tribe of trees, shorter, more umbrageous, and loaded with such wild fruit as mangosteens, mangoes, and jumbus. Beneath and around these again, there's a prolific growth never seen outside the tropics, — palms, rattans, ferns, and indescribable plants, literally woven together, like the "lawyer-hedges" of New Zealand, by a net-work of creepers and parasites. Such a forest is a jungle, the home of the tiger. I never passed one without thinking of tigers and boa-constrictors. Serpents — cold, slimy, treacherous, and poisonous — I loathe and despise. Eden's fable has nothing to do with this inborn dislike to crawling things. Men that tame and handle serpents, and women that pet poodle-dogs, reveal what they might as well conceal!

It was estimated, a few years since, that one man a day fell a victim to the crushing stroke of the tiger in Singapore, an island of about two hundred square miles. These tigers swim across the straits from Johore to the island. The distance is about two miles. The tiger stealthily strikes, and seizes the person by the back of the neck. Like other wild beasts, he is too cowardly to face a man. The Malays have the saying, "If you will only speak to a tiger, and tell him he can get better food in the jungle, he will spare you."

SPICY GROVES. — BEGGARS UNKNOWN.

Descriptions of cinnamon-trees, clove-trees, and others of this nature, might be interesting. Let a brief sketch of the nutmeg-tree suffice. Handsomely formed, and beautiful in proportion, it grows from twenty-five to thirty feet high, and is thickly covered with polished dark-green leaves, which continue fresh the year round. The fragrant blossoms are thick, wavy bells, resembling the hyacinth or lily-of-the-valley. When the fruit is ripening, it might be mistaken, say the old cultivators, for the peach, bating the pink or yellow cheek. When the nut inside is ripe, the fruit splits down, remaining half open. If not now picked, it soon falls. On the same branch — as with the orange — may be seen the bud, blossom, and the ripening fruitage. Nutting-fields in the Singapore region have nearly gone to decay. A careless blight has rendered their spice-gardens unprofitable.

Want of energy in the Malay Islands, and other portions of the East, has become a proverb. There is little inducement to labor where Nature is so unsparing. All individuals are about as lazy as they can afford to be! Two hours of daylight in the Malay Peninsula is enough for a native to build a decent "shanty," and thatch it. Beggars are unknown away from seaports and cities. They have but to lift the hand, to pluck plenty of fruit. Most delicious pine-apples sell for fifty cents a hundred in the Singapore market.

VOLCANIC BELTS, AND MINERALS.

One of the great volcanic belts of the globe stretches along across these Malayan Islands. The breadth of the belt is about fifty miles. Java alone has over forty active volcanoes. Borneo and New Guinea are just outside of the volcanic zone. Peru and South-American coasts faintly compare with these islands in terrible lava upheavals. The Javanese eruption occurring at Mount Galunggong, in 1822, destroyed twenty thousand inhabitants. A gentleman just from Batavia informs me that there has recently been another serious convulsion upon the island. Instead of liquid lava, as at Vesuvius, heated sands, stones, and red-hot ashes were thrown up with great violence. "Why," is it asked, "do Europeans live upon these islands?" The love of money, is the only answer. Gold in this century is god.

A granitic mountain-chain runs the whole length of the Malay peninsula. It has thermal springs, but no active volcanoes. The mountains are not over a third as high as those in Sumatra and Java. This region is famous for minerals, — iron, copper, tin, and gold. Malacca and Siam are said to be the greatest tin countries in the world.

I met several times "Charlie Allen," the young man who accompanied Mr. Wallace during his prolonged explorations in the East Indies. He had just come down from the Chindrass gold-mines in Malacca. These are forty-five miles from the old city of Malacca, and fifteen from Mount Ophir. They promise "rich," as Californians say. "Oh for American energy to work them!" exclaimed Mr. Allen.

What interested me more than the quartz specimen he exhibited, was the description of an ancient, yet substantially built road during some important excavations. It lies embedded deep under a modern thoroughfare, yet revealing an entirely different kind of constructive conception. Who, what people, built it? Echoing ages are dumb.

BIRD'S-NEST SOUPS.

As turtle-soup is a great dainty with English epicures, so are bird's-nest soups among Chinamen at Singapore and elsewhere. The Indian Archipelago, and adjacent rocky isles, are the harvest-fields for these delicacies. The nests, a sort of gluey, gelatinous substance, seen in China markets, are found along the rocks, in deep and damp caves, and are the choicest if gathered before the birds have laid the eggs. The nests resemble in shape those of the chimney-swallows in America. The finest qualities of nests are when they are clear and white as wax: the poorest are those gathered after the young birds have flown away.

THE UPAS.

That terrible *Gueva Upas*, — the valley of poison, — written about many years ago by a Dutch surgeon at Batavia, and afterwards by others, without inspecting the locality, proved to be a hoax. True, there is a valley, grim, bare, and as destitute of vegetable as animal life, caused by the deadly nature of the carbonic and sulphurous acid gases that continually escape from the crevices and soils in this volcanic region. There are numerous plants and shrubs more poisonous than the Upas. Geographies, as well as Bibles, need revising.

BETEL-NUT. — GUTTA-PERCHA. — COCOANUT-GROVES.

The bewitching betel-nut, used by and so staining the lips and teeth of the natives, is common in Cochin China, Sumatra, Java, and tropical Indies. Its exhilarating fascination is said to excel even tobacco. Penang is the more common name of the nut; accordingly Pulo-Penang signifies betel-nut island. While growing on the graceful and slightly tapering trees, they look something like nutmegs. When ripe, and broken into small pieces, the natives prepare them with the siri-leaf and the unslacked lime of shells. Though producing a dreamy, stimulating effect, it must necessarily injure the membranous surfaces of the mouth.

Gutta-percha abounds in both Singapore and Penang. The Malays term the tree *tuban*. It grows large, has a smooth bark and wide-spreading branches. The tree is not only tapped to get the juice, but often literally girdled, destroying the tree itself. This forest vandalism is now forbidden. The juice — life-blood of the tree — is caught in cocoanut-shells, poured into pitchers made from the joints of large bamboos, and then conveyed to caldrons for boiling and the further preparations for sale.

Cocoanut-groves, being planted in horizontal lines, present a most beautiful appearance. These trees, running up some forty feet, unbroken by leaf or branch, are roofed with deep green foliage. The nuts grow in clusters between the roots of the leaves and branches at the top. If not picked when ripe, they drop, and are broken. Planters of large groves tell me that the noise of falling nuts in night-time breaks the silence with sounds " weird and ghostly." Falling upon the skulls of the natives, they sometimes break them. When the oil is sought, they are allowed to ripen. The nuts sell for a penny each. The watery milk within them is considered as cooling and healthy as nutritious.

FIRE-FLY JEWELRY.

Lower races and tribes in all lands are fond of pearls, precious stones, jewelry, — *display* of all kinds. The Malays, unable to purchase diamonds, have a little cage-like fixture, in which they imprison a fire-fly. This, excited, continues to give out perpetual flashes, quite excelling in brilliancy the diamond itself. The natives are sufficiently humane to set them free when the evening party is over. The poor things are not, as some writers have said, impaled on golden needles, that, by increasing the agony, the glitter of the flash may be intensified. The flash has more the appearance of electricity than phosphorescence. But what an idea! — imprisoning harmless insects to attract attention, and minister to human vanity!

OFF TO CALCUTTA, VIA PENANG.

Left Singapore, June 27, on the steamer, "The Statesman," under the command of Capt. Valiant. This line — running between China and Calcutta — is engaged in the opium-trade. The accommodations are excellent; both the captain and his interesting lady, Mrs. Valiant, striving to their utmost to make the voyage pleasant and homelike.

Penang, a nearly circular island, off from the Malacca coast, contains some seventy thousand acres; and its history is the history of the "British East India Company" in its efforts to get a foothold in the Malay Peninsula. The island, laying high claims to beauty of scenery, seems a mass of hills, rising like cones from the water's edge, near the summits of which are the neat, tasty bungalows of the residents, surrounded by palms, pepper-vines, fruit-trees, and cocoanut-groves. In the harbor hardly a ripple dances upon the glassy waters. Crossing it to visit Mr. Hewick, an official over in the Wellsley Province of Malacca, the phosphorescent flames (when returning) flashing up at the dipping of the natives' oars, gave it the seeming of sailing through a sea of fire. Penang, like all the Oriental cities in these latitudes, is peopled with Malays, Chinese, Klings, and other Hindoo derivatives. The town covers about one square mile. The approach to it, through emerald isles, was magnificent.

MOUNT OPHIR.

Rounding the most southern point of land in Asia, and hugging the Malacca coast toward Burmah and India, we had a fine view of Mount Ophir, four thousand feet high. Whether this be the biblical Ophir, or not, is unimportant; but who honeycombed the mountain with shafts? who here searched for gold in the distant past? This is an interesting inquiry. Of the location of the scriptural Ophir, nothing is known that will positively fix the geographical position. It was a place with which the Jews and Tyrians carried on a lucrative trade in the time of Solomon, twenty-eight hundred years since. At this period the Jews were unacquainted with iron, knowing only bronze, silver, and gold. Their bronze they received from the Tyrians. Half barbarous, they had no commerce till David conquered Edom (or Idumea), giving them some coast on the Red Sea. The Jewish crafts that traded with Ophir may have been the "navy of Tarshish;" and this Tarshish may have been a Tyrian port on the Red Sea, — the part known, perhaps, as the Gulf of Suez.

The celebrated German Orientalist, Lassen, places Ophir somewhere about the debouchement of the river Indus. His theory is founded upon resemblances between the Hebrew and Sanscrit names of the commodities brought from Ophir. There is no resemblance, however, between the ancient method of working the Ophir mines, and the copper mines bordering Lake Superior — worked by whom? The mound-builders. But who were the mound-builders?

CHAPTER XIII.

SPIRITUAL SÉANCES ON THE INDIAN OCEAN.

OUT on the waters restless and sea-tossed, deprived of daily journals and libraries, how naturally the mind turns to that inexhaustible field of research, spirit-communion!

Dr. Willis, a medical spirit, controlling the medium, said in his off-hand, epigrammatic manner: —

"Disease is obstruction. Vital phenomena are profound studies. The human system is interpermeated by a very complex network of nerves. The brain, comparable to a sounding-bell, echoes through these nerves the condition of every portion of the physical organism. This is why I touch the head in diagnosing disease through the Doctor. Certain nerves allied to the *medulla oblongata* throw their sensitive branches across the back of the neck. A current of air striking this part is quite certain to produce colds, catarrhs, and serious neuralgic affections. Wearing long hair, therefore, is a preventive. The ancients in Oriental countries understood this. . . . I see no deleterious effects in your abstinence from meat-eating. And yet considering the formation of the teeth, with the make-up of the whole organic structure, I favor it; that is, considering humanity as it is. The system requires oils, as well as materials for muscle. But animal oils are more clogging to the brain than vegetable. . . . Color affects the health. Red should never predominate in the sick-room, especially if the patient is nervously sensitive. It is an excitant. Pale blue and cream colors are quieting. Sunlight is a natural stimulant. Pure air is indispensable. Diet, and the right use of water, are helps. The ancient Romans indulged in tepid baths, followed by sun-baths. The will-power is a wonderful restorative. Our treatment, including the above, is, you know, magnetic and medicinal. Chronic complaints require medicines: *these* we magnetize and vitalize. Nervous affections readily yield to magnetic treatment, providing mediums are healthy, and temperamentally adapted to patients. Promiscuous mingling of magnetisms is deleterious, inducing nervous unbalance, and opening the way for obsessions. Those so inclined pursue the study of medicines in spirit-life, that they may benefit the inhabitants of earth."

SÉANCE II.

Mr. Knight, entrancing, said, —

... "I see, looking at the mental workings of your brain, that the extreme contradictions in the teachings of spirits disturb you. ... In previous conversations, we have told you that the spirit-spheres — hundreds in number — are inhabited by those just adapted to them intellectually and morally; and, as the spheres, such the aims and acts of the spirits peopling them. Death is not a Saviour; nor does it produce any immediate, miraculous change. ... Those basking in the higher conditions of purity, truth, and love, shed or impart the divine influence of the sphere from which they come. And the same law applies to the lower spheres. As there are evil-minded men, so are there evil spirits, selfish, scheming, wicked spirits! And to offer suggestions relative to the means of avoiding the influences of these, is the object of my present visit.

"I. In order to know men, you must try them: so to fathom the real purposes of spirits, try *them*, *test* them by rigid observation and patient experience; and, further, study the effects they produce upon their mediums.

"II. All mediums, not controlled by a fixed and reliable

circle of three or more spirits, are subject to such deleterious influences as low spirits may choose to throw around them. And the control of this class of spirits is often beyond the power of the guardian spirit, who may not have the advantage of an established circle. The immediate power of control lies not in superior intelligence or spirituality, but in magnetic force, or the great will-power of the spirit. Entrancement is the result of the mesmeric influence of spirits; and it excels that of mortals only in this, that it proceeds from spiritual beings, relieved from the grossness of the flesh. The inference is, that persons holding indiscriminate intercourse with spirits through mediums unprotected by circles of pure, exalted spirits, are liable to be flattered, and to receive false communications from spirits under assumed names.

"III. Guardian spirits with fixed circles, and deep desires to promulgate truth, seldom allow their mediums to be controlled by others than members of their own circle. Each mortal has a guardian spirit; and the assistants of this guardian are properly denominated guides. A guardian spirit, giving communications from spirits outside the circle to mortals, — his own circle acting as means of conveyance, — always states his non-responsibility relative to the message.

"The laws of mental science should be diligently studied, and applied to mediumship. And all persons developing as mediums should seek from their *guardian* the immediate formation of a sympathizing circle in which they have faith, and upon whom they can rely. When this is *not* done, mediums, if not seriously injured, are often led into vice and crime, — crimes instigated by low, undeveloped spirits. And, further, they produce perversions, nervous diseases, obsessions, and insanity. Entering upon the career of mediumship, therefore, is treading a pathway of danger and responsibility. Incipient development should be carefully guarded. Much depends upon mediums themselves. They should not only carefully remain away from improper society, but should keep their minds upon subjects high and spiritual, in prayer seeking such controlling intelligences as must necessarily benefit humanity. On the other hand, if they take the opposite course, — seeking such spirits as promise wealth by finding treasures, such as promise fame and worldly glory, or such as will pry into the secrets of others from selfish motives, — they will certainly be led to ruin. As self-denial, as abnegation of good to one's self, and earnest labors for others' benefit, gives that for which one has *not* sought, — *happiness;* so the converse is true, that seeking for comfort and for self-aggrandizement at the expense of others, leads to one's utter defeat and destruction.

"The reality, the philosophy, of spirit-control, then, are matters of almost infinite importance. And the subject should be approached with care and caution, and be used only by the wise, by the pure in purpose, for mental growth and higher spiritual attainments. These ends sought, and humanity will reap the rich reward for which the faithful few have toiled, — the universal ministration of angels, the enlightenment of the races, and the redemption of the world!"

SÉANCE III.

A French Normandy spirit, claiming to have been in the higher existence some three hundred years, coming by permission of the circle, advocated these theoretical dogmas: —

1. "There is no God; *nothing* in the universe of being but matter, and the negative forces in matter."

2. "Annihilation is true; or, a conscious future existence, in the sense of endlessness, is a farce. Spiritual beings, by becoming more pure and etherealized, are finally absorbed in the great ocean of refined matter, — snuffed out, losing their consciousness and their identity."

3. "Fatalism is a truth. Man is not responsible for an act of his life. All things, including men and their actions, are fated, or necessitated to be precisely as they are. Man is a thing."

These exploded theories, once popular among atheists in France, are still taught by this shrewd, intelligent spirit.

They were grounds of sharp debate between us during several sittings. It was a drawn battle. Grant him his premises, and he will succeed admirably in the argument. Dispute them, demanding the proof of his proofs, and the foundation of his premises, and he fails to establish his untenable positions. He is evidently sincere and conscientious, delighting to propagate his metaphysical theories in spirit-life. Can any one conceive of notions that spirits have not taught? The lesson of these controversies was this: Spirits are fallible, and many of them long continue, though disrobed of mortality, to hug their earthly ideas and idiosyncrasies. Therefore, in listening to the teachings of immortals, we must be governed entirely by our intuitions and maturest judgment. Reason is the final judge.

SÉANCE IV.

The spirit Aaron Knight present, the following conversation ensued: —

Now that you have come, I desire your opinion upon the subject of my thoughts for the past few days.

"I should be happy to hear the substance of them."

Spending the winter in London, a few years since, I was deeply interested, listening to Mr. Tyndall's famous lecture upon "Dust," delivered in the Royal Institution. The professor clearly proved that the air is filled with fine atoms and living germs, which, inbreathed, enter the human body. He also explained how dust, and other unseen particled substances, might be filtered away by means of cotton-wool tightly impacted, and worn over the mouth. And M. Pasteur, a French scientist, carrying the investigation a step further, made filters of gun-cotton, using that variety which is soluble in ether. The filters, having done their work, were dissolved in ether; and the solution, when microscopically examined, was found to contain millions of organized germs, — living entities. These could not only be seen, but the genera and species could be detected. Therefore the very atmosphere we breathe is full of air-borne germs and living life-cells. And these, for some wise purpose, must be continually entering into the human organization, must they not?

"Certainly: and you have suggested a subject of vast importance; one relating to, if not involving, the very origin of living beings. Logically speaking, there is *no* creation, — that is, the creation of something from nothing. Surveying earth and spirit-life, I see only evolution or unfoldment; and so pre-existence is true. The minutest monad in space is intelligent on its plane. Intelligence, or mind, is a result, or an effect of essential spirit and matter. But as these were never separated, and as the cause was eternal, so was, and so *must* be the effect also; which effect *was* and *is* intelligence. There are no vacuums. Interstellar spaces are filled with the life-principle, with infusoria, cells, and unseen atoms. Nothing but life can sustain life. Infusorial animalcula, and monadic germ-cells of life, pass into the cranial sensorium by organic attraction and imbibation. In the human organism they become more thoroughly vitalized; and in the brain itself they receive necessary magnetic influences prior to the projected descent by will-power, through the spinal column and seminal glands, to their conceptive destinies. The brain, remember, cradles, rather than generates spermatozoic germs aflame with conscious life. These, pre-existent, were afar back in the measureless past aggregating, throwing off, accreting, pulsing, and passing through various occult processes preparatory to incarnation. As in the acorn, germinally hidden, lies the oak, so in the spermatozoic life-germ, the future man."

SÉANCE V. — QUESTIONS ANSWERED BY THE SPIRITS.

"The cross is the most angular of geometrical figures; and, though connected with the martyred death of Jesus, it originated as an objective symbol in the phallic ages, and referred primarily to generation." . . .

"Emanations electic and magnetic, from the physical and

spiritual bodies, extend outward from the person quite a distance; and, although indicating, they do not unmistakably index the mental characteristics. And so the aural lights, and odylic sprays from the brain, give only the general bent and tendency of the mind." . . .

"Undoubtedly I could go to the planets; but I've no desire to so do. My work as yet is connected with the earth. Parisi's researches lead him in such directions. I think he has visited Jupiter and other planets." . . .

"The future is more important than the past; the destiny than the origin of humanity. Though generally outlined by your guardian angel, your future, morally considered, is not irrevocably fixed. Man is a mental and moral, as well as a physical being. To all moral beings endowed with reflection, there is a field of moral action. You are now paving the highway your feet must press in spirit-life, and laying, too, the foundation-stones of the temple you will inhabit. That chain of pearls was not a mythic farce, but a reality put around your neck when reaching the years of accountability by Parisi Lendanta, who for a time was John's medium. These pearls magnetically reflect, otherwise spiritually mirror, the deeds of your whole life, — deeds and events that you will be necessitated to read when entering the higher state of existence. Personal identity implies memory, and memory retribution. This is the judgment, — the opening of the books." . . .

"Living a celibate life for the purpose of boastingly saying, 'I am a celibate, I am pure: stand by, for I am holier than thou,' is selfish, and therefore morally deleterious; but if in laboring, on the other hand, to save others from passion, from fleshly gratifications, and *all* that opposes chastity and absolute purity, men become virgin celibates pure-minded and spiritual, then are they truly angelic. Such, having been raised from the dead, walk in the resurrection."

SÉANCE VI.

Memory serving me, Mr. Knight, you once informed me that you had been privileged to attend councils of the glorified in supernal spheres, — that you there saw sages, seers, martyrs, and among them the Apostle John, with whom, as a pupil, you had held many interviews. This deeply interested me; and, if consistent, will you answer certain inquiries relating to matters with which John, in his period of time, must have been conversant?

"Certainly, to the best of my ability."

Where was John born?

"In Syria. The Assyrians were once a great and truly enlightened nation, occupying a prominent position in Asia. But, by formidable combinations of foreign powers, their territory was conquered, and their national name abbreviated to Syria. He lived in that mountainous portion of Syria known as Judea; which word was abridged from Jew-deity, so called because of Jewish reverence for Jehovah, the tutelary god of the Jews."

Did he travel in different countries?

"Yes; he traveled not only into the remotest provinces of Assyria, but even into Egypt and Persia. John was a linguist, highly educated for that period, and conversant with the teachings of Plato and Buddha. John and James were most intimately associated in their apostolic life. Occasionally John served as an interpreter for Jesus.

"Returning from a long season of travel in the East, he found his parents in great disrepute from connecting themselves with the Nazarenes, known at that time as Nazarretas, a poorer branch of the Jews, charged with sensualism, with holding intercourse with familiar spirits, and believing in the immediate coming of the Messiah. This sect originated long before Jesus' time."

Did the prophet Daniel impress these visions upon John's mind?

"No: John was not only highly inspirational, but was a trance-medium; often leaving his body, and traveling as a spirit in the highest spheres. Those Apocalyptic images symbolized eras and principles.

"Written in the mystic language of correspondence, and little tampered with by scribes and Christian copyists, John's revelations are capable of an outer and *inner* interpretation. Inspirational men of those times understood them. Jesus and the apostles constituted a sort of secret society among themselves. The similarity of Daniel's and John's visions are traceable to oneness of nationality, and similarity of culture in the schools of the prophets."

What were the "deeds of the Nicolaitans" that Jesus "hated"?

"John was Jesus' medium after he passed to the heavenly life from Calvary; and he inspired John to write to the seven churches, i.e., the seven sympathizing assemblies of believers in Asia. The "deeds of the Nicolaitans" were hypocrisies and the "unfruitful works of darkness." The clan originated with one Nicolas, who sought to compromise the principles of Jews and Christians. They were policy-men, full of flattery, and given to hypocrisies and licentious practices; which 'deeds Jesus hated.'"

Who was Melchisedec, King of Salem?

"There were two, and hence the confusion. One was a spirit. The other, a distinguished personage remote from the tenting Abraham, was called the 'King of Peace,' because baptized of the Christ-spirit. To him Abraham paid tithes. The ancestors of Abraham were Aryans given to war and pillage."

Who were the Essenians?

"A rigid and exclusive people, originally known as Assenians. Strictly constructing the moral law, they were stern reformers, very industrious, and inclined to be self-righteous. Those entering the inner court of the order were diviners and celibates. Joseph, John the Baptist, Jesus, the apostles John and James, and nearly all of the disciples, were Essenes."

Who were the spirit-guides of Jesus?

"He had a large circle, over two hundred attending spirits, — 'a *legion*.' They were mostly from the earlier Jewish prophets; and among them were Moses, Elijah, Isaiah, Jeremiah, as well as sages from India, China, and Persia."

Do the prayers of sectarian Christians affect Jesus?

"Yes: the millions of Christians praying to and persistently calling upon Jesus, very slightly and indirectly affect him; and I must say not pleasurably, because of incorrect ideas concerning him and his mission, and because they ask him to do what they themselves should do. . . . The scriptural records of Jesus are very imperfect. He did not whip the money-changers out of the temple, but so sharply rebuked them that they voluntarily left. Neither did he call men 'swine,' 'dogs,' and 'whited sepulchres;' but said, 'If you persist in your unrighteousness, others will compare you to whited sepulchres.' . . . Jesus was overshadowed by spirit-presences from the sacred moment of conception, and therefore the prophetically expected of the Nazarettas. After the anointing, and descent of the baptismal Spirit, he was Jesus Christ, pre-eminent; the greatest medium ever born upon this earth. And in him, as apostolically expressed, 'dwelt the fullness of the Godhead bodily,' — that is, the full power of the Christ-spirit. And the races will ultimately acknowledge the sublimity of his precepts, as well as his moral superiority among the world's Saviours."

CHAPTER XIV.

INDIA: ITS HISTORY AND TREASURES.

JULY 4, our country's natal day. The republic that is to come will be founded in justice, equality, and peace.

We have spent the day rolling and tossing upon the Bay of Bengal. I shall spell it hereafter Ben*gall*, emphasizing the last syllable. It deserves the bitter epithet. For three full days we endured a terrible monsoon-storm. It was a cyclone, save the rotary motion usually attending these hurricanes. The frightened Jews aboard rushed for Moses and the Prophets, and began to intone the psalms in Hebrew. The wind, increasing, came in maddened gusts; the waves surged and heaved; the lightnings flashed; the rain fell in sheets; the fore-stay-sail struggled in tatters; trunks, tables, upset; the dishes jingled in scattered fragments; the Fates and the Furies seemed, in fact, to have let loose the very artillery of the hells! Oh, it was fearful! The following day we passed a wreck. What became of the crew — what? Our ship, under the command of Capt. Valiant, behaved valiantly. It was a relief to sail into the Hoogly, one of the river-mouths through which the Ganges empties into the ocean.

INDIA.

Oh, marvelous country! Land of tree-worship, serpent-worship, the lotus-flower, and the mystic *ling*-land of the ancient Vedas, and those unparalleled epics the Ramayána and the Máhábharatá with its hundred thousand stanzas! land of the ascetic Rishis, the eighteen Puranas, and the *Tri-Pitaka* of the Buddhists! land of pearl-built palaces, templed caves, marble pillars, dust-buried ruins, walled cities, mud villages, and idolatrous worship! These, *all* these, are among the sights, the lingering memories, of India's mingled glory and shame.

When legendary Rome was a panting babe, and proud Greece a boasting lad, overshadowed by Egyptian grandeur, India was gray-bearded and venerable with years, worshiping one God, and using in conversation the musical Sanscrit, a language not only much older than the Hebrew, but conceded by all philologists to have been the richest and most thoroughly polished language of the ages. Well may India have been considered the birthplace of civilization, and the primitive cradle-bed of the Oriental religions.

APPROACHING THE LAND OF THE BRAHMAN.

Steaming through wind and wave out of the Bay of Bengal, Indiaward, we entered the broad mouth of the sluggish Hoogly, one of the outlets of the Ganges, and consequently to Hindoos a sacred stream. Calcutta is something like a hundred miles from the mouth of this river. Though the banks are low and nearly level, the stretching jungle thickly shaded, and the cultivation only ordinary, the stately palms, cocoanut-groves, and luxuriant vegetation, along this winding Mississippi of the East, rendered the scenery decidedly attractive.

Just previous to reaching the city, we passed the royal mansions of the ex-king of Oude. This prisoner of state, though despising the English, as do the rajahs generally, maintains much of his kingly magnificence, and gets, besides, a yearly stipend from the English government. A Mohammedan in religion, preferring polygamy to monogamy, his social instincts are said to be decidedly animal. Several European women grace — rather *disgrace* — his harem. Within the inclosure of his private, high-walled grounds, he keeps quite a menagerie of wild beasts, and continues in repair a large artificial mound, said to contain two thousand hissing serpents. It was feared, at one time, that he would let loose beasts and serpents upon the city.

CALCUTTA.

On the 7th of July, by the steamer "Statesman," we reached the capital of British India,—the famous City of Palaces. The impertinence of custom-house officers, dilated upon by some of our fellow-passengers, proved a fraud. They were simply gentlemen doing their duty.

The hot, rainy season had just commenced. It was truly oppressive the first few days. In the city, and along the Delta of the Ganges, the mercury frequently rises to one hundred and twenty degrees, reminding one of the sun-scorched clime of Africa. In landing, half-naked coolies clamored loudly for our baggage; actually they excel the New-York hackmen! Dr. Dunn, fighting his way through the crowd bravely, soon saw the trunks safely aboard the *Gharrie* for "The Great Eastern." The rooms in these Asiatic hotels are high, commodious, and Oriental, even to the *punkas*.

TERRITORY AND ENGLISH RULE.

The empire of India, extending over a territory of a million and a half square miles, equals in size all Europe except the Russias. Swarming with two hundred millions of people, exhibiting almost an endless diversity of soils, productions, and climate, the deltas of India's great rivers are befitting granaries for the world. And England, claiming that the sun never sets upon her dominions, holds direct rule over three-fourths of this vast country.

Early in the seventeenth century, British cupidity, looking at the immense wealth of Indian kings and princes, coveted their possessions. Under the pretext of Christianizing, and other reasons, a cause for war was manufactured. Reckless of justice, fraternity, and the New-Testament principles of peace, England, in brief, decided upon a war of conquest for territory and trade, for gold, diamonds, and precious stones. No historian pretends to whitewash Britain's course of crime and infamy in the East. Learned Brahmans understand that history well, and, understanding, secretly hate English rulership. Still they prefer Englishmen to Mohammedans for masters. Disguised in any way, however, slavery is *slavery*, — a condition to be hated!

The "mild Hindoo" is a common term in the Orient; and while the Hindoo is mild, forbearing, peace-loving, and contemplative, the Englishman is ambitious, stern, and dictatorial. The theistic reformer, Keshub Chunder Sen, sensibly said, in a late Calcutta speech, "Muscular Christianity has but little to do with the sweet religion of Jesus; and it is owing to the reckless, warlike conduct of these pseudo-Christians, that Christianity has *failed* to produce any wholesome *moral influence* upon *my countrymen*."

There was a monstrous mutiny in 1756; there have been minor mutinies since; and, mark it well, there is destined to be another, eclipsing in blood and carnage all the others. The Aryan-descended Indians love liberty and self-government.

WHENCE THE HINDOOS?

The Aryan tribes inhabiting Central Asia entered India by the northern passes, and descended first the valley of the Indus, and then that of the Ganges, attaining their full strength and development along the rich alluvial valley-lands of the latter river. They brought with them agricultural implements, some of the fine arts, and the elegant Sanscrit. "Brought it from where? or in what country did it originate?" The inquiry, natural enough, shall be noticed hereafter.

In this great and fertile country, the Aryans — primitive Hindoos — located themselves in comparative security. The aborigines, supposed by some to be of "Turanian descent," fled, in many cases, to the mountain fastnesses before them, as though conscious of their physical inferiority.

The Aryan type, including the pre-historic races of Central and Northern Africa, the Caucasians of Europe, the Assyrians of Western Asia, and the fair-skinned, Sanscrit-speaking people who entered India from the north, developed, wherever it settled, marvelous civilizations. The purest Aryan blood at present is found in Northern India; but wherever within the bounds of the Indian Empire to-day you find light-complexioned, noble-featured Brahmans, you find direct descendants of the ancient Aryans.

The non-Aryan natives, called, in the Rig-Veda, Dasyns, Rakshasas, Asaras, and others with outlandish-sounding names, were dark-complexioned, yet timid, spiritually-minded tribes. Remnants of them, ever the physical inferiors of their northern invaders, are still found in the mountainous districts of Interior and Southern India, known now under the names *Todas*, *Gonds*, *Bheels*, *Kols*, *Korkus*, *Bygds*, *Chamars*, down to the *Pariahs*. Some of these tribes have curly hair and protruding lips. The infusion of the Aryan element into the aboriginal stock took place rapidly; and yet the observant traveler among them will come upon stratum after stratum, showing in a distinct manner the intermediate stages between the two races. Generally, the physical type diverges from aboriginal features and manners towards Brahmanical Hindooism. Some of these aboriginal races have so verged towards the status of Brahmanism that they have assumed the "sacred thread," claiming membership with the "twice-born caste."

GROWTH AND LITERATURE OF THE ARYAN HINDOOS.

None of the other Oriental countries have clung to so many of their primitive customs, retained so much of their early literature, experienced so few internal dissensions, or suffered so little from ancient Vandal invasions, as the Hindoos. Strongly sea-guarded on three points of the compass, the dangerous defiles and mountainous ranges along the northern boundaries of India presented formidable barriers to conquering hordes from Northern Asia. Accordingly, while the nationalities of Central and Northern Africa, in pre-Pyramidal times, as well as the populous countries of Central and Eastern Asia, were engaged in wars both civil and aggressive, destroying, so far as possible, all the historic monuments of antiquity, and exterminating every vestige of literature within the enemy's reach, the Aryans of India seem to have been left in comparative peace and isolation, — left to work out the problem of civilization and mental culture, unaffected by foreign influences or ravaging internal revolutions.

The advancement for a time was all that could be desired. The Aryan Hindoos stood upon the world's pinnacle of progress. This was the era of the Máhabháratá, 1300 B.C., of Manu the lawgiver, and Panini the great grammarian, of the Sanhitas and Brahmanas, of the Vedas and of the Sastras, *all* something like 1000 B.C. Brahmans educated in English colleges, and learned in the Sanscrit, insist that Homer modeled his verses after their ancient poets. Putting it plainer, they boldly *affirm* that Homer's Iliad was "prigged," — largely borrowed from the Máhabháratá.

Though this was the golden age of Aryan learning, mental friction was wanting. The national intellect, at this point, became either stationary, or shaded off into the metaphysical and the speculative. The inductive method of research was abandoned. Mystical theorizing ran rampant. Though the Vedas distinctly taught the existence of one Supreme Being, a dreamy mythology slowly sprung into existence, and fastened its fangs upon the national mind. Chieftains and heroes were made gods. Imagination painted, and tradition ascribed to them valorous deeds and marvelous attributes as unnatural as monstrous. The ignorant masses, carving their images in stone as keepsakes, finally fell to worshiping them; while the higher classes either cultivated philosophy and deductive abstractions, or mentally merged away into a passive self-meditation, looking for final rest in *Nirvana*.

MEN IN THE CITY.

The first movement, after the landing in Calcutta, was to report in person to Gen. Litchfield, the American consul, whom we found a most genial and sunny-souled gentleman. His family residence is Grand Rapids, Mich. Gen. Grant was singularly fortunate in his consular appointments at Calcutta, Singapore, Hong Kong, and Melbourne.

Having made the acquaintance of Keshub Chunder Sen in London, several years since, to inquire about Spiritualism and the progress of the Brahmo-Somaj in India, I sent him my card, receiving in reply a most cordial welcome to his country. Our future interviews, I trust, were mutually pleasing and profitable. Though singularly non-committal upon the causes of Spiritual phenomena, he extends the hand of fellowship to Spiritualism, because a phase of liberalism.

Knowing something of the Unitarian missionary, Rev. C. H. A. Dall, through "The Liberal Christian," and being the bearer of a letter from Rev. Herman Snow of San Francisco, Cal., I called upon him at No. 24 Mott's Lane, Calcutta, where he has a flourishing school for boys, with several native teachers. He has joined, so I was credibly informed, the Brahmo-Somaj, preaching at present little if any. Unitarianism, American-born, had nothing new in the way of religion to send to the Brahmans of India.

Busily counting money, Mr. Dall was at first not very communicative, although he warmed up a bit when the conversation turned upon progress, and the natural relations existing between radical Unitarianism and true Spiritualism. Having read of "free love," "fanaticism," and other rubbish floating upon the spiritual river of life, if not prejudiced, he certainly lacked a knowledge of the Spiritual philosophy. Our chat became quite spicy. In no residence, priestly presence, or princely palace, during these round-the-world wanderings, have I evaded or hidden my belief in Spiritualism. No one principled in truth, or fired with a spark of genuine manhood, would so do, even though shunned by the sham god of the age, — "*society.*" Policy, cunning, and crafty, is kin of the hells. Worldly gain is spiritual loss.

Calcutta, founded by the "Old East India Company," near the close of the seventeenth century, on the site of an ancient city called *Kali-Kutta*, sacred to the goddess Kali, has a population of about eight hundred thousand, some seventeen thousand of which are Europeans.

CITY SUBURBS AND SIGHT-SEEING.

The gardens, the bright foliage, the luscious fruitage, and the palm-crowned suburban scenery generally, win at once the traveler's admiration. The Government House, the High Court, the massive Museum, yet unfinished, and other city buildings, are magnificent structures. The Post Office, imposing in appearance, is built upon the site of the notorious "Black Hole" of mutiny memory, where one hundred and forty-six prisoners, thrust into a room eighteen feet square, were left in a sultry night to smother and perish. Only a few survived. The act was infamous. The Maidán below the gardens, crowned with a Burmese pagoda, is the fashionable resort in evening-time. The drive skirts the river; and, for gayety and costly equipage, Paris can hardly parallel it. Through the kindness of our consul-general, I was privileged with a carriage-ride in the gray of twilight, down the river, and around the square, to the music-stand, where the Queen's Band nightly discourses delicious music. The scenic surroundings, the blending of Occidental style with Oriental grandeur, can not well be described. Many of the costumes were singularly unique, and the social intercourse remarkably free from any stiff provincialisms. All had fashions and styles of their own. The rich *baboos* — Hindoo gentlemen — occupied prominent positions in the gay procession and motley gathering.

Lower-caste Hindoo life is seen in the bazaars; and though there are disgusting sights and rank odors, along the narrow native streets, we neither heard nor saw the Calcutta jackals so often described by romancing writers. Crows, however, may be numbered by myriads. Nestling at night in the ornamental shade-trees of the city, they engage early in the morning at the scavenger business, and often mistake the kitchen for their legitimate field of operations. Tall, stork-like birds, called "adjutants," also do scavenger-work. At night they perch upon the tops of the public buildings, standing like sentinels on guard.

The city is watered from immense reservoirs. The natives bathe in them, wash their garments in them, and then, filling their goat-skins for domestic purposes, and slinging them under the arm, supported by a strap, they trudge moodily away to their employer's residence. Drinking-water is drawn from wells in a very primitive way. Women have but few privileges. They seldom appear in the streets; and then, if married, they veil their faces. One is continually reminded, while studying the Hindoo socially, of Old Testament manners and customs.

RIVER SCENES. — JUGGERNAUT. — THE BANYAN-TREE.

Occupying a place in Gen. Litchfield's barouche, we drove along, early one morning, by the river's side some four miles, witnessing the bathing and worshiping of the Hindoos in the flowing Hooghly. Gesticulating, bowing, sprinkling themselves, and intoning prayers, these worshipers counted their beads much as do the Catholics. Paying no regard to the Christian's Sunday or the Mohammedan's Friday, these sincere Hindoos hold in great reverence festival days of their gods. The English government grants the different religionists of the country some sixty holidays during the year.

Unfortunately, we reached India just too late to see the yearly Juggernaut festival, during which the great idol-car in Eastern India is drawn with such gushing enthusiasm. Believing devotees do not, however, throw themselves voluntarily under this idolatrous engine to be crushed, as falsifying churchmen have widely reported. While the excitement is at a high pitch, careless devotees may accidentally fall under the rotating wheels, and perish. This actually happened the present year. And so similar accidents often occur on Fourth of July occasions in America. That a few impulsive fanatics in the past may have purposely rushed under the ponderous wheels, — much as Christian pilgrims in the Crusade period walked through Palestine with bared feet, to die by the Holy Sepulchre, — is quite probable. Fanaticism has been common to all religions.

But crossing the river on this delightful morning, by the banks of which nestled neatness and filth, — Christly and demoniac men in close proximity, — we were soon strolling through the Botanical Gardens, admiring tropical flowers, with the lilies white, golden, and purple, on our way to the crowning glory of the gardens, the great banyan-tree, *alias* the bread-fruit tree of the East. This grand old tree fully met our expectations, only that it bore berries about the size of acorns, instead of bread. The natives are very fond of them. While this gigantic tree is not tall, it is wide-spreading and symmetrically shaped; and, though not an evergreen, it is clothed in a dark-green, glossy foliage, reflecting at sunrise a thousand vivid tints, varied as beautiful. This Calcutta banyan-tree, throwing down to the soil one hundred and thirty creeper-like limbs, *all* forming trunks, — symbol of the American Union, many in one, — would afford shade or shelter in a light rain-storm for two thousand persons. No traveler in the East should miss of seeing it. Tradition says that Alexander's army of ten thousand, in the fourth century B.C., sheltered itself, while in Northern India, under the far-reaching branches of a princely banyan. Just after leaving this kingly tree, there fluttered up before us, from a clump of date-palms, a fine flock of green-plumaged parrots.

CHAPTER XV.

INDIA S RELIGIONS, MORALS, AND SOCIAL CHARACTERISTICS.

THE higher classes of these Asiatics have fine-looking faces. Tall and rather commanding in person, easy and graceful in movement, they have pleasant, open countenances, dark eyes with long eyebrows, glossy black hair, — of which they seem proud, — thoughtful casts of expression, and full, high foreheads. The complexion is olive, shaded, according to caste and indoor or outdoor exercise, towards the dark of the Nubian, or white of the Northman. In Northern India they are nearly as fair as Caucasians; and, what is more, English scholars have been forced to admit that the Hindoo mind, in capacity, is not a whit behind the European. In hospitality they have no superiors. The lower, oppressed classes, as in other countries, are rude, rustic, and *vulgar!*

As a people I have found the Hindoos exceedingly polite. When two Brahmans meet, lifting each the hand, or both hands, to the forehead, they say, "*Namaskar*" (I respectfully salute you). Sometimes the inferior bows, and touches the feet of the higher personage, the latter exclaiming, "*I bless you: may you be happy!*" The Hindoo, naturally mild, meek, and fond of peace, will sooner put up with oppression than engage in a battle of recrimination and violence. An English ethnologist considers him sufficiently "womanly to be considered effeminate." Certainly, his patience and cool self-possession, inclining him to sail tranquilly along the placid waters of life, present a striking contrast to the impatience, ambition, and dictatorial spirit of Anglo-Saxons. Each and all, however, fill their places in the pantheon of history.

THE KALI GHAUT AND SLAIN GOATS.

Religion, when unenlightened by education and unguided by reason, degenerates into superstition. The Kali temple, situated in the suburbs of Calcutta, sacred to the ugly-looking, bloodthirsty goddess *Kali*, was to me a deeply interesting sight, because showing unadulterated Hindooism in its present low, degraded state. The shrines and the altars, the flower-covered *ling*, and the crimson yard all wet and dripping with the blood of goats sacrificed at the rising of the sun, forcibly reminded me of the Old Testament sacrifices offered as sweet-smelling savors to Jehovah, the tutelary god of the Jews. The bowing of the face to the earth, the kissing of cold stones, the smearing of the face with mud, the liturgical mutterings, and the howling beggary by the wayside, were all repulsive in the extreme. The temple was only a coarse, ordinary structure. Being Christians, we were not permitted to pass the threshold. These temples are not constructed, as are churches, to hold the people; but rather as imposing shelters for the gods, priests, and sacrificial offerings. The worshipers around them are generally of the lower castes. Conversing on the spot with one of these officiating Brahman priests, he assured me that the throng present did *not* worship the Kali image. "It is a symbol," said he, "leading the mind to the higher and the invisible." Doubting his statement, and pondering, I silently said, *Here is retrogression*, for the most ancient of the Vedas taught the existence of one infinite God. The Orientalist, Prof. Wilson, says, "The Aryans believed in one God, who created the world by his fiat, and organized it by his wisdom." After the composition of the first Vedas, with the post-Vedic priesthood, came mythology, and the different castes.

THE BURNING GHAUTS. — CREMATION.

How are the dead best disposed of? Certain American Indians, lifting their dead warriors into forest-trees, leave them to assimilate with the elements; Christians inter the mortal remains of their loved ones beneath the turf; Persians expose the bodies of the dead to the sun on their "towers of silence," while the Hindoos burn theirs in *ghauts* consecrated to this purpose. Many scientists and hygienic reformers consider the last the preferable method. With Gen. Litchfield for guide, we repaired one afternoon to the ashy *ghaut* of flame to witness the burning of the dead. Entering the brick-wall-inclosed arena, the eye fell upon several piles of smoldering ashes; while near by was the corpse of a pleasant-faced young girl of some eleven years, awaiting the priestly preparations for burning. The red-paint spot on the maiden's forehead indicated that she was married. A tearless mother sat by the rude bier, with a naked babe at the breast. A sad stillness pervaded the scene. When the dry hard-wood, intermixed with light sticks of bamboo and sandal, was laid across the shallow trench, and the pile ready for the cremation, the priests anointing the head with oil, and sprinkling the body with sacred water, placed the poorly-clad and ghastly corpse upon the rough pyre. Then, bending the limbs to occupy as little space as possible, and putting seeds, boiled rice, and bananas to the mouth, the lighted torch was applied to the husky bamboo. Soon the fire, flame, and smoke, curling and hissing around the sandal-scented pile, transformed the organized dust to its original dust and ashes. During the burning, the priests paced around the fiery pyre, chanting their prayers of consolation. Thousands flock to the Ganges to die and be burned. Nothing can be sweeter than for a Hindoo to die with his eyes resting upon the sacred river. The funeral pyres of the wealthy are made of the sandal-tree, spice-wood, fragrant flowers, incense, and ointments;

and, while the body is being consumed, priests and distant friends chant the Rig and the Sama Vedas. The immediate mourners stand around, dressed in white. Often the ashes are gathered up, and preserved in urns.

HOW SHALL WE DISPOSE OF OUR DEAD?

Touching the removal of the dead, these have been the common methods: interment, exposing upon towers of silence, mummification, and incinerating or burning upon the prepared pyre. Considering the loathsome changes of decomposition, with the liberation and discharging of poisonous gases into the atmosphere, the burying of deceased bodies is open to serious objections. It is well known that sulphuretted and phosphuretted gases are active poisons; and their influence, when breathed even in infinitesimal quantities, must be deleterious to health. Dr. Walker, a London surgeon, shows in his "Gatherings from Graveyards," that from the surface of the ground, above dead bodies, there are continually rising poisonous miasmas. These impregnate and infect the germ-cells and dust of the air breathed; and thus disease is borne upon the winds. There are few unhealthier places than the cemeteries of crowded cities. In them epidemics and pestilences often originate. People should avoid rather than visit them. In the early history of Judaism, to merely touch a dead body rendered the person "unclean for seven days."

Extravagant coffins, pompous ceremonies, costly monuments, gloved priests, expensive mourning apparel, and bearing corpses long distances for burial, *all* violate the genius of that Spiritual philosophy which sees that the spirit

> "Sings now an everlasting song
> Amidst the trees of life."

The opposition of churchmen to cremation arises from their theological belief that graveyards are temporary resting-places for bodies awaiting the trump of the resurrection. It is evangelical teaching, that the departed are "locked in the embrace of death;" that they have "fallen asleep in Jesus;" or have died "in the hope of a glorious resurrection" of their decomposing, putrefying bodies. As the shirt of Nessus, so clings superstition to the sectarist. The tendency of solid thinkers, however, is turned towards cremation, because a quicker method of turning dust to dust, as by the "refiner's fire" of Malachi; because less expensive than burial; because conducive to the general health; because preserving portions of the ashes in urns is less costly than gravestones; and because it obviates all fear of being buried alive. Science will readily devise means to deodorize the gases given off during the process of burning; while the ashy *débris* will the more readily revert back to usefulness as fertilizers of the soil.

CASTE, AND BRAHMAN PRIESTS.

Under any sky, caste is an unmitigated curse. Buddhism in the sixth century B.C. was a brave inspirational protest against Brahmanical assumption and caste. Though Buddhistic preaching and practice quite checked this caste system for a time, it revived again with the revival of Brahmanism, 200 B.C.; and, intensified by an unrelenting social despotism, it is to-day the scourge of India. Women feel the chains more keenly than men. This great nation is slow to feel the pulsations of progress. English rule has done little, *nothing*, to tone down or overthrow the caste-venom of the ages; and how could it, when caste in English society is nearly as marked as in Hindostan?

This social pest pervades all gradations of life in India. Each servant has his own sphere, and out of it he will not budge. This necessitates in wealthy English families a large retinue of servants. Brahmans, though sometimes poor, never "sink" to be tradesmen! They are generally clerks and draughtsmen. And then there is the messenger, the butler, the cook, tailor, coachman, market-man, washerman, palanquin-bearers, sweepers, and others, down to pariahs.

As is well known, there are four general castes, — *Brahmans*, priests and writers; *Chattries*, soldiers; *Vyshes*, merchants; and *Sooders*, tradespeople and toilers, — with scores of subdivisions. Castes never intermarry, though there is occasionally an elopement. All Brahmans are not priests; but all priests *must* be Brahmans. When a Brahmanian lad reaches the age of nine, a thin, light cord, called *Janeo*, is given him after religious ceremonies and a family festal feast. This, going over the right shoulder, is continually worn around the body. It is symbolical. From the time of its adjustment by the priest, he must abstain from defilement, and engage in stated bathing and worship. Brahmans, living abstemiously, eating no meat, ignoring war, avoiding the sight of human blood, drinking no liquors, and punctually attending to worship, are considered, by the Hindoos, holy men. These Brahman priests, called *Shastris*, read the Vedas and the laws of Manu to the people. They also preside at festivals, celebrate marriages, and affix the sacred cord upon the young.

If a Brahman becomes defiled, losing caste, it can only be regained by the most mortifying penances, and submission to a tedious system of purification. We saw one of these unfortunates doing penance by crawling serpent-like on the ground, and then rising and falling again ; he actually measured his length in the streets on his way to the temple. The poor dupe was pitiably filthy. After his penances comes the bathing for purification.

India originally rooted her caste-system in the priesthood ; England based her caste upon ancestral "blue-blood;" while America is grounding hers upon wealth. The principle is abominable, and means just *this:* three men are ascending a ladder ; the middle one licks the dust from the boots of the one above him, and *kicks* the one below him !

VILLAGE LIFE. — BATHING IN THE GANGES.

The longer that missionaries and merchantmen remain in the "land of Ind," the more do they become attracted to the people, and attached to the country. Old men residing in India can hardly be induced to return to England. Book-making travelers, of the Rev. Prime school, are shamefully partial in their descriptions of the effeminate Orientals. It is chronic with these clergymen to write contemptuously of the "heathen." Idolatry in any form is deplorable; but it is just as absurd to idolize a *book* labeled "holy," as a bit of carved stone.

The native Indians are not only exceedingly social, but trusting and reverential. They are not as moral, however, as they were in the days of Warren Hastings and Sir William Jones. Their habitations, afar back from the great cities, are all clustered in villages. None reside by themselves on farms. Ditches, rather than fences, indicate boundaries. Many of their houses are mere mud hovels, the flooring matting, the furniture scarce and oddly-shapen. The wealthy clothe themselves in costly apparel; while the dresses of the poor are mere breech-cloths, the children sporting in utter nakedness. Wages are exceedingly low. Women do outdoor work the same as men, even to the carrying of dirt in baskets upon their heads, where railroads are in process of construction.

Saying nothing of the filth of the poverty-stricken classes, the Hindoos, as a nation, are noted for physical neatness. Watching them, the other morning, by the river, I silently said, "Your bathing is as natural as your breathing." Brahmans frequently bathe three times per day. The Ganges' banks, along the Ghauts, are often lined by the faithful before sunrise, performing their ablutions. The women are clad in loose, robe-like garments; the men are nude, save close-fitting *lingatees*. These Brahmans, by the way, wearing shoes open upon the top, bathing frequently, being thorough vegetarians, and considering themselves, in consequence, physically sweet and pure, complain that Europeans emit an unsavory smell — a filthy, beef-eating *odor* — from their persons, exceedingly offensive and loathsome to *all* true Brahmans. The Shakers of Mount Lebanon are no stricter peace-men or vegetarians than are these high-caste Brahmans. Often, at the family table, Hindoos stop eating for a few moments, to chant Sanscrit *sloka* — a sort of jolly thanksgiving song.

Genuine Hindoos wear neither pantaloons nor coats, but *dhotars*. Parsees wear trousers, robes, and tall, pyramidal shaped hats; and Mahommedans, long beards and turbans. Noting these costumes, the prominent races of India are easily distinguishable.

The earnest desire of even the lower castes to secure an English education is manifest by their studying along the public streets in Calcutta by gas-light. This is a nightly practice. Such Brahmans as have acquired an education teach others gratuitously. Temperate themselves, wondering at the liquor-drinking customs of Christians, and the downright drunkenness of Western nations, they even blame Jesus for "turning water into wine."

Out of the cities, profanity is unknown among the Hindoos. They have too much reverence for the Christian's "Our Father," and for their own gods, to curse and profane their names. Wealthy Hindoos have their favorite symbol-gods in their houses. A certain room is set apart, flower-perfumed, and consecrated to the household deity, once a hero or saint. On festival days of remembrance, they invite in their European acquaintances. Departing, they put garlands upon their necks, and throw flowers at their feet. In courts of justice, Hindoos brought upon the stand make a *solemn affirmation*. If there are doubts of their speaking the truth, "they swear them by the Ganges, or the sacred *Toolsi-*flower." For some of these singular customs, I am indebted to a personal acquaintance, seven years in India, inspector of schools in Ommeraottix, — famous in England only as a cotton-market.

THE ASIATIC SOCIETY.

No place in Calcutta so completely chained me as the Royal Asiatic Society, with its Museum of Ancient Art and Sculpture. If the command had read, "Thou shalt not covet thy neighbor's library," I should long ago have committed the "unpardonable sin." That eminent scholar, Sir William Jones, who went to India in 1783, established the institution, and Warren Hastings was the first president. In this immense collection of volumes, manuscripts, scrolls, and unread Oriental rolls, are treasured the priceless memorials of the past. The original building, long ago overflowing with its shelved lore, necessitated the storing of manuscripts elsewhere, with many of the precious relics. We found the assistant secretary, a native Hindoo, a most scholarly and gentlemanly man. Gladly we exchanged several books, his treating of Brahmanism, and ours of Spiritualism. All library-books were free to us during our stay in the city. But time was flying. Longingly, regretfully, we left this library, — a very monument of research and reflection, — to penetrate the heart of the country. It was nearly nightfall when we left the City of Palaces, crossing the Hoogly to Howrah, taking the East-India Railway train for the north and west. The depot was dimly lighted, the confusion disgusting, but the cars cool and comfortable. Travelers by English railways painfully miss their accustomed sleeping-cars.

UP THROUGH THE COUNTRY.

The railroad extends along the Ganges Valley up the country in a north-westerly direction, and ultimately reaching Allahabad, between the Ganges and the Jumna, where these rivers form a junction. They both rise in the Himalayas. The scenery, with its vast unfenced rice-fields, clumps of deeply-wooded jungles, hedges of cactus, grazing herds, and nestling native villages, was decidedly attractive, though dulled by sameness. Occasionally broad, rolling ridges reminded us of our fertile prairie-lands in the West. Though camels and elephants are pressed into farming-work, hump-shouldered Asian bullocks do most of the plowing, rather a light *scratching* of the soil. The flocks of sheep along the way were, with hardly an exception, black. Shepherds with bamboo rods, instead of "crooks," tended them. Northern India produces large quantities of wheat and corn.

The cultivation of the Ganges Valley is of an inferior kind. This must necessarily continue till the Hindoos become landholders, owning the proceeds of the fields they cultivate. Though the vast plains of India have scattered groves of acacia, guava, mango, palms, and other Oriental trees, there is a destitution of deep, dense forests, from the fact that, in past centuries, they were ruthlessly cut, and the fields tilled to support the over-population of the country. The telegraph-poles along the way are either of iron or stone, to prevent destruction by white ants. The prying, greedy nuisances soon found their way into our trunks.

BENARES THE BLESSED.

Reaching Mogul Serai Junction, we were soon transferred to the branch-road leading to the river whose waters were anciently thought to insure eternal life. Tread lightly, speak softly; this is the winding Ganges, and that magnificent and moss-crowned city on the western bank, with its temples, mosques, palaces, tapering domes, sacred shrines, and the Golden Temple of Siva, — guardian divinity, — is Benares, *holiest city of the Hindoos!*

All sincere religionists are to be respected. What Mecca is to the Mohammedan, Jerusalem to the Christian, and Rome to the Catholic, Benares is to the Hindoo; and the Ganges, that washes its feet, is the Eden river of immortal life. The grayed pen of antiquity failed to record the names of its founders. But, full two hundred years before the Grecian Plato discoursed in the groves skirting classic Athens, Benares was summering under the sunshine of her palmiest days, boasting of seven hundred flourishing seminaries of learning, with ambitious students from all portions of the Orient. Here metaphysicians, both Brahmans and Buddhists, held their discussions upon philosophy, the duty and destiny of humanity; and, in all probability, no keener logicians ever met upon the field of controversy.

The city of Benares, — anciently called *Kasika*, — having five thousand sacred shrines, is supposed to number some five hundred thousand inhabitants; but during festivals, or in the season when pilgrims flock thither, the population is greatly increased. *Sekrole*, the European part, about three miles from the old city, is handsomely laid out with government buildings, two English colleges, finely shaded streets, and a broad esplanade for military practice and display.

The mention of Sekrole must ever remind us of the hospitality and favors of Dr. Lazarus and his estimable family. His son, a collegiate youth, aflame with genius, informed us that his college class had quite a number of natives, ranging in years from sixteen to nineteen, nearly all of whom were married, some being the fathers of two, three, and four children. "Do these Hindoos keep up with their classes?" we inquired. "Certainly," said this student: "they even excel in mathematics, metaphysics, and moral philosophy, and would be wranglers in English colleges."

EUROPEAN METAPHYSICS OLD IN INDIA.

An English professor in Queen's College, Benares, asssured us that, reading of new methods in metaphysics, or recent mental phenomena in Germany considered *new*, and referring them to the pundits (learned Hindoos in Benares), they would turn to their Sanscrit scrolls, and, finding the same formula in metaphysics, or similar phenomena, they pronounce them *old;* and then, smiling among themselves, would add, "Western scholars are tardily following in the footsteps of our sages who lived full three thousand years ago."

The streets of Benares, as in all old Asian cities, are exceedingly narrow; but the palaces of the wealthy, the mossy ruins, the massive masonry fringing the river, and the magnificent architecture, gorgeous even in decay, beggar description. Taking an open *dinghy*, and drifting down the Ganges one morning by the city, we not only saw floating corpses, but saw them bring their dead to the burning Ghaut; saw them take the muddy waters in their mouths; saw them perform their religious ablutions and immersions, expecting, like sectarian Baptists, to wash away their sins; and saw them bring their offerings, and lay them upon the altars of their gods; and then, climbing a long stone stairway, we went up the Mohammedan Man-Mandil, on the roof of which are astronomical charts, drawn by old Indian sages; then to the Golden Temple, the domes of which are literally washed with gold; and then to the Monkey Temple, sacred to Durgha, where hundreds of monkeys are kept and petted, if not worshiped, by the lower-caste Hindoos.

EASTERN FAKIRS.

Like the dervishes of Islam, these fakirs go by various names, and belong to different orders. Some continually chant praises to Vishnu. Others, inflicting tortures upon themselves, engage in constant prayers; and others still seek to suspend the breath, restrain natural desires, and abstract the mind, preparatory to deeper communion with Brahm. While smiling at their superstitions, let us not forget their sincerity. Their subdued hearts seem to continually sing this sad refrain, —

> "Oh! where shall rest be found, —
> Rest for the weary soul?"

One of these fakirs, stopping for a night in a quiet Hindoo village, is received with profound respect. They consider him a holy man; and, after washing his feet, they supply his wants. Some of these ascetics, renouncing homes, giving away their property, fast, pray, sleep on beds of stone, and practice other severe austerities.

During our second day's wanderings in Benares, we saw in the street, under a burning sun, one of the Hindoo fakirs, — a *Gosain*, holy beggar! This branch of fanatics do penance and work merit for others, by standing on one foot, or holding up one hand, for a term of years; repeating the while pleading prayers. The one we saw, sitting cross-legged, with a three-forked tripod by his side, was exceedingly filthy. His coarse, uncombed hair was sprinkled with ashes, rice, leaves, and lotus-flowers. He kept the index finger open and fixed; his body, nearly naked, was smeared with clay; his ghastly eyes, almost closed, were turned upward; and he seemed striving to cease breathing. He speaks to no one, but "aims," said Hindoo bystanders, "to do works of merit, separate the soul from the body, and commune with God." The next morning, with one of the Benares missionaries, we strolled away some four miles, to the ruins of *Sarnath*, once a very extensive Buddhist establishment, supposed by some to have been the birthplace of Buddha; a grand old monument, with its architectural designs and elegantly carved images, still standing, and commemorating the event. We confess to admiration and veneration for such time-defying ruins. But why so dumb, O tongue of tradition? Speak, and tell us by whom, and for what purpose, were these acres of templed stone and mighty ruins once built!

ALONG THE WAY TO BOMBAY.

It is fifteen hundred miles, by rail, from Calcutta to Bombay, the two rival cities of India. Previous to reaching Bombay from Jubbulpore, famous for marble rocks, there is mountain scenery sufficiently bold and diversified to show a striking contrast to the valley of the Ganges, and others of India's lowlands through which we had passed. The country now rougher and higher, the cultivation of the lands changed, becoming better as we approached the western coast, rice-fields giving place to wheat, millet, and other grains. In Northern India, corn (*Indian maize*) does finely.

There is an extensive network of railroads in this country; and, what may seem singular, they are liberally patronized by the natives. Brahmans, Mohammedans, Sikhs, and poor Christians, rush into the "second-class" cars, riding as cozily as the caged "happy family" of Barnum memory. The steep grades, dark tunnels, dancing cascades, and heavily-wooded hillsides, reminded us of home scenery in New England.

Reaching Bombay in the waning part of the day, a glance convinced us that it was a seaport mart, aflame with business. Numbering over six hundred thousand inhabitants, this city is considered by the unprejudiced the most stirring and progressive of any in India; while the Parsees, whose forefathers brought their holy fire with them from Persia in the seventh century, now constitute one hundred thousand of the city's population. Acquisitive and enterprising, much of the mercantile traffic of the East is under their management. As there are no beggars among Shakers, Quakers, and Jews, so there are none among the Parsees.

Going out leisurely upon the esplanade in early evening, the streets are thronged with multitudes of Hindoos, Mussulmans, Parsees, Indo-Europeans, English half-castes, with occasionally a straggling American; and all either on foot, on horseback, or in *gharries*, or queer, gaudily-decorated and covered-in carriages drawn by bullocks. Costumes are gay and varied. Jewelry, even to rings in the nose, is worn in costly profusion. Wealthy Hindoos are lavish in dress, precious stones, pearls, and diamonds. The bazaars here, with their narrow streets, and filth, their trade and traffic in trinkets, silks, brocades, &c., are but a repetition of those in all Asian cities.

Bombay, built upon a cluster of islands connected one with the other and with the mainland by causeways, forming a sort of peninsula, and fanned by invigorating sea-breezes, is considered the most desirable residence for Europeans in India. The city is supplied with excellent water from Vehar Lake, some two miles out, at the foot of the Salsette Hills. Rich Europeans, and some of the missionaries, reside at the fashionable suburb, Malabar Hill, from December to February; but during the rains and hot weather, from June to September, they migrate to the highland plateaus and cool mountains.

Jesus, worn and weary under Syria's scorching skies, went up on to the mountains, not to escape the heat, and do a bit of cozy lolling around champagne-tables with Peter, James, and John, but to pray, and to heal the sick. It is deliciously comfortable to be a "Christian" in the nineteenth century. But what about that old apostolic word, the "cross"?— "bearing the cross," and suffering for the "truth's sake"?

ORIGIN OF BRAHMANISM.

The Aryans, more properly *Aryas*, meaning, in the Zend language, honorable men, — occupying the high table-lands of Central Asia, known in later times as the Plateau of Iran, — left in the pre-historic past their ancient agricultural seats, traveling westward and southward in the character of emigrants, explorers, and conquerors.

The Aryan conquest of Hindostan, effected before and during the period treated of in the Máhábhárátá, and the Rámayana, was mainly accomplished in the palmy days of those kingly chieftains known as the Máhárájás. These in the pre-Vedic period were their own priests, kindling their own altar-fires. As Thales, Solon, and Socrates were called *Sophoi*, — knowers, — the wise among the Aryans were denominated Rishis, and, in a much later period, Gymnosophists.

It is conceded by Oriental scholars that 1200 B.C. the Aryans were not only a powerful people along the banks of the Indus, but around the mouths of the Ganges, on the extreme east of India. This was the latest period that can possibly be assigned to the Rig-Veda, oldest of the four Hindoo sacred books. And yet these Aryan seers who composed the Veda speak, in their sacred works, of "older *hymns* which the fathers sang," of "ancient sages and elder gods." "They were old," says Samuel Johnson, "at the earliest epoch to which we can trace them. Their religion, like their language, was already mature when the Rishis of the Veda were born." Marriages in this period were performed by the Máhárájás, or by the father of the bride; while the Rishis — seers or wise teachers — instructed the children, offered sacrifices, and spoke comforting words over the dead.

Sacrifices have in them an underlying truth. On the higher planes of thought, they imply the consecration of the dearest possessions to the highest ideal. On the lower, superstitious stratum of life, the term "sacrifice" is made to mean the shedding of blood, and the remission of sins. The primitive Aryans offered three gifts as sacrifices, — fire, clarified butter, and the plant whose juices stimulate to a new life. The Jews offered goats and kids, heifers and rams. Certain superstitious Hindoos, in their degenerate present, engage in similar sacrifices. Enlightened men and women sacrifice strength, ease, comfort, to educate and bless humanity.

Owing to wealth, luxury, and multiplying responsibilities of the earliest Máhárájás, they employed the Rishis as substitutes in religion, — employed them to attend to the sacrificial gifts, and serve as mediums of communication between them and their gods. How natural for Rishis, seers, prophets, to slide into the attitude of priests! Thus employed, these seers, *alias* priests, soon assumed authority, and professed supernatural powers; and knowing something of philosophy, magic, astrology, and seership, they perfected an organization which resulted in the priestly or *Brahman caste*, the features of which were defined in the laws of Manu. As the Brahman priests believed in Brahm, molded the rising thought, and officiated at religious ceremonies, the religion of Hindostan was naturally denominated Brahmanism.

Aryanic in origin, 13.4 per cent of the world's religionists are Brahmans, and 31.2 per cent are Buddhists. These together make a decided majority over any religious sect on the globe. Buddhism bears something the same relation to Brahmanism that Christianity bears to Judaism. I class them together because Aryan in their origin and growth.

BELIEF OF THE ANCIENT BRAHMANS.

"There is," says Max Müller, "a remembrance of one God, breaking through the mists of idolatrous phraseology, — a monotheism which precedes the polytheism of the Veda." * Mr. Müller, who as authority is unrivaled, further says, "A Hindoo of Benares, in a lecture delivered before an English and native audience, defends his faith, and the faith of his forefathers, against such sweeping accusations" as polytheism and idolatry.

"'If by idolatry,' says this Hindoo scholar, 'is meant a system of worship which confines our ideas of the Deity to a mere image of clay or stone; which prevents our hearts from being expanded and elevated with lofty notions of the attributes of God, — if this is what is meant by idolatry, we disclaim idolatry, we abhor idolatry, and deplore the ignorance or uncharitableness of those that charge us with this groveling system of worship. . . . We really lament the ignorance or uncharitableness of those who confound our representative worship with the Phœnician, Grecian, or Roman idolatry as represented by European writers, and then charge us with polytheism in the teeth of thousands of texts in the Purânas, declaring in clear and unmistakable terms that there is but one God, who manifests himself as Brahma, Vishnu, and Rudra (Siva), in his functions of creation, preservation, and destruction.'" †

* Müller's Sanscrit Literature, p. 559.
† Müller's German Workshop, p 17.

It is the common reply of the modern Hindoo to the missionary, when accused of worshiping many gods, "Oh! these are various manifestations of the *one* God; the same as, though the sun be one in the heavens, yet he appears in multiform reflections upon the lake." That there are ignorant Hindoos who worship images, is doubtless true; and equally true that there are Roman-Catholic Christians who worship pictures and the Virgin Mary, and Protestants who worship the Bible, instead of accepting its inspired truths.

Defined in general terms, Brahmans believe in Brahm, the One self-existent, manifesting himself in the relation of creator, destroyer, preserver. Up to the present time, there have been, say these Hindoos, nine incarnations; the ninth is that of Christna, son of the virgin Devanaguy. He was begotten by the thought of Vishnu; and, at the moment of his birth, celestial music filled earth and heaven. Christna signifies, in Sanscrit, *sacred*.

"The initiated Brahman," says Manu, "should take the vow of chastity, that he may present himself at the holy sacrifice with heart and body pure." The Catholic missionary Dubois says in his work entitled "*Mœurs des Indes*," —

"Justice, humanity, good faith, compassion, disinterestedness, all the virtues, in fact, were familiar to them, and taught to others both by precept and example. Hence it comes that the Hindoos profess, at least speculatively, nearly the same moral principles as ourselves; and, if they do not practice all the reciprocal duties of men towards each other in a civilized society, it is not because they do not know them."

The sacred books of the Brahmans are rich in moral teachings; to wit: —

"Love of his fellow-creature should be the ruling principle of the just man in all his works; for such weigh most in the celestial balance."

"As the body is strengthened by muscles, the soul is fortified by virtue."

"As the earth supports those who trample it under foot, and rend its bosom with the plow, so should we *return good for evil.*"

"The virtuous man is like the gigantic banyan-tree, whose beneficent shade affords freshness and life to the plants that surround it."

Brahmans further believe the soul emanating from Brahm to be divine and immortal; and, as it was given pure from all stain, it can not re-ascend to the celestial abode till it shall have been purified from all faults committed through its union with matter. They teach universal charity, —teach that self should be secondary, and, that selfishness leads to hells and re-births; while happiness and ultimate redemption come through purity and entire self-renunciation. Benevolence and good deeds lead to homes among the gods. Some of the Vedic "hymns are addressed to deified men who had attained their divinity through beneficent work." Other of these ancient hymns treat of charity and good works as means of salvation. Listen: —

"He who keeps his food to himself has his sin to himself also."

"He who gives alms goes to the highest heavens, — goes to the gods."

"To be kind to the poor is to be greater than the greatest there."

"Mortal life ended, go thou home to the fathers, and, if thou hast deserved it, dwell in a shining body with the gods."

CHAPTER XVI.

THE RISE OF BUDDHISM IN INDIA.

BUDDHA, of the family of the Sakyas and clan of the Guatamas, was not properly a Brahman by birth, but belonged to the line of royalty. History pronounces him the son of a rajah of Kapilavastu, a kingdom probably in Nepál, near the foot of the Himalaya Mountains, north of Oudh. As a boy he was beautiful and brilliant, as a youth remarkable for his candor and contemplation. His wife was the accomplished Gopá.

Riding as a prince in his father's city, in a chariot, observing the poverty, misery, and death around him, and contemplating upon the vanity of earthly things, he contrasted all this anxiety, this misery, with the calmness and true freedom of a religious devotee, a sort of an ascetic beggar, sitting at the city gate. The sight opened in his soul a new fountain; and, though a proud prince, he threw aside his royal attire, crushed caste under his feet, and retired to a hermitage for six years.

Brahmanical theology, with its sacrifices, ceremonial practices, and Pharisaic conceits growing out of caste, early disgusted this religious enthusiast. The world was selfish and hollow. He renounced it, — renounced all pleasure, and, through humiliation and meditation, sought to conquer himself. Subjecting the lower nature to the higher, engaging in fasting, prayer, and penances, he was blessed with ecstatic visions which pointed to true knowledge — the way of salvation. Soon he became divinely illumined, and claimed the title of *Buddha*.

His first public ministry, attended with spiritual marvels, was at Benares, where he made many converts. This accounts, in all probability, for the Buddhistic ruins at Sarnath, near this sacred city of the Hindoos.

Scholars generally agree in placing his death 543 B.C.

BUDDHISTIC ETHICS.

The gist of Buddha's teaching was this: all earthly objects, cognized by the senses, are unreal. All is change, all is vanity. There's nothing but sorrow in life. This sorrow is caused by ignorance, and the flow of the passions. Accordingly, the passions must be subdued, the affections toned down, the mind enlightened, and the life consecrated to good works: *these* moral and meritorious altitudes gained, and the soul is at the threshold of salvation, the gate of divine repose, conscious rest and peace in *Nirvana*.

In addition to its prohibitory commandments, not to kill, nor steal, nor commit adultery, nor lie, nor be drunken; it enjoined such positive virtues as purity, charity, integrity, contemplation, forgiveness of injuries, equanimity of temper, and self-abnegation. In brief, holiness of life released from further transmigrations, and secured eternal salvation. *Nirvana!* Buddhism was never nihilism or atheism. Nirvana — derived from the negative *nir*, and *va*, to blow as the wind — implies calm unruffled, the peace and rest of a spent breeze, perfect felicity. Until this high position is attained, transmigrations are moral necessities.

"Buddhism," says Dr. Wuttke, "stands in history as a religion not of one people, but of humanity. It conceived in the commencement the grand idea of peacefully converting the world." While maintaining the right of religious freedom, its rejection of war and bloodshed has been absolute.

Priests and others, both men and women, ministering in spiritual things, must live celibate lives. Buddha's doctrines spread rapidly. After his death, some 543 B.C., occurring while sitting under a sàl-tree, the first general council of his followers was held to settle theological dogmas. At a third council, held in the reign of King Asoka, commencing 263 B.C., when Buddhism had become the state religion of India, the canon, or holy Scriptures, — *Tri-Pitaka*, — of the Buddhists, were drawn up, and pronounced canonical.

THE REV. MURRAY'S "CIVILIZED HEATHEN."

This distinguished Congregational clergyman, in a lyceum lecture delivered through New England upon the "Civilized Heathen," said in substance: —

"Christian civilization might profit from Buddhism, and New England and Boston might go to school to China and Canton. The underlying idea of Buddhism is a belief in the infinite capacity of the human intellect; belief in the availing of true merit, and in the development of all the human faculties. It is not a heavy, sensual religion, but one purely rational, appealing to consciousness and intellect for support. While Old England and New England have used the rack, the cell, the dungeon, the inquisition, and thousands implements of torture, there were twenty-three hundred years of Buddhism with not a drop of blood in its onward march, nor a groan along its pathway. It has never persecuted. It has never deceived the people, never practiced pious fraud, never discouraged literature, never appealed to prejudice, never used the sword. If the Buddhists are heathen, are they not *civilized heathen?* . . . Their priests depend upon voluntary subscriptions. We have homes for the sick, the poor, and the aged. But the heathen Buddhists go one step farther, and provide hospitals for sick and worn-out animals. They plant shade-trees along the way to shelter men and animals from the scorching sun. Grazing herds and all insect-life represent the divine thought. All life in their eyes is sacred. Christians entertain travelers at hotels if they pay their bills. You are respectfully received by the wealthy if you bring with you letters of introduction from aristocratic circles; but the door of the Buddhist is ever open to the stranger, with the mat and waiting pot of rice. The Burmese missionary Smith, said he 'could traverse the whole kingdom without money;' and during his missionary stay he saw no drunkenness, not an indecent act, nor an immodest gesture. Compare this with the gross, filthy, night-walking prostitution of New York or London. Unselfishness, or forgetfulness of self, is a cardinal virtue. Struggles, sufferings, and sacrifices for others' good, purify and prepare the soul for heavenly rest." And these, *these*, are the heathen Buddhists, whom Orthodox theologians have for centuries preached to perdition for not believing in Christianity, — this American Christianity that speculates, loans money, persecutes heretics, rents pews, cheats, fights, and gambles at fairs and festivals, for religion's sake. I am not writing of the Christianity of Jesus, but the civilized Christianity of America, that sends missionaries to Asia's coral strand "to convert the Buddhists."

BUDDHA AND JESUS.

The Buddhists consider Sakya Muni Guatama Buddha a much greater Saviour than Jesus Christ; because the latter, born in poverty, a carpenter's son, sought, upon Jewish authority, to enthrone himself as king; while Guatama Buddha, a king's son, laying aside royalty and a prospective crown, humbled himself, walking the companion of beggars, that he might the more effectually break down caste, reaching and enlightening the lowest classes of humanity. In preaching, Buddha continually magnified the "wheel of the law," the four great principles: —

I. There is sorrow, want, pain.
II. Examining the source of pain, he found it to be selfish desire.
III. Pain was destroyed by regulating the natural demands of life, and destroying selfish desire by self-control.
IV. The means of destroying it, in the sense of extirpation, were meditation, self-abnegation, and the practice of every virtue.

A Brahman accusing Guatama Buddha of idling away his time, neither sowing nor reaping, was met with this reply: "I do plow and sow, reaping thence fruit that is immortal."

"Where are your implements, O Guatama?"

"My field is the law; the weeds I clear away are the cleaving to life; my plow is wisdom; the seed I sow is purity; my work, attention to the precepts; my harvest, *Nirvana!*"

TEACHINGS OF BUDDHA AND HIS DISCIPLES.

"The taint worse than all others is ignorance."

"In a corrupt world each ought to be a lotus without spot."

"So long as the desire of man towards woman is not subdued, so long is his mind in bondage."

"Sin will come back upon the sinful, like fine dust thrown against the wind."

"The way of release is through the practice of the virtues."

"When the just man goes from this world to another, his good deeds receive him as friend greets friend."

"Thyself is its own defense, its own refuge; it atones for its own sins; none can purify another."

"Master thyself; so mayest thou teach others, and easily tame them, after having tamed thyself; for self is hardest to tame."

"Let us live happily, free from greed among the greedy, — *happily*, though we call nothing our own."

"Proclaim it freely to all men, — my law is a law of mercy for all. . . . Whoever loves will feel the longing to save not himself alone, but all others."

"The talk of the 'high and low castes,' of the 'pure Brahmans, the only sons of Brahma,' is nothing but sound: the four castes are equal."

"Are the Buddhas born only for the benefit of men? Have not Wisakha, and many others, entered the paths? The entrance is open for women as well as for men."

"Of all the lamps lighted in Buddha's honor, one only, brought by a poor woman, lasted through the night."

"Forsake all evil, bring forth good, master thy own thought; such is Buddha's path to end all pain."

"And you yourself must make effort. The Buddhas are but preachers."

"The good delights in this world and the next; he delights in his own work, and is happy when going on the good path."

"All we are is the result of what we have thought. If a man speaks or acts with evil thoughts, pain follows, as the wheel the foot of him who draws the carriage."

"'Better than ruling the world is the reward of the first step in virtue."

"Not even a god, not Mára nor Brahma, could change into defeat the victory of a man over himself."

The Dhammapada, otherwise "Path of Virtue," is put down as among the oldest records of the Buddhistic doctrines. Most of the above precepts are taken from it, as stars from shimmering skies. The erudite, especially of the East, believe that they either refer directly to, or fell from the inspired lips of, Guatama Buddha himself. These and other sacred writings were carefully transmitted, as canonical, by the son of King Asoka, the Constantine of Buddhism.

DECLINE OF BUDDHISM IN INDIA.

Though Buddhism arose in India, it soon spread into Ceylon, Thibet, Burmah, Siam, China, Mongolia, and the extreme north of Asia. There are few or no Buddhists at present in India. The decline commenced in certain portions of India, about 200 B.C. The subsequent *Jaina* religion, denying the authority of the Vedas, was a modified Buddhism. While the Brahmins use no language in their sacred writings but the Sanscrit, the Ceylon Buddhistic Scriptures are in *Pali*, a rich, poetical language, attaining its highest refinement near the advent of Buddha, something like 588 B.C. This *Pali*, of which Max Müller so frequently speaks, is little more than the Brahminical Sanscrit melted down to the softness of the Italian.

It was in the palmy days of the Buddhistic period that the Greeks under Alexander invaded India, 327 B.C.; shortly after which, Grecian orators visited, and Greek ambassadors resided at, the court of a distinguished Indian king. Subsequent to these invasions, Greek historians, while giving very interesting descriptions of the Brahmanical caste system, the wealth of the country, the republican tendencies of government, and the great learning of the Indian scholars, expressed the most surprise at the self-abnegation and asceticism practiced by the hermits of India. They further speak of schools of prophets, or communities where men lived abstemiously and peaceably, holding "all things in common."

The Greek and Persian invasions into India, several hundred years before Jesus' advent, opening up an interchange of learning and letters, put into our hands keys to be used in the elucidation of religious questions, growing out of the *Alexandrian School* in Egypt, where the Indian philosophy, Hellenism, and Judaism grasped in deadly conflict, affecting and coloring the future Christianity of the ages.

THE WORLD'S RELIGIONS.

Religion as a soul emotion is universal; but the expression as a sentiment, owing to organization and racial tendency, manifests itself in several great sects. The most primitive worship of all is Fetichism, or Sabaism.

This is professed by	100,000,000.
The religion of Zoroaster and Confucius	40,000,000.
Brahmanism, the original faith of India	60,000,000.
Buddhism, the reformed faith	170,000,000.
Mohammedanism	90,000,000.
Judaism	4,500,000.
The Greek Church	62,000,000.
The Roman Church	130,000,000.
The sects of Protestantism	60,000,000.

These numbers profess to be approximations only. The Tauists of China, numbering millions, are not mentioned. The Buddhists, here estimated at one hundred and seventy millions, far outnumber any other sect of religionists upon the globe. This admits of no doubt.

THE ELEPHANTA CAVES.

Shri Gunesha-aya-Namaha! — To glorious Gunesha, salutation! Gunesha, the elephant-god of India, is connected with literature as well as worship. When first reading that unrivaled work, Godfrey Higgins's Anacalypsis, I was peculiarly struck with his reference to the "Elephanta Caves of India." They are situated upon the island of Garipurix, only a few hours' sail from Bombay.

Landing, a long, winding stone stairway leads to this mountain of sculptured marvels. A stroll through these churchal-looking caverns, old Buddhistic temples, cut into a yielding, yet solid mountain rock, was a sight truly impressive, a day long to be remembered. The ceiling to the first we entered was about twenty feet high, the depth back to the rock-carved gods, Brahma, Siva, and Vishnu at the rear, something like one hundred and fifty feet by perhaps one hundred and twenty in width. The divisions, compartments, pillars, aisles, alcoves, and niches, filled with exquisitely-cut gods, and panoramic festival scenes, grim as grand, kindling the wonder of travelers, *all* literally charmed me: it was tradition in earnest, a feast to my love of antiquity. In one compartment is symbolized the Trinity, — Brahma, Siva, Vishnu, — the Christian "Three in One." In another division is Christna, with emblems referring to his incarnation. Behind the left thigh of this *god* is carved — what? the *cross*, or a heavy-hilted *sword*, which? No matter whether cross or sword, it can not fail to remind one of Abraham's position when taking an oath.

Every thing connected with these caverns inspires one with the grand and the reverential. Scores of lifelike figures, from twelve inches to fifteen feet in height, elegantly carved *in* and forming a part *of* the original rock, with corridors and tapering columns, *all* exhibit a high order of architectural talent, considering that it antedated the Christian era by several hundred years. These Buddhistic monasteries, though conceived and constructed long before the birth of Jesus, and still the resort of Hindoo pilgrims, are admirably adapted to religious meditation and anchoretic life. Many years since, the Portuguese anchoring on an adjoining island, shelled these caves for sport. "May God have mercy on their souls, and all other such Christian vandals!" Dr. Bháu Daji, a Hindoo scholar, and vice-president of the Asiatic Society of Bombay, takes a deep interest in exploring and explaining the histories of cave-cathedrals in India, to all lovers of antiquarian studies.

CHAPTER XVII.

THE BRAHMO-SOMAJ AND PARSEES. — SPIRITUALISM IN INDIA.

"THE FRIEND OF INDIA," published at Serampore, had among its selections, just before our arrival, this telling paragraph: —

"The Bombay papers contain accounts of a mania for spirit-rapping, which they say has set in among the natives there. If the statements are correct, it would not be surprising if the mania ran through India. Every thing connected with the spirit-world is a profound mystery to the native of India. He has no definite ideas as to the future. He confesses at once that it may be this or that, — he knows not what. A city with golden pavement astonishes him, but really the definiteness is what puzzles him. If spirit-rapping finds its way among such a people, we shall have queer revelations by and by. They will intensify a hundred-fold all the mysteries, and will make a thousand more. Religion will not stand in the way in the slightest degree. A Hindoo is free to examine any thing on the face of the earth, and speculate to his heart's content."

A rare tissue this of the true and the false! Hindoos, thank Heaven! are "free to examine any thing on the face of the earth." And this confession, all unwittingly made, should put to shame the churchman's bigotry. "Every thing connected with the spirit-world," however, is not a "profound mystery to the native of India." Converse with spirits is as old as the Vedas, while Indian Oriental writings generally are freighted with the teachings of inspired seers and sainted Rishis.

Opening Capt. Forsyth's volume on "Central India," I find important passages on p. 362 and others. Here is the substance: —

"Theirs — the *Bygás* — it is to hold converse with the world of spirits, who are everywhere present to the aborigines; and theirs it is also to cast omens, call for rain, and charm away disease. The Bygá — medicine-man — fully looks his character. He is tall, thin, and cadaverous, abstraction and mystery residing in his hollow eyes. A great necklace, carved from forest-kernels, marks his holy calling. Ghosts are supposed to be ever present, inciting to either good or evil. Many profess to see them. . . . These Bygá medicine-men further possess the gift of throwing themselves into a trance, during which the afflatus of the Deity is supposed to be vouchsafed to them, communicating the secrets of the future. I am thoroughly convinced [says the captain], by evidence from other quarters, that this *trance is not mere acting.*"

Mr. Tscherepanoff, a Russian scientific man, published in 1854 at St. Petersburg the result of his investigations with the lamas — Buddhist priests — in Thibet. He says, "The lamas, when applied to for the discovery of stolen or hidden things, take a little table, put one hand on it, and after nearly half an hour the table is lifted up by an invisible power, and is carried to the place where the thing in question is to be found, whether in or out of doors, where it drops, generally indicating exactly the spot where the missing article is to be found."

The missionary M. Huc says, —

"When a living Buddha is 'gone,' i. e., deceased, it is not a subject of mourning in the lamasery, for all know he will soon come back."

THE CALCUTTA SPIRITUALISTS.

Readers of the "Banner of Light" remember to have heard me speak of receiving India letters from Peary Chand Mittra, a commission-merchant, writer, and Spiritualist. It can well be imagined that it gave me much pleasure to clasp the hand of this Hindoo thinker, author, and Spiritualist; and the more so when I found his soul deeply absorbed in spirituality as against the vices of this sensuous life. The Brahmanical tinge permeating his Spiritualism had for me a thousand charms. He was for a time a writing medium; but at present his gifts pertain more to spiritual insight. He assured me that his ascended wife was as consciously present, at times, as though in her body. Parting with this excellent man, he gave us, besides other presents, a small volume from his pen entitled "The Development of the Female Mind in India." Perusing, I find it rich in historic references to woman's independence in the Vedic period,—the golden age of the Aryans.

Mohindro Saul Paul and Romanath Senx—two interesting young gentlemen connected with the higher castes—called upon us several times to converse of Spiritual phenomena in America, and the best methods of holding private séances. Conversant with the Spiritualistic literature of England through James Burns, these young men are Spiritualists; and yet they have never witnessed a shred of the phenomenal. A correspondence was agreed upon with these gentlemanly Hindoos. Are we not brothers *all?*

Shibchunder Deb—another devoted Spiritualist, introduced by P. C. Mittra—presented us a neat volume that he had recently published upon Spiritualism. It contains liberal extracts from American authors; in fact, the works of Davis, Tuttle, Sargent, Denton, Edmonds, and others, are well known in India. This gentleman has also translated Emma Hardinge-Britten's "Spiritual Commandments" into the Bengalese language; and they are now being circulated as a tract in India. We saw several Hindoo *healers* relieving the sick in the streets.

Expressing regrets that I had not a copy of the "Seers" to tender him in turn for his valuable volume, smiling, he said, "I have read 'The Seers of the Ages,' and others of your later works, quite a number of which have reached our country from Mr. Burns's publishing house in London." So courage, brave fellow-workers all, courage! Your pens preach where your eloquent tongues are never heard.

India's better class of minds — metaphysical and contemplative — are singularly adapted to accept the harmonial philosophy. It is a common saying that "Hindoos, educated in English colleges, return to India theists and pantheists." Though willing enough to believe in Jesus as one of the Asiatic saviors and prophets, they can not believe in the immaculate conception and vicarious atonement. Oh that there were self-sacrifice, sufficient liberality, generous enthusiasm, and missionary spirit, among Americans, to send Spiritualist papers, pamphlets, books, and lecturers even, to India, to disseminate the beautiful principles of brotherhood, free thought, and a present spirit ministry! The seed has already been sown by the angels; there are many Spiritualists in different parts of this great country: can they, *will* they not perfect organizations, and thus come into working order?

THE ABORIGINES OF INDIA. — A SAGE-LIKE SPIRIT'S COMMUNICATION.

As the present is born of the *past*, I am ever anxious, so far as possible, to get at the foundations of the old civilizations and religions; and for the reason that many of them were so far in advance of ours in this boastful nineteenth century. Comparative philology, coins, and inscriptions upon monuments, with the testimony of ancient spirits, — *these* must decide upon the *status* of the pre-historic periods. Sitting one evening by the side of Dr. Dunn aboard the steamer "Aretusa" in the Arabian Sea, reflecting how the rude, stalwart Northmen descended upon cultured Rome in the long ago, and pondering upon the thought that physical "might makes right," the doctor all unexpectedly became entranced. The controlling spirit, bowing low after the Oriental manner, said, —

"Good evening, stranger. I see you are wrapped in meditation; perhaps my coming is an intrusion."

Not in the least, sir; am glad to welcome you.

"The origin and destiny of races is a subject of vast import. I lived in *Hindusta*, the land of plenty, — now called India, — about four thousand years ago. We spoke the *Sansar*, the language of the sun, — vulgarized into Sanscrit. It was the language of sounds, and compassed the uttered emotions of man, beast, insect. The most learned *savants* of my time professed to understand the out-breathed and meaning sounds — pleasure, pain, desires — of all animated life. Generally poets understood one part, Rishis another, metaphysicians still another; but none knew it *all*, for it was the study of more than a single life. Our government, embracing a portion of Africa, Egypt, Assyria, Persia, and India, was patriarchal; the emperor being considered a father, under whom were kings over smaller divisions, lords of cities, and head men of villages. This extensive government, having no coin currency, and transacting business, even of a commercial character, upon the principle of *equivalents*, was largely sustained by voluntary contributions. A moderate competency was regarded a sufficiency with my countrymen.

"Indeed, it was a maxim among us that man wants only what he lives upon; and accordingly at the end of the year each city, village, and family paid over to the government all its surplus produce and treasures of every kind. And then, in times of scarcity or famine, the government, upon the principle of compensation, supported the people from its public granaries and accumulated stores. Disputes were settled by arbitration. Capital punishment was unknown among us.

"The Aryans, or rather the *Aryas*, who came down from the north, were among the first of the blood-spilling nations. They were the lower, athletic classes, the rovingly disposed, in Central and Northern Asia, speaking a mongrel Sanscrit. Their descent into India was long after my time. Our system of marriage was monogamic; after this came polyandry, the marriage of one woman to many men, of which your histories speak; still later came polygamy, which, as you are aware, continues in many countries. We worshiped one God, incarnate in all things. The pyramids, of which in due time you shall know more, were built before my time on earth."

Pardon me, but had you commerce in that age?

"Yea: we not only carried on shipping with Africa and other foreign countries, but had extensive canals through India, Egypt, and other portions of Africa. Some of these countries have been greatly changed by convulsions since I left the body. We counted time by sun-changes, and long periods by the reigns of emperors. Literature was patronized among us, and beggary unknown. I lived through about eighty *sun-changes*, or years according to your reckoning. We understood spirit-communion, and many of us held mediumistic converse with spirits. I was cognizant, long after my ascension to the heavenly life, of the spirit-world's raising up, some two thousand years since, through inspirational and magnetic processes, an Israelitish Nazarene, a *prophet*, to spiritually enlighten his people, and afterwards the nations of the earth. He was guarded by angels, and guided by the spirit of truth. There have been many ages of iron and ages of gold. Nations are ever rising and descending as do waves upon fathomless oceans."

There, reader, is the communication — the sentiments, at least — with much of the language *verbatim*. Take it as I did, with all other spirit communications, for what it is worth, weighed by reason, and sound, practical judgment.

"Is there any historic evidence," says one, "of non-Aryan races with culture and literature, inhabiting India long before the Aryans came down from the north?" Certainly there is. We have room for only this from Prof. E. Lethbridge, M.A., Oxford, and now professor in a Calcutta College. He says (" History of India," pp. 17, 18) : —

"Remnants of a large population, non-Aryan in origin, yet hardly, if at all, less civilized and polished than the Aryans, are found among the hills and river-basins south of the mountain-ranges. Their personal appearance testifies that they are not connected, by descent, with the Aryans; while their language proves decisively that they belong to an entire different race. It has been called Dravidian, — the language *Telugu;* others term it *Támil.* . . . The architectural and other remains that are scattered over the country, and the state of the language, confirm the traditions that the Tamilian race attained a high state of civilization in *very remote ages, probably long before the Aryan invasion of India.*"

ALLAHABAD.

"India of the East, o'er whose valleys sweet
Too quickly pass my ever-wandering feet,
Ere yet your shores in lengthening distance fade,
Let faithful Memory lend my pen her aid."

Unfortunately, it was long after nightfall when we crossed the magnificent bridge spanning the Jumna, to enter *Allahabad,* "the City of God," anciently called by the Hindoos *Prayaga.* Here, at the junction of the Ganges and Jumna, is the great fortress, built on the ruins of an old Hindoo fort by Akbar, a Mogul emperor, reigning about three hundred years ago. Travelers consider this — because of wide, well-shaded streets, beautiful avenues, mausoleums, and marble domes, commemorating Mohammedan glory — the handsomest city in India.

Historically speaking, it should be remembered that there were five Mohammedan invasions into India, the first being one of disgraceful plunder and downright murder. Mussulman power was not established to any great extent till nearly the twelfth century. Sultan Mahmoud, of Ghazin, fought seventeen distinct campaigns in India, carrying away immense treasures to enrich his country. His zeal in destroying idols gave him the name of "Iconoclast," — *the image-breaker*. There is a deep, silent hatred existing between the Hindoos and Mohammedans, and yet they peaceably worship side by side.

Allahabad is a wonderful resort for pilgrims. It is said that a million are sometimes encamped about the city. Some of the Brahmanical priests are evidently very saintly men; others, doubtless, encourage these pilgrimages and festivals from avaricious motives. Priestcraft is the same in all countries. It is two hundred and fifty miles from Allahabad to Agra, world-famed for the Taj, — a tomb of exquisite and unparalleled magnificence. The structure, peerless and unrivaled, was built at a cost of fifteen million dollars, to immortalize the memory of a woman, — Noor Mahal, — the favorite wife of Emperor Shah Jehan. This Mogul ruler was the grandson of Akbar, who was sufficiently enlightened to patronize literature, and tolerate all religions. Nowhere on earth has human dust been buried in style and grandeur so sublime. Here at the Taj lie the forms of emperor and empress beneath a splendid dome, "each in a couch of almost transparent marble," set with precious stones, topaz, ruby, jasper, carnelian, chalcedony, all beautifully inwrought in running vines and blossoming flowers. It is said that the whole of the Koran in Arabic is most skillfully wrought in gemmed mosaics into this templed tomb; and *all* for what? To perpetuate in memory the pitiable pride and vanity of mortals even in death! Were there no ignorant to be educated, no hungry to be fed, and no thirsty to give a cup of water, in Shah Jehan's time? Looked down upon from the spirit-land, this tomb can only be a sting!

THE BRAHMO-SOMAJ WORSHIPERS.

As progress in all countries necessarily interests Americans, they must like to know more of the Brahmo-Somaj, — "Society of God," and real theistic church of India, — originally founded by Rajah Rahmohun Roy, a distinguished Hindoo reformer of the Brahman caste. Being a fine scholar, versed in the *Sanserit*, he became convinced that the earliest Vedas taught a system of pure theism. Thus believing, he wrote against the "idolatry of all religions," encouraged education, advocated free thought, and opposed *suttée*, — voluntary widow-burning, then a common practice in India. Universally esteemed, Rahmohun Roy died while on a visit to England in 1833.

These first Hindoo reformers, though exceedingly liberal in most matters, firmly believed the Vedas to be the infallible word of God. Ere long, however, some doubting the infallibility of the Vedic scriptures, four young yet scholarly pundits were sent to Benares to study and copy from the four Vedas. This research dispelled the gathering fog of infallibility; and the Brahmo-Somaj, numbering many of the choicest intellects in India, ceased to be a Vedantic church. From this time the sacred books of all nations were taken for what they were worth, and no more.

No band of reformers, whether in India or America, can expect to ever sail on sunny seas. Storms, petty dissensions, will arise; some within, others without. Social persecution from orthodox Hindoos lifted its hydra head; and a partial eclipse came on, followed by indifference to the interests of theism.

At this critical hour there came upon the stage a caste Hindoo, and graduate from the Presidency College, *Baboo Keshub Chunder Sen*. This religiously inclined scholar, reading and admiring English literature, and the works of Theodore Parker, soon shook off every vestige of idolatrous superstition, becoming a stanch theist. Connecting himself with the Brahmo-Somaj, he quite unconsciously found himself in a short time a leader in their ranks. Expressed in a sentence, these Brahmo-Somaj worshipers are simply radical Unitarians, practicing the same order of Sunday worship, only engaging in more singing. Among their innovations are the equality of women, the ignoring of caste, the rejection of the "sacred thread," and the performance of the marriage ceremony without absurd Hindoo rites.

When proud Brahmanical Hindoos found that these iconoclastic Brahmos not only denied the infallibility of the Vedas, but did not respect the custom of child-marriage, nor cherish faith in Hindoo theology generally, they reproached them as heretics. On the other hand, "when Christians find," says Keshub Chunder Sen, "that Brahmos call in question the authority of the Bible, dispute the divinity of Jesus, and freely criticise Christian doctrines held in reverence by the best and wisest of Europe, an utter *contempt* is felt for the poor, misguided, presumptuous theists of India, whom the Rev. Dr. Duff styled as 'striplings on the banks of the River Ganges.'"

Here are sketches from their articles of belief: —

"God is spirit, not matter. He is perfect, infinite, and eternal. He is omnipresent, omnipotent, omniscient, all-merciful, all-blissful, and holy. He is our Father.

"The soul is immortal. Death is only the dissolution of the body: the soul lives everlastingly in God. There is no new birth after death: the life hereafter is only the continuation and development of the present life. Each soul departs from this world with its virtues and sins, and gradually advances in the path of eternal progress while realizing their effects.

"Brahmoism is distinct from all other systems of religion; yet it is the essence of all. It is based on the constitution of man, and is therefore ancient, eternal, and universal. It is not sectarian, not confined to age or country.

"All mankind are of one caste, and all are equally entitled to embrace the Brahmo religion. Every sinner must suffer the consequences of his own sins sooner or later, in this world or in the next; for the moral law is unchangeable, and God's justice irreversible.

"It is the aim of the Brahmo religion to extinguish caste hatred and animosity, and bind all mankind into one fraternity,—one brotherhood of *souls*."

The Brahmos, having quite a number of organizations in India, publish a theistic annual, print six or seven journals, and send out missionaries into different parts of the country. They also have branch associations in England, Belgium, Holland, Italy, Spain, and the United States; the president of the latter being Rev. O. B. Frothingham, and the secretary, Rev. W. B. Potter. The attitude of these Indian Liberalists is exceedingly friendly and cordial toward Spiritualism.

This religious movement, originating as it did among the Brahmans of India, is one fraught with vital importance. And while tendering to the Brahmos of the East and all parts of the world the hand of hearty fellowship; hoping for their growth in peace, purity, and that charity which crowns the Christian graces,—I sincerely pray that they may "add to their faith" *knowledge*, knowledge of a conscious immortality through the present ministry of spirits; thus preparing them to "go on unto perfection," holding "all things in common," and living daily the "resurrection life."

Already more than a year has passed since leaving my native home. Time flies. August days are upon me; and I must take my departure from this ancient mother-country of civilizations and religions. Egypt and Palestine are before me. But, dear old India! land of my early dreams, receptacle of Oriental learning, and the most interesting of all the countries my eyes have yet seen, I leave you reluctantly, sorrowingly. Peace, *peace*, be unto you,—*peace* from God and his good angels!

THE PARSEES.

Youth is the dreamland of life. Reading, when an academic student, of the famous Persian King Darius, contemporary of Buddha, leading an invading army into India, and also of Zoroaster the great Persian religionist, implanted in my soul a deep desire to know something practically of Persian character and religion. Next to Central Persia itself, India, containing over a hundred thousand "fire-worshipers," was just the place, inasmuch as they tenaciously retain most of the customs of their ancestors. Exceedingly clannish, dressing in Oriental, robe-shaped apparel, generally white, the Parsees do not intermarry with other nations, nor do they like to eat food prepared by other people. They consider themselves the chosen of God, and the subjects of special angel ministry. Fair-complexioned, their general appearance is graceful and commanding. They are the Jews of Bombay, the bankers, the money-lenders, the traders. On Malabar Hill they have great wealth and elegant villas. Pious Parsees pray sixteen times each day, maintain their own schools, and take care of their own poor.

ZOROASTER, FOUNDER OF THE PARSEE FAITH.

It is difficult to determine with exactness the precise period of the world's saviors. That eminent Oriental scholar, M. Haug, puts Zoroaster — Zarathustra Spitama — 2300 B.C., thus antedating Moses. But far better authorities than Haug or Rénan are the earliest Greek writers. It is a momentous consideration, that all the Greek authors who wrote upon the Magi and the Parsee religion, previous to the Christian era, put Zoroaster back to a period of full six thousand years B.C.

Xanthos of Lydia, one of the first writers upon the subject, living about 450 B.C., was a younger contemporary of Darius and Xerxes. His reckoning makes Zoroaster to have been living at a period nearly 6500 B.C.

Aristotle, the philosopher and teacher of Alexander the Great, states that Zoroaster lived about six thousand years before the death of Plato (348 B.C.), which would carry us to about 6350 B.C. Eudoxus, Harmodorus, and other Grecian writers, made similar calculations.

Hermippus of Smyrna, one of the most ancient authorities among the Greeks upon the religion of the Magi, lived about 250 B.C., making the Zoroastrian books the study of his life. This Hermippus, according to Pliny, was informed by his teacher, Agonakes, a Magian priest, that Zoroaster lived about five thousand years before the Trojan war, occurring 1180 B.C. This would take Zoroaster back to 6180 B.C.

That there was a Zoroaster in the time of Hystaspes, Darius' father, is not disputed. Zoroaster was a common name in Persia, as was Jesus in Syrian countries. But Zoroaster of the Avesta, the prophet and founder of the Parsee religion, flourished more than eight thousand years since.

RELIGIOUS DOCTRINES OF THE PARSEES.

Conversing with Ichangir Burjorji Vacha, a Parsee Oriental scholar of Bombay, and perusing the books he so kindly presented, the following is submitted as a general statement of their religious opinions: —

They believe in one God, eternal, invisible, — Ahura-Mazda, unity in duality. Ormuzd, the "highest of spirits," was a tutelary divinity, as was the Jehovah of the Old Testament. This God, Ahura-Mazda, infinitely wise and good, punishes the sinful, and rewards the virtuous for their good deeds. Their theology knows nothing of any sin-atoning Saviour. Their fire-temples have no pulpits. Their priests are teachers, abounding in prayers.

Zoroaster was the exalted prophet, the chief of the wise, who wrought miracles, who taught men to pray with their faces towards the light, who enjoined upon men to practice good deeds, and look for a reckoning on the fourth morning after death.

There are both good and evil spirits. The wise ask the protection of their guardian angels. The truly pious guard the sacred fire, bathe often, avoid pollution, encourage knowledge, and perform acts of beneficence. The Kusti and the Sudra form the badge of the Parsee worshipers. The Sudra is a plain, robe-like vest reaching to the knees; the Kusti a hollow woolen cord, woven by women of the priest-caste only, and consisting of seventy-two threads in the warp. The Kusti, blessed of the priests, is tied over the Sudra, and wound three times around the waist. The *Nirang*, or the use of Nirang during the first morning prayer, is not enjoined in the Avesta; nor is it practiced by the progressive Parsees of Bombay or Persia. Previous to prayers, they wash the face and hands. Each month of the year is named after an angel. All prayers are recited in the Zend language. The Parsees are not polygamists, but strictly monogamists.

PARSEE CEMETERIES, AND THE VULTURES THAT DEVOUR THEIR DEAD.

The Persian method of disposing of their dead must, to an American believing in the evangelical doctrine of the resurrection of the body, be absolutely revolting. The Parsee cemetery in Bombay, *Dokma*, situated several miles from the center of the city, is designated by some writers "the Tower of Silence." The area devoted to this purpose is located on the north-east crest of Malabar Hill, and surrounded by thick walls some thirty feet high, within which are walks, flowers, seats for meditation, and tall, round stone towers, capped with descending, concave-shapen gratings. Upon these the bodies of their dead are placed, and left to return to the elements, or be devoured by the scavenger-birds of the East. Flocks of these filthy, flesh-eating birds are said to be ever in waiting for a corpse. All avenues to these "*Towers of Silence*" are carefully guarded. Parsees themselves, even the mourners, are not permitted to enter the gateways leading to these cemeteries: only priests and a certain caste, "bearers of the dead," officiate within the walls. When suns and rains have changed, and ugly vultures torn and devoured, the flesh of these exposed bodies, the bones slide down into deep sepulchral vaults.

Owing to diet and bathing, the Parsees are long-lived. They eat neither pork, beef, nor meat of any kind. Holidays are employed in prayers and feasts. When a Parsee dies, prayers are offered at the house. The soul goes to heaven, and the body must not be tainted with corruption. Therefore it is at once washed, purified, dressed in white, and borne by the dead-bearers to the Towers of Silence. There are six of these within the walled inclosure, which overlook bungalows, public buildings, forests of palm-trees, Elephanta, and other mountain-islands studding the deep waters.

THEIR TEMPLES, ALTAR, AND FIRE.

There is little in style or architecture to outwardly distinguish a Parsee temple from a Jewish synagogue. Their edifices in all countries are considered consecrated to worship, to prayer, and the "sacred fire" originally from heaven through their prophet Zoroaster. They do not worship this *fire*, but consider it, as they do the sun, a symbol of the infinite Light, that "*eternal fire*" which must ultimately burn up the dross of the universe. Though the mosaic floors of Parsee temples are never paced by unholy feet, nor their perpetual fires seen by infidel eyes, the following description, paradoxical as it may seem, is dictated by one who has explored their temples, and gazed upon their sacred fire, ever burning in the innermost sanctuary: —

Within their temples are three courts, Parsees themselves entering only the outer. The high priest with veiled face, that his breath even may not pollute, approaches alone to see and feed the fire with sandal, precious woods, and fragrant spices. Those in the second, or intermediate court behold a dimmed reflection; while those in the inner court only catch a glimpse of the light from the altar, and freely breathe the incense-fumes of the spice-woods. Their altars are of stone, and parallelogram-shaped; some rough-hewn, and others choicely polished, shining like alabaster. On the top of the altar is an excavation, or hollowing-out for the fire. On one side of the altar is an exquisitely carved figure of the sun; on the opposite side, creation, or chaos unfolding into *Kosmos;* on one end is a high tower, with a human form chiseled thereon, catching the first rays of the rising sun, signifying the entrance of the spirit into the light of immortality; and on the other side is a shadowy reflection of the sun fading away into total darkness, prefiguring *Hades*, the under-world of darkness and destruction. As no good Mohammedan drinks wine, nor Jew eats swine's flesh, so no Parsee smokes tobacco. Such a use of *fire*, applied to a weed, would be both a disgrace and a desecration.

CHAPTER XVIII.

FROM INDIA TO ARABIA. — ADEN AND THE ARABS.

THE usual sailing distance from Bombay across the Indian Ocean to Aden, a seacoast city of Arabia, is some seventeen hundred miles; but our Austrian captain commanding the steamer "Aretusa," considering the fierceness of the monsoons at this season, decided upon the southern course, making the route full twenty-five hundred miles, and subjecting us to an eighteen-days' drag upon the deep!

This Aden in "Araby the Blest" is called the "Gibraltar of the East," because so thoroughly fortified, and consequently prepared to manage any military movements on the Red Sea. Though once held by the Portuguese, afterwards by the Turks, and now by the English, it has ever been a city of sand, nestling at the feet of volcanic peaks, and destitute of vegetation, even to a blade of grass.

Dreary and desert-looking, Aden claims a population of twenty thousand; the cantonment portion of which, being five miles from the landing, is cozily located in the crescent-shaped crater of an old, extinct volcano. It is a great mart for ostrich-feathers. Rumor declares that it rains here but once in three years.

Owing to the protracted droughts, those holding this barren place in the sixth century excavated immense reservoirs in the rocks at the foot of the mountains, for the tardy yet heavy rains to fill. Still in preservation, and called the "ten tanks," they are largely utilized to supply the present demands of the city. Standing upon heated sands, by the lowest of these tanks, surrounded by donkeys, camels, and Arabs, never did water taste sweeter to parched lips.

Back into Arabia, about seven miles from Aden, there begins to be quite a show of vegetable life. Oases multiply and widen, till farther on are green fields, small trees, and living streams, along which Arabs pitch their nightly tents. Thirty miles from the city is a fine river, which English enterprise thinks of turning into Aden.

Arabia is not the vast, barren desert once supposed. In the interior, and among the mountainous portions, are beautiful rivers, dense forests, vast pasture-lands, with choice fruits and grains.

ARABIC LITERATURE.

No traveler can say much in favor of the Arab character. The Bedouins, athletic, stout, treacherous, and roving, — wild men of the desert portions, — are the degenerate sons of Araby's better days. Like all Eastern countries, this, too, had its golden age, its period of literature and fine arts.

While the sacred canon of the Mohammedans was in Arabic, the great bulk of their general literature has been in the flowing and more musical Persian. During the latter part of the dark ages in Europe, the Arabs were the chief cultivators of science; their literature having previously attained a high stage of development. They excelled in chemistry, mathematics, history, and poetry. One of their poets, Ferdansi, has been compared to Homer.

Whewell, in his "Ethics of Sir James MacIntosh," says : —

"In the first moiety of the middle ages, distinguished Mohammedan Arabians, among whom two are known to us by the names of Aviesura and Averroes, translated the ancient Peripatetic writings into their own language, expounded their doctrines, in no servile spirit, to their followers, and enabled the *European Christians* to make those translations of them from Arabic into Latin, which in the eleventh and twelfth centuries gave birth to the scholastic philosophy."

This is Aug. 8, and we ship this afternoon for the Red Sea and Egypt.

> "We'll away to Egypt, and rest awhile
> In palm-girt palace beside the Nile,
> And watch from our roof Canopus rise
> In silver splendor 'mid opal skies."

PARTING: STEAMING ALONG THE RED SEA.

We sailed into the Red Sea through the Straits of Bab-el-Mandeb, — "the gate of tears," — so named, doubtless, from the dangers of the sea; which, while lacking a sufficient number of light-houses, abounds in African coast-winds, rough coral-reefs, and half-hidden rocks, ever the terror of navigators.

Steaming northward, the third day out, and rising with the gray gleams of morning, I had another magnificent view of the Southern Cross, hanging low in the hazy south-west distance. A few nights and mornings thereafter, and it faded from our sight forever; or, at least, till seen by us with unsealed eyes from the evergreen shores of the Morning Land.

The withering heat upon the Red Sea was almost beyond human endurance. The winds, sweeping from African sands west of us, fell upon our panting persons at noonday like breaths of fire. Thermometer measurements showed that the mercury stood in the sea-water at 90°, and in the air, from 95° to 115° in the shade.

Approaching the terminus of this sea, and standing upon the ship's deck in the Gulf of Suez, one sees, lying to the east and west, bald, arid deserts, and shrubless mountain ridges, warm in each morning's glow, and at noon a tremulous *mirage* of burning, glistening mirrors. Farewell, O sea of fire!

For several miles out from the Suez landing, the sea is only from a mile to two and three miles in width. A roughly-cut and rugged mountain shuts in the desert upon the left; while from a projecting tongue upon the Egyptian side, to a corresponding point upon the Arabian, the Israelites, led by Moses, are supposed to have crossed. Soundings at the present time show six fathoms of water. Sands are ever shifting in these Eastern seas: accordingly, a few thousand years ago, there might *not* have been six *feet* of water at this point. And then, again, the heavy north winds pushing, piling the waters southward with a six-feet ebb tide, the Israelites might easily have crossed upon dry land. On the other hand, a sudden change of wind, the inflowing tide, with a *not* uncommon "water-whirlwind," would naturally overwhelm and submerge the advancing Egyptians. Admitting the literal truth, therefore, of the scriptural record, no miracle was necessary for the preservation of one, or the destruction of the other party. Miracles, defined as abrogations of natural laws, are simply impossibilities.

SINAI.

Naturally skeptical, unbelief arose when our kind-hearted captain of "The Aretusa" — who, by the way, is an Austrian Spiritualist, well read in the works of Allan Kardec — pointed out to us the mountain that, 'mid reported convulsions of nature, saw the "law inscribed on tables of stone." Doubts in abeyance for the time being! Previous to reaching Suez, there loomed up in the haze upon the Arabian side grim and bald mountainous peaks, the highest and most forbidding of which is pronounced to be the Mount Sinai of the Pentateuch. Hushed forever are those thunders; lost are the voices of the Syrian prophets; and the land once flowing with milk and honey is but a desert waste. Near the foot of this ragged Sinai range is the site of Moses' wells; and bright, green spots they are, — the only verdure visible. Here it was — so say Jews and Mohammedans — that the Israelites quenched their thirst, while Jehovah displayed his power in drowning the wicked Egyptians. This Jehovah of the Old Testament, the war-god of Christians, must have been an incorrigible sinner, if the peace principles of Jesus are divine.

SUEZ AND ITS SANDS.

Mostly a straggling mass of low mud houses, this city of ten thousand inhabitants, including some three hundred Europeans, is surrounded by a desert region, and naturally repulsive to an American. One good hotel, the "Suez," with any number of disreputable ones, a tall mosque tower, a square with no shrubbery, and bazaars full of Oriental goods, with Copts and Arabs for salesmen, tell the story of the place. Not to mention fleas and lizards, one becomes disgusted while looking at the sand-clad children who brush the flies from their sore, gummy eyes, to look upon the traveler, and cry "Backsheesh!" Evidently the glare of the noonday sun, and the flying sand, have as much to do with the eye-diseases of Egypt, as syphilis and other scrofulous taints. Begging is a profession in Suez. Healthy Arab lads will follow you, shouting, "Backsheesh!" while old men, hoary, ragged, and toothless, hobble along after one, muttering, "Backsheesh!" It is not strange that the Israelites wanted to leave this part of the country.

THE SUEZ CANAL.

Just previous to dropping anchor at Suez, our eye caught a glimpse of a faint blue thread stretching away into the desert toward the north. It was that modern triumph of genius, the Suez Canal. Observing ships dragging slowly around the coast of Africa and the Cape of Good Hope, and through the Indian Ocean, for the East, that enterprising French engineer, M. F. de Lesseps, proposed to Mohammed Said to re-open the ancient canal of Sesostris. Be it remembered that two, three, and five thousand years ago, when Europe had no history, Egypt not only had her *canal* through the lakes across the isthmus, — remnants of the ruins still remaining, — but proud old Egypt had other canals, with an extensive commerce.

This canal, uniting the Mediterranean with the Red Sea and the vast waters of the Indian Ocean, one hundred miles in length, three hundred and twenty feet in width at the top, two hundred and forty-six feet at the bottom, and twenty-six feet deep, was formally opened on the 13th of October, 1867. At this time, as fortune would have it, we were in Constantinople, privileged to see the Austrian Francis Joseph, the Prussian Frederick William, the Italian Amadeus, now ex-King of Spain, with others in authority, on their way to the *fêtes* and festivities consequent upon the interesting occasion. Prophetic politicians, Lord Palmerston, and English aristocrats, to the contrary, the Suez Canal is a grand success.

Formerly five thousand vessels sailed to India every year around the Cape of Good Hope. Now over a thousand of these pass through the Suez Canal; and the number will increase, especially since the tolls are so fairly assessed. By this canal the distance between London and Bombay has been reduced to 3,050 miles, from 5,950 by the Cape. This canal, a colossal work, was built at an expense of sixty millions of dollars, one-half of which was contributed by the Khedive himself. Such ambition is laudable.

Considering the shifting nature of the sand, the heated barrenness of the desert, the difficulty in procuring fresh water, no one can gaze upon the numerous steamers — English screws of two thousand tons and more — driving along this desert-cut furrow filled with water, and not admire the skill of the French engineer, and the enterprise of the Khedive. Egypt that was, and then was *not*, is now waking from the dreamy slumbers of weary centuries.

FROM SUEZ TO CAIRO.

The Dead, Red, and Mediterranean Seas evidently constituted, in the almost measureless past, one body of water. At a later period the Red and Mediterranean Seas were united, as the sandy contour of the country each side of the isthmus plainly indicates.

It is about one hundred and fifty miles, if memory serves me, by railway from Suez to Cairo, much of the way lying across vast sand-plains, with only an occasional oasis. Let us hasten. Here is a patch of palms: how drooping they look! There is a slowly-pacing caravan: how patient the poor camels! There are tenting Arabs; there a lonely pelican; there camels and donkeys browsing on a sort of sagebrush; there a squad of Egyptian soldiers; there a storm of sand whirling across our track; and here a mud-built village, a very hive of squalid humanity. Around it cluster dates, figs, plums, and flourishing vegetation, the results of energy and irrigation. Many of the desert tracts of the East may, by this and other methods, be reclaimed, and made to blossom as the rose.

But see! there are piles of old, moldering ruins; there crumbling walls, and prostrate pillars! What a field for exploration! How often ancient spirits have told us of sand-buried cities! Surely, this was not once the picture of desolation that it now is. Oh the sand, the scorching sand! On this August day the thermometer stands at 136° Fahrenheit. It is living at a poor "dying rate!"

But we are on the way to the Nile. Wonder if this is the route the patriarch Abraham took when going down to Egypt to escape the famine? And was it anywhere in this locality that, returning from the "slaughter of the kings," he met Melchisedec, the king of peace, the baptized of Christ?

Worn and weary, this day's railway travel across sands reminded me of the Arabian sheik's prayer. "An Arab," says Saadi, "journeying across a vast desert, wearily exclaimed, 'I pray that, before I die, this my desire may be fulfilled: that, a river dashing its waves against my knees, I may fill my leathern sack with water!'"

CHAPTER XIX.

THE CITY OF CAIRO. — EGYPT.

DELICIOUSLY gratifying was it to gradually leave the sands, and approach, with the lengthening shadows of the day, the wide and fertile Valley of the Nile. It was nearly twilight when the train reached the city; and yet, on our way in the carriage to the Oriental Hotel, we caught a distinct view of Cheops and Belzoni, — two of the great pyramids. The sight shot a thrill of satisfaction into my being's core.

August 18. — This, in one sense at least, was an auspicious time to reach Cairo, because the third night of the yearly illumination in honor of the Viceroy of Egypt. The estimated expenditure for the display was half a million.

They dine in the East at eight o'clock. Strolling out in evening-time, after dinner, accompanied by an Egyptian guide and Dr. Dunn, I mentally asked, "Is not this dreamland? the lotus-clime of the poet? the palace realm of the 'Arabian Nights'?" Bright globed and various colored lights were distributed through the gardens, and along the streets, arching the avenues, whitening the pavements, flickering in the branches, and sending silvered shafts down into playing fountains; while rockets, serpents, revolving wheels, and other kinds of fireworks, blazed out upon the night, half paling, for a time, torch and lamps. Not only were triangular and pyramidal-shaped figures hung with glass lanterns, trimmed and illumined, but theaters, palaces, mosques, up to the very summits of their minarets seemed all ablaze with a weird, gaseous brightness. The streets and lanes, fringed for miles with flags, banners, and costly tapestry and transparencies, were literally thronged with carriages and giddily-gaping multitudes, some in rags, some in silks and satins, and others in the gilded trappings of state. Seen externally, it was a most magnificent pageant. Considered spiritually, it was the quintessence of babyish folly, — the glittering pampering so pleasing to vain royalty. This half million, worse than squandered, should have been spent in educating ignorant subjects, freeing the country from slavery, and feeding the wretched street-beggars.

Disgusted with the confusion, the wild excitement, and the sham of the show, I returned to my apartment to meditate.

Is it a dream? or am I really in Egypt, the country of Hermes, Trismegistus, and Menes the founder of Memphis? Am I in the land of ancient symbolical art, of hieroglyphs, obelisks, pyramids, and paintings, of monoliths, sarcophagi, and templed tombs? Changed, oh, how changed during the devastating decades of two, three, and five thousand years! The sacred Nile still moves on in silent majesty; but no wandering Isis weeps, searching for the dead Osiris.* The shadow of Typhon's frown falls no more upon the tremulous waves of this great rolling river. The lips of Memnon, touched, smitten even by rising sunbeams, remain voiceless as the sphinx that gazes coldly out upon the vast granary-valley of Egypt. Cleopatra and the kingly Ptolemies are only dimly, dreamily remembered; but those marvels of towering masonry, those *pillared Pyramids*, though stripped of their marble casings, continue to stand in peerless grandeur, the wonder of the races, the riddle of the ages!

THE KHEDIVE AND HIS PURPOSES.

Ismael Pasha, Khedive of Egypt, formerly resided in a magnificent palace on the Bosphorus, surrounded by lawns and gardens, *all* arranged in the highest style of Oriental elegance. He was educated in Paris. The clear complexion and light blonde hair, that he inherited from his Circassian mother, give him more the appearance of an Anglo-Saxon than an Oriental. He is of medium height, stately in gait, with a full forehead, gray eyes, and shrewd expression of countenance.

He is immensely rich, virtually holding the land of Egypt in fee simple; his subjects working it on *his* terms. The proceeds fill his purse too, rather than the pockets of the fellahs. Irrigation-canals are bringing a vast amount of barren land under cultivation; four thousand miles of telegraph stretch from the Delta over the Nile Valley in every direction; and surveys have been made for the purpose of rendering the Nile navigable its whole course. There will be, within a few years, a continuous line of railway from Alexandria to Khartoum, near the site of the ancient Meroe at the junction of the Blue and White Nile, a distance of fifteen hundred miles. Ere long the confines of Egypt will be extended over Darfour, Abyssinia, and the Soudan, to the Mountains of the Moon, — countries burdened with heavy forests, and abounding in medicinal plants, in gold, silver, iron, and copper, in cotton, rice, and other productions of great commercial value. It is said by the Khedive's ardent admirers that wherever he pushes his conquests he abolishes the slave-trade. This is seriously doubted. Domestic slavery, and polygamy, are common in most Mohammedan countries.

THE CENTRAL AFRICANS AS THEY ARE.

English scientists sitting in their cozy homes, consulting the reports of sea-captains, slave-buyers, and the tales of ivory-dealers, write glibly of Africa, and the degraded African tribes. Opinions derived from such sources are utterly worthless, as compared with the testimonies of Sir Samuel Baker, Prof. Blyden of Liberia, Dr. Livingstone, and other distinguished men, long residents in Africa. Dr. Livingstone says, —

"If I had believed a tenth of what I heard from traders, I might never have entered the country. . . . But fortunately I was never frightened in infancy with 'bogie,' and am not liable to 'bogiephobia;' for such persons in paroxysms believe every thing horrible, if only it be ascribed to the possessor of a black skin." *

After speaking of the insight and practical good sense of the Bushmen, Livingstone remarks, —

"We all liked our guide Shobo, a fine specimen of that wonderful people, the Bushmen." †

Referring to the race of Makololos, he observes, —

" Their chief Sebituane came a hundred miles to meet me, and welcome me to his country."

This is an intelligent, kind-hearted race, having no fear of death, because believing in immortality. " When I asked the Bechuanas to part with some of their relics, they replied, 'Oh, no!' thus showing their belief in a future state of existence. The chief boatman often referred to departed spirits who called a Placho." ‡ Treating of the Bakwains, a large inland tribe of Africans, Livingstone says, —

"Though rather stupid in matters that had not come under their observations, yet in other things they showed more intelligence than is to be met with in our own uneducated peasantry. . . . They are well up in the maxims which embody their ideas of political wisdom." §

Mentioning the keenness of perception manifest among the tribes north of the Zambesi, he says, —

"They all believe that the souls of the departed still mingle among the living, and partake in some way of the food they consume. . . . They fancy themselves completely in the power of disembodied spirits." ‖

---

* Livingstone's Africa, p. 542. † Ibid., p. 47. ‡ Ibid., p. 121.
§ Ibid., p. 21. ‖ Ibid., 283–287.

Describing the far inland Manyema men, he pronounces them, —

"Tall, strapping fellows, with but little of what we think distinctive of the negro about them. If one relied upon the teachings of phrenology, the Manyemas would take a high place in the human family. . . . Many of the Manyema women, especially far down the Lualaba, are very pretty, light complexioned, and lively."

Speaking of another race in the interior of Africa, Dr. Livingstone says, —

"They are slender in form, having a light olive complexion. . . . The great masses of hair lying upon their shoulders, together with their general features, reminded me of the ancient Egyptians. Some even have the upward inclination of the outer angles of the eyes."*

"The London News," commenting upon Livingstone and Stanley, expresses the conviction that "enterprising travelers will soon find a full confirmation of those old Egyptian traditions handed down to us by Herodotus, which until recently were supposed to be romance rather than actual fact. The account of the races that Livingstone met indicates that the inhabitants of Central Africa have a civilization little dreamed of by European anthropologists. And then, the whole country is exceedingly fertile, especially in those resources which repay commercial enterprise."

Sir Samuel Baker in his Cambridge lecture made this observation: "Central Africa will awake when the first steam-launch is seen upon the Albert Nyanza;" and he added, "Nowhere in the world does scenery exist more beautiful, or soil more fertile, or climate more healthy to the temperate and strong, than those vast and diversified highlands of Central Africa, which inclose these glorious, sparkling seas of sweet water, and feed the mighty rivers whose course is so far-winding that to this day no man has yet traversed them from mouth to fountain."

The mayor of Monrovia, Liberia, confirming the above

* Livingstone's Africa, p. 296.

statements of Dr. Livingstone and Sir Samuel Baker, assured me that the lowest of the Africans were found along the sea-coasts; while, the farther one ventured into the interior, the finer and more intelligent races he found. "Some of the tribes," said he, " in Central Africa, bear little or no resemblance to negroes; being tall, light-complexioned, ingenious, and thoughtful men." Of what racial division of humanity are these tribes the lingering remnants? What of their origin? And when was their palmy period?

AFRICA THE BIRTHPLACE OF THE SANSCRIT.

None interested in the "lost arts," or conversant with the matchless grandeur of the past, need be informed that the ancient Greek and Babylonian historians ever reverted to Africa as the once garden of the world. And, marvelous as it may seem, many of the root-words. applied to the rivers and mountains in Africa are directly traceable to the Sanscrit language. Wise spirits, of remotest antiquity on earth, have assured us that the Sanscrit in distant, prehistoric periods, was, if not the universal language, the language of the cultured Africans. It was in Africa that this, the most perfect of written languages, according to Sir William Jones and other Orientalists, originated. Those primitive peoples, acquainted with agriculture, mechanics, art, literature, and withal becoming as ambitious as populous, moved slowly off in time, through those regions denominated in later periods Mizraim (Egypt), Assyria, Iran, Media, into Central Asia, where, multiplying, they were called Aryas. In a long-subsequent era, they swarmed out from those high table-land localities in all directions. A branch of them met and mingled with the progenitors of the Cathayans. The Malays sprang from this intermixture. The more warlike division of these Aryas that moved southward, invading India, came to be known as the *Aryans*.

This country, protected by mountains on the north, and oceans on the south, largely escaped the vandal influences.

of war. Prospering, they modified and reconstructed their literature, preserving it from entire destruction. What remains is known as the ancient Sanscrit of India, a reflex wave of which ultimately returned to Egypt. Fading remnants of this fairer race, degenerate descendants of the original African Aryas, still exist in Central Africa. Dr. Livingstone describes them as " tall and slender, olive complexioned, and as intelligent to-day as the peasantry of Britain."

SWEDENBORG'S MOST ANCIENT OF ALL BIBLES.

Those African Aryas not only possessed a literature, but a Bible rich in nature's teachings. Was not this the veritable Bible referred to by the Swedish seer?

Swedenborg, giving an account in his " Memorable Relations " of what he saw and heard in the world of spirits, says, " There was a Bible far more ancient than the Jewish Scriptures, harmonizing perfectly with the revelations of nature, most of which was lost. But some scraps were gathered by Moses, and preserved, appearing in what is now termed the Old Testament. In this remote period of time people talked in the language of correspondence; afterwards the symbolic, or pictorial; this degenerated into the hieroglyphical; and this again into the various dialects spoken by the Semitic races." He further says (A. C. 1002). " The people of these most ancient times never on any account ate the flesh of any beast or fowl, but fed solely on grains, fruits, herbs, and various kinds of milk." Referring to the degeneracy of men, he says, " In the course of time, when mankind became cruel and warlike as wild beasts, they began to slay animals, and eat their flesh."

CAIRO AS A CITY.

The Cairo of to-day, including the old city and the new, has an estimated population of four hundred thousand. The mixture of races puts to defiance the classifications of ethnologists. Under the administration of the Turkish Khedive, or reigning viceroy, the city is rapidly improving. The palaces, the public buildings, and the substantial bridge across the Nile, are fine specimens of architectural masonry. Old Cairo is three miles from the new, and yet there is no real break of buildings between them. Modern Cairo seeks its model in Paris, not only in extravagance, fashions, and luxuries, but in its amusements, gardens, sparkling fountains, marble walks, mosaic pavements, and reception-rooms inlaid with porphyry and alabaster. The viceroy is still building for himself new palaces. Those who wish to see the Cairo of the past should not delay. The weird old houses, with their polished and fantastic lattice-work, are fast disappearing. All day long the remorseless chipping and hammering of the mason is heard. The constructor is upon his heels; and soon boulevards and flowering gardens will cover alike the ruins of the Christian Coptic and the more ancient Egyptian.

THE CITADEL AND THE MUSEUM.

Rising above the rest of the city, is the grand mosque, called the citadel. Standing by this Mohammedan structure, one may catch a panoramic view of the whole plateau; the Nile, fringed in living green, rolling at your feet; at the right the tombs of the old caliphs and Mamelukes; on the left the ruins of ancient Cairo; in the distance emerald islands, dotting the now swollen Nile; and, farther off, scores of monuments and pyramids pushing their gray shafts up toward the heavens. The prospect is magnificent.

During the day we visited one of the old Coptic churches, said by our guide to have been built in the seventh century. The paintings of Bible scenes were unique and fantastic, the crypts cold and gloomy.

Among objects of deep interest to travelers is the Egyptian Museum, situated upon the banks of the Nile, and enriched with rarest specimens from ancient Memphis, Heliopolis, and hundred-gated Thebes. Many of the museums of Europe abound in the rare curiosities of old Egypt, and yet her ruins are not exhausted. New discoveries are constantly being made, both in Upper and Lower Egypt. Walking through the cabinets of this museum in Cairo, free to the public, one may read the history of Egypt for five thousand years, — its religion, its art, and domestic life.

WHAT A SPIRIT SAID TO THE CLAIRAUDIENT EAR.

While studying the relics of antiquity in this museum, and wondering what this and that hieroglyphical figure meant, an ancient Egyptian spirit came, and explained them clairaudiently to Dr. Dunn. Referring to the manners and customs characterizing his period, he said, among other things, that the "Great Pyramid, constructed upon mathematical and astronomical principles, with its seven well-aired chambers, was built for a *granary*, and the *coffer* for a measurer. Others in after periods were constructed for different purposes." Speaking of the hieroglyphs, he said, "The hawk symbolized war; the deer fleetness; the triangle, trinities; the *yoni*, purity, also generative life; and the circle, immortal existence."

Though the opinion may be considered a wild one, I venture the belief that the original Sanscrit was simply phonetically abbreviated hieroglyphs. The ancients, instead of carefully chiseling the whole hawk, would naturally, after a time, convey the thought by drawing the head of the bird, then the bill, then the bill-shaped curve, which *curve* would signify war, and emphasized a *warrior*.

THE NILOMETER AND NILE.

Opposite Old Cairo, nestling in the Nile, lies the little isle of Roda, the north part of which is occupied by beautiful gardens. Arabic tradition assures us that it was here that Pharaoh's daughter found "Moses in the bulrushes." If these guides are sincere, they deserve only pity.

The famous Nilometer — *Nile-measurer* — is located upon this island. It did not strike me as any thing very wonderful. It consists of a square well, in the center of which is a graduated pillar, divided into cubits, and surrounded by circular stones with inscriptions upon them. Along the arches are passages from the Koran in sculpture. The whole is surmounted by a dome. The Nile begins to rise the latter part of June, reaching its maximum about the 25th of September. It is watched during this period with intense interest, because, if rising too high, it produces inundations, destroying crops; and if not high enough, filling the canals and reservoirs, the means of irrigation fail, causing infertility and famines. The yearly rise is from twenty to forty feet, depositing over the fertile valley a rich sediment of nearly two inches in thickness. It is to be hoped that before our Stanley leaves Africa, the sources of the Nile will no longer be geographical problems. Strabo, the ancient geographer, mentions the Nilometer. Diodorus informs us that it was in use during the period of the Pharaonic kings; and Herodotus speaks of its measuring the Nile waters when he visited Egypt twenty-three hundred years ago. Though not a vestige of rain has fallen now for nearly six months, the river at the present time is very high and muddy. During inundations the rise is proclaimed daily in the streets of Cairo. The rainy season lasts about three months.

CHAPTER XX.

EGYPT'S CATACOMBS AND PYRAMIDS. — APPEARANCE OF THE EGYPTIANS.

In physique the Egyptians of to-day are larger and much stouter in organic structure than the Hindoos, yet evidently lack their intellectual activity. Physically they are a well-formed race, with an expressive face, retreating forehead, jet black eyes, full lips, prominent nose, broad shoulders, and beautiful teeth. Their complexions — strangely blended — vary; the darkest are doubtless the descendants of the pyramid-builders. Those having an infusion of Arabian blood in their veins are exceedingly hardy and stalwart. The women veil their faces, *all* except their eyes. A certain class, however, as do some Syrians, veil their faces completely. The reasons assigned refer to the harem, and the "look" of temptation.

Dress, with Egyptian men, consists of trousers, — literally a red bag through which the feet are thrust, — a tight undershirt, probably white when clean; a short, flying overjacket; a heavy, sash-like fold of cloth about the waist; and a red-tasseled "tartouche" upon the head, around which is twisted a fanciful coiffure. All classes wear the tartouche, even those who otherwise doff the European dress. Travelers frequently put it on, thinking to pass for old citizens. Have they forgotten the "brayer" in the "lion's skin"? Could I speak but one word to the Khedive of Egypt, that word should be *education*, — educate the people!

THE PYRAMIDS, THE PYRAMIDS!

A picnic from Cairo to the pyramids is one of the easiest things, nowadays, in the world. The Great Pyramid, Cheops, is only some ten or twelve miles from the city, and a fine carriage-road; but this is not the route for tourists desirous of seeing other pyramids, the ruins of Memphis, Heliopolis, and the tombs at Sakkarah.

Accompany us. It is seven o'clock in the morning, carriage at the door, the lunch-basket filled, the guide ready. The streets are yet comparatively quiet. Starting westward, we cross the bridged Nile, and pass along its banks, under overarching acacias, by a palatial structure of the viceroy's, in process of completion, by quaint buildings of less prominence, by mud-built huts, toward Geezah. Here we alight, and take to the cars as far as the Bardshain station, where, finding mules and muleteers, we are off through crooked paths to the ruins of Memphis. Donkey-riding is doleful business for a tall man, inasmuch as feet dangling in the sand become neither grace nor comeliness. But see those heavily-laden camels on their way to the market, those toilers winnowing grain by fickle wind-gusts, and, beyond, those beautiful groves of date-palms, reddening and ripening to load the tables of the rich!

Now we are upon the threshold of the Memphian ruins. Though level with the ground, or buried in the sand, they cover a vast plain. Egyptian priests informed Herodotus that Memphis was founded by Menes, a very ancient king of Egypt, and noted for having turned the Nile from its course, making a large tract of dry land upon which to build a city. In hieroglyphs, Memphis was styled Manofre, the "land of the pyramids," the "city of the white wall." According to Diodorus, this wall was seventeen miles in length, girdling and guarding the city against armies, and the annual overflow of the "Eternal River." The city, once or twice rebuilt, had suffered terribly from the Persians when Herodotus saw it. Among its most magnificent temples was that of *Phtah*. Near this temple, at the gate, were statues, one fifty feet high, made of light-colored silicious limestone. At the entrance of the east gate, there lies, at present, the statue of a Memphian god, two-thirds buried in the sand. It is red granite, about twenty feet in length, beautifully chiseled, highly polished, and lies nearly upon the face. Other statues and unique relics have been found in this vicinity. If you look at them, however, a swarm of beggars, with their attending flies and fleas, fasten to you. The pest of travelers are these begging Bedouin Arabs. Their bullying, gesticulating, importuning impertinences are supremely contemptible. Giving them less or more, they are still unsatisfied.

Let us on, over brick-dust, broken pottery, carved images, and shifting sands, some two miles to Sakkarah, the vast subterranean tomb-lands of the old empire, called the " Sakkarah plateau of the dead." With the exception of a single modern stone building, Sakkarah is a grassless, shrubless, houseless cemetery of robbed tombs. Acres are honey-combed and mummiless; and still nearly a thousand men, under the auspices of government, are employed excavating and digging for relics and antiques. The treasures found daily are kept secret.

Ascending a little hill, the eye could take in, at a single sweep, eleven pyramids. They are neither of the same size nor shape, nor have they the same angles. One very large one before us is square, yet pyramidal-domed. Others, square at the base, are nearly round up a little distance, and pagoda-storied near the summit, *all* clearly indicating that they were built at different periods, and for diverse purposes. Travelers mention about one hundred and forty pyramids, and all within nearly one degree of latitude, clustering in and along through Middle Egypt. Thebes, on the same side of the Nile as Cairo, is about ten days up the river. They measure distances here in the East not by miles, but by hours and days.

Let us go into the Memphian catacombs. The ponderous gate of death swings on its rusty hinges. The guides light their tapers. The main passage, several hundred yards in length, is cut in a solid limestone rock. To the right and left of this arched avenue are niches filled with large sarcophagi. These, chipped and hewn from the hard granite, are beautifully polished and hieroglyphed, but empty. Vandals of the past robbed them of their embalmed remnants of mortality. There were twenty-seven of these sarcophagi, one of which, resembling pure porphyry, was constructed by King Bis for his last resting-place. History puts him down as a vain, ambitious ruler. Might he not, in his dying hour, have uttered the following? —

> "Farewell, a long farewell, to all my greatness!
> This is the state of man: to-day he puts forth
> The tender leaves of hope; to-morrow blossoms,
> And bears his blushing honors thick upon him;
> The third day comes a frost, a killing frost,
>   .   .   .   .
> And then he falls, as I do. I have ventured,
> Like little wanton boys that swim on bladders,
> This many summers in a sea of glory.
>   .   .   .   .
> Vain pomp and glory of this world, I hate ye!"

A little distance from this range of catacombs, we visited the excavated cave-tombs of *Seri-biana*. The mummied forms, with the gaudy casing and linen wrapping, had been removed. Approaching the grim cavity, a fox leaped out, and fled into the distance. It reminded me of Hosea Ballou's famous "Fox Sermon," from the passage, "O Israel, thy prophets are like the foxes in the desert!" This was a magnificent tomb, with the two pillars at the entrance arranged in Masonic order, and twelve others surrounding the sarcophagus, each full four feet, made of a magnesian limestone composition, hard as rock, and decorated with hieroglyphics. Egypt wrote her public history on walls, towers, and obelisks. But in these tombs are inscriptions setting forth the names and titles of the deceased, followed by an address to Anubis, guardian of tombs, and also to the gods beyond the river of death, asking them to be favorably disposed toward the individual in his journeyings to the Elysian lands of the blessed.

Wandering among the subterranean temples and tombs of Sakkarah, site of the ancient Memphis, and reflecting upon the gigantic size of these rock-cut granitic graves, long since ruthlessly deprived of their mummied wealth, the wonder increased how such huge masses of stone were ever brought here so finely cut, and each fitted to its place. Those ancient Egyptians certainly had mechanical knowledge, and powers of moving immense blocks, of which we are comparatively ignorant. And, by the way, these Ramsean temples and tombs were as much a marvel to the Grecian Herodotus as they are to us.

"SIX MILES TO CHEOPS!"

So sings out our jolly guide. It seems very much nearer. The sun is slowly declining; let us hasten. Any thing but a contrary donkey for locomotion! Effort is useless: the stupid brute will hunt his own sand-path. Now we pass a herd of breeding camels, with their young; there a miserable mud-built Bedouin camp; there a little patch of crisped vegetation; and, just beyond, a turbid-looking back-water cove from the swollen Nile. This we must drink, or thirst. Surely, —

"Every pleasure hath its *pain*, and every sweet a *snare*."

But here we are, under the shadow of the Sphinx, hewn, cut, and polished, from a reddish solid limestone rock, and resting in its original position. With the body of a lion, and the head of a man, emblematic of strength and wisdom, it has gazed coldly, with prophetic eye, for thousands of years, upon the fertilizing Nile. The rough-featured face, shamefully defaced, conveys the impression of thoughtfulness and a fixed resolution. The architect evidently fashioned it to represent *Che-ops-sec*, the builder of the Great Pyramid. Cheops, *alias Che-ops-sec*, was deified after his death as " Ramses the Great!" Ram, Rama, Ramses, are famous names in India to-day, as well as historic landmarks in the palmier days of the Asia and Africa of the dreamy past. On the Sphinx was hieroglyphed the name of this *great king of the world*, " RAMSES THE GREAT!"

The figure, according to the measurement of Prof. C. P. Smyth, Sir Gardner Wilkinson, and other distinguished explorers, is thirty-seven feet above the sand-surface, and something like thirty-seven feet below. It is twenty-nine feet across the wig, for the image, remember, has a colossal beard. The lips and protruding lower jaw typify a deficient moral organization. Owing to the perusal of imaginative and overdrawn descriptions of the Sphinx, it quite disappointed me, both in size and the architectural elegance of the workmanship. Still it is a wonder, — a deathless monument guarding a desert waste!

One quarter of a mile more to the foot of Cheops. Who would tarry long at the Sphinx? Off and away, donkeys! They become spirited. See, they actually gallop! But, " ha! *ha!* " here we are at the base of the Great Pyramid! Casting an eye toward its dizzy summit, language proves inadequate! Every fiber of my being flames with the grand, the majestic, the inexpressible! Come, Beverly, — mad philosopher of New Zealand, — *come*, bringing your diagrams and figured calculations, and let us explore them together. Do you not remember, friend Beverly, how we nightly talked of the pyramids, last winter, till the clock struck ten; ate fruit, and talked on about the Pyramids; turned the slate, stirred the fire, and still talked about the old Pyramids? *Hark!* the bell rings out upon the clear midnight air, — *Twelve!* and still the pyramid-mania rages. You, Mr. Beverly, in the estimation of the ignorant Dunedin rabble, was a crack-brained enthusiast; and self, a crazy Spiritualist just loose from some American madhouse. Laughing at all such pious rage, we remembered, that, when Bunyan's lions became too old and toothless to bite, they gratified their vicious dispositions by growling. Sectarians, harmless nowadays, can only growl.

But the pyramids! Cheops, built strictly upon geometrical and astronomical principles, faces due north, south, east, and west. And, according to the measurement of Col. Howard Vyse, the base of this pyramid is 764 feet, and the vertical height 480 feet, with a basical area of thirteen acres, one rood, and twenty-two poles. The quantity of masonry is 89,028,000 cubic feet, with a weight of 6,848,000 tons; the space occupied by chambers and interior passages being something over 56,000 cubic feet of the immense mass. Greek authors state that 500,000 laborers, comprising government captives and bondsmen, were employed during a period of twenty-five years in putting up and completing the structure. To fully realize the magnitude of this desert Titan, one should walk around it, and then, looking up to its dizzy height of five hundred feet, reflect that the granite blocks which furnish the outside of the third, and a portion of the inside of the first pyramid, came, if not manufactured on the spot, all the way from the first cataract; and that outwardly these monumental giants were originally covered with silicious limestone, or marble, highly polished. These facts considered, and the magnificence, the pristine splendor, begin to become manifest.

UP, UP TO THE APEX.

Our dragoman engaging three Bedouin Arab assistants for each, we were ready for the ascent. Full of pluck, we start up the stony steep, scaling block after block. A stout Arab clasps each of our hands firmly. Getting weary, the third "*boosts*," — if there's a more classic word to convey the idea, use it. Though fun at first, fatigue and exhaustion soon follow. "Bravo! a third of the way up: take a rest," shout the guides. Another start, but not so gay and gritty as the first. Up, and still upward; the air seems too light for breathing. Pity be to the short-winded! blessings to the long-legged! all deformities have their uses. 'Tis done! Our feet press the summit! Hallelujah! The apex, seen at a distance as a point, proves to be an area full twelve feet square, from which the view is absolutely magnificent Northward, you look down the river upon the Delta, with its patches of green, groups of palms, and long files of patient camels. Southward, you gaze up the river, fringed with waving date-palms, penciled in gold against the delicate sky; fields of vegetation, green and yellow; flocks of black and brown sheep, with attending shepherds; peasant-women bearing water-jars upon their heads; and, farther on, the ashes of the ancient Memphis. Eastward, upon Cairo, with its glittering domes, minarets, labyrinthine streets, dazzling bazaars, public squares, coffee-houses, three hundred mosques for Mahometan prayers, and the gracefully-towering citadel, grand and gorgeous, crowning the whole. Westward stretches in the clear distance the African Sahara, undefinable and immeasurable; while at your feet, seemingly, rolls the majestic Nile, great river-god of the old Egyptians, whose sculptured figures they wreathed with lotus-flowers, and filled his extended arms with their ripened fruits and grains. Let us linger upon this desert Mount of Transfiguration, and meditate. But where — *where's* the doctor?

A SÉANCE ON THE PYRAMIDS.

Sunny and joyous, Dr. Dunn and his Arab aids started first to make the ascent; but for some unaccountable reason they have not yet reached the pinnacle. Looking over the precipitous stone terraces, there he was, full a third of the way down. "What's the matter?" we inquired. "Why those gesticulations, and why the delay?"—"Dun no," was the Arab response in broken English. "Well, go down and help them." A shrug of the shoulders said *No!* Becoming alarmed, I exclaimed with strong emphasis, " *Go down after them!*" They stood mute and stolid as statues. Impulsively taking all the silver from my pocket, — a precious little, — and giving it to the leader, I repeated, " Go to the rescue!" Down they went. Alone now upon the Pyramid! what a moment! But here the whole party comes; Dr. Dunn unconsciously entranced, and the Arabs, all excited, frightened at his " fits." The mystery was solved. Michael O'Brien, the controlling spirit, said, —

" Faith, Jammie, I saw these beastly fellows pulling away at the madeum, and I thought I would just lind a hand."

Well, you probably did more hurt than good.

" More hurt than *good!* and is that the way you talk to a fine Irish jintleman?"

But you alarmed me : what did you entrance him for?

" Sure, and don't I understand my own business? and don't I want to see the *round towers* of ould Ireland?"

These are not the round towers of Ireland.

" Well, didn't I know *that?* These are the pyramids, and I wanted to see 'em, that I might compare them with those round towers of my native country, that puzzle *you* and everybody else. But I must out of this, for here's one of those old long-haired spirits, who lived a while after this pyramid was built. He wants to talk to you. The top of the morning to you, Jammie!"

A change; owing to inharmonious conditions, the entrancement is spasmodic. How the Arabs stare! It is difficult to keep them at a distance.

But listen: another spirit has taken possession. What dignity in the attitude! and what a deep-toned voice! —

" Traveler, you stand now upon the summit of one of the world's wonders, — a mountain of stone rising from trackless sands. I once lived under these skies, vestured in a mortal body. The same majestic river rolled through the valley; but winds, storms, shifting sands, and maddened convulsions, have changed all else. This pyramid, upon which I often gazed, was even *then* more a matter of tradition than history. It must have received its final cap-stone over ten thousand years since. Our time was measured by ruling dynasties. My years on earth seem now like a half-forgotten dream. Starry worlds have faded; islands have risen from the ocean; continents have disappeared; thronged cities have perished; conquering kings have been born, ruled, died, and been forgotten; but this Titanic monument of the desert still stands in stately solitude. And yet nothing earthly is immortal; this pillared pile of composite, of granite, and of porphyry is slowly, surely crumbling. Only the undying soul, the templed pyramid of *divinity* within, is eternal. See, then, O stranger and pilgrim! that every thought, deed, act, — *each* a 'living stone' placed in the spiritual temple you are constructing, — is polished, and fitted to its place with the master's 'mark.'

"But you wish to know the purpose of *this*, the oldest of the pyramidal structures. The aim was multiform. Carefully considering the constellations, the position of the North Star, and the shadow cast by the sun at the time of the equinoxes, it was built upon mathematical principles, to the honor of the *Sun-God* that illumines and fructifies the earth; built for the preservation of public documents and treasures during wars of invasion, and built as a storehouse for *grains* during famines and devastating floods, with that mystic *coffer* in the center, as an exact measurer for the world. A universal system of weights and measures, a universal currency, and a universal government, were Utopian theories of the ancients before my period of time. This pyramid was not built by forced toil, and at a great sacrifice of life, but by gratuitous contributions, the servants of the wealthy doing the manual labor. There are seven granary apartments in the structure, with shafts leading from each to the common granary of the coffer, now called the King's Chamber. These shafts have not yet, to my knowledge, been discovered.

"During long rains and terrible floods, ancient Memphis was twice swept away, — once even to its walls, with all its inhabitants, in a single night. Convulsions of nature, and terrible floods, were then common. Immediately after one of these, this pyramid was commenced, requiring more than a generation in the construction. It was completed before the great flood, and the wars of the shepherd kings.

"Once in my time the water rose, and rolled over the very apex of these stones. It rained *forty-five consecutive days;* and, while torrents swept down the Nile Valley from the south, stout, heavy winds from the Mediterranean drove the water up the country, piling wave upon wave, till this structure was completely submerged. But, though thus buried in the flooding waters, the treasures and well-filled granaries remained to feed, when the waters subsided, the famishing people who had fled southward to the hilly country. There seems to be less water upon the face of the earth now than then. Liquids are becoming solids, and change in every department of being is doing its destined work. Only pyramids of **truth, constructed of immutable principles, are eternal.**

"*Che-ops-see*, the great king of the world, died in Thebes. Embalmed by the priests, he was placed, after a time, in this pyramid, as a mark of *honor* for having conceived and planned a monument serving as the savior of his subjects. Finally, the sarcophagus removed, he was godded, or deified, *Ramses the First;* and the Sphinx, that calm, weird, unreadable face, now mutilated by a degenerate people, was designed to hand the outlines of his physiognomy down to posterity. I must leave. Stranger from a foreign country, do well the work appointed you, that, when ashes and sands claim their own, you may be prepared for the fellowship of those ancient spirits of whom you seek counsel."

We have reported this Egyptian spirit's ideas and words as best we could. Take them for what they are worth, making history, hieroglyph, and reason the umpire of decision. Powhatan, the good Indian spirit, came, and, noting the waning of the western sun as a symbol of the fading-away of the aboriginal tribes before a merciless civilization, said they went down like setting stars, to rise into the better conditions of the Morning Land.

CHAPTER XXI.

STUDY OF THE PYRAMIDS. — SIGHT OF THE GREAT PYRAMID.

THOUGH in no wise smitten with the pyramid mania, still I must say that the image of the Great Pyramid, sitting so kingly upon the African side of the Nilotic Valley, can never be effaced from the picture-gallery of my soul's memory chambers.

WHEN? — WHAT OF IT?

"I asked of Time: 'To whom arose this high,
  Majestic pile, here moldering in decay?'
He answered not, but swifter sped his way,
With ceaseless pinions winnowing the sky.

. . . .

I saw *Oblivion* stalk from stone to stone:
  'Dread power!' I cried, 'tell me whose vast design' —
He checked my further speech in sullen tone:
  'Whose once it was, I *care not*: now 'tis *mine!*'"

Strangely, and with widely different eyes, do men of culture look at the tablets, carvings, memorials, and teaching monuments of antiquity. Many surface-thinking Americans have sneered at them; while others have scoffingly mocked the fading memories of their inspired constructors. A New York journalist, while traveling in the East a few years since, spotted a bit of clean manuscript paper with this paragraph: "These old pyramids, useless and crumbling, are only ugly piles of stones, covering a few acres of howling desert." This style has been too common with the flippant, the facile, and the ambitious, from the time of Pliny, down to the novelist Sir Walter Scott.

It is needless to remind the historian that the old Greeks were exceedingly indignant with their distinguished traveler, Halicarnassus, who, after having explored, extravagantly praised the pyramids.

"What!" said these vain Greeks; "does not our own divine Greece possess monuments more worthy of intelligent admiration? Had not Greece the *omphalos*, or navel-stone of the whole earth, to show in the temple of Delphi, in order to prove that Greece was the center of the vast world's plain? Were not Greek rocks and hills, Greek fountains and groves, all hallowed by the presence of Grecian gods and goddesses of every degree? And were not the then inhabitants of Greece descended by direct line from those superhuman beings? What need had a Greek to go to distant Egypt, and admire any thing not erected by genius of Grecian artists?"

Still, in the face of the most virulent opposition, in spite of the boastful Greeks 500 B.C., in spite of Rome's proud Cæsars, in spite of twenty-five hundred years of persistent attempts to sneer down and write down these monarchs of the ages, there they stand, *irrepressible*, — absolutely refusing to be driven or scribbled into oblivion!

OPINIONS OF THINKERS AND SAVANTS.

Saying nothing of German and French scholars who have visited, measured, and written of the pyramids, — nothing of Prof. John Greaves, Col. Howard Vyse, Sir Gardner Wilkinson, and other men of letters, — we turn with pride to Prof. C. Piazza Smythe, Astronomer Royal of Scotland. When this erudite and eminent gentleman proposed to make accurate measurements and scientific observations touching Egypt's pyramidal glories, his fellow professors in the university exclaimed, "What! you, too, a believer in the pyramids? Can you imagine for a moment that the ancients had a knowledge of mechanics, of science, lost to moderns? You will lose your reputation as an astronomer if you begin to meddle with the pyramids!" Prof. Smythe replied thus in substance: —

"As a university professor, I deem it strictly in accordance with the methods of modern science to test any and every material thing whatever by observation, by measure, and by the most rigid examination. These ever-recurring questions demand rational answers: Why hangs there so much historic lore about the Great Pyramid? Why is it referred to in the legends of nearly all the Eastern nations? Why has it so often been claimed as a treasure-house of scientific information? What need, upon the Egyptian-tomb theory, had the corpse of a king for a thorough and complete system of ventilation to his sarcophagus-chamber? Why was the interior of the king's tomb so perfectly plain, and void of all ornament of carving, painting, or hieroglyphics, when his subjects reveled in such things up to the utmost extent of their wealth? Why were the passages leading to the supposed secret sepulchral chamber lined with white stone, as if to lead a would-be depredator, and without a chance of missing his way, right up to the very place where, on the sepulchral theory, he ought not to go? Why was so different a shape employed for a king's tomb to all his subjects' tombs, prince and peasant alike? Why did pyramid-building cease so early in Egyptian history, that it had become a forgotten art in the times of Egypt's chief greatness under the so-called new empire at Thebes, Luxor, and Karnak, yet an empire earlier than the siege of Troy; when the Egyptian kings, too, were richer, more despotic, and more fond of grand sepulture, than at any former period of their history?"

To investigate, and, if possible, rationally answer these pressing inquiries, Prof. Smythe, collecting and packing his measuring instruments, sailed — accompanied by his brave wife — on a stormy November's morning, for Egypt, to spend the winter in the study of the pyramids. Consulting the viceroy, "his royal highness" granted him twenty men to remove *débris*, clear the passages, and otherwise assist in the measurements.

Fixing his abode in the eastern cliff of Pyramid Hill, the professor, in due time, with lamps, measuring-rods, note-books, and Arab assistants, went into the entrance-passage on the north side, forty-seven inches high by forty-one wide, to commence the all-important work of exact measurements. These were necessary steps in order to draw the legitimate deductions. And the whole enterprise was worthy the Scotch astronomer, and the occasion.

THE GLORY OF GHEEZEH.

Reaching the great pyramid of Gheezeh, across the desert from Sakkarah, quite late in the afternoon, we lost no time in commencing the work of sight-seeing. The general mass of this giant edifice, covering, as it does, over *thirteen acres* with solid masonry, is rather roughly, yet substantially built. The blocks of stone upon the outside — the largest, I should judge, being four feet in width, by six or eight in length — are handsomely squared, keyed to each other, and cemented on their surfaces. The material is mostly limestone; and the blocks have the appearance of "made material," — a composition of magnesian limestone, sand, and cement. These constituents constitute a species of rock much like that now being made in the city of Alexandria to outline and bulwark the harbor. It is the opinion of many that all the blocks were chemically manufactured by the ancient Egyptians. This class of writers put the construction of the pyramids back in the past some twenty thousand years. Such of the polished stone blocks as are worked into the astronomically-constructed entrance-passages are hard, and almost as white as alabaster. These evidently came from the *Mok-at-tam* Hills on the Arabian side of the Nile; while those enormous granite slabs in the interior must have been brought — if not manufactured on the spot — from the Syene quarries, five hundred and fifty miles up the Nile.

"Recount to me the beauties of the Nile:
 No more of Tigris and Euphrates sing;
 Those days of joy in Gheezeh and the Isle,
  Their memories ever round my heart will cling."

THE INTERIOR STRUCTURE.

Though the climate of Egypt is tropical, and generally dry, time with its disintegrating forces has rapidly changed the pyramidal monument of Gheezeh since the outside casings of polished limestone and marble were torn off by the Arab sultans of Cairo. Entering the pyramid at a descending angle of twenty-seven degrees, and wending our way downward at first half-bent, led by Arab guides, and then up the ascending passage for a long distance, we entered the King's Chamber, the floor of which rests upon the fiftieth course of stone forming the whole pyramidal mass. This chamber is a magnificent oblong apartment thirty-four feet in length, seventeen feet broad, and nineteen feet high, formed of monstrous yet elegantly polished blocks of granite, but utterly destitute of ornament, painting, or every thing save that plain, puzzling, yet time-defying coffer. The glaring lights gave the room a dismal appearance; and our voices sounded fearfully strange and sepulchral. The granite walls of the chamber surrounding the *coffer* are divided into five horizontally equal courses; and there is also a sign of the "division into five" over the doorway outside. Five, it is well known, is the ruling and most important number in mathematics.

THE PORPHYRITIC COFFER.

But this hollow, lidless, rectangular box, chest, or coffer of imperishable stone in the center of the King's Chamber,—what of *this?* Why so very plain? Why lidless, and minus any inscriptions? And, further, why much of the pyramid made as though in subserviency to it?

When this pyramid was first broken into, remember, by Caliph *Al Mamoon*, more than a thousand years since, he expected to find immense treasures, with the key to all the sciences. Tradition has it that this pyramid had been previously discovered, explored, and robbed by the ancient Romans. Be this as it may, the Moslem caliph, to his great disappointment, found nothing but the empty porphyry coffer, — the riddle of riddles!

CONTINUED INVESTIGATIONS.

Dropping all preconceived theories, this Edinburgh professor, after noting the sloping key-line stones in the passage, the mystic number five, and the seven overlappings of the grim walls, began his series of measurements by measuring the size, shape, and position of every stone in the passages; also the walls, the floor, the roof, and the ceiling of the King's Chamber; and, to guard against any possible error, he repeated these measurements at three different times. "It was not until after two months of apprenticeship at pyramid mensuration," says this *savant*, "that I undertook that most important question of the precise angle of the grand gallery." The mathematical mensuration finished, he ordered his assistants to carry the boxes containing the instruments — the large altitude azimuth circle and telescope — to the top of the structure, that, in connection with his geometrical calculations, he might make the necessary astronomical observations. This must have been a sublime spectacle! — a profound scholar studying the rising and culminating positions of different stars, those stellar milestones along the ethereal spaces, in the silent night-time, under those clear and cloudless skies of Egypt.

RESULTS OF RESEARCH.

Besides solving puzzling problems, these investigations of John Taylor, Profs. Greaves, Smythe, and others, with the mathematical calculations of A. Beverly, Esq., Dunedin, N. Z., demonstrate, clearly demonstrate, the marvelous foresight and wisdom of the most ancient Egyptians, especially in the application of symbolism, by a speaking arrangement of parts to science, and to pictorial expressions of the recondite principles of nature.

I. — The heaviest winds of the Orient, especially in the

monsoon seasons, are from the south-west and north-east. These strike the corner angles, rather than the facial fronts of the pyramids, thus tempering the storms to the preservation of the structures. And then they are located in that latitude best designed to prevent the African sands from swooping down upon certain fertile localities of the Nile. Further, the form of their structures is founded upon the *extreme* and *mean* ratio, so well known to geometricians.

II. — The size of the Great Pyramid, Cheops, is so nicely proportioned upon mathematical and architectural principles, as to indicate the number of revolutions made by the earth on its yearly axis in terms of a certain unit of linear measure; while *other numbers* measure the length of the semi-axis of the earth's rotation.

III. — The angle of inclination towards its central axis is such that its vertical hight is to the continued length of the four sides of its base as the radius to the circumference of a circle; and this is a fractional quantity lying at the very base of mathematics.

IV. — This unit of linear measure, *alias* unit of length, was the same as the cubit of the Hebrews, and identical with the inches of our ancestral Anglo-Saxons, and the present British inch, into less than a thousandth part. Practically, then, the unit of linear measure in the pyramid is the same in length as the American inch. Thus may our mensuration be traced through Britain, Rome, Greece, to Egypt of the pyramidal era.

V. — The geometrical knowledge of the pyramid-builders began where Euclid's ended; for Euclid's forty-seventh problem, said to have been discovered by Pythagoras, and to have caused the sacrifice of a whole hecatomb of oxen, is common all through the pyramids.

> "When the great Samian sage his noble problem found,
> A hundred oxen dyed with their life-blood the ground."

VI. — The subterranean chamber shows the extraordinary way in which it points out the pyramid's axis, thus indicating a solution of the problem which has occupied the attention of geometers in all ages, viz., the trisection of angles; while the *metrical square* shows how the unit measures of the pyramid are related to one another, to the earth's radius of curvature in lat. 30°, and the pyramid as a unitary structure.

VII. — The polished coffer in the heart of the pyramid, representing the cube of a marked linear standard, is based upon principles referring to the specific gravity of all the earth's interior substance; and, to use the language of the celebrated John Taylor, " It precisely measures the four *cheoners* of the Hebrews, and also the one chalder, or four quarters, of the Anglo-Saxon system, to such a nicety, that the present quarters " in which British and American farmers measure their wheat are the veritable quarters of the stone coffer in the King's Chamber.

In brief, while the Great Pyramid indicates astronomically that the "North Pole is moving toward Eastern Asia," the coffer not only shows the method of dividing the circle into degrees, and bisecting angles generally, but this porphyry coffer is the standard measure to-day of capacity and weight with the two most enlightened nations of earth, — England and America, — "ruling," as Prof. Smythe says, "the approximate size of our British quarters, tons, and pounds. These admissions furnish the key-proofs, that, while the coffer was designed by the king for a standard measure, the hollow chambers were built for *granaries*, and the receptacle of *treasures* and *records* during wars and floods. Further explorations will discover other chambers, making seven, and all ingeniously connected with the King's Chamber."

This Edinburgh professor, treating of his astronomical observations, says, " I have ascertained by recent measures, much more actually than was known before, that the Great Pyramid had been erected under the guidance of *astronom-*

ical science, . . . and that the entrance-passage had been pointed at the star *á Draconis* when crossing the meridian below the pole, at a distance of 3° 42′; . . . accordingly this star's closest approach to the pole, and within only ten minutes thereof, occurred about the year 2800 B.C." Upon the hypothesis of the *á Draconis* observation and epoch, taken in connection with the precessional displacement, the Great Pyramid was built 3400 B.C.; but Lepsius puts it 3500 B.C.; the French Rénan 4500 B.C. That learned man, Baron Bunsen, in his world-famous volumes of "Egypt's Place in Universal History," claims a duration of six thousand seven hundred years of a civilized, well-governed, and prosperous Egypt, previous to their kings of the so-called Manetho's fourth dynasty.

Dr. Rebold, a French archæologist, treating of the Greek historians visiting Egypt in the fifth century B.C., makes the following observation: —

"From the date 13300 B.C. until the year 4600 B.C., when the zodiac was constructed and set up in the temple of Esneh, there occurred four periods; to the first is ascribed the reign of the gods, and to the last the consolidation of the lesser kingdoms into three large kingdoms, acting in concord with some thirty or forty colleges of the priests. . . . Hermes observing the star Aldebaran 3360 B.C., and writing upon astrology, and the certainty of immortality, said in dying, 'Until now I have been exiled from my true country, to which I am about to return. Shed no tears for me. I return to that celestial country whither all must repair in their turn. *There* is God. This life is but the death.'"

It can not be supposed that the Egyptians *suddenly* built their walled cities, carved and ornamented their monuments, established picture-writing, — the language of the stars, — and constructed their pyramids upon the principles of science, with a standard measure for their cities and all the adjoining countries. Did it not take a long period to invent those tools, to construct machinery for raising such immense weights, to establish laws to govern workmen for general concert of action? — and profound learning too, to build with such exactness upon principles geometrical and astronomical? And yet what grand results! Those pyramids are perpetual light-houses in the desert, speaking histories of once marvelous civilizations; mighty monuments, serenely, proudly overlooking the fading ruins of nearly-forgotten ages.

The learned Gliddon in his "Ancient Egypt" sensibly asks, —

"Can the theologian derive no light from the pure primeval faith that glimmers from Egyptian hieroglyphics, to illustrate the immortality of the soul? Will not the historian deign to notice the prior origin of every art and science in Egypt, a thousand years before the Pelasgians studded the isles and capes of the Archipelago with their forts and temples? — long before Etruscan civilization had smiled under Italian skies? And shall not the ethnographer, versed in Egyptian lore, proclaim the fact that the physiological, craniological, capillary, and cuticular distinctions of the human race existed on the first distribution of mankind throughout the earth?

"Philologists, astronomers, chemists, painters, architects, physicians, must return to Egypt to learn the origin of language and writing; of the calendar, and solar motion; of the art of cutting granite with a *copper* chisel, and of giving elasticity to a *copper* sword; of making glass with the variegated hues of the rainbow; of moving single blocks of polished syenite, nine hundred tons in weight, for any distance, by land and water; of building *arches*, round and pointed, with masonic precision unsurpassed at the present day, and antecedent by two thousand years to the 'Cloaca Magna' of Rome; of sculpturing a *Doric column* one thousand years before the Dorians are known in history; of *fresco* painting in imperishable colors; of practical knowledge in anatomy; and of time-defying pyramid building.

"Every craftsman can behold, in Egyptian monuments, the progress of his art four thousand years ago; and whether it be a wheelwright building a chariot, a shoemaker drawing his twine, a leather-cutter using the selfsame form of knife of old as is considered the best form now, a weaver throwing the same hand-shuttle, a whitesmith using that identical form of blowpipe but lately recognized to be the most efficient, the seal-engraver cutting, in hieroglyphics, such names as SHOOPHO's, above four thousand three hundred years ago, — *all these*, and many more astounding evidences of Egyptian priority, now require but a glance at the plates of Rosellini."

When newspaper scribblers, when blatant talkers, pronounce Egypt of "little account," pronounce the pyramids "useless piles of stones, the largest covering four or five acres of sand," they will permit me to pleasantly express a pity for their egotism, and a scathing contempt for their ignorance.

Evidences difficult to gainsay incline many to the belief that the oldest pyramids are nearer twenty than five thousand years old. That eminent Egyptologist, Bunsen, concedes to Egypt an antiquity of twenty thousand, and to China a larger period.

HOW DID THE OLD EGYPTIANS MOVE SUCH MOUNTAINOUS MASSES OF STONE?

In Sakkarah Catacombs, near the site of the present Memphian ruins, are beautifully polished granite slabs, constituting the tombs of the kings, twelve feet in length, eight feet wide, and six feet high. Such sarcophagi are actually mammoths. In them I could and *did* stand erect. And yet these are but playthings compared to some of the obelisks, granite needles, and pyramidal stones, characterizing the Egypt of remotest antiquity. This one thing is certain: either the mechanism of ancient Egypt was vastly superior to ours, or these huge stones and pillars were manufactured where they now stand.

"Pliny describes some of the arrangements connected with an obelisk a hundred and twenty feet high, erected at Alexandria by Ptolemæus Philadelphus. A canal was dug from the Nile to the place where the obelisk lay. Two boats were placed side by side, filled with pieces of stone having the aggregate weight of the obelisk. These pieces were in masses of one cubic foot each, so that the ratio between the quantity of matter in the obelisk, and that held by the boats, could be determined by a little calculation. The boats were laden to twice the weight of the obelisk, in order that they might pass under it, the two ends of the mighty monolith resting on the two banks of the canal. Then, as the pieces of stone were taken out one by one, the boats rose, until at last they supported the obelisk. They were finally towed down the canal, bearing their burden with them. So far, Pliny's account is clear; but he tells us little or nothing of the tremendous task, performed ages before, of originally transporting such masses from the Syene quarries to Thebes and Heliopolis.

"An account is given by Herodotus of the transport of a large block of granite to form a monolith temple. The block measured thirty-two feet long, twenty-one feet wide, and twelve feet high; its weight is estimated to have been not less than three hundred tons. The transport of this huge mass down the Nile, from Syene to the Delta, occupied two thousand men for three years."

Several comparatively inferior Egyptian obelisks have been brought and reconstructed in Rome. The Luxor obelisk, borne from Egypt by the skillful M. Lebas, at an immense outlay of money and men, and put up in the Place de la Concorde, Paris, 1833, weighed less than two hundred and fifty tons. This is but a babe, compared to those remaining. There are single blocks, in that land of marvels, estimated by Glidden and others to weigh nine, and even twelve hundred tons. Tell us, engineers, tell us, O moderns, how they were removed, and placed in their present positions!

CHAPTER XXII.

ANCIENT SCIENCE IN EGYPT. — ASTRONOMY OF THE EGYPTIANS.

THE ancients swarming the Nile Valley seem to have excelled in astronomy, as well as in mechanics. Smythe, the astronomer royal of Scotland, sustains this position. And in a lecture delivered in Philadelphia by Prof. O. M. Mitchell, and reported for the press, he said, —

"Not long since I met, in St. Louis, a man of great scientific attainments, who for forty years had been engaged in Egypt in deciphering the hieroglyphics of the ancients. This gentleman had stated to me that he had lately unraveled the inscriptions upon the coffin of a mummy now in the London Museum, and in which, by the aid of previous observations, he had discovered the key to all the astronomical knowledge of the Egyptians. The zodiac, with the exact positions of the planets, was delineated on this coffin; and the date to which they pointed was the autumnal equinox in the year 1722 B.C., or nearly 3600 years ago. Accordingly I employed his assistants to ascertain the exact positions of the heavenly bodies belonging to our solar system on the equinox of that year (1722 B.C.), and sent him a correct diagram of them, without having communicated his object in so doing. In compliance with this, the calculations were made; and to my astonishment, on comparing the result with the statements of his scientific friend already referred to, it was found that on the 7th of October, 1722 B.C., the moon and planets had occupied the exact points in the heavens marked upon the coffin in the London Museum."

HELIOPOLIS.

What Oxford is to England, and Yale to New England, Heliopolis was to Egypt in the fifth century B.C. It is only two hours and a half from Cairo by carriage. They tell me that in winter-time it is a very pleasant drive, over a splendid road bordered with orange, lemon, acacia, and olive trees. The gardens of ancient Heliopolis were famous, as the historian knows, for their balm-of-Gilead balsams. What think you, my countrymen, remains of this sacerdotal, this university city of antiquity, where Moses studied the "wisdom of the Egyptians," where Joseph's father-in-law officiated as a priest in the temple, where Plato the Grecian graduated, and where Herodotus, in his travels, sought counsel from the "wise men of Egypt"? Its colleges, its magnificent temples, are but isolated mounds now; and all that remains to determine the locality is a beautiful granite obelisk. This, fixing the site of the Temple of the Sun, is thought by some Egyptologists to have been erected by the Pharaoh of Joseph's time, bearing the name of Osirtasen I., founder of the twelfth dynasty. When the geographer Strabo visited this grand old country, Egyptian scholars pointed out the residences of Eudoxus and Plato during the thirteen years they remained in Egypt under the searching tuition of the priests of Heliopolis. Though relentless time long since transformed Plato's Egyptian palace to dust, it has not effaced the hieroglyphics from Heliopolis's stately obelisk.

The obelisk in the Hippodrome at Constantinople, which I visited several times while in Asiatic Turkey, is supposed to be the work of the fourth Thotmes. Those in Rome, brought from Egypt, bear inscriptions of various Pharaohs. But, of all the obelisks, the largest and most beautiful is that of Karnak, at Thebes, cut by Queen A-*men-see*, about 1760 B.C. It is a single towering shaft of the purest and most exquisitely polished syenite, in height about ninety feet, and in weight over four hundred tons.

In hieroglyphical symbol-writing, Heliopolis means "the abode of the sun;" and, as a celebrated seat of philosophy, its hierophants and seers professed to enlighten the world

After mentally and architecturally enriching other cities, the reputation of Heliopolis began to fade soon after the conquest of Egypt by Greece; the Grecianized city of Alexandria taking its place.

THE ROSETTA STONE, AND COPTS.

When visiting London the first time, nothing interested me more than the Rosetta Stone in the British Museum. Rosetta, in Arabic, Rasheed, is handsomely located on the west bank of the Nile, near its mouth. This modern town, founded by a caliph, 870 A.D., is built upon the site of some ancient city. Its present archæological celebrity was acquired by the finding of the trilingual stone, known as the "Rosetta Stone," discovered by the French in 1799, while digging foundations for a fort. This invaluable tablet contained a decree made by the priests of Egypt in honor of Ptolemy Epiphanes, 196 B.C. It was written in hieroglyphic, enchorial, and Greek. This gave the key to the Egyptian alphabet, the old Coptic, and to the reading of the hieroglyphical inscriptions. Copt is the language written on most of the monumental walls in Egypt.

The Arabic is the vernacular of the country to-day, though there are many dialects spoken in the various parts of Egypt.

The Coptic Church is the national church. Its archbishop of Alexandria, though residing in Cairo, is said to be the direct successor of Mark the Evangelist. So run these theological threads; the Catholics looking to Peter, the English Church to Paul, the Coptic Church to Mark, and the Greek Church to the embodied wisdom of the apostolic fathers. The liturgy of the Copts is in the ancient Coptic. Their forms of worship resemble the Catholic; but they utterly deny the authority of the Pope.

None doubt the Copts, so numerous in Middle and Upper Egypt, being the direct descendants of the ancient Egyptians. Their brown complexions, almond-shaped eyes, and heavy lips, resemble the face of the Sphinx, the ancient paintings, and sculptured portraits; and, further, they are slightly under the medium size, as are the exhumed mummies.

ALEXANDRIA.

In the palmy days of the Ptolemies this city numbered full half a million: it has to-day about one hundred and fifty thousand. Bating Pompey's Pillar and Cleopatra's Needle; broken columns, cisterns, aqueducts, traces of walls, unexplored catacombs, porphyry, portions of Cæsar's palace, fragments of statues, and library ashes, are all that remain of this ancient magnificent city, founded by Alexander the Great soon after the fall of Tyre, 333 B.C. Strabo gives a brilliant description of the streets, avenues, libraries, museums, obelisks, groves inclosing retreats for learned men, and temples of marble and porphyry that ultimately enriched Rome and Constantinople.

The same architect, Dinocratus, who acquired such fame from planning the Temple of Diana at Ephesus, was employed by Alexander in the construction of Alexandria. Upon the death of this Macedonian monarch, he became governor of Egypt, and finally assumed the title of king 304 B.C. Ptolemy Philadelphus, while adding much to the grandeur of the city, and increasing its libraries, built a marble tower, upon the summit of which a fire was kept continually burning as a direction to sailors. At this period, and long after, it was the great cosmopolitan seat of theological controversy and moral philosophy. One links with it precious memories of Proclus, Plotinus, Ammonius, Saccas, the Alexandrian school, and its modifying influences upon Christianity.

THE ALEXANDRIAN LIBRARY, DESTROYED BY WHOM?

This massive collection of literature was shelved in the Temple of Serapeion. Most of its rolls and scrolls were originally brought from India. Ptolemy Sotor has the honor of being its founder. Ptolemy Philadelphus enlarged it. Others increased it to over seven hundred thousand volumes. To further add thereto, the following unique plan was devised: " Seize all books brought into Egypt by Assyrians, Greeks, and foreigners, and transcribe them, handing the transcriptions to the owners, and putting the originals into the library."

Book-burning is a business common to both ancients and moderns, Christians and Mohammedans. In an article on Alexandria, " The Encyclopædia Britannica " says, —

" This structure [alluding to the Serapeion] surpassed in beauty and magnificence all others in the world, except the Capitol at Rome. Within the verge of this temple was the famous Alexandrian library, . . . containing no fewer than seven hundred thousand volumes.

" In the war carried on by Julius Cæsar against the inhabitants of the city, the library in the Brucheion, *with all its contents*, was reduced to ashes. The library in the Serapeion, however, still remained, and here Cleopatra deposited two hundred thousand volumes of the Pergamenean library. These, and others added from time to time, rendered the new library of Alexandria more numerous and considerable than the former; *but, when the Temple of Serapis was demolished under the archiepiscopate of Theophilus, A. D.* 389, *the valuable library was pillaged or destroyed ; and twenty years afterwards the empty shelves excited the regret and indignation of every intelligent spectator."*

The blinded zealots of the agone ages strove to obliterate every vestige of that historic knowledge which distinguished the nations of antiquity. John Philaponus, a noted Peripatetic philosopher, being in Alexandria when the city was taken, and being permitted to converse with Amrou the Arabian general, solicited an inestimable gift at his hands, — *the royal library.* At first Amrou was inclined to grant the favor; but upon writing the caliph, he received, it is said, the following answer, dictated by a spirit of unpardonable fanaticism : " *If those ancient manuscripts and writings of the Eastern nations and the Greeks agree with the Koran, or Book of God, they are useless, and need not be preserved ; but, if they disagree, they are pernicious, and ought to be destroyed.*" The torch was applied, and a wretched barbarism was for the time triumphant. Sensations of sadness thrilled my being's core, while walking over ashes and ruins that were once ablaze with the literature of the East. Never for a moment have I felt that "it was all for the best," the burning of the Alexandrian Library.

Travelers visiting the present Alexandria naturally rush to see Cleopatra's Needle, a solid block of reddish granite, said to have been originally brought from Syene. This granite needle is sixty feet high, having to the top three columns of hieroglyphical inscriptions. Its twin column is buried in the sand near by. Not far distant is Pompey's Pillar, a single graceful column of pink granite, one hundred and fourteen feet high, and twenty-seven feet in circumference. During the reign of Tiberius, A. D. 14 to 37, these "obelisks were brought from Heliopolis to Alexandria." But how were they brought? Ay, that's the question. It would be absolutely impossible for moderns to do it. The method is among the "lost arts." Was not this pyramidal stone estimated to weigh nine hundred tons? were not these obelisks manufactured where they stand, historic opinion to the contrary?

Just at the dawn of, and after the initiation of the Christian era, the history of Alexandria became singularly intermingled with that of Jerusalem, Greece, and Rome, in which the Ptolemies and Cæsars, Philo Judæus, Pompey, Cleopatra, and St. Anthanasius, all play conspicuous parts. Here I am reminded of Gen. Lytle's lines referring to Cæsar, Pompey, Antony, and Cleopatra:—

> "I am dying, Egypt, dying!
> Ebbs the crimson life-tide fast,
> And the dark Plutonian shadows
> Gather on the evening blast.
> Let thy arm, O queen! support me,
> Hush thy sobs, and bow thine ear,
> Hearken to the great heart secrets,
> Thou, and thou alone, must hear.

Though my scarred and veteran legions
  Bear their eagles high no more,
And my wrecked and scattered galleys
  Strew dark Actium's fatal shore,
Though no shining guards surround me,
  Prompt to do their master's will,
I must perish like a Roman,
  Die the great triumvir still.

Let not Cæsar's servile minions
  Mock the lion thus laid low.
'T was no foeman's hand that slew him:
  'T was his own that struck the blow.
Here, then, pillowed on thy bosom,
  Ere his star fades quite away,
He who, drunk with thy caresses,
  Madly flung a world away.

Should the base plebeian rabble
  Dare assail my fame at Rome,
Where the noble spouse, Octavia,
  Weeps within her widowed home,
Seek her: say the *gods have told me*, —
  Altars, augurs, circling wings, —
That her blood with mine commingled
  Yet shall mount the throne of kings.

And for thee, star-eyed Egyptian,
  Glorious sorceress of the Nile,
Light the path to Stygian horrors
  With the splendors of thy smile;
Give the Cæsar crowns and arches;
  Let his brow the laurel twine;
I can scorn the Senate's triumphs,
  Triumphing in love like thine.

I am dying, Egypt, dying!
  Hark! the insulting foeman's cry:
They are coming; quick, my falchion!
  Let me front them ere I die!
Ah! no more amid the battle
  Shall my heart exulting swell.
Isis and Osiris guard thee!
    Cleopatra — Rome — farewell!"

It is supposed that the two obelisks called Cleopatra's Needles once decorated the palaces of the Ptolemies. One of these has been presented to England by the Egyptian Government. It is questionable if decaying Britain has sufficient energy to transplant it upon her shores.

When Amrou conquered Alexandria, he was so astonished at the magnificence of the city, that he wrote to the caliph, "I have taken the City of the West. It is of immense extent: I can not describe to you how many houses it contains. There are four thousand palaces, four thousand baths, twelve thousand dealers in fresh oil, forty thousand Jews who pay tribute, and four hundred theaters, or places of amusement."

Bidding Egypt, the Mizraim of the Hebrews, farewell, I have to say, O Egypt! your reigning viceroy is an ambitious Mohammedan polygamist; your government in its taxation is oppressive; your slavery is a blotch upon the face of the nineteenth century; your religion is a gaudy show; your people are terribly ignorant; your guides are shameless liars; your donkeys are hopelessly impenitent; your "backsheesh" crying beggars are a disgrace to any country; and your hungry fleas and flies more numerous, if possible, than they were in the times of the biblical patriarchs. On the other hand, those pyramidal Titans standing in somber majesty; those hieroglyphical records, defying the wear and waste of time; that magnificent museum of antiquities upon the bank of the Nile; those far-stretching groves of palm; those broad fields of cotton, coffee, and rice, dotting the Nilotic valley; those gardens of fruits and flowers; those gorgeous sunsets of crimson and gold, translated into myriads of flashing jewels, to gradually melt away like Cleopatra's pearl into a sea of purple; and those skies so clear and golden by day, so blue and delicately studded with constellations by night, reminding one of that city immortal with the twelve gates of pearl, as seen by John in vision,—these, *all these*, are to be set down to the sunny side of the Egypt of to-day.

TALKERS. — EASTERN LIARS. — MARK TWAIN.

These everlasting talkers, who run all to tongue, continually put one in mind of a swinging sign on the hotel abandoned. They are the Cheap-Johns of civic life. Sap drizzles and drops. Limber-lipped talkers talk what they know, and what they do not know ; talk what they imagine, what they suspect, what they infer, what they dream, what they have done, and what they intend to do, making themselves the heroes of all tales told. Men like Alcott and Emerson, substantially great, are retiring and modest. Deep rivers roll silently. The lightnings are voiceless. God never speaks. Any thing, then, but a talkative, self-conceited egotist, who, to put it alphabetically, shows off at A, spills out at B, slops over at C, runs sediments at D, and then repeats and re-repeats, commencing with the *ego*, and all — *all this* — to seem " smart ! "

If David in his " haste " said, "All men are liars," I say it deliberately of all the " dragomen " and guides employed by us in the East. Many would both falsify and steal. Charity compels the opinion, however, that some of their misstatements were grounded in ignorance, rather than willfulness. Take this sample : Standing near the dome of the Grand Mosque in Benares, and surveying the city circling the bend of the Ganges, we inquired of our guide the number of the population. " Six millions ! " was the prompt reply. " What ? " we doubtingly inquired. " Six — *six millions*, sir ! " was the emphatic response. It was provokingly annoying. London, the largest city in the world, has less than three millions and a half. When looking up to the summit of Pompey's Pillar in Alexandria, Dr. Dunn inquired the hight. " Ten miles : he be ten miles high," was the ready answer. This Arab guide neither knew the real hight, nor the use of the English language. His professed guidance, therefore, was an imposition.

Mark Twain does full justice to the "sheiks," to the

"dragomen," and to the beggars generally, of the Levant and the East. Generously admitting the genius of Twain in some directions, I nevertheless feel to say that, while *wit*, if original, is well; while fiction has its place, and romance its legitimate use, — still truth and falsehood, sacredness and sacrilege, history and tradition, indiscriminately mixed, and bound between two covers with no lines of demarcation, reveal not only a silly conceit, but show a lack of solid literary culture. Such "Innocents-Abroad" books of travel, read trustingly and believingly, lead the unwary strangely astray. True, their pages may excite interest: so do Gulliver's. They may produce laughter: so do clowns. And such volumes, too, may sell: so also does the Jack Sheppard style of novels. But is this the only object of bookmaking?

SPIRITUALISM IN THE EGYPT OF ANTIQUITY.

The *gods*, the guardian angels of the ancient Egyptians, were once mortal men. Sanchonianthon, whom accredited historians place before the time of Moses, wrote in the Phœnician. Philo of Byblus translated a portion of his works into Greek. Here follow a few lines: —

"Egyptians and Phœnicians accounted those the greatest gods who had found out things most necessary and useful in life, and who had been benefactors when among mankind."

Hermes Trismegistus acknowledged that the "gods of Egypt were the souls of dead men." And Plutarch informs us that the "Egyptian priests pointed out where the bodies of their gods lay buried." The eloquent Cicero wrote, —

"The whole heaven is almost entirely filled with the human race: even the superior order of gods were originally natives of this lower world." And with these gods, angels, *spirits*, the Egyptians of remotest antiquity held constant converse. They also thoroughly understood psychological science. On their tombs, towers, and obelisks, are pictured mesmerists, in the act of pathetizing subjects.

The papyrus of Sne-frau, predecessor of Cheops, abounds in the marvels of a gifted priestess. On a papyrus-scroll from Thebes is a symbol of death; and just over the mummied form is hovering the resurrected spirit, with eyes turned towards the scales of justice and truth. In the distance are the expected mansions of rest. Several chapters in the ritual of the "Book of the Dead" treat of magic, trance, and magnetic healing. There are also pictorial illustrations of the different magnetic states, and operators with upraised hands mesmerizing their subjects. Aural rays are seen streaming upon the patient's brain; and consecrated priests stand by, holding in their right hands croziers, warding off the psychological influences of dark-hued, undeveloped spirits. The study and practice of Spiritism must have been common in the period of the pyramid-builders. The Hebrews obtained their knowledge of psychological science in Egypt.

SPIRITUALISTS IN CAIRO.

The Angel of Spiritualism has sounded the resurrection trumpet of a future existence in every land under heaven. Madame Blavatsky, assisted by other brave souls, formed a society of Spiritualists in Cairo about three years since. They have fine writing-mediums, and other forms of the manifestations. They hold weekly séances during the winter months. Madame Blavatsky is at present in Odessa, Russia. The lady, whose husband keeps the Oriental Hotel, is a firm Spiritualist. Fired with the missionary spirit, I left a package of pamphlets and tracts in her possession, for gratuitous distribution. "And, as ye go, *teach*," was the ancient command.

CHAPTER XXIII.

FROM ALEXANDRIA TO JOPPA AND JERUSALEM. — THE CITY OF JOPPA.

AUSTRIAN steamers leave Alexandria three times a week for Jaffa, *alias* the Joppa of the New Testament. The passage requires two or three days, stopping only at Port Said, the northern terminus of the Suez Canal. This city contains hardly seven thousand, — a motley.gathering of all nations, the Arab element largely predominating. It has an artificial harbor, the huge blocks of which are manufactured of limestone, sand, and cement, and then transported to their position, forming a breakwater sufficiently substantial to insure the safety of ships. Unless money were the object, few would fix a residence in this sandy city.

Aug. 24, Sunday morning, six o'clock, Joppa — the Joppa of my Sunday-school dreams, with its domes, minarets, palms, and suburban orange-gardens — loomed up in the distance like an amphitheatre from the ocean. To the right and left of the city only a sandy beach was visible. Joppa — a city of fifteen thousand, literally a "city set upon a hill," and the natural landing-place of Jews, Christian and Mohammedan pilgrims to Jerusalem — has a very insecure harbor. Remnants of an old Phœnician harbor are yet traceable; but the precise spot where Jonah shipped for Tarshish, — probably *Tarsus*, — to "flee from the presence of the Lord," is not pointed out even by credulous monks. The clergy of the East, knowing the nature of the finny tribes that sport in the Mediterranean waters, consider it no heresy to doubt the whale-story of the Old Testament.

It was at Joppa that the Lebanon timber from Hiram, king of Tyre, was landed for the building of both the temples at Jerusalem. It was here that the Tabitha whose name "by interpretation was Dorcas" lived, whom Peter, by his mediumistic powers, "raised to life," and where this apostle also had the remarkable vision recorded in the tenth chapter of Acts. The "*Acts* of the Apostles" should have been denominated the practices and spiritual experiences of the apostles. Tradition points to the very house where lived "Simon the tanner, by the seaside." Certainly we visited this spot, as do all pilgrims. The "seaside" is still there: further, "deponent saith not." Houses perish, but the good, never. Peter still remembers his vision.

NEW-ENGLANDERS IN JOPPA.

Considerable interest attached to Joppa, a few years since, from the attempted settlement there of some Maine and New-Hampshire "Church of Messiah" religionists, under the leadership of the Rev. G. H. Adams, well known in some of the New-England States. This colonizing movement proved, however, a complete failure. Adams — originally an actor, a Mormon, a pretender — became dissipated; the colonists lost their property; an officious consul (since dismissed) took the fleece; and the flock became scattered, only a few of the original settlers remaining in the country. The tract of land secured and taken up by these New-England enthusiasts is now owned principally by Germans. Some of these American settlers became so poor that they actually begged bread of the Arabs. Contributions sent to them were appropriated by Adams and his wife. Only twelve of the original one hundred and fifty-six that went to Joppa remain. Adams is in England; and Mrs. Adams, the least respected of the two, is in California. The whole story is a sad one, the details of which will hereafter be given in full.

But how can we longer tarry in Joppa, when Jerusalem, once the "city of the great king," is only thirty-five miles distant, and that over an excellent road, considering the mountainous nature of these Syrian lands?

IN JOPPA, BOUND FOR JERUSALEM.

While yet in Cairo, Egypt, we unwisely engaged an Arab dragoman, at so much per day, to conduct us through Palestine; *unwisely*, because better guides can be employed in Jaffa at the same price. Mr. Rolla Floyd, a very candid, competent American gentleman, and an energetic young man named Clark, both thoroughly acquainted with the whole country, will prove excellent guides. They are remnants of the Jaffa colony, and quite conversant with the Arabic and the Palestinian dialects. I am particular to note these facts, because, in the Egypt of to-day, famous for flies, fleas, and falsifiers, they are sure to tell travelers that no guides can be procured in Jaffa. Our Cairo guide — Mahomet Selim — was a failure so far as intellectual guidance was concerned, yet a good and faithful "dragoman" in other matters. It is cheaper traveling in this than in the winter season. The dry and rainy seasons remind one of California.

Selim, having secured his sheik, well-armed, his muleteers, his horses, donkeys, and tents, we were off at ten o'clock on a sunny morning, horseback, for Jerusalem. Our horses were good ones. Passing through the bazaar, the narrow streets swarming with glittering raggedness, and the walls grayed with age, we emerged from this Oriental city buried in noble groves of orange-trees, out into the main thoroughfare, which was lined for some distance with irrigated gardens, lemon-orchards, and orange-groves. Suburban Jaffa is beautiful. The roadside, for a long way toward Ramleh, is fenced with cacti, and fringed with gardens. Residents tell us that these gardens in March and April are literally enchanting, the air being loaded with mingled fragrance of apricot and orange, lemon and quince, plum and china tree blossoms. During the dry season, lasting from May till November, these gardens are kept fresh and green by irrigation.

> "In Eastern land they talk in flowers,
> And tell in a garland their loves and cares:
> Each blossom that blooms in their garden-bowers
> On its leaves a mystic language bears."

But we are galloping away from garden and grove over vast plains, the biblical plains of Sharon. How flash upon the mind now the poetical phrases, "Carmel and Sharon," "the rose of Sharon, and the lily of the valley"! Who are these? "Pilgrims," says Selim, "coming back from Jerusalem and the Jordan." Some were Catholics, some Greek Christians, and others Mohammedans, *all* either riding camels, donkeys, or afoot, weary and dusty. Most of the traveling at this season is done in the night-time. Syrian, like Egyptian women, veil their faces. It is said that when the Sultan of Turkey was at Paris, in 1867, Louis Napoleon inquired of him, "Why don't you have roads in *your* country?" adding, "The empress wishes much to visit Jerusalem." "There shall be a road within a year," was the Sultan's reply; and so there was, a handsome carriage-road, twenty-five or thirty feet in width, the work of forced labor.

Sharon has not, as Isaiah prophesied, become a "howling wilderness." Its extensive plains, rounding up now and then into swells and long ridges, are very fertile, judging from the cultivated fields we passed, covered with corn and wheat stubble. Reapers and gleaners gather the harvests in June, or early in July. These plains, so eminently fertile, constantly reminded me of Sacramento and other rich valley-lands in California.

On this route from Jaffa to Ramleh, three hours distant, there are several little villages in orchards of olives, figs, pomegranates, and mulberries. These mulberry-trees, like those of Australia, are grown not for the silk-worm, but for their fruit, the berries of which, while resembling the largest blackberries, have a sharper acid taste. From the mountains of Judea and Samaria to the sea, and from the foot of Carmel to the more barren lands of Philistia, lie spread out the plains of Sharon, in spring-time like a flower-flecked island, beautiful as vast, and diversified as beautiful, fascinating the eye, and enchanting the imagination. It must have been paradisaic when Israel's king sang of Sharon's rose.

RAMLEH.

This old city, mostly in ruins, is said by Eusebius and St. Jerome to have been the Arimathea of Joseph, the Joseph into whose new tomb they put the body of Jesus. It was and *is* customary for Jews in distant localities to have tombs and burial-places in the immediate vicinity of Jerusalem, the holy city. This Ramlehan city of ancient buildings, cisterns, and subterranean vaults, has a grand old tower, believed by some to have been a minaret; others think it originally the campanile of a magnificent church. That it has an Arabic inscription, bearing date A.H. 710, A.D. 1310, proves nothing, as there are similar vaunting inscriptions on castles and temples in Syria much older than the Mohammedan religion. Among the old stone houses of this city rises a palatial Latin convent, the monks entertaining travelers. The kindness of these celibate monks is proverbial.

THROUGH THE JUDEAN COUNTRY.

"We have turned us away from the fragrant East,
  For the desert sand and the arid waste."

"Selim," our guide, announcing himself ready with horses watered, bridled, equipped, we are again snugly in the saddle under a scorching sun, on the way from Ramleh to Jerusalem. It is several miles yet across the plains of

Sharon to the foot-hills that fringe the more mountainous regions. The landscape is diversified and beautified with olive-orchards, the leaves resembling those of the willow, only more soft and delicate. This is a common tree in the south of France, in Greece, and Syria. The beautiful plain of Athens, as seen from Hymettus, appears almost covered with olive-trees. Olive-oil, quite an article of export in Syria and Asia Minor, is eaten with lettuce and other salads all through the East. The fruit is plucked by the hand, reduced to a pulp in the olive-mill, put into sacks of coarse linen, and subjected to a crushing pressure. This tree in portions of the Orient, like the oak in the West, is held in a sort of veneration. It was an olive-branch that the dove brought to the legendary ark; while in Greece the wreaths that crowned the victors in the Olympic games were woven from the slender branches that tremble upon the leafy olive.

The road winding, the country now wild and desolate, we gallop along quite reckless of the thought that this portion of Palestine, storied in song and trodden by apostles, had given birth to Jeremiah, witnessed the duel of David and Goliath, and the recorded standing-still of the sun on the plains of Ajalon. Passing old stone villages and rude tombs, we meet more pilgrims. It is nearly noon, a burning August noon, and the way begins to seem long to the "city of the great king." Through ravines and cañons, how rugged the country, and barren too, save the orchards of figs and olives that dot the valleys, or terrace the hillsides. What strange geological formations! Giving our panting horses a little rest, we lunch to-day in an olive-grove, and have delicious prickly pears plucked fresh from a cactus hedge, and brought us by some sore-eyed Syrian girls, living a little distance from the wayside. "Selim," our dragoman, provides well, but the day seems long. Other hills and mountains are scaled, and Jerusalem is still before us. This is novel and odd-looking, surely. "What?" Why, this summer threshing-floor in the open field, the grain being trampled out by the stamping of oxen. It is decidedly primitive. The Egyptians have a similar method.

Traversing these regions, one naturally asks, "How do the people live?" Only in dreams could it have been called a land "flowing with milk and honey;" and yet when irrigated there are tasty oases, and numerous vineyards too, burdened with white and purpling clusters. Cities and villages, built upon hillsides, frequently crown their summits. Thus situated, these warlike inhabitants of Scripture records could better see the approaching enemy, and defend themselves in battle. Terraced up toward the steep hilltops, many streets are on a range with the stone houses below. And then these tile-roofed buildings are generally flat. Some are handsomely grassed over. In several places we saw goats and cattle feeding upon the housetops.

But see! here's a *restaurant!* Two men come out, American dressed. They speak English. One of them, originally connected with the American colonists to Jaffa, is now employed by the Palestine Exploration Society on the east side of the Jordan, in the land of Moab. These explorations are certainly confirming Jewish history. Our horses are weary and worn: so are their riders. The sun has now dipped his disk in the Mediterranean.

GLIMPSES OF JERUSALEM.

There's not a cloud in sight. The skies are aflame with departing sun-rays, crimson and golden. Only "this hill to rise!" Ay, there — *there* it is! the very Jerusalem over which "Jesus wept." Some poet sings, —

> "Jerusalem! I would have seen
> Thy precipices steep;
> The trees of palm that overhang
> Thy gorges dark and deep.
> Around thy hills the spirits throng
> Of all thy murdered seers;
> And voices that went up from it
> Are ringing in my ears."

The fading light throws over the city a gray, somber, shadowy appearance; and yet you see around its entire circuit a lofty wall with beautiful parapets; and within, white roofs, balustrades, domes, minarets, majestic churches, and the Mosque of Omar crowning Mount Moriah. Though situated upon a mountain-top, Jerusalem is surrounded by still loftier mountains. It surprised us, however, that a city so historically famous should be so small. Pictures and Sunday-school teachings had impressed us with the belief that it must be marvelously great, because built and adorned by King Solomon. Nevertheless it is large and rich in Semitic associations. Here Abraham dwelt. Here patriarchs and prophets had their pastures, their wells, their tents, their tombs, and their altars. Here Jesus performed many of his spiritual marvels. Here apostles sat at the feet of their divine Teacher. Here disciples learned the commandment, "Love ye one another." And here the tender, sweet-hearted John lovingly leaned upon Jesus' bosom, giving to all these hills and mountains an associate sacredness. Well might Whittier write, —

> "And throned on her hills sits Jerusalem yet,
> With dust on her forehead, and chains on her feet;
> For the crown of her pride to the mocker hath gone,
> And the holy shekinah is dark where it shone."

OTHERS' IMPRESSIONS OF JERUSALEM.

Lieut. Lynch, of the navy, approaching Jerusalem, writes, —

"I rode to the summit of a hill on the left, and beheld the holy city. Men may say what they please; but there are moments when the soul, casting aside the artificial trammels of the world, will assert its claim to a celestial origin, and regardless of time and place, of sneers and sarcasms, pay its tribute at the shrine of faith, and weep for the sufferings of its Founder."

Prof. Osborne observes, —

"Though weary from the day's ride in the saddle, and exhausted as were the pilgrims by the way, it was near night when we obtained the first view of the city with its mosques and towers. How unspeakably charming was that moment's vision! Never did silence and loneliness appear so gratifying."

Believing as firmly in Jesus' suffering, bleeding, and dying a martyr to a principle, as in Socrates' draining the hemlock draught, the sight of Jerusalem had for me a thousand charms.

> "Here circling vines their leafy banners spread,
> And held their green shields o'er the pilgrim's head;
> At once repelling Syria's burning ray,
> And breathing freshness on the sultry day."

To Strauss, Jesus was a wise rabbi; to Rénan, a moral teacher; to Fourier, a warm-hearted socialist; to Fénelon, the most rapt of mystics; to Paine, the most sincere of philanthropists; to Müller, the harmony of all history; to Emerson, a true prophet seeing the mystery of the soul; to Parker, a fellow-brother and self-sacrificing reformer; while to me he was the marvel-working medium of the East, the baptized of Christ, and the great Syrian *Spiritualist* sent of the gods to bear "witness to the truth." Previously I had looked upon the Isle of Samos that gave birth to Pythagoras; I had stood upon the spot where Socrates was imprisoned for corrupting the youth; I had wandered over the fields of Sarnath, where Buddha's feet had pressed the soil; I had traversed the land where Plato taught in the Athenian groves; and *now* I was at the gates of the city where Jesus had toiled and taught, healed and suffered, wept, and died with the prayer upon his purpling lips, "Father, forgive them!" The sainted John Pierpont sweetly wrote,—

> "A lonelier, lovelier path be mine;
> Greece and her charms I'd leave for Palestine;
> There purer streams through happier valleys flow,
> And sweeter flowers on holier mountains blow;
> I'd love to breathe where Gilead sheds her balm;
> I'd love to walk on Jordan's banks of palm;

> I'd love to wet my foot in Hermon's dews;
> I'd love the promptings of Isaiah's muse;
> In Carmel's holy grots I'd court repose,
> And deck my mossy couch with Sharon's blooming rose."

This is Aug. 24. We enter Jerusalem by the Jaffa Gate, and follow " Christian Street " to Mount Zion.

JERUSALEM AS IT NOW IS.

How often in life does sunshine fade away into cloudland, poetry into dullest prose! So Jerusalem, which was so beautiful an hour ago in the softening, fading light of the setting sun, shrunk away to a trafficking Turkish city the moment we entered within the gates. The city has at present a population of some twelve thousand, of whom three thousand four hundred are denominated Christians, three thousand Jews, and five thousand Mohammedans; each class largely occupying separate quarters. The streets are narrow, dirty, and poorly paved. The houses, built of stone, look like fortresses, presenting in front little more than blank walls. Morning and evening they are crowded with Turks and Arabs. The bazaars were sparsely supplied, with the exception of fruits. The principal trade of the city consists in beads and coins, crosses and relics. There are no gaslights, as in Alexandria; and therefore it was impossible to see much of the city in evening-time. Stopping at the Mediterranean Hotel on Mount Zion, kept by Mr. Honstein, — a Free-Mason and a free-thinker, — we had a delightful night's rest. Waking rested and refreshed, we could say most heartily, "Pray for the peace of Jerusalem; they shall prosper that love thee. Peace be within thy walls, and prosperity within thy palaces."

OUR FIRST DAY IN THE CITY.

Out in early morning upon the housetop I saw the sun rise from beyond the Jordan. After a delicious breakfast of eggs, bread, honey, and several kinds of fruit, we started, with a guide, for the Church of the Holy Sepulcher. Fronting it is a neatly paved square, reached from the street by descending a flight of worn stone stairs. This area is usually thronged with Syrians, Abyssinians, Armenians, Greeks, Copts, and Turks, as well as Europeans. Monks and tradesmen also frequent the place daily to sell amulets and cheap relics. The Holy Sepulcher is open to all religionists except the Jews. These, with an intolerance unpardonable, are excluded. There is little doubt but that the "new tomb" of Joseph of Arimathea was in this mountainous eminence. It was so designated in the first, and confirmed by the fathers of later centuries. The magnificent dome of the Church of the Holy Sepulcher has been erected directly over this white-marble sarcophagus under which is the veritable rock-hewn "tomb." Near the sepulcher is a marble slab on which it is said they anointed the body of Jesus; and to the east of it is a small door, requiring a stooping posture to enter, made, in all probability, to harmonize with St. John's account, "And, as she wept, she stooped down, and looked into the sepulcher." About the tomb and the altar are gifts of precious stones, wreaths of pearls and diamonds, from the Christian sovereigns of Europe, and lamps of gold and silver kept continually burning. These, glittering with the smoke of the incense, the perfume of spices, and the attar of roses, induced in us a strange, weird sensation. Silently we said, "Jesus and the poor; Jesus and the beggar by the wayside; Jesus, once treading the wine-press alone, without 'where to lay his head,' now a *god* with a costly, garnished sepulcher, and the poor of the nineteenth century begging, starving, dying!" Jesus was genuine: Christianity is a sham.

The crucifixion upon Calvary, the stone of anointing, the burial sepulcher, and other holy places, to say nothing of the Greek, Latin, Armenian, and Coptic departments of worship, are all included under the roof of the Church of the Holy Sepulcher. Mount Calvary, within a stone's-throw of the sepulcher, is reached by climbing a flight of eighteen stone steps, introducing us into a richly decorated chapel. In this chapel is quite a rock with a hole therein, said to have received the foot of the cross; and a tablet, showing where the " mother of Jesus stood " during her son's agony. Descending a rugged stone stairway, we entered the Chapel of St. Helena, mother of Constantine; where, three hundred years after the crucifixion, it is pretended were found the " three crosses " in a state of perfect preservation.

It is claimed that the Armenian Church covers the site where John was beheaded; and close by they pointed us to Adam's grave, and a picture of his skull. They also showed where the cock stood and "crowed three times" before Peter's denial; showed us the Judgment Hall; the place where Jesus, leaning against the wall when weary, made an indentation in the rock; the spot where he fell under the cross, calling upon Simon of Cyrene; the place where they scourged him; the cleft in the rock, made when he yielded up the ghost; and, what is more, they identified the exact locality where the angel stood that appeared to the Maries. Further, they pointed to the tomb of Melchisedec, the palace of Herod, the place where Stephen was stoned, the house of Dives, the dilapidated stone shanty of Lazarus, and the prints of Jesus' footsteps where he stood when confounding the "doctors of the law."

Naturally incredulous, the fixing of these localities with such cool precision disgusted me. Tradition and superstition are the handmaids of ignorance. The truth is, the most imaginative genius can not reconstruct Jerusalem as Jesus saw it, and Josephus and other Jewish writers describe it. The demon of war, crimsoning its streets, too often sacked the city. It has been burned, built, and rebuilt. The localities of towers and tombs, pools and sepulchers, therefore, are mostly hypothetical; and yet the general topographical outlines of the city and immediate country are as clearly marked as they are ineffaceable.

"THE WALL, AND THE GATES THEREOF."

The present wall, with its five gates, surrounding Jerusalem, is about two and a half miles in length; and portions of it evidently occupy the line of the ancient *first wall*. Some fifteen feet thick, and from twenty-five to forty feet high according to the location of the ground, this wall has salient angles, square towers, battlements, and a breastwork running around upon the top, furnishing a fine promenade for tourists. Standing upon the topmost stones, and surveying the scenery, we were shown a horizontally projecting column upon which Mohammed is to "stand when he comes to judge the world." It was interesting to examine the excavations of Capt. Warren, who, commencing some fifty yards outside the walls, pushed a shaft under them, discovering the foundations of the *old Temple*, the pillars and arches of which are marvels.

Visiting the gate that is called "Beautiful," and then passing out of St. Stephen's Gate, we descended the steep hillside to the vale of Kedron, just by the Valley of Jehoshaphat. No water flows along the bed of the Kedron, save during the rainy season. Previous to beginning the ascent of Mount Olives, we come to the garden of Gethsemane, a pleasant bit of level ground about fifty yards square, surrounded by a high wall, and containing, besides several old, scraggy olive-trees, some flowering shrubs, plants, and semi-tropical flowers, carefully cared for by Latin monks. Over this "Garden of Agony," Greek and Romish monks, fired with rivalry and jealousies, have not only wrangled, not only fought with their tongues, but they have several times actually come to blows and bloodshed. Turkish officials, in the name of the *Allah* of the prophet, were compelled to interfere. Behold how these Christians "love one another"!

THE MOUNT OF OLIVES.

Though the stones were rough and rolling, the nimbleness of our Arab steeds made us feel safe while climbing up the steep hillsides of Mount Olives from the Garden of Gethsemane. Jesus and the apostles must have often left the passing imprints of their bare feet along this winding way. Upon the summit we had reached, is a miserable, dirty village, whose dark-hued inhabitants greatly resemble, both in dress and appearance, the Mussulmans of India. The women, sitting at the doors of their low stone houses, partially covered their faces as we passed by; and the children chased us, calling for money as a matter of right, rather than charity. Upon the top of this uneven mount, guides, showing the impress of a large foot legibly stamped upon the face of a stone, declare that the indentation was there made when " Jesus ascended to heaven." Saying nothing of the unnaturalness of the imprint, the alleged ascension was not from Mount Olives, but from Bethany. Accordingly, the Evangelist Luke says, " Jesus led out his disciples as far as Bethany, and blessed them ; and, while he blessed them, he was parted from them, and carried up into heaven."

> " ' Peace I leave with you!' From days departed
> Floats down the blessing, simple and serene,
> Which to his followers, few and fearful-hearted,
> With yearning love, thus spake the Nazarene, —
> *'Peace I leave with you!'* "

CHAPTER XXIV.

CITY OF PROPHETS AND APOSTLES. — JESUS AND JERUSALEM.

> "The panting pilgrim's heart is filled
> With holiest themes divine,
> When first he sees the lilies gild
> The fields of Palestine."

JERUSALEM, literally the city of peace, built and destroyed, buried and resurrected, was plundered by the Egyptian conqueror Shashak; besieged and taken by Nebuchadnezzar, king of Babylon; robbed by Syrian kings from the north; subjected, with all Judea, to Roman rule 63 B.C.; destroyed by Titus; devastated by crusaders; and savagely sacked by the Saracens in the seventh century. Standing on Mount Olives, perhaps near where John leaned upon Jesus' bosom, and reflecting upon the above historical events, while an Arab lad was gathering some olive-branches as evergreen symbols of the angel-song "Peace on earth," my thought flashed backward o'er the waste of nearly twenty centuries, to the occasion that called forth Jesus' plaintively tearful appeal to his kinsmen. As a psychometrist knowing the murderous persecutions of the past, and as a seer foreseeing the future of the city of the prophets, he wept, saying, —

"O Jerusalem, Jerusalem! thou that killest the prophets, and stonest them which are sent unto thee! how often would I have gathered thy children together, even as a hen gathereth her chickens under her wings,

CITY OF PROPHETS AND APOSTLES.

and ye would not! Behold, your house is left unto you desolate. For I say unto you, Ye shall not see me henceforth, till ye shall say, Blessed is he that cometh in the name of the Lord."

As the summit of Olives is some three hundred feet higher than Jerusalem, the prospect, especially from the Bethany side, is magnificent. Eastward nearly twenty miles are the Jordan and the Dead Sea: the surface of the latter is said to be the lowest point of water upon the face of the globe, being one thousand three hundred and twelve feet lower than the Mediterranean Sea.

Travelers accustomed to the wide distances of America are astonished to find how near together nestle the Palestinian cities, so famous in the Scriptures. Bethlehem is but six miles south from Jerusalem; while Bethany, the place with which are associated many of the sweetest and tenderest memories of Jesus, is but two or three miles from the city. It was from Bethany, then embowered in olive and palm, acacia, fig, and pomegranate, that the Nazarene commenced his triumphal march over the rising hills on which "much people that were come to the feast, when they heard that Jesus was coming to Jerusalem, took branches of palm-trees, and went forth to meet him, and cried, Hosanna!"

Monks here show the cave-like grave from which Lazarus, who had fallen into a deep, unconscious trance having the appearance of death, was raised. Deep and damp, it was reached by several descending steps. Naturally skeptical touching "sacred spots," we did not care to enter. Here in Bethany lived Martha and Mary, whom Jesus so loved.

"BUT DID JESUS EXIST?"

It is too late in the day of historical erudition to raise such an inquiry. Intelligent spirits without exception, — so far as I am aware, — thinkers and *savants* in all countries, admit that Jesus lived and taught, was persecuted, and martyred upon Calvary. Gerald Massey, in commencing his lecture upon the " Birth, Life, and Marvels of Jesus Christ," in Music Hall, Boston, Jan. 18, said, —

"The question of the real *personal existence* of the Man is settled for me by the references to *Jesus* in the Talmud, where we learn that he was with his teacher, Rabbi Joshua, in Egypt, and that he wrote a MS. there which he brought into Palestine. This MS. was well known to the rabbis; and I doubt not it contained the kernel of his teachings, fragments of which have floated down to us in the Gospels."

Aaron Knight, one of my spirit teachers, assured me, several years since, that from conversing with the apostolic John, and other ancient spirits, he had learned that Jesus, between the years of twelve and thirty, visited Assyria, Egypt, and Persia, there studying spiritual science. In consonance with this, "The London Human Nature" of 1872 (published by James Burns) has a picture (through the artistic mediumship of Mr. Duguid) *of*, and a communication *from*, the Persian spirit who on earth was the traveling companion of Jesus during his pilgrimage into Persia and India. The narration is thrillingly interesting.

While in Jerusalem, we visited a learned and venerable rabbi, to ascertain what the Talmud said of Jesus. He kindly read and translated for us, and also loaned us for the day a portion of the translation. From this "Talmudic pile" we gathered the facts that the *Mishna*, or repetition of the law, relating to governments, laws, customs, and events, transpiring long before and after the Christian era, contained the opinions of one hundred and thirty learned rabbis. The compilation of this was finished in A. D. 190, and is considered by the Jews in all Oriental lands as divine. Certain comments annexed to the Hebrew text of the Mishna constitute the work known as the "Jerusalem Talmud." But the Neziken of the Mishna in one of its seventy-four sections (Order IV. chap. 10) while treating of the Sanhedrim, or great Senate and House of Judgment at Jerusalem, makes special mention of Jesus of Nazareth, — his "indifference to the law of Moses," his "pretended miracles," his "stubborn waywardness," his "kingly ambition," and "repeated blasphemies." These testimonies are befitting *addenda* to "Jesus: Myth, Man, or God?" *

THE MOSQUE OF OMAR.

It is common for Arabian and Indian Mussulmans, after visiting Mecca, sacred to the birth of Mohammed, and Medina, holy because holding the ashes of Araby's prophet, to visit Jerusalem, praying in the Mosque of Omar. This famous edifice, as an architectural structure, is unique, massive, and eminently rich in consecrated antiquities. Its overshadowing dome, its porcelain, blue enamel, crimson canopies, elaborately gilded texts from the Koran, and weird shrines of the patriarch, give the building a grand and imposing appearance. Mohammedans, ever hating Christian leather, require "infidels" from the West to enter their temples of worship with bared feet, or in slippers presented at the vestibule. But as workmen, last autumn, were repairing this mosque, — the crown of Mount Moriah, and original site of Solomon's Temple, — we were allowed to enter well shod ; when our guide, recounting the old and silly myth, pointed to the "stone," the rock of *El Sakara*, a large, irregular, limestone rock surrounded by an iron railing, and said to be "miraculously suspended." Passing by (without a thought) the loadstone suspension, this is declared to be the rock upon which Abraham sacrificed the "ram," the one that Jacob used for a "pillow," and the one, say Mussulmans, from which Mohammed made his miraculous flight to heaven upon his celestial steed *Barak;* and, as proof, they point to the marks of the horse's hoofs in the rock.

This mosque has parted with much of its past splendor. Ibn Asâkir saw it in the twelfth century. Then it was a

* This volume referred to by Mr. Peebles, "*Jesus: Myth, Man, or God?*" giving the historical evidences of Jesus' existence, as well as drawing damaging comparisons between the results of sectarian Christianity, and the moral effects of the "heathen philosophy" so called, is for sale at the "Banner of Light" office.—ED. BANNER OF LIGHT.

building of beautiful proportions, having fifty doors, six hundred marble pillars, fifteen domes, four minarets, and three hundred and eighty-five chains, sustaining five thousand lamps. Not until 1856 were Jews and Christians allowed to enter this mosque. Mohammedans believe that angels keep nightly watch about the lofty dome, bringing with them, to breathe, the air of Paradise.

THE JEWS' WAILING-PLACE.

Admitting, which seems reasonable, that the present western wall, and a portion of the northern wall circling Jerusalem, occupy the very line of the *ancient first wall*, it is perfectly natural that Eastern Jews should meet at the base of the wall upon the west side to weep and wail over stones there placed before Herod's time. Though there are some present each day, Friday is the great wailing-day. Assembled, —

The rabbi begins, "On account of the Temple which has been destroyed, and the glory which has departed" —

"*We sit here and weep.*"

"Because our prophets and holy men have been slain, because Jerusalem is a desolation, and because our Messiah long promised has not come" —

"*We sit here lonely weeping and praying.*"

Both sexes were present. The aged women, bowing, sighed and wept; young maidens bathed the hallowed walls in their tears; old men tottered up to the stones, prayers trembling on their lips; while others wailed aloud as though their hearts would break. Seeing them made my soul sad. And oh! how I wanted to tell them, Messiah has already come. Your Messiah, like the kingdom of God, is within you; while the Christ-spirit has been coming during all the cycling ages! This locality along the outer wall may well be termed "the Jews' wailing-place."

IN HELL AS PROPHESIED.

Leaving the close-communion Calvinistic craft while my cheeks were yet crimson, and hair flaxen, the clergyman, in a rage over my irrepressible infidelity, told me I would "go to hell." And it was true, — infinitely truer than *his* Sunday preaching, for I went, *yes*, went to hell; and that, too, while seeking Jesus, or, rather, his footpaths round about Jerusalem. After passing for half an hour under a scorching sun along the brow of Mount Zion, dotted with here and there an olive-tree, I suddenly found myself in the Valley of Hinnom, *Gehenna*, Hell; the place referred to in Mark ix. 45, 46, —

"And, if thy foot offend thee, cut it off: it is better for thee to enter halt into life, than having two feet to be cast into hell, into the fire that never shall be quenched; where their worm dieth not, and the fire is not quenched."

This Valley of Hinnom, on the south-east side of Jerusalem, is nearly one mile and a half in length; and in ancient times there was an image here standing dedicated to Moloch, to which idolatrous Jews offered human sacrifices, even their own children. After King Josiah had partially purged the land of idolatry, this valley became the common receptacle of rubbish from the city, and of the dead bodies of notorious criminals, upon which festering filth worms reveled. And to stifle the stench, and prevent pestilential diseases, a fire was there kept continually burning; hence this place of fire, or hell-fire. The term Gehenna (Hell), composed of two Hebrew words, *Gee*, a valley, and *Hinnom*, the name of the man who once owned it, was used by Jesus figuratively to describe a state of deep, conscious misery. I do not agree with Theodore Parker that "Jesus taught the eternity of future punishment." The whole drift of his moral teachings and parables is against such a conclusion. True, he employed the phrase, "*The fire that shall never be quenched;*" but he used it in the limited sense of the Orientals. Strabo the geographer, treating of the Parthenon, a temple at Athens, says, "In this was the inextinguishable or unquenchable lamp," and yet this lamp was quenched ages since. Josephus, speaking of a festival of the Jews, writes, "Every one brought fuel for the fire of the altar, which continued always unquenchable;" and yet the fire was long ago quenched, with altar and temple in ruins. So in this valley of Hinnom, — this Gehenna-*Hell* of the New Testament, — the grass in spring-time is green, and the flowers bloom; olive and fig trees bear their fruit; while near by bubbles the Pool of Siloam. Hell, theologians to the contrary, is more a condition than a locality.

BETHESDA'S POOL AND MEDICINES.

This Pool of Bethesda, literally the "house of mercy," pointed out as within the city, near St. Stephen's Gate, is thus spiritually referred to in John's Gospel: —

"Now, there is at Jerusalem by the sheep-market a pool, which is called, in the Hebrew tongue, Bethesda, having five porches. . . .

"And an angel went down at a certain season into the pool, and troubled the water: whosoever then first after the troubling of the water stepped in was made whole of whatsoever disease he had."

There are strange traditions connected with this pool. In Old-Testament times David, walking upon the housetop, saw the beautiful Bathsheba, wife of Uriah the Hittite, bathing in Bethesda's limpid waters. And this "man after God's own heart," being touched with the infirmity of "affectional freedom," sent messengers, and "took her." The remainder of the story need not be told. This reservoir of sanative waters was "troubled," that is, magnetized by an angel, or band of spiritual presences, something as certain modern media will, by holding, so "trouble" a goblet of water that the color will change, and medicinal properties be imparted. The spirit-world is, in a measure, made up of the invisible essences of roots, plants, and minerals. Divine physicians know their uses. When the angels spiritually magnetized Bethesda's waters, the "blind, halt, and withered" stepped in, and were healed. Give intelligent spirits the conditions, and I dare set no bounds to their power. Intermittent springs, pools, and reservoirs, owing to earthquakes and other frequent convulsions of nature in tropical climates, often spasmodically rise and fall, and occasionally for ever cease to flow. September last, Bethesda was a dirty, sunken cesspool, with simply a show of shallow, turbid water.

THE DATE OF THE CRUCIFIXION.

A London critic has recently given Disraeli the Israelite, and present leader of the Tory party in Parliament, a terrible flagellation for the chronological blunder of putting the crucifixion in the reign of Augustus Cæsar, when the event transpired in the twentieth year of the reign of the Emperor Tiberius, son-in-law and successor of Augustus Cæsar. Herr Kaib, the great German *savant*, in a lately published work, shows that

"There was a total eclipse of the moon concomitantly with the earthquake that occurred when Julius Cæsar was assassinated on the 15th of March, B.C. He has also calculated the Jewish calendar to A. D. 41; and the result of his researches fully confirms the facts recorded by the Evangelists of the wonderful physical events that accompanied the crucifixion. Astronomical calculations prove, without a shadow of doubt, that on the fourteenth day of the Jewish month Nisan (April 6) there was a total eclipse of the sun, which was accompanied in all probability by the earthquake, 'when the veil of the temple was rent from the top to the bottom, and the earth did quake, and the rock rent' (Matt. xxxii. 51); while St. Luke describes the eclipse in these words: 'And it was the sixth hour (noon); and there was a darkness over all the land till the ninth hour (three o'clock P. M.), and the sun was darkened' (Luke xxi. 44).

"This mode of reckoning corresponds perfectly with the result of another calculation our author made by reckoning backward from the great total eclipse of April, 1818, allowing for the difference between the old and new style; which also gives April 6 as the date of the new moon in the year A. D. 31. As the vernal equinox of the year fell on March 25, and the Jews ate their Easter lamb, and celebrated their *Frib Passoh*, or feast of the passover, on the following new moon, it is clear April 6 was identified with Nisan 14 of the Jewish calendar, which moreover was on Friday, the *Paraskevee*, or day of preparation for the sabbath; and this agrees with the Hebrew Talmud. Thus by the united testimony of astronomy, archæology, traditional and biblical history, there can be but little doubt that the date of the crucifixion was April 6, A. D. 31."

Jesus, the Syrian seer, a radical reformer and divine teacher, died a martyr to the sublime principles he taught, — died with a prayer of forgiveness trembling upon his quivering lips. May we not say with the Revelator, " Worthy the Lamb "?

"THE STAR OF BETHLEHEM."

" The star in the east took its place in the choir;
While the seraphs sang alto, the angels sang air;
They sang, and the cadence is lingering still, —
' Be our peace evermore to the *men of good will*.' "

As melody marries the words of a song, so truth marries the cycling ages. The priest officiating at the altar is history, — the issue, wisdom. But was this Bethlehem star a new star? Was it a comet? Was it a transient meteor? Was the brilliancy caused by planets in conjunction? Was it an atmospheric luminosity? Was it an angel assuming an astral appearance? Or was it a sudden stellar eruption similar to that witnessed by Tycho Brahe in 1572, when a star appeared suddenly, and increased to such an astonishing magnitude that it was visible at noon, maintaining much of its splendor for seventeen months? The French Academician, Alphonse De Lamartine, said that —

" Chinese astronomers, whose observations are noted for their accuracy, and extend back thousands of years, record that a bright comet did appear in the year 4 B.C., and remain visible seventy days during the vernal equinox. This is a curious fact, and it corroborates the assertion made by most chronologers, that the nativity occurred four years before the time usually assigned to it; so that we should now be in A. D. 1878, instead of 1874."

Though accepting the *fact* of the star on that auspicious evening, we utterly repudiate the theories of both astronomers and miracle-believers. Those philosophers and astronomers who saw the star were, according to Matthew, "wise men from the East," — *Magi;* and the term "Magi," from *Mag* in the Pehlvi language, implies a mystic, a visionist, a dreamer of dreams. Pliny and Ptolemy mentions *Arabi* as synonymous with *Magi.* Accordingly the more learned of the second century believed that the Magi who brought the offerings of "frankincense and myrrh" came from Southern Arabia, where these productions abound. But, whether they came from Arabia or Persia, those "wise men" were media gifted with clairvoyance; and the star was a brilliant psychological presentation guiding them to the birthplace of him who, when mediumistically developed, spiritually educated, and baptized of the Christ, "went about doing good."

BETHLEHEM THE BIRTHPLACE OF JESUS.

Biblical commentators to the contrary, it is of little consequence whether the Nazarene was born in a peasant's house, a cave, or a dismal grotto. Along the Nile in Egypt they build of mud, but in Syria of stone; a limestone rock underlying, if not overtopping, most of the country. Bethlehem, a city of six thousand inhabitants, built of stone, has many houses hewn in the rocks, cave-like. It stands upon a hill, the sides of which are terraced with vineyards. The suburbs are bleak and wild. As a whole, the city is more tidy and cleanly, however, than most of the Syrian villages.

Reaching Bethlehem about noon, we hurried to the Church of the Nativity, said to have been constructed over the cave-stable in which Jesus was born. The edifice is shaped like a cross, and was erected A. D. 325 by the Empress Helena. We rested and lunched in the Latin convent. The monks were very kind, and their rooms cozy and quiet. These Franciscan monks entertain travelers free of charge,

—a common practice in the East. At one o'clock we saw these monks feed a flock of poor children gratis. It was a beautiful sight; and in our soul we said, *Heaven bless these Roman-Catholic monks!* The country surrounding Bethlehem is full of interest. It was around these hills that the youthful David learned to make the lute and the harp. Here were the border-lands of Boaz; here Ruth gleaned the barley-fields; here was the wilderness of Judea, in which John preached repentance; here were the plains where shepherds were abiding when they heard the angel-song of "Peace on earth;" and here, too, was born Jesus, the Shiloh of Israel, and the "Desire of all nations."

When crossing these unfenced "shepherd hills," so called, said our spirit-friends, in Jesus' time, we noticed flocks feeding on a dry, hay-like substance, and shepherds watching them. Observing and meditating upon this, I thought of the hymn, — the *fugue* my mother used to sing in those sunny days of a New-England childhood, —

> "While shepherds watched their flocks by night,
> All seated on the ground,
> The angel of the Lord came down,
> And glory shone around."

Oh the lingering melody of that mother's voice! its tender echoes can never die away from my soul. Further reflection brought to memory the sweet lines of our Quaker Whittier: —

> "Lo! Bethlehem's hill-site before me is seen,
> With the mountains around, and the valleys between;
> There rested the shepherds of Judah, and there
> The song of the angels rose sweet in the air.
>
> I tread where the twelve in their wayfaring trod;
> I stand where they stood with the chosen of God, —
> Where his blessings were heard, and his lessons were taught;
> Where the blind were restored, and the healing was wrought.

Oh, here with his flock the sad Wanderer came!
These hills he toiled over in grief are the same;
The founts where he drank by the wayside still flow;
And the same airs are blowing which breathed on his brow."

WHY DID NOT CONTEMPORARY GREEKS AND ROMANS REFER TO JESUS?

This inquiry has little force. Why did not contemporary Hindoo historians choose to notice the presence of Alexander the Great in India? Why do prominent European writers deny the existence of the Grecian Pythagoras; alleging, among other reasons, that the name is traceable to the Sanscrit *Pitha-gura*, the schoolmaster? Why did not Homer, the contemporary of Solomon, make mention of him or of the Hebrews? Why do the writings of Thales, Solon, Democritus, Plato, Herodotus, Xenophon, and others, contain no references whatever to the Jews? Do such omissions prove the non-existence of patriarchs and prophets? It should be remembered that those were not the eras of a world-wide toleration and appreciation, nor of special telegrams and morning newspapers.

Saviors are fated to non-recognition by their fellows. Prophets have never had where to lay their heads. The proud and the erudite do not notice them. Thorns leave crimson kisses upon their pale foreheads. Jesus "the Galilean" was of this number. Neither rabbi nor Roman helped him to "bear the cross." But Greek and Roman writers of the second century make direct mention of him and the "superstitious vagaries" of the Christians. Historians of the coming century may deign to make records of the present exponents of the Spiritual philosophy.

SOLOMON'S POOLS.

These, by the winding road we went, are ten miles from Jerusalem. The place is called El Burak. The dilapidated old castle here standing was built upon Masonic principles.

The two pillars, the arch, the breastplate, the trowel, and the star inclosed in the circle, are plainly visible. The construction of these three gigantic pools, or cisterns, is ascribed to Solomon. If he was not the builder, who was? The one farthest east is six hundred feet in length, two hundred in width, and fifty feet deep. The proudest man-of-war that ever plowed the ocean might float thereon. The first of these pools is fed from a living fountain. During the rainy season the upper pool, overflowing, fills the others. The water from these immense reservoirs, carried through an underground aqueduct around the hills a little to the east of Bethlehem to Jerusalem, and used originally in the various services of the sanctuary, is at present used by the Mohammedans about the Mosque of Omar, who bathe their hands and faces before worshiping.

FROM JERUSALEM TO THE JORDAN.

Rising early from a good night's rest upon Mount Zion, breakfasting upon eggs, bread, grapes, figs, and honey, — *minus* the locusts, — and finding our sheik, and guide Selim, well armed, the muleteers and tenting apparatus in readiness, we were speedily in the saddle, wending our way through the vale of Kedron, by the tomb of Zechariah, the tomb of St. James, and the battered tomb of Absalom, which to this day, when the Jew, passing, especially upon a funeral occasion, picks up and hurls a stone thereat, exclaiming, "Cursed be the son who disobeys the father's commands!" The hills in this vicinity are literally honey-combed with graves and old tombs.

Reaching a rugged eminence a little distance from the city, Mr. Knight, a spirit-friend, spoke to Dr. Dunn's clairaudient ear, saying, "Along that valley to the right, Jesus and his disciples used to come into the city from Bethlehem; . . . and farther, on that palm-crowned hill, lived a warm personal friend of Jesus, with whom he frequently tarried over night." Spirits of the apostolic age, accompanying, directed us to such localities as were yet magnetically aflame with ancient marvels. Not a spoken word of Jesus was lost; not a touch dies away into nothingness; the universe knows no annihilation. To this, psychometry is a living witness. While Mr. Knight was conversing with us, this passage flashed upon my mind like a sunbeam: —

"Did not our hearts burn within us while he talked with us by the way, and while he opened to us the scriptures?" (Luke xxiv. 32.)

MAR SABA AND THE DEAD SEA.

Journeying Jordan-ward, we met crowds, with their heavily-laden donkeys and camels, on their way to Jerusalem. The morrow was market-day. Syrian women still bear burdens upon their heads. Late in the afternoon we came to our tenting-place in a grassless, shrubless valley, rimmed around with sharply-defined hills. Near us was *Mar Saba*, a weird convent castle. No pen-picture can do justice to this Oriental edifice, with adjoining gorges, perpendicular cliffs, and rock-hewn chambers, where monks nightly mouth their midnight prayers. Within this half-martial, half-churchal structure are not only numerous small chapels, covered with old pictures and Greek inscriptions, but St. Saba's sepulcher, and a vault filled with fourteen thousand skulls of martyred monks.

The country is indescribably rough, ragged, and mountainous; the results of terrible convulsions are everywhere visible. Repairing to our tent-apartment from Mar Saba, just at dark, an Arab lad, nearly naked, brought us specimens of bituminous rock; it seemed filled with a species of petroleum. These dark, dismal, pitchy cliffs, with the bitumen, sulphur, niter, and phosphoric stones found in all this region, account for the plains of fire, or the destruction of the "five cities of the plain," — Sodom, Gomorrah, Admah, Zeboim, and Zoar, — upon purely natural principles. Having seen burning Ætna, stood upon sulphurous Vesuvius, walked upon Solfatara's cooled yet tremulous crater, as well as utterly extinct volcanoes in different countries, I discover no satisfactory evidences that the Dead Sea was once the crater of an extinct volcano: rather should I consider it originally a fresh-water lake. But, reflecting upon the millions of years that have rolled into the abysmal past since the beginning of earth's mighty geological upheavings, who dare define conditions, or fix bounds to ancient rivers, seas or oceans? Immutable law governs all things. Explorers, as well as roaming Arabs, tell us that along the southern extremity of the Dead Sea are several bubbling hot springs.

Notwithstanding the nasal music, the multitude of fleas, and the doleful shriek of night-birds, we slept comfortably well in our tottering tent, guarded by sheiks and their heavily-armed attendants.

Tuesday morning, Aug. 26, four o'clock found us approaching the Dead Sea upon the north, near the entrance of the Jordan. It was yet starlight. Never did the stars appear so brilliant. We felt the presence of spirits. It is cool and comfortable traveling at this hour, even in half-tropical Palestine. Riding our jaded horses to another frowning summit, we caught a full view of this memorable sea. Its crystal waves, lying tremulously at our feet, were bathed in the sun, now rising gorgeously over the brown hills of Moab. The Dead Sea, resembling externally a beautiful American lake, is some seventy miles in length, and from three to twenty in width. Its waters presenting a silvery, transparent appearance, are a little bitter, and salt even beyond the ocean. They act something like alum in the mouth, and cayenne in the eye. Birds sail over its blue depths; while rank shrubbery, graceful reeds, and flowering plants, grow down to the very sands upon the brink. If there are no abrasions upon the skin, bathing in the Dead Sea is exquisitely delicious. Owing to its great specific gravity, twelve hundred, — distilled water being one thousand, — effort to remain upon the surface is needless, sinking impossible. Coming out from our swimming excursion in these clear yet bitter, briny waters, there was a saline crystallization upon the beard, and an irritable, uncomfortable feeling upon the cuticle, till, galloping away over the plains six miles, we bathed in the soft, rippling waters of the Jordan.

> " On Jordan's stormy banks I stand,
>   And cast a wistful eye "

to *America*, — the noblest, grandest country in the world.

> " Breathes there the man with soul so dead,
> Who never to himself hath said, —
>   'This is my own, my native land'?
> Whose heart hath ne'er within him burned,
> As home his footsteps he hath turned
>   From wandering on a foreign strand?"

CHAPTER XXV.

PRESENT GOSPELS.

ALL countries have had their inspired chieftains, all dispensations their prophets, and all recurring cycles their apostles. Many evangelists besides those of the New Testament have written gospels, — good messages of peace, love, and "good will to men."

It is perfectly natural that Rénan, while traveling in Palestine, should exclaim, "I have before my eyes a fifth Gospel, mutilated, but still legible."

Though the Ganges is sacred to the Hindoo, the Nile to the Egyptian, and the Jordan to the Christian, the liberal and the more intelligent of this century, rising above the special into the beautiful border-lands of the universal, see in every flowing stream a Jordan, in every sunny vale a Kedron, in every day a sabbath day, in every soul a temple for prayer, in every tomb a forthcoming Savior, in every healthy country a Mount of Transfiguration, and in every heart an altar of religious devotion, where the incense of aspiration is, or *should* be, kept continually burning.

WHY JESUS WAS BAPTIZED IN THE JORDAN.

All the Oriental religions had their regenerating rites. Egyptians were washed from their iniquities in the Nile. Upon sarcophagi and hieroglyphical scrolls Osiris is represented pouring water upon candidates in a kneeling position. The Avesta ceremonials of the Persians abound in directions for baptismal ceremonies. Even proud Romans practiced the rite; and accordingly Juvenal criticised and satirized them for seeking to wash away their sins by " dipping their heads thrice in the flowing Tiber." Jesus, a Palestinian Jew, born subject to the law of Moses, must needs be circumcised and baptized for the washing-away of sin according to the Israelitish understanding of ordinances in that era. But if Jesus was not consciously imperfect, was not a sinner, why should he submit to baptism by water? Matthew says, " Then went out to him Jerusalem, and all Judea, and all the region round about Jordan, and were baptized of him in Jordan, confessing their sins;" while Mark assures us that " John preached the baptism of repentance for the remission of sins." And John baptized Jesus in the Jordan. Therefore, as baptism was understood to be the " washing-away of sin," it is clear that Jesus was considered a sinner. Nothing upon theological grounds could be more absurd than the baptism of a *saint!*

Jesus, conscious of his imperfections, said, " Call not thou me good." The New Testament further declares that Jesus " learned obedience by the things he suffered," that he was " made perfect through suffering," and that he was called the " first begotten from the dead;" but how begotten from the dead unless *himself* once dead in trespasses and sins?

After Jesus confessed, and was baptized, — the water being a symbol of purification, — the " heavens were opened," and the Christ-spirit from the heaven of the Christ-angels descended upon him, and a voice came saying, " This is my beloved Son, in whom I am well pleased." Now we have Jesus Christ " our exemplar;" Jesus Christ standing upon the basis of eternal principles, Jesus Christ the anointed and illumined, ministering the tenderest sympathy and love. Those parables are inimitable; the Sermon upon the Mount stands out unparalleled; while that pleading prayer upon the cross, breathing forgiveness toward murderers, proves the Nazarene divine.

JORDAN'S SOURCE AND SCENERY.

The Jordan of the Evangelists, originating at the base of snowy Hermon, passes through the Galilean lake; through a rich valley-strip of land southward some two hundred miles; through shaded banks of willow, sycamore, and such reeds as were shaken by the wind when the mediumistic John there stood baptizing *Him* who afterwards baptized with the Christ-spirit; and finally falls quite precipitously into those crystal depths of brine and bitumen, the Dead Sea. Though vineyards, balsam-gardens, and palm-forests have disappeared; though the climate is bleaker, and the face of the country considerably altered, — still this saline sea, with river and mountain, sufficiently mark these Meccas of biblical history.

Easily fording the Jordan, we should call it in America an ordinary stream, nothing more. Tasting, I found the water soft, of an agreeable flavor, and great limpidity. Drinking freely, it wanted but one quality, — *coolness*. After quenching our thirst, cutting canes, gathering specimens, wading, bathing, and splashing in the waters, we lunched in the cooling shadows of rose-laurels and junipers, probably the same species of juniper as that under which Elijah sat when the angel came, and touched him (1 Kings xix. 4).

WHAT SPIRITS SAID OF JORDAN AND JERICHO.

Accompanying us in this wild region were exalted spirits who lived in the Nazarenean period, — royal souls then, angels now. These assured us that, during the past twenty centuries, rightly denominated a cycle, terrific convulsions had left their footprints upon the face of all that country known as Assyria. The Jordan itself is a much smaller stream now than then. Anciently it had two series of banks, one of which was annually overflowed from the melting of Hermon's and Lebanon's snows with the heavy rains of the winter season. The channel, deepening, especially near the

Dead Sea, has also changed its course. This the old bottom-land gravel-beds abundantly demonstrate. Portions of these flat lands have at the present time an exceedingly rich soil; and it only requires industry, irrigation, and cultivation to make the plains of the Lower Jordan fruitful as the orange-gardens of Sharon.

Dr. Thomson, after thoroughly exploring the whole Judean country, says: —

"Thus treated, and subjected to the science and the modern mechanical appliances in agriculture, the valley of the Jordan could sustain half a million of inhabitants. Cotton, rice, sugar-cane, indigo, and nearly every other valuable product for the use of man, would flourish most luxuriantly. There were, in fact, sugar-plantations here long before America was discovered; and it is quite possible that this plant was taken from this very spot to Tripoli, and thence to Spain by the crusaders, from whence it was carried to the West Indies. Those edifices to the west of 'Ain es Sultan are the remains of ancient sugar-mills, and are still called Towahin es Sukkar."

Pitching our tent near sundown, Aug. 27, adjoining Rihi, a village of squalid Arabs, we sat down for journal-writing and reflection. Squads of curious Arabs continually prowled about our camp. These Bedouin-tenting denizens of the desert are coarse, rough, and often high-handed robbers. Many shades darker than the same class on the mountains, they subsist largely upon plunder, as do gypsies in some portions of the East.

JERICHO AND THE GOOD SAMARITAN.

Early rising is both commendable and healthy. The morning of Aug. 28, five o'clock, found us in the saddle approaching Jericho, anciently called the city of palm-trees; but the last palm, that a generation since stood by the old tower, a solitary sentinel, fell at last, and not a vestige of the date-palm now appears in the vicinity. Riding over lines of ancient walls, feet-worn pavements, mounds, fallen aqueducts and arches, bits of brick, and moldering piles, a feeling of sadness brooded over my entire being. Is it possible that this was the magnificent Jericho of antiquity? — the Old-Testament Jericho, whose walls fell before those echoing ram's-horn blasts sounded by seven mediumistic priests; the Jericho that many times saw the weary Nazarene on his way from the Jordan up to Jerusalem; the Jericho that takes in the great fountain of *'Ain es Sultan*, and so famous in religious memory as connected with the parable of the "Good Samaritan," and the lesson of universal brotherhood? Is this teaching practiced by either Spiritualists or sectarists? Is there simplicity, confidence, purity, peace, and brotherhood in the ranks of fashionable Christians? Why, Christianity has become the synonym of pride, fashion, plunder, persecution, and war! When the blood of seventy thousand Mohammedans by the hands of crusading Christians had crimsoned the streets of Jerusalem, the prayerful murderers, in the name of religion, went and kissed the cold stone that covered the tomb of him termed "The Prince of peace!" Hate of Christian priests for philosophers kept the Roman Emperor Julian with the old Pagan religions. "Ere I leave the worship of the gods," said he, "let me see a better state of society emanating from Christian teachings."

RETURNING TO JERUSALEM.

Our spirit-friend Mr. Knight — referring, as we passed along, to Jesus' aptitudes at teaching from nature, and then commenting upon the sheep and the goats, the barren fig-tree, the lilies of the field, and other Nazarenean illustrations — said that twenty centuries had wrought marvelous changes upon the face of Palestine. Volcanic countries were ever liable to sudden commotions. The topographical, climatic, and electric conditions were *all* considerably different. Something like two thousand years constituted a cycle; and a cycle had passed since the later Hebrew seers and poets, standing upon the mount of vision, foretold the desolation that should come. The causes were then in operation. All prophecy, however, is within the realm of causation.

Poetically speaking, Syria was once a land flowing with milk and honey. Its undulating valleys rejoiced in waving fields of corn; its crystal streams were bordered with palms and roses; its mountains were covered with olives, figs, mulberries, pomegranates, and clustering vines; and its rocky cliffs with grazing flocks and herds.

The present population of Palestine, estimated at two hundred thousand, is scattered over mountains dotted with mingled masses of rocks and ruins. It seems impossible that this country, now under the sultan's rule, once sustained three millions of prosperous people. And yet it is evident that there have been great natural and desolating convulsions since the days of Hillel, Philo, Josephus, and Jesus. Agricultural pursuits were abandoned for war, denuding mountains of their woody vestures, and hills of their figs, olives, and grazing herds. Shortly after the crucifixion, the country was wasted by famine, cursed by civil dissensions and foreign wars instigated by ambition and a merciless cupidity.

But we are again approaching the city so holy to Jews, Christians, and Mohammedans, — the seventeen times besieged, rebuilt, and re-ruined Jerusalem, which to-day is little more than a gathering of rival bishops, ecclesiastics, monks, artisans, and traders, selling relics, and supplying the temporal wants of religious pilgrims, who thither flock to see the magnificent sepulcher and costly shrines dedicated to an inspired reformer, — a reformer who, when on earth, was considered by arrogant Pharisees as a wandering, sabbath-breaking, blaspheming, false "prophet of Galilee." Draining the cup of sorrow, drinking to the dregs the chalice of agony, he sadly said, "The foxes have holes, and the birds of the air have nests; but the Son of man hath not where to lay his head."

EXPLORING PALESTINE.

Why not, in a broad cosmopolitan spirit, explore Palestine, Tyre, Troy, and the once peopled isles of the ocean?

In 1848 Lieut. Lynch was sent out by the English Government to go down the Jordan from Galilee, through the windings of that river to the Dead Sea. Capt. Warren's excavations in Jerusalem, and discoveries relating to ancient localities, entrances to Solomon's Temple, subterranean passages, winding aqueducts, wells, tanks, canals cut in solid rock, pottery, weights, seals, gems, and inscriptions in the Phœnician characters, and historical sites mentioned by Josephus, are exceedingly valuable to archæologists.

Prof. Palmer of Cambridge, and Mr. Drake, have recently explored the country lying between the peninsula of Sinai and Palestine, — desert of the Exodus, — in which the "Israelites wandered forty years." The country was covered with a brown, parched herbage. The route was interesting from the discovery of ruins, mounds, fortresses, and localities retaining the names they had in the days of David.

The American Steever's Expedition reached Beirût in 1873. Mr. Paine there discovered important Greek inscriptions. In March they went to Edom and Moab. Here was found the celebrated Moabite stone, shedding more light upon the invention of our alphabet than anything yet discovered. The learned Dr. Deutsh said, "It illustrates to a hitherto unheard-of degree the origin and history of the art of alphabetic and syllabic writing as we possess that priceless inheritance." The purpose of this company is to determine traditionary places, discover inscriptions, secure relics, and make an accurate map of this whole Syrian country. Besides the usual surveys, they also take astronomical observations. They have already discovered the famous Mount Nebo and Mount Pisgah. Those who have read "The Book of Moab" will be deeply interested to know what they say about Zoa of Pentapolis memory. It is to be hoped that this expedition, considering the growing demands of science, will not be used in the furtherance of sectarian interests. When will our American Congress furnish funds to equip expeditions to unearth the treasures hidden in the mounds of the south-west, to penetrate the non-explored ruins of Yucatan, and the dust-buried temples of Peru?

NON-PRACTICABILITY OF REFORMERS.

Apollonius, the rival of the Nazarene, was a mediumistic "mendicant;" Cleanthes was a "vagrant;" Jesus "impracticable." *These* are the frisky judgments of pert, mole-eyed men. Seen from the slough of selfishness, and measured by a miser's standard, Jesus was decidedly impracticable. Listen: "Lay not up for yourselves treasures on earth." "When thou makest a dinner or supper, call not thy friends, thy brethren, thy kinsmen, nor rich neighbors to the feast, but call the poor, the maimed, the lame, and the blind." Nothing to a vain externalist could be more unnatural, nothing more egregiously impracticable to fashionable, Pharisaic worldlings.

The beautiful hymn of Cleanthes to Jupiter, from which Paul quoted this to the Athenians, "*For we are also his offspring*," will live on the page of poesy for ever. And yet poor, kind-hearted Cleanthes, who gratuitously taught philosophy and religion, was, upon the complaint of an envious and pompous Greek, brought before the tribunal of Areophagus, and charged with having no visible means of support. Shadow-days have their compensations: justice is ultimately done. The moral teachings of Jesus, and Cleanthes' hymn, are in literature immortal; while the names and memories of their persecutors are rotting to nothingness in a resurrectionless oblivion.

CHAPTER XXVI.

THE CHRISTIANITY OF THE AGES. — PLATO AND JESUS IN CONTRAST.

THE Grecian Plato was the prince of philosophers; the Syrian Jesus, of inspired religionists. What a vivid contrast of birth, education, and country, these celebrated chieftains present to the rational thinker! Plato was well born, his mother a descendant of Solon. Among his ancestors were several erudite and wise Athenians.

His birth occurred in the palmiest period of the most distinguished country of antiquity. His education was the best that Athens could afford. Neither body nor mind was neglected. Muscle, imagination, taste, and reason were equally cultivated. While yet a youth he became a disciple of Socrates, meeting the most brilliant spirits of the age. That splendid yet extravagant genius, Alcibiades, the solid, clear-headed Xenophon, the keen, sophistical Protagoras, the logical and philosophical Crito, and other eminent scholars and statesmen, could but educe all that was divinest in man. The very air of classic Athens seemed to breathe the genius of art, science, and poetry; while the wit of Aristophanes, and the tragedy of Euripides, moved the masses as do the winds the forest-trees. Then Plato traveled, studying under Euclid at Megara, under Theodorus at Cyrene, under the Pythagoreans at Tarentum, and under the Hierophants and Egyptian priests twelve years at Heliopolis. He ate but once a day, or, if the second time, very sparingly, abstaining from animal food. He maintained great equanimity of spirit, and lived a celibate life. Returning to his native country, laden with the intellectual riches of the East, he opened an academy at Athens, in the Gardens of Colonus, where he lived in contact with the greatest men of the period, and died at a ripe old age, leaving a school of thinkers and orators to perpetuate his philosophy. Clad now in the shining vestures of immortality, he walks a royal soul in the republic of the gods.

Jesus was born a peasant. Mary was good and pure-minded. Joseph was a country carpenter. Judea, geographically insignificant, and numerically small, was at this time in a condition of political and religious decadence. The whole land had nothing to inspire faith. Its shekinah was eclipsed, its prophets dumb, and its very memories like the embalmed mummies of Mizraim. An alien race sat upon the Syrian throne. A Roman official presided in the judgment-hall. Roman soldiers paraded the streets, Roman officers levied and collected the taxes, and Roman coins circulated in the markets. The Jews at this period were narrow, selfish, proud. Hatred of Gentiles was a virtue; help for suffering foreigners, little better than a crime. Religion was a form; fasts fashionable; and a broad cosmopolitan charity unknown.

Jesus lacked early culture. John and James were scholars. Though uneducated in dialectics and the classics, Jesus was nevertheless clairvoyant, clairaudient, and marvelously intuitional. Accompanied by a legion of heavenly angels, he stood above human laws, a law unto himself, unique, emotional, incomparable. The schools of the rabbis being but conservatories of traditions, Jesus, inspired by his spirit-guides, traveled in foreign countries, Egypt, Assyria, Persia, studying the mysteries of the seers, and listening to the voices of ascended gods. He sat at the feet of religious mystics, Magi, and gymnosophists; Plato, at the feet of orators and logicians. Jesus, whose daily psalm was love, whose touch was a blessing, and presence a benediction, cultivated the sympathetic, the self-denying, the *religious faculties;* but Plato the perceptive and the philosophical. Centuries have rolled into the abysmal past. Now millions march under the banner of the cross, made memorable by the martyrdom of that religious enthusiast and radical Palestinian reformer. The once thorn-crowned Jesus Christ is now companioned with those celestial angels, the presence of which make radiant the kingdom of God. The preeminent greatness of Jesus consisted in his fine harmonial organization; in a constant overshadowing of angelic influences; in the depth of his spirituality and love; in the keenness of his moral perceptions; in the expansiveness and warmth of his sympathies; in his unshadowed sincerity of heart; in his deep schooling into the spiritual gifts of Essenian circles and Egyptian mysteries; in his soul-pervading spirit of obedience to the mandates of *right* manifest in himself; in his unwearied, self-forgetting, self-sacrificing devotion to the welfare of universal humanity, and his perfect trust in God.

CHRISTIAN TEACHINGS BEFORE THE TIME OF JESUS CHRIST.

The patriarch Abraham, when returning from the "slaughter of the kings," convicted of the sin of war, met Melchisedec, King of Salem, priest of the most high God, and received his blessing. Abraham, conscious of the superiority of this so-considered "heathen" King of Salem, King of Peace, paid tithes, giving him at once "a tenth of all." But "who was Melchisedec?" Why, he was the king of some contiguous nation, the peace-king of Salem, the baptized of Christ; in a word, a Christian. This Christ-spirit, or Christ-principle, is truly " without father or mother, without descent, having neither beginning of days nor end of life, a continually abiding priest."

There were Christians in those pre-historic periods, Christians in golden ages past, Christians long before the

Old Testament patriarchs traversed the plains of Shinar, and Christians who spoke the ancient and mellifluous Sanscrit. Many of the most genuine and self-sacrificing Christians on earth to-day are Brahmans and Buddhists. All great souls, under whatever skies, and in whatever period of antiquity, baptized by the Christ-spirit of peace, purity, and love, and illumined by the divine reason, were Christians.

Dean Milman admits that

"If we were to glean from the later Jewish writings, from the beautiful aphorisms of other Oriental nations which we can not fairly trace to Christian sources, and from the Platonic and Stoic philosophy, their more striking precepts, we might find, perhaps, a counterpart to almost all the moral sayings of Jesus." *

Bigandet, the Roman Catholic bishop of Ramatha, and apostolic vicar of Ava and Pegu, says, —

"There are many moral precepts equally commanded, and enforced in common, by both the Buddhist and Christian creeds. It will not be deemed rash to assert that most of the *moral truths* prescribed by the gospel are to be met with in the Buddhistic Scriptures. . . . In reading the particulars of the life of the last Buddha, Guatama, it is impossible not to feel reminded of many circumstances relating to our Saviour's life, such as it has been sketched out by the Evangelists."†

St. Augustine, treating of the origin of Christianity, affirms that —

"The thing itself, which is now called the *Christian religion*, really was known to the ancients, nor was wanting at any time from the beginning of the human race, until the time when Christ came in the flesh; from whence the true religion, which had previously existed, began to be called *Christian;* and this in our day is called the Christian religion, not as having been wanting in former times, but having in latter times received its name."

---

* Dean Milman, Hist. Christianity, B. I. c. iv. § 3.
† Bigandet, Life of Buddha, p. 494.

The Emperior Hadrian, writing to Servianus, while visiting Alexandria, and referring to the religion of the old Egyptians, assures us that —

"The worshipers of Serapis are also Christians; for I find that the priests devoted to him call themselves the bishops of Christ."

Clemens Alexandrinus, so eminent in the early Church, admitted that —

"Those who lived according to the true *Logos* were really Christians, though they have been thought to be atheists, as Socrates and Heraclitus among the Greeks."

The Rev. Dr. Cumming of London, in his discourse upon the "Citizens of the New Jerusalem," says, —

"It is a mistake to suppose that Christianity began only eighteen hundred years ago: it began nearly six thousand years ago: it was preached amid the wrecks of Eden."

The Rev. Dr. Peabody (Unitarian) pertinently asks, —

"If the truths of Christianity are intuitive and self-evident, how is it that they formed no part of any man's consciousness till the advent of Christ?"

The learned Baboo Keshub Chunder Sen, whom I have met several times both in London and Calcutta, said in a discourse just previous to leaving England for India, —

"The Hindoo, therefore, who believes in God, is a Christian. If purity, truth, and self-denial are Christian virtues, then Christianity is everywhere where these virtues are to be found, without regard to whether the possessors are called Christians, Hindoos, or Mohammedans. Hence it comes that many Hindoos are far better Christians than many who call themselves so. The result of my visit is, I came as a Hindoo, I return a confirmed Hindoo. I have not accepted one doctrine which did not previously exist in my mind."

This rational position lifts the Christianity of the ages out of the slough of sect, out of the realm of the partial, and places it upon the basic foundation of the universal. Seen from this sublime altitude, all true Spiritualists are Christians, recognizing the evangelist's affirmation, that "Christ had a glory with the Father before the world was;" and, furthermore, that "Christ is the chief among ten thousand, and the one altogether lovely."

THE MEDITERRANEAN AND ITS ISLANDS.

The sapphire waves of the Mediterranean, rippling under cloudless skies in star-lit hours, lift the thoughts to the "isles of the blest." A shade deeper than the sky, the islands that stud these waters called to mind early readings of the East.

Rhodes, — "Laudabant alii claram Rhodon," as Horace sings, the sunny Rhodes of which Pliny records that the Rhodians never lived a day without seeing the sun; and Scio, that may have been the birthplace of Homer as well as any other of the nine cities that contend for the honor, — *these*, and other isles, gladdened my vision.

In Cyprus, held by Egyptians and Iranians before the time of Greece, excavators have recently discovered a colossal statue of Hercules, holding before him a lion. It was found at the old town of Amathus, said to have been colonized by the Phœnicians.

We anchored off Syra, a beautiful isle, set in a sea smooth and green as polished malachite. Here was born Pherecydes, one of the oldest Greek writers.

Rhodes will remain ever connected with the Knights of St. John, and the Colossus, one of the seven wonders of the world. Overthrown by an earthquake, it remained where it fell for over nine hundred years; ultimately it was cut up for old métal, and borne away by the Mohammedans. Its size was doubtless greatly exaggerated by Greek visitors. This island has much to interest antiquarians. Syracuse, founded in 734 by the Corinthians under Archias, upon the ruins of an ancient Phœnician settlement, is all aglow with classical memories. It was the most extensive of the Hellenic cities. Strabo states that it was twenty-one miles in circumference. Connected with its history were such men as Æschylus, Pindar, Epicharnius, Thrasybulus, Dionysius, Demosthenes, and Archimedes, slain by a soldier who did not know his value either as mathematician or philosopher.

The modern Greeks, peopling these islands, have the reputation of being the worst exaggerators on earth. They are generally tall, having fine complexions, sharp noses, and still sharper eyes. Their perceptive are much larger than their reflective brain-organs. Like the Jews, and not very unlike Americans, money is their god. On deck are a few Nubians, dark as night; Syrians, with Jewish visages; several Cretans; one Arab trader, tall, thin, and withered; and two or three Armenians, who are more European in their characteristics. The strange garments of these people are more diversified than their complexions. To a traveling pilgrim, how frail and fickle seem fashions! Who are those that summer and winter under the fez, the turban, or pointed hood, under those flowing trousers, embroidered vests, red sashes, and multiformed cloaks, sacks, and robes? What are their aspirations and life employments?. These are the practical questions that throng the mind. They are brothers of Oriental lands, brothers with the same beating, pulsing hearts as ours, and destined to the same immortality.

SMYRNA.

"And unto the angel of the church in Smyrna write, These things saith the first and the last, which was dead, and is alive:

I know thy works, and tribulation and poverty. . . .

Behold, the Devil shall cast some of you into prison that ye may be tried.

Fear none of those things which thou shalt suffer: but be thou faithful unto death, and I will give thee a crown of life. — JOHN THE REVELATOR.

Smyrna, golden with the memories of early Christian teachings, sits to-day like a queen upon the border-lands of the Orient.

Our entrance into the broad, beautiful bay was just before sunset. The city lies at the very extremity, and partly upon the hill-side to the right, as you approach the shore. The site of ancient, historic Smyrna was on the left, at the foot of the mountains, and some little distance from the modern. Earthquakes have effected serious changes in much of the topography of this country. The Mediterranean at this and other points is continually receding.

Excepting Constantinople, Smyrna is the most important commercial city in the Turkish Empire. Though sending large quantities of opium yearly to the United States, most of its export trade is carried on with Great Britain, consisting of cotton, carpets, wool, fruits, and opium. This latter article is raised extensively in the back country, and brought in upon camels for exportation, after inspection. How, in what way, is so much of it used in America?

Passing the Greek church, a modern structure, the Armenian houses, and a drove of burdened camels, to the suburbs of the city, I commenced ascending the hill towards the old castle, accompanied by a dragoman. It was nearly noon when I reached the tomb of Polycarp, the ancient Smyrnian bishop, the good Christian martyr, the acquaintance and fervent admirer of the Apostle John. This tomb, held semi-sacred by both Mohammedans and Christians, overlooks the one hundred and fifty thousand souls that constitute the present city of Smyrna.

Every thing in this country — cloths, fruits, potatoes, vinegar, firewood — is bought and sold by the pound. The figs and grapes of Smyrna are famous for size, quality, and abundance. It seemingly adds to the exquisite flavor of olives, oranges, and figs, to pluck them fresh from the trees. This I was privileged to do in several fields and gardens in Smyrna and the Grecian Isles. Doubtless the best figs never see America.

There are a number of prominent Spiritualists in Smyrna. Among the most active are C. Constant and M. E. H. Rossi.

Calling at Mr. Constant's palatial residence, in front of which is a beautiful garden fringed with fig, lemon, and orange trees, we were, after taking our seat upon a most inviting divan, treated to a cup of Turkish coffee, fruits, and delicious preserves. This is the Oriental custom. Everywhere in the East, hospitality is as profuse as commendable.

The Smyrnian bazaars, though much inferior, are very similar to those in Constantinople. One Turkish city typifies all others, — dirt, filth, decay, narrow streets, and a mixed population. How sad that such a profusion of fruitage, that such a clear atmosphere and sunny sky, should look down upon so much stagnant, dozing shiftlessness! When Americans have peopled the prairies and the broad millions of the Far West, they may safely turn their eyes towards Asia Minor, and the over-estimated desert-lands of the Orient.

CLIMATE AND COSTUMES.

The Smyrnians, like multitudes in the East, seem to live out of doors. The warm climate invites to a free and easy life. They eat but little meat, subsisting almost entirely upon vegetables and fruits. Dining at the hospitable home of Consul Smithers, there came upon the table, after soup, fish, and other courses, seedless sultana raisins, different varieties of nuts, grapes, pomegranates, figs, apricots, and delicious oranges. Asia Minor is certainly the paradise of fruits. The variety of costumes renders a walk in the streets exceedingly interesting. With the national Greek or Albanian, the costume consists of a high fez, with a long blue tassel, red jacket with open sleeves, and richly embroidered; shirt with wide and flowing sleeves; a leathern belt, with pouch for weapons; short pants, and white fustanella. The Turkish costume is somewhat similar, only they wear short, wide trousers, dark-colored jackets, and shoes with buckles. The fez is almost universal. The old style of turban is seen only engraved upon tombstones, or worn on the heads of old men in the back country. Some of the young Turks wear the French style of hats. The Persians wear tall, pyramidal-shaped turbans; and all wind sashes around their waists. Strangers generally engage a "cavasse," — that is, a sort of Turkish guide, having a certain police power. Going back into the country, these are necessary, as there are Greek brigands lurking in the mountains. The "cavasse," clothed in full authority, doffs a tall Turkish fez, sack-legged trousers, mock jewelry, flowing mantle lined with fur, a belt with three pistols, several knives and dirks, and a sword dangling by his side. One far away from the city is in doubt which to most fear, — the guide, or the mountain brigands. Nothing, for a time, more attracted my attention off in the country from Smyrna, than the camels, — patient, faithful creatures! Sometimes there were hundreds in a train, each following the other, led by a lazy Turk astride a donkey, and all heavily burdened with cotton, madder-root, olive-oil in goat-skins, opium, figs, and other products from the interior. The caravans farther east are more extensive, and exceedingly profitable in their line of traffic.

EPHESUS, AND THE APOSTLE JOHN.

"Unto the angel of the church of Ephesus write, These things saith he that holdeth the seven stars in his right hand, who walketh in the midst of the seven golden candlesticks:

"I know thy works, and thy labor, and thy patience, and how thou canst not bear them which are evil: and how thou hast tried them which say they are apostles, and are not, and hast found them liars.

"Thou hatest the deeds of the Nicolaitanes, which I also hate. . . .

"To the angel of the church in Thyatira write, . . . I have a few things against thee, because thou sufferest that woman Jezebel, which calleth herself a prophetess, to teach and to seduce my servants. . . .

"Him that overcometh will I make a pillar in the temple of my God, and he shall go no more out: and I will write upon him the name of my God, and the name of the city of my God, which is New Jerusalem, which cometh down out of heaven from God: and I will write upon him my new name.

"And I will give him the morning star." — JOHN THE REVELATOR.

Sailing up the Mediterranean I saw Samos, — literally "sea-shore height." This island, at an early period of history, was a powerful member of the Ionic Confederacy. Pythagoras left it, to travel in foreign countries, under the government of Polycrates. A future view of this classic isle from St. Paul's prison and Mount Prion, around which was grouped ancient Ephesus, famed as the seat of the most eminent of the old Asian churches, was very fine. Not far distant was the beautiful island of Cos, with its mountainous peaks, vine-clad hillsides, and pleasant-appearing homes, embowered in evergreen foliage. And there peered above the horizon Patmos, sainted Patmos, seat of John's visions and revelations. Banished from the world's bustle, and frequently in the "spirit on the Lord's Day," he became the recipient of truths and illuminations that streamed in glory down through all the sunrise hours of the Christian dispensation.

Determined to see the ruins of this old Ionian city, Ephesus, once noted for its commercial prosperity, for its stadium, theaters, and Temple of Diana, as well as for the place where the Apostle John spent his last years, I left Smyrna Nov. 7, 1870.* It was sixty miles distant to Isaalouke, a disagreeable Arab town.

The English own this railway. An hour's ride on wretched horses dropped us down with a party of pilgrims to the rim of the Ephesian ruins. The original city was evidently built around the base of Mount Prion. Crumbling remnants of custom-house and ware-houses are yet visible. But the Mediterranean waters have so receded, that bay, harbor, and landing have given place to a broad basin covered with grasses and weeds, through which winds a small serpentine stream. The employees of J. T. Wood were putting down shafts between Prion and St. John's

---

* Descriptions in this volume relating to Smyrna, Ephesus, Constantinople, Rome, Naples, Pompeii, Herculaneum, &c., are taken from notes made during a previous visit to Europe, Turkey, and Asia Minor.

Church, in search of Diana's Temple, which was in process of completion when Alexander passed into Asia, 335 B.C. This temple was erected to succeed the one set on fire the night of Alexander's birth, 356 B.C. The labors of Mr. Wood were crowned with success; and portions of those magnificent columns may now be seen in the British Museum, with the gods and goddesses of that period, beautifully modeled and chiseled.

THE APOSTLE'S BURIAL-PLACE.

A pilgrim under a scorching Asian sky, resting, I leaned upon one of the pillars that Christian and Moslem tradition unite in declaring marks the Apostle John's tomb. It was a consecrated hour. While standing by his tomb, on the verge of Mount Prion, looking down upon the marbled seats of the Ephesian theater, — relic of Hellenic glory, — with my feet pressing the soil that once pillowed the mortal remains of the "disciple that Jesus loved," ere their removal to Rome, no painter could transfix to canvas, no poet conceive suitable words to express, my soul's deep emotions. The inspiration was from the upper kingdoms of holiness; the baptism was from heaven; the robe was woven by the white fingers of immortals; while on the golden scroll was inscribed, ' *The first cycle is ending: the winnowing angels are already in the heavens. Earth has no secrets. What of thy stewardship? Who is ready to be revealed? Who, who shall abide this second coming? Who has overcome? Who is entitled to the mystical name and the white stone? Gird on thine armor anew, and teach in trumpet tones that the pure in heart, the pure in spirit only, can feast upon the saving fruitage that burdens the tree of Paradise.*"

From the summit of Mount Prion, the Isle of Samos may be distinctly seen. Gazing at this in the distance, and nearer to the winding course of the little Cayster towards the sea, at the scattered remnants of temples, marble fragments, broken friezes, and relics of every description,

I could not help recalling the prophetic warning of John, in the Book of Revelation, "I will come unto thee quickly, and will remove thy candlestick out of its place, except thou repent" (Rev. ii. 5).

It is generally admitted that the Apostle John lived to one hundred and four years of age; and all we know of his later days is linked with Ephesus, — accurately described by Herodotus, Pausanius, Pliny, and others, — outside the records of the Church fathers. It is not known how long St. John resided in this portion of Asia: suffice it, that his memory still lingers here, enshrined even in the Turkish name of the squalid village about two miles from the ruins of the old Ephesian city, "*Ayasolouke*," which is a corruption of the Greek "*Agios Theologos*," the holy theologian, the name universally given to this apostle in the Oriental Church.

The mosque here, which is magnificent, even though in partial ruin, was undoubtedly an ancient Christian church, probably the identical one which the Emperor Justinian built on the site of an older and smaller one, dedicated in honor of St. John, who at Ephesus trained the disciples Polycarp, Ignatius, and Papius to preserve and disseminate apostolic doctrines in Smyrna and other cities of Asia. In the erection of this church edifice by Justinian, upon the spot where the venerable apostle preached in his declining years, were employed the marbles of Diana's temple. Visiting these scenes, Asian cities, and churchal ruins, strengthens my belief in the existence of Jesus, the general authenticity of the Gospels, and the profound love-riches of John's Epistles. It is the land of inspiration, of prophecy, and of spiritual gifts. Even the skeptical Gibbon, writing of the "seven churches in Asia," virtually admits the fulfillment of the apocalyptic visions. (Gibbon's "Decline and Fall," chap. lxiv.)

Eusebius and others tell us of the profound reverence that all the early believers in the doctrines of Jesus had for this aged and loving saint, who sorrowed with Christ in the garden, stood by him at the cross, received in charge Mary the mother of Jesus, and clairvoyantly beheld him ascend to the homes of the angels. This sentence from his pen will live for ever: "God is love." When he had become too weak and infirm to walk to the old primitive church edifice in Ephesus, his admirers, taking him in their arms, would bear him thither; and then, with trembling voice, he could only say, "Little children, love ye one another." These and other well-attested historic recollections, rushing upon my mind, lift me on to the Mount of Transfiguration.

The sun of the New Testament epistles is John, — the sainted John, that lovingly leaned upon Jesus' bosom. In youth he was my ideal man. To-day he is that angel in heaven whom I most love. Not Arabia, then, nor Palestine, but classic Ephesus, is my Mecca.

The poet Joaquin Miller sings thus of the "Last Supper:" —

"Ah! soft was their song as the waves are
  That fall in low, musical moans;
And sad, I should say, as the winds are
  That blow by the white gravestones.

What sang they? What sweet song of Zion,
  With Christ in their midst like a crown?
While here sat Saint Peter, the lion;
  And there, like a lamb, with head down, —

Sat Saint John, with his silken and raven
  Rich hair on his shoulders, and eyes
Lifting up to the faces unshaven
  Like a sensitive child in surprise.

CHAPTER XXVII.

TURKEY IN ASIA.—IONIA AND THE GREEKS.

THE ancient cities of Ionia were wonderfully well situated for the growth of commercial prosperity. The Greeks of to-day have superior talents for finance, and all else that relates to sharpness and downright persistency. They cherish ardent expectations of becoming some day the masters of the Mediterranean. To this end, with an eye on Constantinople, they are busy in devising schemes for the more complete consolidation of their empire. For acuteness, shrewdness, and exaggeration, they are said to excel any people in the world. It is a common saying in Levantine cities, "He lies like a Greek."

The modern Greeks are handsome. They step quick, are gay and airy, have clear complexions, classical faces, fine frames, and a noble carriage, that constantly excites increasing admiration. Their national costume, a seeming blending of Scotch and Turkish, is quite indescribable, though, on the whole, decidedly Oriental. They are fond of heavy cloaks, long gaiters, close-fitting trousers, fancy colors, and *all* picturesque effects. Proud of their past history, they delight to remind the citizens of the Occident that the greatest man the Teutons ever had tells us, "The sun of Homer shines upon us still;" and another eminent man of the Anglo-Saxon race informs us that "it is Plato's tongue the civilized world is even now speaking, and Plato's landmarks that fix the boundaries of the different provinces of art and science." During the past forty years the Greeks have built over three thousand villages, fifty towns, and ten capitals. In Athens, in all the isles of the Archipelago, where the Greeks have either a governmental foothold or influence, strenuous efforts are being made to revive the written language of the country, — the old Hellenic. The Greek language they now use bears far more resemblance to ancient Greek, than does the present Italian to Latin. The periodicals printed in Athens to-day may be read with perfect ease by such scholars as are well acquainted with the Greek of Xenophon and other classical writers of that period. The Greeks and Turks are implacable enemies all through the East. In the Levantine cities, each reside in their own quarters. If they mingle, it is for trade and traffic. Both need to learn that "in Christ Jesus," — that is, the Christ-principle of brotherhood, — "there is neither Jew nor Greek," but all are heirs of a common Father's care and inheritance. "God," said the apostle, "is no respecter of persons."

CONSTANTINOPLE.

It was in the gray of early morning that we sailed calmly along the Dardanelles. Oh the glory of that October morning! The ideal becomes the real. The sun now colors the eastern sky with gold. Rising, it tips and turns the minarets to fire. The buildings, the vessels, the mosques, are all illuminated. Surely we may exclaim with Byron, —

"'Tis the clime of the East, 'tis the land of the sun."

If Genoa has been called the proud, and Naples the beautiful, Constantinople may rightly claim for herself the title of magnificent. Seated in gardens upon one of seven hills, it is not strange that Constantine should have desired to move the capital of the Roman Empire to the site occupied by the imperial city. No soul alive to the beautiful in nature, or the exquisite in art, could fail of admiring its lofty and imposing position, its domes, its minarets, its sheltering groves of cypress, its hills in the distance, now crimsoning into the sear of autumn, and the blue waters that lie at the feet of these Moslem splendors. The Golden Horn is all that pen painters have pictured it. The Sea of Marmora is deep and beautiful. Hardly a ripple danced upon its surface during our passage over its crystal depths. What a magnificent harbor it would make, with Constantinople for the central capital of Europe, Asia, and Africa!

How rich in historic association is this city crowned with mosques! Belisarius sailed from here into Africa, and along the Italian coast, while Justinian in 558 was erecting the present St. Sophia. On the opposite Asian shore, at Scutari, the Persians, after their conquests in Egypt and Syria, sat for a dozen years threatening the city. Here Tartars, Turks, and Croats first planted their unwelcome footsteps in Europe, inspiring the beginning of those fearful crusades. The first passed through Constantinople in 1097, Alexis reigning. About the year 1200, Baldwin conquered the city; and in the fourteenth century the Ottomans in Asia Minor laid the foundations of the empire that now extends so far into Europe. In 1453 Mohammed II. entered this Christian city in great triumph, and transformed it as if by magic into a Moslem capital. It is said by the historian, that, entering the gates, he steered straight for St. Sophia, to discover the priests who were hiding in the cathedral. They having escaped by a subterranean passage, he hacked off the head of the brazen serpent with his sword, to manifest his hate of images, and all forms of idolatry.

WALKS IN THE CITY.

How true of this great cosmopolitan city of a million souls or more, that "distance lends enchantment to the view"! On the deck of the ship in the harbor, the gigantic tower at Pera, the flotilla upon the Golden Horn, the Bosphorus with its suburban villages, the palaces of the sultan, the architectural effects of the mosques shooting up like marble pillars, the dark plumes of the cypresses, the peopled hillsides upon the Asian coast, and the stately, massive hospital, scene of Florence Nightingale's noble, womanly work during the Crimean war, thrilled my soul with intense delight. But landing, and seeing the ruin, the filth, the dogs in the streets, the mixture of races, the crowded, dirty bazaars, our poetry speedily chilled to rigid prose. Surely, —

"Things are not what they seem."

Decline and decay characterize the sluggish Turkish nation. A deathly torpor has seized its vitals. It is truly the "sick man" of the Orient. Russia wants the vast domain. England and France say, "Hands off!" Germany and the central nations of Europe, think it well to maintain the balance of power as it is. May not the modernized phase of Turkish theology have something to do with this stupor? The Moslems are *fatalists*. One article of their faith reads thus : * —

"It is God who fixes the will of man, and he is therefore not free in his actions. There does not really exist any difference between good and evil; for all is reduced to unity, and God is the real author of the acts of mankind."

"The old Turk residing in the interior of the empire," said Mr. Brown, secretary of the American Legation, "is a very different man from these modern Turks that linger around the capital. The former wears his full trousers and flowing robes, surmounts his head with the old-fashioned turban, winds his shawl or girdle around his waist, carries his pipes and pistols, prays to Allah five times a day, and, despising trick, treachery, and duplicity, is sincere and truthful."

In point of honesty, truthfulness, and self-respect, nearly all travelers unite in saying that the Mussulmans of the Orient are superior to Christians, — the Christian masses of

* See J. P. Brown's Derv., p. 11.

Italy, Spain, Russia, or even England. "Behold the crescent!" say the Mohammedans: "see how it has triumphed over the cross. Is not *Allah* great?" For nearly twelve centuries Mohammed and the Koran have held the religious and political destinies of the East; and at this hour Islamism is rapidly extending in Northern Asia, Central Africa, and along the borders of the Caspian Sea, affirming there is "*one God, and Mohammed is his prophet!*"

TURKISH HOSPITALITY.

It requires little physical labor to live in these Eastern countries. Hills and plains are burdened with fruits. The climate invites the people to out-of-door life, which cheapens home, and renders them content with slovenly and ill-furnished accommodations.

The Turks are justly famed for their hospitality. Entering one of their low, flat-roofed houses in the country, they immediately bring a cup of coffee, and exclaim with great earnestness, "My father is your slave, my mother your bondwoman, my wife your servant: my home is yours, — *all I have is yours*." This, of course, is Eastern, and to some degree figurative; but they really mean by it generosity and hospitality. Besides the dragoman and donkey, it costs little or nothing to travel in Asia Minor.

Expenses, however, are increasing each year. Europeans are teaching the Orientals shrewdness and selfishness.

LANGUAGE. — SOCIAL CUSTOMS. — WORSHIP.

The Turkish language is made up of some two parts Arabic, one Persian, one Tartar, and the remainder from the Turkistan dialect, a difficult language to learn. The Arabic, a magnificent language, is termed by linguists the Latin of the East; the Turkish is compared to the French; and the Persian to the Italian, liquid and flowing.

The Turk never eats with his wife. "*Man was first made, then woman*," says Paul. This the Mohammedan quotes as glibly as the Christian minister produces other passages from this apostle to bear against woman.

No good Mohammedan touches swine's flesh, or wines of any kind: these alcoholic drinks he terms "fire-draughts of hell." If you reprove them for polygamy, they at once refer you to the practices of Abraham, Jacob, Solomon, and other biblical characters praised by Christians.

The government of Turkey is an absolute monarchy. The sultan's will is law. He is the supreme head of the Mohammedan faith. These Mohammedans believe that the Koran came direct from heaven, through the Angel Gabriel, and that divine inspirations came to Mohammed from Allah the same as in past times to Jesus and Moses.

I visited a large number of mosques.

Taking off the shoes before entering is expected and demanded. The imams (priests), facing Mecca, lead in the prayers to the one God, — Allah. Their sermons are highly moral, explaining the Koran, and its relation to the Old and New Testaments. Mohammed, though permitting a plurality of wives in imitation of the Hebrew patriarchs, recommended but one.

Extravagance is thinning the ranks of the harems. Few Turks care to support more than one wife to display her richly-colored garments in the bazaars. Though silks, satins, and fine plain merino cloths, are worn, the Levantine women, as well as those of the extreme East, are as fond of gay trimmings as they are of their ease. French styles are rapidly creeping into all Turkish countries.

The muezzin's calls sound from the minarets of the mosques five times a day, — at the break of morning, at twelve o'clock, at two hours before sundown, at the going-down of the sun, and again two hours after sunset. We recollect ascending the minaret of a mosque, that, like most of the ancient structures of the East, had long passed its age of beauty. The Oriental coloring had faded; the pavements were sunken, and the mosaics crumbling, and dropping from the wall. Still the lofty hight, the majesty of the columns, the immense dome, deeply impressed us, and will other beholders for centuries to come. It was near the hour of twelve. Soon the muezzin came out from near the summit of the minaret, summoning to prayer in these words: "*Allah akbar, Allah akbar, La illah il Allah, Mohammed resoul Allah, Allah akbar.*" (God is great. There is no God but God, and Mohammed is the prophet of God. Come to prayer; come to security and peace. God is most great: there is no God but God.) They intone these prayer words of invitation in a plaintive, half-singing style, often varying them to suit the occasion. In the morning they usually cry, "Awake, awake and pray. It is better to pray than to sleep. There is but one God, Allah." At noon the piteous, pleading voice falls upon them, "God is great; the world is wicked. Come to prayer. There is but one God, Allah the merciful."

It is almost an absolute impossibility to convert a Mohammedan to evangelical Christianity. They can not subscribe to the Trinity; can not comprehend how Jesus Christ can be "very God," and yet the "Son of God;" can not understand how Jesus existed before his mother, and is of the same age as his Father. It is not quite plain to us!

TURKISH WOMEN.

Polygamy, or any form of "social freedom" involving promiscuity, is a practical hell in any country. Envies and jealousies abound. The caliphs have for weary years maintained more or less eunuchs as attendants in their harems.

The general characteristics of Turkish women may be best studied on Moslem festival-days.

They are not so really dressed as draped in a flowing robe, over which hangs a loose mantle, nearly covering the lower portion of their trousers. Their feet are small, and show very distinctly while walking. Over their yellow slippers they wear an ugly-looking overshoe, which they slip off when going into a mosque to worship. Indulging in the luxuries of the Turkish bath, they have the appearance of being exceedingly neat. Notwithstanding their veils, and professed seclusion from society, there is no difficulty in seeing them or their faces. Their features are generally small and delicate. Their veils are made of very transparent muslin, covering all but the eyes and upper portions of their neatly-painted cheeks. As a rule it is safe to infer this: the more symmetrical and beautiful the features, the more thin and gauze-like the veil.

The time was when the facial veils of Turkish ladies were really opaque: now, unless the woman is exceedingly lean and ugly, they are as thin as those through which the blushes of American brides may be seen, really enhancing the beauty they pretend to conceal.

Silly vanity is seen in all countries.

Though these women's eyes are hazel and handsome, they sparkle with no great life-purpose; their motions in walking are ungraceful; their figures resemble bundles of foreign drapery; and they are said by those who know them the most intimately to be exceedingly ignorant, helpless, insipid, and shiftless. Since polygamy is the rule, since they are the slaves of men's pleasures and passions, what otherwise could be expected? And these wives, these women, are to be *future mothers.*

As the Turk, who can have many wives, can have but *one* mother, the sultan's mother is virtually queen. The mistress of the treasury is next in honor to the queen, filling an intermediate place between the sultan and women of the harem. The Turks are very fond of the blonde Circassians. Purchasing them is now forbidden.

MOHAMMEDAN DERVISHES.

What Shakers and Quakers are to evangelical Christians, dancing dervishes are to Mohammedans. They believe in Allah, and in present inspirations and revelations. The elders are seers and celibates. Their lodges are retired homes. Their worship is unique; their so-called dancing being more properly whirling. The healing dervishes, reducing themselves physically by subsisting upon two and three olives a day, perform the most remarkable deeds during their holy month of Ramazan. We saw them form their circle for the healing of the sick. When prepared by gesticulation, whirling motions, chants, and prayers, the sheiks, that is the elders,—healed by touch, by the use of "Mohammed's brass hand," and by treading, literally *treading*, in this state of ecstasy, upon the crippled limbs and diseased bodies of the sick, some of which were infants. If disease were located in the eyes, throat, or brain, they pathetized them. The Crown Prince of Prussia stood by our side " unshod," after the Mohammedan custom, while witnessing the healings, and the magnetic and instrumental feats, of this primitive people in their consecrated room.

Through my interpreter, who spoke Arabic and Syriac, as well as Turkish and English, I held long conversations with the sheiks concerning the origin of their orders, their worship, their visions, their knowledge of the spirit-world, and their gifts of healing.

SPIRITUALISM IN TURKEY.

There are excellent mediums and many Spiritualists in Constantinople. During the winter season they hold regular circles in Pera, the European part of the city. Writing and trance are the usual forms of manifestation. These spirits, with a few exceptions, teach re-incarnation. Invited, we addressed the Spiritualists in the hall of the *Chambre de Commerce*. The attention they gave, and the interest they manifested, were truly inspiring.

The Hon. John P. Brown, connected with the legation, and a thirty-years' resident of Turkey, I found to be a firm Spiritualist. In a letter written to the "Universe," he said, —

"Many Moslems also fully believe in a power or faculty of the spirit of man to see, behold, or have an intuitive perception of, things invisible by the ordinary organs of sight. This assertion they sustain by the frequent examples of individuals having the most correct and exact knowledge of events occurring at a vast distance from them, — of visions in which they behold, like pictures passing before their eyes, scenes of which they have never had any previous knowledge or perception. . . . These Turkish Spiritualists are always people of well-known purity and virtue, animated with the highest degree of benevolence, and deeply interested in the spiritual welfare of others. This belief is often acted upon and exercised in such a manner by others as to lead some persons to suppose that Spiritualism and animal magnetism are one and the same thing; for the pious Moslem believes that he can effect cures, or at least give relief from bodily sufferings, by prayer, and the imposing of his hands on the invalid."

CHAPTER XXVIII.

ATHENS.

"Dream on sweet souls in purpling seas
Till we reach the land of Pericles."

IN life's golden time, when listening to the academic declamations of students upon the heroism of the ancient Greeks, we dreamed of treading the shores of the classic land, — land once pre-eminent in poetry, philosophy, painting, and the fine arts, and whose republics voiced the heaven-winged words of equality and freedom. But the Greeks of to-day are ancient Greeks no more. Civilizations move in cycles and epicycles. The Grecian mind has been tending downwards for full two thousand years. Its present glory consists of its ancient ruins. A wizard hand, grayed and grim, ever points backward to lost arts, lost grandeur!

Do we not remember Byron, whose lamp of life faded under the Grecian skies he so enthusiastically loved? How musical his lines! —

"Know ye the land where the cypress and myrtle
Are emblems of deeds that are done in their clime, —
Where the rage of the vulture, the love of the turtle,
Now melt into sorrow, now madden to crime?

. . . .

'Tis the *clime* of the *East*, — tis the land of the *Sun:*
Can he smile on such deeds as his children have done?"

Piræus is the prominent port of Greece. Athens is five miles distant from this landing. There is a railroad. But here, *here*, is the once classic city.

Never can we forget our sensations when casting a first glance at the Acropolis. Passing up the Propillion, or grand entrance, we had a fine view of Mars Hill, where Paul preached the "Unknown God" to the Athenians. Two massive pillars of the Temple of Bacchus are still standing. There was a subterranean passage leading from this temple of mystic rites into the vast amphitheater. The Temple of Minerva and the Temple of the Winds are nearly piles of ruin. The Temple of the Muses, nine figures of choicest marble, must have been very beautiful. To the right of the Acropolis, massive and stately, is the Temple of Jupiter Olympus, many of whose proud columns, having defied the storms and devastating forces of time, remain as standing signals of architectural splendor and perfection. England has rifled some of these old temples to supply its museums with models for modern sculptors and artists.

Among the most celebrated of the ancient oracles was Delphos. Princes and philosophers flocked thither for consultations. Upon the hights of Mount Parnassus stood the magnificent Temple of Apollo; while at the foot was the spring of Castalia. Of this fountain, the Pythia, or priestess, drank; and in its crystal waters she bathed before invoking the presence of the gods. Then clothing herself in white, emblem of purity, she was magnetized by spirits, and spoke under their influence.

Nestling near the base of Mars Hill is the prison-cave where superstitious Greeks confined that ancient Grecian philosopher and Spiritualist, Socrates. The coarsely constructed iron gate, nearly wasted away, is still shown the traveler. The dingy, chalky apartment seemed cut into the side of the hill, — a gloomy den to converse with a Crito and an Alcibiades. Greece and Judea awarded to their inspired teachers crosses and hemlock-draughts. Such was gratitude. Have the times, only in methods, materially changed?

It was our purpose to have visited the plains of Marathon; the ruins of Corinth; the isle of Salamis, memorable for the great battle in which the Persian fleet of Xerxes was defeated by the Greeks 480 B.C.; and Eleusis, which introduced the famous Eleusinian mysteries into Athens as early as 1356 B.C.; but brigandage presented a formidable obstacle. Political outlaws are a perpetual scourge to the country. The government, though practically absolute, fails to institute and perpetuate law and order. In sorrow we turn from modern to ancient Greece.

NAPLES.

The Bay of Naples lifts the soul in thought to such shimmering seas as are said to dot the summer-land scenery of angel realms. The city itself, crescent-formed, is backed by an amphitheater of hills and mountains, the rocky slopes of which are covered with sunny villas, and sprinkled with orange and lemon, with fig and oleander. Fanned by invigorating sea-breezes, and walled in the distance by the Apennines, Naples sits a very queen upon the edge of crystal waters, unrivaled for the beauty of her situation.

The streets are paved with lava, and in the winter season thronged with strangers. Traveling the narrow sidewalks, one feels continually cramped, and sighs for the roomy promenades of prairie cities in the West.

Terraced toward St. Elmo, some of the houses seem clinging to rocky cliffs. Certain streets actually lie hundreds of feet above their immediate neighbors. The dearth of fresh, handsome buildings, and modern works of art, creates a soul-longing, for which the magnificent discovery of Herculaneum and Pompeii, with their matchless treasures of antiquity, only in some measure compensate. The narrow, dingy streets, the high, palace-shaped, yet badly constructed dwelling-houses, with huge iron gates in front, flat roofs, and balconies projecting from nearly every window; the never-ceasing noise, the interminable rattling of wheels during the hours of day and night; the insolent importunities of carriage-drivers, with hordes of pitiable beggars combining the most cringing manners with malicious attempts and devices at extortion, — all present a life-picture any thing but attractive.

GARIBALDI AND THE MONKS.

Standing in the Palace Square one day with Signor Damiani, he pointed us to the balcony from which Garibaldi, in 1860, uttered this stirring sentence to an immense multitude: —

"*Brothers*, believe me, the greatest foe to freedom, the greatest enemy of Italy, is the Pope of Rome."

This liberator of the people, Garibaldi, drove into Naples, Sept. 6, in an open carriage, directly past the fortified barracks of the Carmine, where soldiers were still holding out for Francis II. Not a hair of his head was harmed. Victor Emmanuel offered to make him a duke, and give him a large pension. He declined the dukeship, declined all honors, only caring to see Italy free, united, and happy.

Moping, brown-garbed, barefooted monks, a class of men that neither work nor wash, are as thick in Naples and the adjoining country as office-seekers in Washington. Italy was a clover-field for gowned monks, and a veritable paradise for priests, till Garibaldi, a few years since, partially aroused the people from their dream of submission. Thank God! say students and the young Italians of to-day, the number of these churchal orders is lessening each year. Many of these monks literally live by begging. Lifting their greasy caps, and exposing their shaved heads, they plead by the wayside for a penny. Beggars and priests are the products of Roman Catholic Italy. Papal Rome is the hub of this ecclesiastic wheel.

Out of between twenty and thirty millions of Italians, hardly seven millions can read and write! The bare statement of such a *fact*, in connection with the stupid ignorance and wretched beggary of the middle and lower classes, is of itself a scathing condemnation of Roman-Catholicism. I had the honor of being present at the Anti-Council, or *Congress of Free-Thinkers*, called by Count Ricciardi, a Neapolitan deputy in Parliament, at Naples, on Dec. 8, 1869, the day on which was convoked the Council of the Vatican.

Noble and high-minded as was this body of men, the police, interfering, dispersed the delegates. They met afterwards in secret. The Pope shorn of his temporal power, speech is now free in Naples.

THE MUSEUM IN NAPLES.

This massive building, commenced in 1587 as a university, was finally adapted by Ferdinand I., in 1790, to a museum. Enriched with Etruscan vases, papyrus manuscripts, and Egyptian antiquities, as well as recently excavated treasures from Pompeii and Herculaneum, it is one of the most interesting museums in the world. The library contains about two hundred and fifty thousand volumes, and nearly three thousand manuscripts, some of which date to the eighth and tenth centuries. What interested us more intensely was the antiquities found in Herculaneum and Pompeii, buried for nearly two thousand years. The surgical implements, agricultural implements, ear-rings, brooches, chains, combs, gold lace, and ornaments of every kind, show clearly to what a high state of civilization the Pompeiians had attained before the Christian era. Not only these, but loaves of *bread* with the baker's name thereon stamped, honeycomb, grains, fruits, eggs, bottles of oil and wine hermetically sealed by the Vesuvius eruption of 79, are now exhibited in a wonderful state of preservation in this museum. In the Royal Library attached to this building are more than seventeen hundred papyri found in Herculaneum. These, with nearly as many found in Pompeii, are being unrolled and deciphered, preparatory to publication.

ITALY. 383

POMPEII AND HERCULANEUM.

Cinder-shingled Vesuvius buried these cities on the 24th of August in the year 79 of the Christian era. Their origin is lost in the misty regions of mythology. They were prosperous and famous more than two thousand years since. Livy speaks of their harbors as "magnificent naval stations." Fifty years before the advent of the Nazarene, the geographer Strabo praised the excellence of Pompeii's grain and oils. Roman patricians had embellished adjoining landscapes with splendid villas. Marius, Pompey, and Cæsar had residences in these cities.

Here, too, Cicero had a charming villa. He speaks of its beauty in a letter to Atticus, associating it with Tusculum. Pliny, the naturalist, was in charge of the Roman fleet stationed at Misenum when the catastrophe transpired. Striving to save others, he lost his life. To the younger Pliny are we indebted for a most graphic description of the scene. Ruthless as was this destruction, an index finger pointed to a compensation; for, if Vesuvius destroyed, it also shielded and preserved. Beautiful are the paintings and statues *lapilli*-entombed for nearly two thousand years. The excavations were commenced in 1748. During the exhumations, about one thousand bodies have been found, and with them papyrus, coins, cups, keys, necklaces, bracelets, rings, seals, engraved gems, beautiful lamps, gauzy fabrics, and even well-preserved blonde hair.

Pompeii is now almost completely unearthed. The resurrection is quite perfect. It was good for me to be there. Walking its Roman-paved streets, I felt introduced to the citizens and customs of an ancient civilization. And yet Pliny characterized this period as the age of "dying art," — dying as compared with those artists, Apelles and Protogenes, living nearly five hundred centuries earlier. Pompeii and Herculaneum are bridges spanning the gap of centuries, and holding together as with a golden link two civilizations. Studying the wisdom of the ancients compels us to recognize the spiritual unity of the race, that grand central truth around which the moral world revolves.

ITALIAN CHURCHES.

The real pride of Italy is her relics and churches. They are certainly rich in the artistic work of the masters. These paintings excite the most lively feelings of taste and fancy, as well as intensify reflections of a deeper nature, connected with the illustrious of past centuries. Still for devotional purposes they do not compete with the Gothic structures of Northern Europe. Churches exhibit national character. Floods of sunbeams through stained glass, mosaic pavements, variegated pillars, costly ornaments, priestly robes, smoking incense, airs that breathe of gayety, and

> "Light quirks of music, broken and uneven,
> That waft the soul upon a jig to heaven,"—

are among the indispensables of joyous, impressional Italians. Italy's church-edifices to-day are absolutely magnificent; but with the decline of Roman-Catholicism, and the increase of knowledge, they will gradually assume the Protestant type, ultimating into elegant places of resort for educational purposes and scientific lectures.

ROME.

And this is Rome, — proud, seven-hilled Rome! The principal street is Corso. To the left of the Pincian Hill is the Tiber, rolling along its muddy tide as in old historic periods. Not far from its banks is the column of Trajan, and also that of Marcus Aurelius Antoninus one hundred and twenty-two feet high, and crowned with a statue of St. Paul; while there rises the dome of the Pantheon, and the cupolas and towers of costly churches. On the other bank of the Tiber, just over the bridge, is the massive tower of Hadrian's Mausoleum, or Castle of St. Angelo; and, beyond, the grand old

Palace of the Vatican, from whence have gone edicts shaking kingdoms, and making crowned heads tremble.

The population of the Eternal City is about one hundred and eighty-five thousand. Of this number, nearly ten thousand are ecclesiastics of some kind. Only think, — one to every eighteen of the people! The streets are thronged with cardinals in scarlet, priests in shining black, and barefooted monks in hideous brown.

On Christmas Day, 1869, there were seven hundred and sixty-five church dignitaries in the city, connected with the Ecumenical Council. Of these, there were fifty-five cardinals, eleven patriarchs, six hundred and forty-seven primates, archbishops, and bishops, six abbots, twenty-one mitred abbots, and twenty-eight generals of monastic orders.

Never will the scene fade from our memory, of standing, and seeing these seven or eight hundred fathers of the Church reverently bow, and kiss the brazen toe of that ugly-visaged, speechless statue of Jupiter, *christened St. Peter*. Around Peter's tomb lamps are kept perpetually burning. Devout visitors to the Vatican, from America even, frequently kiss the genuine, though elegantly slippered, toe of the pope. The act is said to symbolize obedience and submission. The kisses of the faithful have worn the cold foot of the bronze statue of St. Peter to the thinness almost of a knife's edge. Praying and kissing continually abound in St. Peter's, while without the templed walls beggars are pleading for crusts of bread.

WANDERINGS IN THE ETERNAL CITY.

Rome must be judged by its own standard. It can not be compared with other great cities. It has no commerce, no manufactures, no enterprise, — *nothing* of what is considered essential to life in London or New York. It is the home of Popery, the center of a Judaized Christianity; and hence its very life is death, — the "second death," so difficult of resurrection.

Roman manufactures consist of ecclesiastic bulls, edicts, commentaries, and creeds; of mosaics, cameos, scarfs, and copies of pictures. She imports her cloths, cottons, railway materials, cutlery, china, carriages, and military weapons. Teeming with the accumulated treasures of ages, she encouragingly allows her destitute children to be assisted by infidel foreigners, whose heretical books she confiscates, and whose souls she consigns — or would, had she the power — to eternal torments.

The Pantheon is one of the best preserved monumental buildings of this ancient city. On the day of our visit, the Piazza was dirty, and crowded with market-women. Rome would do well to wash her devotees. The edifice has sixteen columns of granite; each surmounted by a frieze and entablature, containing an inscription, which informs us that this "heathen temple" was founded by Agrippa, the friend of Augustus, 27 years B.C.

The Coliseum is considered the greatest wonder of Rome. Its magnitude surpassed all my previous conceptions. The circumference of its area is over one-third of a mile. It has four stories, each of a different order, — the Doric, Ionic, Corinthian, and the Composite, — terminating by a parapet. It is estimated that it would comfortably seat ninety thousand people. Masses of stones have been taken from these ruins to build palaces in the modern city; and yet the structure is so immense, their absence is hardly noticeable. The Coliseum and Forum should be seen by moonlight, say travelers. Midnight hours might throw a mysterious drapery around these ruins, concealing their imperfections, and hightening their grandeur; still I am sufficiently practical to prefer sunlight and daylight. The Coliseum was commenced in A.D. 72, by Vespasian, and completed eight years after by Titus. Much of the work was done by captive Jews. The opening festival scene, say historians, lasted a hundred days. Almost two thousand years has it stood a monument to Roman enterprise and muscular barbarity.

And yet recent excavations reveal pavements, marble statues, and finely finished granite columns, thirty feet below the level of the arena. Evidently there was a previous building of massive dimensions on this site, the constructors of which were pre-historic.

ST. PETER'S AND THE BEGGARS.

The first sight of this most gorgeous of earthly temples strikes the traveler with a sense of unspeakable grandeur. This increases with each succeeding visit, till you stand under the firmament of marble, and cast your eye along the richly-ornamented nave, along the statue-lined transepts, and up into that circling vault, — that wondrous dome, supported by four piers, each 284 feet in periphery, and then you feast upon the fullness of its magnificence. The building stands on a slight acclivity in the north-western corner of the city. It is built in the form of a Latin cross, the nave being in length 607 feet, and the transept 444 feet. The east front is 395 feet wide, and 160 feet high; whilst the pillars composing it are each 88 feet high, and $8\frac{1}{4}$ in diameter. The hight of the dome, from the pavement to the top of the cross, is 448 feet. In front of the church there is a large piazza. The church occupies the place of Nero's circus, and is erected on the spot where St. Peter was martyred. It occupied a period of one hundred and seventy-six years in building, and required three hundred and sixty years to perfect it. It cost ten million pounds; it covers eight English acres; and is kept in repair at a cost of six thousand three hundred pounds per annum.

Raphael's "Transfiguration" is in the Vatican. The great master put his soul into this production. It was his last work; and, while executing it, he seems to have been conscious of standing upon the very verge of the summer-land. He died before finishing it, at the early age of thirty-seven years. After the departure of this great master-painter, the "Transfiguration" was suspended over his corpse. He now ranks a star in the art-galleries of heaven.

But who are these? Why such a troop of beggars at our heels? Is this not a Christian city? Does not the vicegerent of Christ here reside? Did not Peter and Paul here preach? Was there not a special epistle addressed to the *Romans?* Did not Jesus command his followers to sell what they had, and give it to the poor, and follow him? Is this the fruit of nearly two thousand years of Christian teaching and practice? When among the heathen Indians of the great north-west, with the Congressional committee, I saw little begging; but here, near the feet of the *visible Christ*, Pius IX., I am surrounded by filth, beggars, and rags, or the scarlet of cardinals. While working for the downfall of Antichrist, my constant prayer is, " Thy kingdom come, and thy will be done on earth as it is in heaven."

Just under the shade of Pincian Hill, in a magnificent park, musical from flowing fountains, and dotted with palms and flowering-plants from the tropics, I took leave of Prince George de Solms, the personal kindnesses of whom I can never forget. Rome, its ruins and relics, its glory and its shame, I leave with the prayer of faith. If the pope has been pronounced "infallible," his temporal power is gone forever. Roman-Catholicism is waning in Europe; and Rome, city of the Cæsars, is dreaming of a resurrection.

FLORENCE.

Southern Europe is grim with the ghosts of dead cities. Florence, the glory of the middle ages, and formerly capital of Tuscany, is built in the form of a pentagon. Its population is something over one hundred and thirty thousand. This city was for a season the scene of the brave yet fiery Savonarola's labors. A kind of second Calvin, he was called the Catholic reformer of Florence. The pope trembled under his thunderbolts. Through the city flows the Arno. The suburban eminences are crowned with charming villas interspersed with clumps of olive-trees. These grow in such luxuriance that they called out one of Ariosto's sweetest songs.

Just out of this city, under cypress-trees shading a plain brown-marble monument, reposes all that is mortal of one who, not only in America, but in all enlightened lands, lives on earth immortal. The slab has only this: —

THEODORE PARKER.
BORN AT LEXINGTON, MASS., U. S. A., AUG. 24, 1810.
DIED AT FLORENCE, MAY 10, 1860.

Standing by the grave of this man, who was too broad for a sect, and too noble for a priest, strange and deep emotions thrilled my being's center; and I was proud that I had personally known him in life. Near by is the monument of Elizabeth Barrett Browning with simply the plain initials, "E. B. B." The inscription, exceedingly unassuming, seems a veritable prophecy from herself in these lines:—

> " A stone above my heart and head,
> But no name written on the stone."

Among other distinguished Italians, I here met Girolamo Parisi, the editor and publisher of the " Aurora," a well-conducted periodical, printed in Florence, and devoted to Spiritualism, psychology, phrenology, and moral philosophy. Its pages are rich in sound, substantial teachings. In doctrine, it accepts the re-incarnation system of the French school.

Happy were the hours I spent in the society of Baron Kirkup. Encircled by distinguished men of rank, having a massive library of books treating of magic and the unsystematized philosophy of the mystics, and being a practical mesmerist withal, the baron was brought into the fold of Spiritualism over eighteen years since; and he has never shrunk from a frank avowal of his principles. His daughter is the principal medium he consults. Some of the manifestations he has witnessed are absolutely astounding.

Our poet Longfellow, attending a séance at Baron Kirkup's residence, avowed himself a believer in the present ministry of angels.

Appreciating the baron's labors in the restoration of the painting of Dante, there was conferred upon him by royal decree, *La Corona d' Italia*. He had previously been "knighted" by Victor Emmanuel.

CHAPTER XXIX.

EUROPE AND ITS CITIES.

ORIENTAL life has a never-ending charm; the charm of beauty, of tropical freshness, and perpetual summer. Humboldt declares in his "Cosmos," that a man once residing in the spice-lands of the palm and the banana, the cactus and the orange, can never be content to live again in the colder latitudes.

We reached this Austrian city, Trieste, the 15th of September. The cholera was prevalent, and the American consul absent in Vienna. Next to Naples, the harbor of Trieste is the most beautiful in Europe. The city is eminently commercial. Italian is the language most spoken. Nearly all nationalities may be seen in Trieste. The Greeks retain their turbans and flowing robes. Dark-haired, black-eyed Italians do the shop-keeping. Occasionally a German blonde threads the streets. The wealthier class of citizens reside in beautiful villas high up the mountain-side, and a little north of the city.

Leon Favre, the Consul-General of France, and a devoted Spiritualist, resides in Trieste. Unfortunately he was absent. Happy were the hours we spent with this gentleman and scholar, several years since, in Paris.

Signor G. Parisi, another eminent Spiritualist, whom we first saw in Florence, meeting us in the street, embraced us with a love paternal and fraternal. It is as customary in Southern Europe for men to embrace and kiss as for women. "Greet ye one another with a holy kiss" (2 Cor. xiii. 12).

Capt. Richard Burton, noted in literature, known as a visitor to Mohammed's tomb, and a traveler in Africa, is the British consul in this city. So far as the captain has any religious bias, it is towards Spiritualism. If he visits America next season, we may accompany him on a tour to Yucatan, and various ruins in South America.

VENICE, QUEEN OF THE ADRIATIC.

"I heard in Venice sweet Tasso's song,
By stately gondola borne along."

This is decidedly an odd city, a city built upon over a hundred little islands, a city with canals for streets. Only think of being taken from the depot, and rowed about the city in search of a hotel; think of seeing front-doors open on to the water; think of the queer taste that could select such a site for a city. Byron's ecstasies over Venice puzzle us.

The Venetian Republic elected its first doge, or president, A.D. 697. Its armies ultimately conquered the Genoese. The hundred Catholic churches of Venice, though rich in paintings, look interiorly dark and gloomy; the streets are narrow and tortuous; the marbled palaces are grayed and grim; and the "gay gondoliers," who propel those four thousand licensed gondolas, are very much like other men that work for money. By a Venetian law dating back three hundred years, the gondolas are painted black. This gives them a hearse-like appearance. The aristocratic classes have their palaces on the Grand Canal, and keep their gondolas as our wealthier citizens keep their carriages. The city has three hundred and seventy-eight arched bridges of either iron or marble, and high enough for the passage of gondolas under them.

To religionists, St Mark's Cathedral is the charmed center; to poets and sentimentalists, the Bridge of Sighs, rendered famous in Byron's "Childe Harold,"—

"I stood in Venice, on the Bridge of Sighs,
A palace and a prison on each hand."

The hundred old palaces gracing the Grand Canal are named after their founders. Many of them are magnificent even in decline. By paying a small fee, the doctor and self were permitted to stroll through one of these splendid palaces, so unique, so rich in furniture and paintings, golden mirrors, and specimens of antiquity. Venice boasts the largest painting in the world. Venetian ladies, going to church, wear veils upon their heads. They are exquisite singers. Guides and gondoliers show the house from which Desdemona eloped with the Moor, and the residence of Shylock, who dealt so mercilessly with the Merchant of Venice. Enough of fiction: give us facts.

MILAN.

Northern Italy is transcendently beautiful. Most of the distance from Venice through Verona to Milan presents a continuous scene of luxuriant vegetation. The fortified towns, the chain of mountains on our right, terraced with vineyards, the lovely Lake of Garda linking Italy to Austria, and the irrigated lawns and landscapes, made our soul all the day sunny with gladness. Milan, considering the state of civilization and progress, is evidently the finest city in Italy, and the best-paved city in Europe. It is walled, with the gradings, gardens, and ornamental shrubbery so arranged that it seems surrounded with a park. The center of attraction to strangers is the world-renowned cathedral, a full description of which is impossible. To be appreciated it must be seen. Built in the form of a Latin cross, its length is four hundred and ninety feet, and its breadth one hundred and eighty feet. Its rich marble tracery, its forest of spires, its seven thousand statues, its aisles, pillars, and lofty arches, present a wilderness of magnificence absolutely indescribable. From the summit the Alps, with Mont Blanc in the blue distance, are clearly visible. As a monument of elegant and costly architecture, it must for ages stand unrivaled; and yet it is but a pygmy compared with St. Peter's at Rome.

PARIS AND THE COMMUNE.

Our route from Milan lay through Turin and Mont Cenis. Does not this Alpine tunnel — marvel of enterprise and engineering — prophesy of tunneling the English Channel? Paris, proudest city of Europe! Previous visits to the French capital under Napoleon only fanned the desire to see it since the Prussian victories, and the reign of that Commune which raised its spiteful hand against palaces, monuments, works of art, and rare old libraries, — a Commune that madly fired its own city! Strange way to actualize the grand theories of "liberty, fraternity, and equality," by obliterating all evidences of former genius and culture!

Arriving at Paris in early morning, the first glance showed no signs of the war, nor of Communistic vandalism. A longer stroll lifted the veil, and revealed the reality. The Tuileries, Hotel de Ville, Chateau du Palais-Royal, the Louvre, the library of the Louvre, and hundreds of other buildings, were either fired or burned to ashes. Men and women of the baser sort vied with each other in scattering petroleum and mineral oils. Parisians proved themselves worse enemies of France than Prussians.

The Hotel de Ville was famous not less for its antiquity and architectural beauties than for having been the place where the mayor of Paris handed the tricolor cockade to good King Louis XVI.; where they arrested Robespierre July 27, 1794; and where the festival was held of the marriage of Napoleon I. with Marie Louise.

The pen that writes of Paris between the 18th of March and the 28th of May, 1871, should, to correspond with the scenes, be dipped in blood. Barbarians have burned cities, and annihilated the books and art-treasures they could not understand. But the Commune outdid this, destroying indiscriminately museums, libraries, and granaries. The burning of Paris was discussed and openly decided upon in the councils of the Commune. The decree was published in "The Official Journal." Rigault, Billivray, *et al.*, spent their leisure with their mistresses; while even Paschal Grousset, appointed delegate for foreign affairs, gave himself up with other leaders to bacchanalian excesses. While shouting, "Down with the house of Thiers, and confiscate his property," decrees went forth, "Use petroleum," "Repeal all law," "Fire the churches," "Suppress the newspapers," "Abolish marriages;" and all this in the name of *liberty, fraternity, freedom*, — "social freedom," *par excellence!*

Doubtless the Thiers government was in some respects oppressive; but did this justify the atrocities of the Commune? Burning a barn to kill a weasel, demolishing a costly edifice to get rid of a wasp's nest under the eaves, would be a ranting diabolism paralleled only in folly by French Communism.

Excepting Flourens, the leading members of the Commune seemed inflated with ambition; inspired with the love of money and pleasure, wine and women.

The Franco-Prussian war, and the Commune, quite effectually paralyzed Spiritualism. It is now re-gathering its scattered forces. At Mrs. Hollis's séance, held in the apartments of Mrs. Mary J. Holmes, near the Champs-Elysées, I had the pleasure of meeting that gifted author, Victor Hugo. He wept like a child when receiving a communication from a loved friend in spirit-life.

ILLEGITIMATE CHILDREN.

Official returns from Parisian hospitals last year showed, that, of the births in the city, fifteen thousand three hundred and sixty-six were illegitimate. Boxes called *tours* are established in various parts of Paris, each of which revolves upon a pivot, and, on a bell being rung, is turned around by the proper person inside, to receive the child that may have been deposited. No attempts are made to ascertain the parents. These children never know a father's care, a mother's love. Nurses are secured from the country.

The suburban villas of Paris send into the foundling hospitals annually over four thousand of these illegitimate children, a large portion of which are received by the *Hospice des Enfants Assistés*, founded in 1640. Virtually twenty thousand illegitimate children, abandoned by their parents, plead yearly in Paris for paternal recognition, and maternal tenderness, — plead in vain. This is the legitimate outcome of French socialism.

GOETHE AND BARON GULDENSTUBBE.

Neither genius nor true greatness can be entirely disconnected from angel ministrations. Poets, philosophers, all, are inspired of the gods. The following, from "Lewes's Life of Goethe," refers to the poet's last hours: —

"The next morning he [Goethe] tried to walk a little up and down the room, but after a turn he found himself too feeble to continue. Reseating himself in an easy chair, he chatted cheerfully with Ottilia on the approaching spring, which would be sure to restore him. He had no idea of his end being so near. It was now observed that his thoughts began to wander incoherently. 'See,' he exclaimed, 'the lovely woman's head — with black curls — in splendid colors — a dark background!' Presently he saw a piece of paper on the floor, and asked how they could leave Schiller's letters so carelessly lying about. Then he slept softly, and, awakening, asked for the sketches he had just seen. They were sketches in a dream."

An eminent professor, intimately connected to Goethe's family, refers to noises, whistling sounds, and voices, heard near the close of this great man's life. These are his words: —

"It seemed as if, in a less frequented part of the house, a door either unknown, or long forgotten, slowly opened, creaking on its rusty hinges. Then a beautiful female spirit-figure appeared, bearing a lamp burning with a light-blue flame; her features were surrounded by a halo of glory. She gazed calmly upon the the terror-stricken witnesses, sang a few stanzas of some angelic melody, and then disappeared; the door, closing behind her, presenting the same sealed appearance as before. In solemn silence the observers retraced their footsteps to the chamber of mourning, and there learned that the spirit had returned to God, who gave it. The last words audible were, "More light!'"

When in Paris the first time, guest of Mr. Gledstanes, the French Consul Leon Favre accompanied me to the residence of the Swedish Baron Louis Guldenstubbe. This gentleman, a distinguished Spiritualist, was related to a Scandinavian family of great renown. "Two of his ancestors, Knights of the Order of the Grand Templars, and of the same name, were burned alive in 1309, in company with Jacques de Molay, by order of Pope Clement the Fifth."

If it be true, as is sometimes asserted, that the country of one's birth and hereditary descent are not without influence upon mediumistic qualities, the baron was favored in both these respects. The mother who gave him birth in the country of Swedenborg, the mystic Scandinavia, prone to Spiritual belief, early initiated him in this kind of reading. When quite young he was remarkable for presentiments and visions.

He published several volumes relating to his researches in the science of positive and experimental pneumatology, besides a deeply interesting contribution upon " direct spirit writing." Both himself and sister were mediums. The baron recently passed to spirit-life, esteemed highest by those who knew him best.

ALL CITIES REPUDIATED.

As wens and warts to human bodies, so are cities to a country. Unnatural, they are the cesspools of crime, competition, and avarice. While Nature has lavished her gifts with prodigal hand, men should make community-villas, and gardens of hill and dale, each and all earning their bread by honest toil. Rome, grim and grand, unites the dead past and living present. The Papal Church is the most logical of any. It has an infallible God, an infallible Lord Jesus, an infallible Church, an infallible Douay Bible, and an infallible Pope; and all communicants have to do is, to attend mass, confess their sins, pay their priests, and go to glory!

Threading the streets of Naples, and the suburban villages, one wonders how six hundred thousand inhabitants can here live. Lazzaroni are thick as flies around pools. Jews, Quakers, and Shakers take care of their own poor. Lyons, the Lowell of France, is alive with silk manufactories. Paris is handsome and proud, showy and sinful. Berlin is rich in historic and artistic attractions. The cathedrals are open at all hours of the day in these cities. On their feet-worn floors, prince and peasant meet as equals. Gardens in European cities and hamlets are enjoyed by the people as by the proprietors. Visitors do not presume to meddle with plant or flower. The citizens generally are better mannered and more polished than in America. Our caste is based upon wealth. Our boasted individuality has degenerated into a selfish rascality. Our laws punish little, and pardon great criminals. New-York City only a year since had sixty thousand children of school age that had never been inside a schoolroom. American self-conceit and English caste are both abominable. As nations they are antichrist.

LONDON.

Crossing the English Channel from France to Dover, a few hours through the fertile fields of Merry England brought us to the heart of London, the city of cities, with a population almost equal to that of the whole State of New York. Individuals may drive sixteen miles in a straight line upon any one of London's diameters. The seven parks have been termed, not inaptly, the lungs of London. They lie chiefly at the West End. The Richmond Park, owned by the crown, has two thousand two hundred acres, and is eight miles in circumference. Hyde Park claims four hundred acres. Victoria Park, named in honor of the Queen, is comparatively new, but exceedingly beautiful with lake and pleasure boats. The Parliament Buildings, Gothic in form, and covering over seven acres, are as queer as magnificent, Westminster Abbey, venerable structure where have taken place all the coronations since Edward the Confessor, is visited more for a sight at the tombs of Shakspeare, Milton, Addison, Campbell, Dickens, and other distinguished authors, than for worship. Crystal Palace, embracing several hundred acres, with broad avenues, extensive gardens, floral embellishments, and within the building statues, paintings, and unique marvels, presents rare attractions. Madame Tussaud's wax-works are not as admirable as have been represented. The Tower of London is stern and gloomy, — the traditions repulsive. In one of these towers is a large iron cage, containing a collection of jewels estimated at twenty million dollars. The great Koh-i-noor diamond is among this collection. " The crown of her Majesty Queen Victoria is a cap of purple velvet, inclosed in hoops of silver, surrounded by a ball and cross, all of which are resplendent with diamonds. In the center of the cross is the 'inestimable sapphire,' and in front of the crown is the heart-shaped ruby said to have been worn by the Black Prince."

Remembering the teaching, "Lay not up for yourselves treasures on earth," why not dispose of those jewels and diamonds at once, using the proceeds to procure homes for the homeless, and bread for orphans?

The British Museum is an institution of itself. Blessings upon all old book-shops! English parsons think Oxford the mother of the best English. Americans quote Boston as authority. The English excel in justice, simplicity of faith, and solid friendship; Americans in tact, originality, and audacity. The Latin race is bad at colonizing; but, wherever Englishmen go, they create a new England. Their individuality, like the sponge, excels in absorbing. Their houses are their castles.

The English have more German characteristics than we. In their travels they go to Germany, Italy, or the East. Americans rush to Paris. A gulf separates the working people of England from the nobility. The latter clutch dead bones to knock the life out from progressive souls. And, further, boasting of a titled ancestry, they search at the roots of trees for fruits, — *such* fruits as burden only the topmost branches. Though the Nile has many mouths, it has no discoverable head. A privileged few own nearly all the soil. These have yet to learn that legitimate production is the only basis of ownership. What men by faithful toil make to grow or produce is theirs, and nothing more. There's a tendency in London and throughout England to co-operation and a practical communism.

HOMEWARD. — THE SPIRITUAL OUTLOOK.

Belief often blossoms out into knowledge. Traveling westward as a missionary, I circumnavigated the globe, and know the world to be round. Progress is the key-word of all nationalities, and Spiritualism God's witness of a future existence, in the Pacific Isles, and all portions of the Orient, as in the Occident. Believe me, it was joy unbounded almost, after this long, perplexing voyage, to be dropped down in London, to walk familiar streets, look into friendly faces, clasp cordial hands, listen to the ringing accents of good solid English, and receive such a cordial public reception at the "Spiritual Institution" under the supervision of Mr. James Burns.

English Unitarianism is icy, arrogant, and cultured. Orthodox theology is a spent force. Spiritualism is a living gospel power; and the English are making rapid strides in the dissemination of its heavenly principles. I could but exclaim, How changed since James Burns and self strolled through London's labyrinthine streets in search of the Cavendish Rooms, to commence a series of Sunday meetings! Competent editors, erudite essayists, eloquent speakers, and superior mediums for demonstrating the reality of the phenomena, are now *all* doing substantial work upon the temple of truth.

Books, journals, Spiritualist literature of all kinds and gradations, are rapidly increasing in England and the British Empire. Under this head, the most unique, and the most wonderful too, in some directions, are a series of books by ——, entitled the "Book of God," "Book of Enoch," "Apocalypse," &c. For acquaintance with Brahmanism, Buddhism, and other Oriental religions, together with research into the mysteries of the East, these volumes stand quite unrivaled.

SUGGESTIONS TO TRAVELERS.

As a tourist, have some higher purpose than mere pleasure.

"O happiness! our being's end and aim,"

though good poetry, is wretched philosophy. Happiness should be no man's "aim." It would be the quintessence of selfishness.

While packing your trunk (*one* is enough), store away in your soul's silent chambers a choice stock of good temper and patient forbearance. Passports are no longer necessary, even in Turkey or Egypt. In case of accident or trouble, however, they might be convenient for identification. Take as little clothing as possible; it is cheaper in most countries than America. Guide-books are indispensable; while guides are often a pestilence and a prey. The Bank of England is best known in the East; but a "circular letter of credit" from any responsible house in New York or Boston is negotiable in the prominent cities of foreign countries. If there should be any difficulty, our consuls will remedy it. In the Asiatic cities secure, for sleeping, an uppermost room: you will find better air, and less fleas.

Fire-arms of all kinds should be left at home: it is generally the most cowardly that carry them. Dogs fight because they are dogs. Few men are sufficiently brave to run, rather than fight. That Miltonian war in heaven was a myth; and all fighting is anti-Christian. The cost of travel depends altogether upon tourists. Bating the beggars, and the to-be-expected fleecing of travelers, the average hotel charges are much cheaper in some parts of Europe, and equally as cheap in Asia, as America.

SUNRISE AROUND THE WORLD.

It is no marvel that sun-worship was once common in the East, nor that modern Parsees look upon the sun as the symbol of universal light, the divine Intelligence of the universe. How true that, in the modified language of another, the "morning dawns on the isles of the Pacific, where the palm-grove, the coral-reef, and the lagoon are to be seen. Westward it moves, irradiating at once Australia and Japan, the gold-diggings of the Briton, and the summer gardens of the Tycoon. Next Java seas and Chinese waters reflect the morn; the one studded with spicy isles, the other teeming with ships of antique form. On it goes, lighting up the populous cities of China, the shrines of Siam, and the temples of Burmah, until the tops of the Himalayas reflect the first rays of coming day. Brighter grows the light upon its lasting snows, and wide it spreads on either hand, o'er ocean's waves and Tartar land,

> 'O'er many an ancient river,
> O'er many a palmy plain,'

until jungle and city, deep defile and Hindoo temple, are flooded with the light of day. Onward still it moves, over Afghanistan and Persia, until the snows of Ararat are suffused with a crimson glow. Brighter grows the light, until surrounding seas reflect the day, until the camel's shadow is projected on the sand, and the mosque and the minaret are revealed on Zion's Hill. Onward still it advances in ceaseless march, illumining the classic shores of the Mediterranean, and spreading far away to Caffre hut and Lapland burrow; embracing at once Zambesi and Nile valleys, Grecian isles, and Russian steppes. At length the Alps are all aglow, and the shadows of night chased from the valleys. Darkness retires from the scene, and reveals the rolling Rhine, the plains of France, and the hills of Spain. The British Isles, too, are all in view, — the greensward of England, and Scotia's rugged strand. Having lighted up the Old World, westward it moves to seek a New. The waves of the Atlantic are irradiated from pole to pole. Ten thousand sails mirrored on the deep, or rocked by the tempest, reflect the day. A New World comes in view, from the shores of the Amazon to Labrador; wide savannas, emerald isles, populous cities, mighty rivers, and pine-clad hills, embrace the day. On marches the morn over fertile plains and dark primeval forests, over the banks of the Amazon, the windings of the Mississippi, the network of railways, and the waters of the great lakes, until beyond green savanna and rolling prairie it glows on the snows of the Andes, and the tops of the Rocky Mountains, where the condor trims his plumage, and the grizzly bear skulks to his lair. Down the mountain-side it pours, until Chilian cities and Californian sands are mirrored in the waters of the Pacific. Again its march is o'er the deep, until, amid the beauteous isles where day began, it resumes its glorious course of sunrise round the world."

THE JOURNEY SUMMARIZED.

Travel is a school of trial; and traversing Oriental lands requires considerable pluck, perseverance, and determination. Though passing through diverse experiences, though subjected to strange mixtures of diet; though often sweltering in torrid climes; though scattering Spiritualistic literature among missionaries and mandarins, Brahmans and Buddhists; though resorting to donkeys, camels, and elephants in the line of locomotion, as well as sedan-chairs, palanquins, railways, and ill-ventilated steamers, still we met — thanks to God and ministering spirits — with no serious disaster by land or sea. And, further, if we except custom-house annoyances, and the begging proclivities of pariahs and other lower classes in the East, all the races and tribes with whom we had to do, Maoris and Malays, Hindoos and Arabs, treated us with considerations of kindness and good will.

Sitting quietly now in my library-room, and retrospecting the year and a half's absence consumed in this round-the-world pilgrimage, it seems hardly possible that I've seen the black aborigines of Australia, and the tattooed Maoris of New Zealand; that I've witnessed the Hindoos burning their dead, and Persians praying in their fire-temples; that I've gazed upon the frowning peak of Mount Sinai, and stood upon the summit of Cheops; that I've conversed upon antiquity and religious subjects with Chinamen in Canton, Brahmans in Bengal, Parsees in Bombay, Arabs in Arabia, descendants of Pyramid-builders in Cairo, and learned rabbis in Jerusalem; that I've seen Greece in her shattered splendor, Albania with its castled crags, the Cyclades with their mantling traditions, and the Alps impearled and capped in crystal.

The Spiritual séance that we held upon Mount Zion, in Jerusalem, when ancient spirits that personally knew Jesus after the "days of Herod the king" came and conversed with us, was to me the most consecrated hour of life. It was the door, the very gate to heaven, and *that* ajar! The particulars and preparations for the séance, with the teachings, the inquiries, and responses, will be written out in the future. The time is not yet. We are living in the Second Coming, the continuous coming of Christ, a coming in judgment, in " power and great glory ! "

As midnight hours are lighted by starry hosts; as grasses and grains, fruits and yellowing harvests, first freshen, then come to maturity through the warmth and light of the sun, so comes the soul's salvation through Christ. " We are saved by his life " (Rom. v. 10). Christianity — that is, the Christ-principles enunciated by Jesus Christ — stands upon an imperishable basis. With its everlasting arms of tenderness, it infolds the world, and pours forth a crystal flood of love as boundless as inexhaustible.

It is difficult to realize that I've been in Bethlehem, walked in the Garden of Gethsemane, stood upon Mount Olives, bathed in the Jordan, breathed the air that fanned the serene face of Jesus when weary from travel under the burning skies of Palestine, looked thoughtfully upon the same hills and valleys clothed in Syrian spring-time with imperial lilies, and had the same images daguerreotyped upon my brain that impressed the sensitive soul of the "man of sorrows,"— the teacher sent from God.

As the voyage of mortal life must end some time, so must the record of these travels. If those who have followed me have been edified, and morally benefited, then am I satisfied. The "greatest word," said Confucius, "is 'reciprocity.'" Writing in haste, we may have committed some minor errors, or expressed opinions without sufficient research; but the endeavor has been to treat the subjects referred to candidly, bringing to our aid the most reliable information; and *all* to impart correct ideas of the millions peopling the East.

Though each nation has its individuality, and each zone its peculiar attractions; though there are choicer antiquities, and more classical lands; though there are sunnier skies, and tropical fruits mellowing in one eternal summer, — still I admire my native land. And yet standing upon the mount of vision, illumined by the principles of the Spiritual philosophy, I know no rich, no poor, no Asia, no America, no caste, no country; but *one divine humanity*, resting upon the beating, loving bosom of God.

TABLE OF CONTENTS.

PAGE.
PREFACE iii

CHAPTER I.

HAMMONTON TO CALIFORNIA.

Uses of Travel. — The Western Route. — Indians on the Plains. — Salt Lake City. — Joseph Smith's Visions. — Why Mormons practice Polygamy. — Brigham Young and his Wives. — Strange Doctrines concerning Sexual Life. — How to deal with Polygamy. — Its Destiny. — California Fruits and Products. — Treatment of Chinamen. — Religious Tendencies. — Inharmonies of Harmonial Philosophers . 1

CHAPTER II.

THE SANDWICH ISLANDS, SOUTH-SEA ISLANDS, AND SÉANCES AT SEA.

Our German Princes. — Identification of the Spirit Aaron Knight. — What is the Soul? — When does it begin to exist? — The Moon's Inhabitants. — Natives of the Sandwich Islands. — Their Habits and Morals. — Hawaiian Spiritism. — Recent Phenomena. — Decrease of the Native Population 22

CHAPTER III.

THE POLYNESIAN RACES.

The Ocean Outlook. — Beauty of the Pacific Islands. — The Samoan Group, and the United States. — The Feejees and their Customs. — How were these Islands peopled? — How Civilized Nations have treated these Islanders. — Lost Islands of the Ocean . . . 34

CHAPTER IV.

OCEANICA TO AUCKLAND.

Gorgeous Sunsets. — Souls as Exiles. — Louis XII. and Shaving. — Sports of the Passengers. — Spirit and Matter. — A Spirit-Chief of Oahu. — Sights in the Depths of the Ocean. — The Uses and Abuses of Spiritual Séances. — Parisi the Italian Teacher. — Reaching Auckland, New Zéaland. — The Climate and the People 44

CHAPTER V.

AUSTRALIA.

Sydney: its Population and Parks. — Landing at Melbourne. — Appearance of the City. — Its Morals and Amusements. — The Climate and Fruits. — The Gold Discovery in Australia. — Rushing to the Mines. — Excess of Male Population. — Our Reception by Spiritualists. — Persecutions by the Victorian Press. — Appealing from the Press to the Public. — Lecturing in the Prince of Wales Theater. — Mandarin Chinamen organizing for Missionary Effort among Christians. — Spirit of the Christian Church in Australia. — Spiritualism in the Provincial Cities. — The Black Man of Australia. — Their Religion and Social Characteristics. — Whence their Origin? — What their Destiny? . 51

CHAPTER VI.

NEW ZEALAND.

Mountainous Appearance of the Country. — The Scotland of the South. — The Beautiful Climate and Fruits. — The Gold-Fields. — Botanizing. — The Moa-Bird. — Mineral Springs. — Akaroa and Christchurch. — Wine at a Funeral. — Cannibalism. — Is Man-Eating Natural? — Theological Cannibalism. — The Lord's Supper of Unleavened Bread approved. — The Maori Race of New Zealand. — Their Domestic Habits. — From whence came they? — Tattooing. — The Spiritual Experiences of the Maoris. — The Tohunga. — Spiritualism in Dunedin. — A Challenge for Discussion. — Dunedin Presbyterianism. — Racial Influences 81

CHAPTER VII.

FROM NEW ZEALAND TO CHINA.

What is Time? — Too Trusting, or not? — Selfishness of Worldly Men. — Trimming to the Breeze. — Plato's Republic. — More's Utopia. — Fourierism. — The Communism of Robert Owen. — The Great Communist Jesus. — The Chinese praying for Wind. — The Southern Cross. — Our Lost Day. — Longings for Land. — A Fight among Chinamen. — An Eclipse at Sea 105

CHAPTER VIII.
SÉANCES ON THE OCEAN.

Delicacy of Conditions. — Compliance with them Indispensable. — Teachings of Spirits. — How they read Thoughts. — The Length of Time that Man has inhabited the Earth. — Spirits passing through Matter. — Selfishness in Spirit-Life. — Where are the Spirit-Spheres located? — Can Spirits pass to the Planets? — Obsessing Spirits of the Lower Spheres. — Are there Animals in Spirit-Life? — Do the Spheral Belts, encircling, revolve with the Earth? — The Occupations in Different Spheres. — The Christ-Sphere of Purity 121

CHAPTER IX.
CHINA.

Hong Kong. — The Face of the Country. — The Past History of China. — Its Ancient Names. — Early Efforts to Christianize the Chinese. — Up the Pearl River to Canton. — The Chinese Temples. — Magicians. — Streets. — Sedan-Chairs. — Customs. — Benevolent Institutions before the Presence of Missionaries. — Chinese Literature. — The Coolie Trade. — Christian Kidnapping. — America long known to the Chinese. — Why the Coolies came to California. — Consulting Spirits before leaving. — Chinese Cemeteries. — Pagodas, and why they were built 133

CHAPTER X.
CHINESE RELIGIONS AND INSTITUTIONS.

Confucian Examination-Hall. — The Great Wall, and Walled Cities. — Eating Rats and Puppies. — Chinese Books of Morals. — Lau-tsze the Superior of Confucius. — Extracts from his Teachings. — How they reckon Time. — Buddhism. — Its Teachings. — Chinamen as Emigrants. — Do they murder their Infants? — Their Retorts on Christians. — The Deification of General Ward. — His Career with General Walker in Nicaragua. — The Tai-ping Rebellion. — Tea. — Secret of Mr. Burlingame's Influence in China. — Chinese Spiritualism. — What Missionaries say of it. — Methods of Converse. — Very Ancient among the Chinese. — The Moral Influence of Spiritism upon the Nation. 151

CHAPTER XI.
COCHIN CHINA TO SINGAPORE.

The Anamites. — Saigon. — The Anamite Customs and Religion. — French Fashions and American Independence. — Singapore. — The Tropical Beauty of the Island. — The Malays of the City. — The Malays an Old Race. — Their Color, Dress, and General Features. — Whence came they? — How did they reach America? — Customs Common to the Malays and our Indians. — Religion of the Malays. — The Orang-Utan. — Darwinianism. 178

CHAPTER XII.
MALACCA TO INDIA.

Johore. — Visit to the Maha-Rajah. — Extensive Forests. — Sawmills in Asia. — Jungles. — Tigers. — Serpents. — Abundance of Fruits. — Volcanic Belts. — Gold-Mines. — Bird's-Nest Soups. — The Upas. — Cocoanut-Groves. — The Betel-Nut, and how used. — The Gutta-Percha Tree. — Spice-Field Breezes. — Calcutta *viâ* Penang. — Passing Mount Ophir 192

CHAPTER XIII.
SPIRITUAL SÉANCES ON THE INDIAN OCEAN.

Communication from Dr. Willis on Disease. — Meat-Eating. — How Color affects Health. — Sun-Baths. — Mixture of Magnetisms and Obsessions. — Undeveloped Spirits. — How to avoid their Influence. — Crimes instigated by Low, Scheming Spirits. — Teachings of a French Normandy Spirit. — Breathing in Life-Germs and Living Cells. — Origin of Intelligence. — From whence the Cross? — Auras as an Index to Character. — Constructing our own Future Homes. — Living Celibate Lives. — Place of John's Birth. — His Travels. — His Visions. — What the Deeds of the Nicolaitanes were. — Who was Melchisedec? — The Essenians. — Who were Jesus' Guides? — His Present Position in the Heavens 201

CHAPTER XIV.
INDIA: ITS HISTORY AND TREASURES.

Approaching the Land of the Brahman. — English Territory and Rule in India. — Whence the Hindoos? — Nature of the Aryans. — Growth and Literature of the Hindoos. — The Vedas. — Walks about the City. — City Suburbs and Sight-Seeing. — River Scenes. — Juggernaut. — The Banyan Trees. — Condition of the Country . . . 211

CHAPTER XV.
INDIA'S RELIGIONS, MORALS, AND SOCIAL CHARACTERISTICS.

Social·Tendencies of the Hindoos. — Ghauts for burning their Dead. — Shall we burn, or bury? — Origin of Castes. — The Brahman Priests. — How they do Penance. — Bathing in the Ganges. — Their Manner of Dress. — Their Natural Politeness. — The Royal Asiatic Society. — Up through the Country to Benares. — Metaphysics Old in India. — Fakirs and their Practices. — Along the way to Bombay. — The Supposed Birth-place of Budha. — Origin of Brahmanism. — Age of the Rig Veda. — Meaning of their Sacrifices. — Belief of the Ancient Brahmans. — Christna the Ninth Incarnation. — Brahmanical Maxims . 222

TABLE OF CONTENTS.

CHAPTER XVI.
THE RISE OF BUDDHISM IN INDIA.

History of Buddha. — The Ethics of Buddhism. — The Rev. Murray's Civilized Heathen. — The Reason why Buddhists consider Guatama Buddha a Greater Man than Jesus Christ. — The Doctrines of the Buddhists. —Teaching of his Disciples. — Their Sacred Writings. — The Decline of Buddhism in India. — The World's Religions. — The Elephanta Caves 241

CHAPTER XVII.
THE BRAHMO-SOMAJ AND PARSEES.

Spiritualism in India. — Believers in Calcutta. — Communication from an Ancient Spirit of India. — Allahabad. — The Brahmo-Somaj Worshipers.— Keshub Chunder Sen. — The Parsees. — The Ancient Zoroaster. —The Religious Doctrines of the Parsees.— Their Strange Method of disposing of their Dead. — Their Temples and Altars for the Sacred Fire 250

CHAPTER XVIII.
FROM INDIA TO ARABIA.

Aden and the Arabs in the Country. — Arabic Literature. — The Heat upon the Red Sea. — How the Israelites crossed the Sea. — The City of Suez. — Filth of the People. — The Suez Canal. — Across the Desert to Cairo 265

CHAPTER XIX.
EGYPT AND ITS WONDERS.

The City of Cairo. — The Khedive of Egypt. — His Ambitious Purposes. — A Railway Fifteen Hundred Miles up the Nile.—The People in Central Africa. — The Testimonies of Travelers concerning them. — Reasons for thinking the Sanscrit originated in Africa. — Swedenborg's Belief founded upon the Teachings of Spirits as to an Ancient Bible in Africa. — The Museum in Cairo. — Spirits explaining the Hieroglyphs. — The Nilometer. —Strabo's Mention of it. — The Fertility of the Nile Valley 272

CHAPTER XX.
EGYPT'S CATACOMBS AND PYRAMIDS.

Personal Appearance of the Egyptians. — The Pyramids. — Ancient Description of them. — The Catacombs of Memphis. — The Tombs of Sakkarah. — From Sakkarah by Donkeys over the Sands to Cheops. — The Sphinx. —The Great Pyramid. — Its Hight. — Its Amount of Masonry. — Climbing to the Apex. — Spiritual Séance on the Pyramid. — Communication of the Spirit 282

CHAPTER XXI.
STUDY OF THE PYRAMIDS.

Different Estimates of the Pyramids. — What the Old Greeks said of them. — What Present Scientists think about them. — Prof. C. Piazza Smythe's Examination of these Monuments. — The Internal Structures. — The King's Chamber. — Careful Measurements. — Results of the Researches. — The Great Age of the Pyramids. — Gliddon's Testimony. — How did the Ancients move such Blocks of Stone? — Were they moved, or manufactured in Places where they are found?. 293

CHAPTER XXII.
ANCIENT SCIENCE IN EGYPT.

Astronomy of the Egyptians. — Heliopolis, the College of Priests. — The Obelisk in Constantinople. — The Rosetta Stone. — The Ancient Copts. — Ancient Alexandria. — Destruction of the Library. — Book-Burning by Mohammedans and Christians. — Cleopatra's Needle. — General Lytle's Poetic Lines. — Eastern Liars. — Mark Twain's Extravagance. — Spiritualism in Ancient Egypt. — Mesmerism pictured on their Papyri. — Spiritualists in Modern Cairo 305

CHAPTER XXIII.
FROM ALEXANDRIA TO JOPPA AND JERUSALEM.

The Appearance of Modern Joppa. — Scriptural References to it. — The New-England Colony in Joppa. — Fanaticism. — Engaging Dragomen. — Whom to engage. — The Gardens of Joppa. — On the Way to Jerusalem. — Wheat-Stubble on the Plains of Sharon. — Ramleh and its Convent. — The Roughness of the Route towards Jerusalem. — Glimpse of the City. — Natural Emotions. — Others' Impressions. — Estimates of Jesus. — Jerusalem as it now is. — Its Walls, Filth, and Shrines. — Localities pointed out by Monks. — Mount of Olives . . 316

CHAPTER XXIV.
CITY OF PROPHETS AND APOSTLES.

Did Jesus exist? — What are the Proofs? — Gerald Massey's Testimony. — What a Rabbi said to us in Jerusalem. — The Mosque of Omar. — The Wailing-Place of the Jews. — What they say. — Walking in *Gehenna*. — Hell. — Trees there growing. — Bethesda's Pool. — Magnetic Waters. — The Date of the Crucifixion. — Bethlehem's Star. — Astronomical Confirmation. — The Birthplace of Jesus. — Present Appearance of the City. — Shepherds still watching Flocks there. — Why did not Greek and Roman Writers refer to Jesus? — Solomon's Pools. — Route from Jerusalem to the Dead Sea. — The Jordan. — Spirits pointing out Places and Paths where Jesus journeyed . 330

TABLE OF CONTENTS.

CHAPTER XXV.

PRESENT GOSPELS.

Present Inspirations. — Why Jesus was baptized in Jordan. — Did he confess his Sins? — Peculiarities of the River Jordan. — What the Spirits said of Jordan and Jericho. — Robbers in the Vicinity of Jericho. — The Good Samaritan. — Present Population of Palestine. — Explorations in the Country. — The Book of Moab. — Non-Practicability of Reformers 346

CHAPTER XXVI.

THE CHRISTIANITY OF THE AGES.

Plato and Jesus in Contrast. — Who has the Pre-eminence? — Christian Teachings before the Time of Jesus Christ. — Testimonies in Proof. — The Mediterranean Waters. — Islands of Rhodes and Cyprus. — Characteristics of Modern Greeks. — Smyrna. — The Ancient Smyrnian Church. — Spiritualists in Smyrna. — The Climate and Costumes. — Visit to the Ruins of Ephesus. — Place of John's Death. — Isaalouke 354

CHAPTER XXVII.

TURKEY IN ASIA.

The Grecian Isles. — Constantinople. — Walks in the City. — The Kindheartedness of the Turks. — Their Language, Social Customs, and Worship. — The Koran. — The Muezzins. — Turkish Women, and their Vanity. — The Mohammendan Dervishes. — Their Belief, and Way of Worship. — Spiritualism in Turkey 368

CHAPTER XXVIII.

MODERN GREECE, ROME, AND NORTHERN ITALY.

Athens. — Byron, and his Love of Greece. — Mars Hill, and the Prison of Socrates. — The Mediterranean Waters. — Naples. — Garibaldi's Entrance into the City. — The Beggary in Naples. — The Congress of Free-Thinkers. — The Museum and its Treasures. — Pompeii and Herculaneum. — The Marvels there found. — Italian Churches. — Rome. — Wanderings in the Eternal City. — The Pantheon and Colisenm. — St. Peter's Church. — Raphael's Transfiguration. — Begging under the Shadow of Christian Churches. — Florence. — Spiritualism in Florence 378

CHAPTER XXIX.

EUROPE AND ITS CITIES.

Trieste. — Venice: its Canals, Gondolas, and Palaces. — Milan: its Cathedral and Modern Improvements. — Mont Cenis Tunnel. — Paris and the Commune. — Fire the Churches, and abolish Marriage. — A Séance in Paris. — Illegitimate Children. — Baron Guldenstubbe. — All Cities and City Life repudiated. — The Characteristics of Different Cities. — London. — Westminster Abbey. — The Queen's Wealth. — Crystal Palace. — The British Museum. — The Aristocracy of England. — Spiritualism in England. — Homeward looking. — Suggestions to Travelers. — Sunset around the World. — The Journey summarized. 391

www.ingramcontent.com/pod-product-compliance
Lightning Source LLC
Chambersburg PA
CBHW030554300426
44111CB00009B/975